ASIAN STUDIES ASSOCIATION OF AUSTRALIA

Southeast Asia Publications Series

THE CONTOURS OF MASS VIOLENCE IN INDONESIA, 1965–68

ASIAN STUDIES ASSOCIATION OF AUSTRALIA
Southeast Asia Publications Series

Since 1979 the Southeast Asia Publications Series (SEAPS) has brought some of the best of Australian scholarship on Southeast Asia to an international readership. It seeks to publish leading-edge research by both young and established scholars on the countries and peoples of Southeast Asia across all disciplines of the humanities and social sciences with particular encouragement to interdisciplinary and comparative research.

SEAPS is now published for the Asian Studies Association of Australia by NUS Press, a unit of the National University of Singapore, in alliance with the University of Hawaii Press in North America and the Nordic Institute of Asian Studies (NIAS) [non-Indonesia titles] and the KITLV Press [Indonesia titles] in Europe.

Website: http://iceaps.anu.edu.au/asaa_publications/southeast_asia.html

THE CONTOURS OF MASS VIOLENCE IN INDONESIA, 1965–68

Edited by

Douglas Kammen and Katharine McGregor

Asian Studies Association of Australia
in association with
UNIVERSITY OF HAWAI'I PRESS
HONOLULU

Published in Singapore by:
NUS Press
National University of Singapore
AS3-01-02, 3 Arts Link
Singapore 117569

Published in North America by:
University of Hawai`i Press
2840 Kolowalu Street
Honolulu, HI 96822 USA
www.uhpress.hawaii.edu

Library of Congress Cataloging-in-Publication Data

The contours of mass violence in Indonesia, 1965–68 / edited by Douglas Kammen and Katharine McGregor.
p. cm. – (Southeast Asia publications series)
"Published in Singapore by NUS Press."
Includes bibliographical references and index.
ISBN 978-0-8248-3743-3 (pbk.: alk. paper)

1. Political violence – Indonesia. 2. Indonesia – History – Coup d'état, 1965. 3. Gerakan Tigapuluh September. 4. Partai Komunis Indonesia. 5. Indonesia – Politics and government. I. Kammen, Douglas Anton. II. McGregor, Katharine E. III. Series: Southeast Asia publications series

HN710.Z9V537 2012
303.609598 — dc23 2012022217

Cover image: Reproduced with permission from David Jenkins

Printed by Mainland Press Pte Ltd

Contents

List of Maps vii

List of Illustrations vii

Preface and Acknowledgements ix

Chapter 1 Introduction: The Contours of Mass Violence in Indonesia, 1965–68 1
Douglas Kammen and Katharine McGregor

Chapter 2 The September 30th Movement: The Aporias of the Official Narratives 25
John Roosa

Chapter 3 International Dimensions of the 1965–68 Violence in Indonesia 50
Bradley Simpson

Chapter 4 The Army Para-commando Regiment and the Reign of Terror in Central Java and Bali 75
David Jenkins and Douglas Kammen

Chapter 5 East Java and the Role of Nahdlatul Ulama in the 1965–66 Anti-communist Violence 104
Greg Fealy and Katharine McGregor

Chapter 6 Anti-communist Violence and the Ethnic Chinese in Medan, North Sumatra 131
Yen-ling Tsai and Douglas Kammen

Chapter 7 South Sulawesi: The Military, Prison Camps and Forced Labour 156
Taufik Ahmad

Chapter 8 South Blitar and the PKI Bases: Refuge, Resistance and Repression 182
Vannessa Hearman

Chapter 9 West Bali: Experiences and Legacies of the 1965–66 Violence 208
Mary Ida Bagus

Chapter 10 Mass Graves and Memories of the 1965 Indonesian Killings 234
Katharine McGregor

Glossary and Abbreviations 263

Bibliography 268

Contributors 286

Index 288

List of Maps

Map of the territory of modern Indonesia xiii

Planned route of military "victory" convoy through Central Java 96

Map of East Java 113

Map of North Sumatra and Aceh 135

Map of South and Southeast Sulawesi 164

Map of the area of Blitar in East Java 189

Map of Central Java and grave locations 239

List of Illustrations

Political prisoners in front of the Moncongloe prison camp 175

Grave of Pak Kardi, Budeng, Jembrana, Bali 228

Forensic expert Dr Handoko at the Wonosobo excavation site 241

Preface and Acknowledgements

When, as sometimes happens, crucial and well-known historical events are left grossly under-studied for decades, there are usually good reasons that should serve as a warning to the unwary newcomer. Such is the case with the counter-revolutionary violence committed against the political Left in Indonesia in the 1960s. While both the circumstances in which the violence was perpetrated and the regime that emerged out of that violence have been the subject of serious academic study and debate, we know very little about the violence itself. Many of the most basic questions remain largely unanswered: When did mass violence begin in each locality and province? What variation was there in the perpetrators by region? Why were more people killed in some locations while more detainees survived elsewhere? What was the relationship between the struggle over the central organs of the state and localised violence?

As Geoffrey Robinson noted 15 years ago, one would have thought that violence on this scale would be the subject of serious investigation. But this has not been the case. It was not until two decades after the pogroms that the first (and last) academic workshop was held to discuss the killings; three years later, under the careful editorship of Robert Cribb, a valuable volume was published by the Monash University Centre of Southeast Asian Studies under the title *The Indonesian Killings of 1965–1966: Studies from Java and Bali*. Since then, a number of excellent monographs and articles have addressed aspects of the violence in locations ranging from Aceh and North Sumatra to East Java and Bali, and a slightly larger number of academic articles have begun to flesh out knowledge of the violence elsewhere in the archipelago. Since 1998, an increasing number of young Indonesian scholars and activists have begun to research the violence against the political Left.

Building on the work of Robert Cribb, Harold Crouch and others, this volume is a modest attempt to further our understanding of the counter-revolutionary violence in Indonesia between 1965 and 1968. Drawing together recent work by scholars based in Indonesia,

Singapore, Taiwan, Australia, the United States and Canada, this book seeks to contribute to our understanding of the broad contours of the attack and the regional peculiarities of the violence.

As is so often the case, this book is the product of chance, unwary curiosity and a failure to foresee the long road that lay ahead. While a visiting fellow at the Asia Research Institute (ARI) at the National University of Singapore, Katharine McGregor suggested to Anthony Reid, then the director of ARI, that it was high time an international conference was held on the mass killings in Indonesia. Anthony liked the idea, but with Katharine due to return to the University of Melbourne, he needed someone in the Faculty of Arts and Social Sciences to step forward. Over a drink in the Guild House, Vedi Hadiz (then in the Department of Sociology) and Jamie Davidson (Department of Political Science) wisely declined, leaving Douglas Kammen as the last one with his hands (somewhat foolishly) on the table. It proved to be a fruitful crossing of paths. Katharine, trained in history, has been interested in the topic of the violence of 1965–68 for many years and had researched the politics of memories of 1965 and official Indonesian military historiography. Douglas, trained in political science, had researched the Indonesian military during the late Suharto years.

Nine months later, after consulting with mentors, colleagues and friends, Douglas, Katharine, Anthony and Vannessa Hearman convened a three-day conference at the National University of Singapore. Over 30 scholars and activists presented papers at the conference held in June 2009. We would like to thank all of them for their encouragement and their interest and input in the resulting volume. They are: Asvi Warman Adam (LIPPI, Jakarta), Taufik Ahmad (Universitas Negeri, Makassar), Yudhi Andoni (Universitas Andalas, Padang), Robert Cribb (ANU, Canberra), Leslie Dwyer (Haverford College), Diah Ariani Arimbi (University of Minnesota), Theodora Erlijna (ISSI, Jakarta), Steven Farram (Charles Darwin University, Darwin), Greg Fealy (ANU, Canberra), Robert Goodfellow (Brisbane), Vannessa Hearman (University of Melbourne), Yew Foong Hui (ISEAS, Singapore), Mary Ida Bagus (University of Newcastle), David Jenkins (Sydney), Nurkholis (Komnas HAM, Jakarta), Yen-ling Tsai (Taiwan), Putu Oka Sukanta (Jakarta), Anne Pohlman (University of Queensland, Brisbane), John Roosa (UBC, Vancouver), Laurie Margot Ross (UC Berkeley), Degung Santikarma (Bali), Sentot Setyosiswanto (Yogyakarta), Bradley Simpson (Princeton University), Priyambudi Sulistiyanto (Flinders University, Adelaide), Nasir Tamara (ISEAS,

Singapore), Adrian Vickers (Sydney University), Saskia Wieringa (IIAV, Amsterdam), Winarso (SEKBER 65, Surakarta), Mark Woodward (University of Arizona), and Narny Yenny (Universitas Andalas, Padang). We were sorely disappointed that Ruth McVey, Geoffrey Robinson and Agung Ayu Ratih were unable to attend.

We would like to thank the organisations and individuals who made the conference possible. The Asia Research Institute provided a generous grant, and Anthony Reid and Lily Kong supported the conference and the publication of this volume. Valerie Yeo and her team from ARI made impeccable arrangements and ensured that the conference ran smoothly. The Faculty of Arts and Social Sciences at NUS and the Australian Research Council Asia Pacific Futures Network also provided generous funding that made the conference possible.

A number of individuals provided guidance and encouragement during the organising stages. These include Benedict Anderson, Jamie Davidson, Vedi Hadiz, Hilmar Farid and Ruth McVey. We extend a special thank you to Robert Cribb for putting us in touch with other researchers in the field and for giving the keynote address. In addition, we want to thank Robert Lemelson and Putu Oka Sukanta for screening their films on the 1965–68 violence and its legacies. In addition to those who helped with the conference, we also want to note the service performed by Robert Cribb and Michele Ford, who took the initiative to profile some of the research from the conference in a special edition of the magazine *Inside Indonesia* (Issue 99, January 2010) devoted to the Indonesian killings.

This book brings together a selection of the conference papers. These have now been through several rounds of revision, and we thank our contributors for their patience in responding to feedback and comments from reviewers. We owe special thanks to the anonymous reviewers, both for their encouragement and for their detailed comments. In preparing this manuscript Vannessa Hearman deserves special mention for her research assistance and for translating one chapter that was originally written in Indonesian. Bradley Simpson kindly shared his collection of declassified diplomatic documents from the United States and United Kingdom. Several other colleagues provided assistance with the manuscript along the way: Robert Cribb, Harold Crouch, Hilmar Farid, Vera Mackie and Ryan Tans. We would also like to thank Carolyn Leslie, Wong Wee and Sunandini Arora Lal for their editorial assistance, and Lee Li Kheng from the NUS Department of Geography, who kindly produced the elegant maps. We thank the photographers who provided copyright permission for images used in the volume, and Stanford University Press and the Cornell University Southeast Asia Program for copyright permission for material used in Chapters 3, 5 and 8.

Very special thanks are owed to Howard Dick, editor of the Asian Studies Association of Australia's Southeast Asia Publications Series, for his direction and patience in waiting for the manuscript. In addition, Paul Kratoska from NUS Press provided important early support and saw this manuscript through to press.

We have used modern Indonesian spelling throughout, except in cases where the name of a person or place continues to follow the old spelling. The one exception to this is that we have opted to use the modern spelling Suharto, despite the fact that he himself used the "oe" spelling. All monetary amounts indicated are in US dollars unless otherwise indicated.

Douglas Kammen
Katharine McGregor

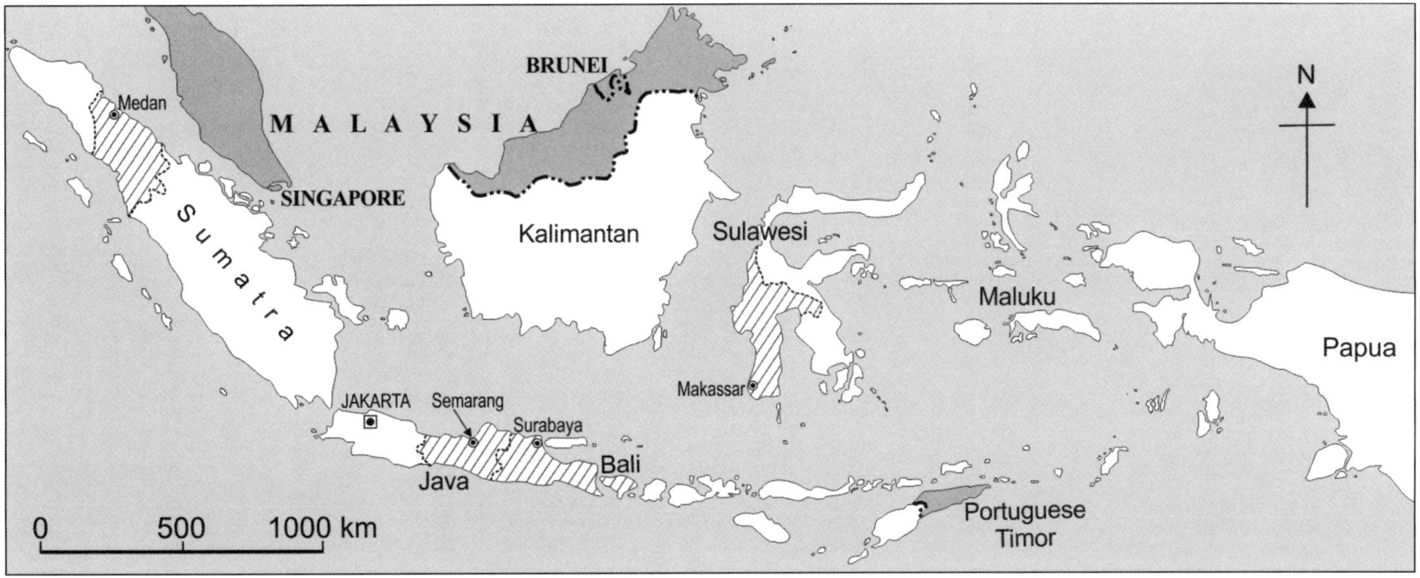

Map of the territory of modern Indonesia. Provinces covered in this volume are shaded.

1

Introduction: The Contours of Mass Violence in Indonesia, 1965–68

Douglas Kammen and Katharine McGregor

In the early hours of 1 October 1965, a small group of conspirators in the Indonesian Army abducted and murdered six high-ranking generals and a lieutenant, then buried the bodies in a dried-up well near Halim Perdanakusuma Air Force Base, on the outskirts of Jakarta. At 7:15 a.m. that day the national radio station broadcast an announcement, prepared by the conspirators, that a self-proclaimed September 30th Movement (Gerakan 30 September), led by Lieutenant Colonel Untung, had acted to safeguard President Sukarno from a coup planned by a CIA-backed Council of Generals. Listeners were asked to remain calm and forewarned that further actions would follow. The broadcast provided the cue for fellow conspirators to seize control of key cities in Central Java. Later that day the Movement announced the formation of a Revolutionary Council. By then, however, Major General Suharto, the commander of the Army Strategic Reserve, had initiated counter-operations to crush Untung's movement. At the time, all actors were uncertain about what had happened as well as what to call the incident.

Suharto and his allies crushed the Movement in Jakarta within a day and promptly banned all newspapers except for those owned by the military. Over the next week, the Army-controlled press condemned the September 30th Movement — now abbreviated G-30-S — as "counter-revolutionary", fabricated stories that members of the Communist Party-affiliated Indonesian Women's Movement (Gerwani) had gouged out the eyes and mutilated the sex organs of the generals, and called for the Indonesian Communist Party (Partai Komunis Indonesia, PKI) and its affiliates to be banned. But it was not until 8 October that the Army newspapers presented what was to become the official line: Untung's movement, now branded GESTAPU (an acronym derived from the slightly rearranged name Gerakan September Tiga Puluh), had been masterminded by the PKI. The acronym, coined by the director of the Armed Forces' news daily, was intended to equate the conspirators, including the PKI, with the Nazi Secret State Police.[1] The reference was meaningless to the vast majority of the population but was well understood by members of the political elite and foreign observers.

The second week of October saw a tense tug-of-war between President Sukarno and the surviving Army leadership over what had happened, who had the authority to take action, and what that action should be. Suharto played his hand carefully. On 10 October he announced the establishment of a new Operations Command to Restore Order and Security (Komando Operasi Pemulihan Keamanan dan Ketertiban, abbreviated Kopkamtib). Four days later Sukarno, under increasing pressure, announced that Major General Suharto would be appointed commander of the Army. The installation ceremony was held two days later. Having seized full authority over the Army, cowed the other service branches, and inflamed bloodthirsty calls for the destruction of the PKI, Suharto was ready to take direct action. The next day he ordered troops from the Army Paracommando Regiment (Resimen Para Komando Angkatan Darat, RPKAD) to depart overland to Central Java to initiate operations against the remnants of the September 30th Movement and the Communist Party's huge following, now collectively demonised as "Gestapu-PKI". Mass killings of Communist Party members and sympathisers commenced.

Outraged by the lies and horrified by the violence unleashed against the PKI, President Sukarno challenged the Army's version of

[1] "Inilah tjerita kebinatangan 'Gestapu'", *Angkatan Bersendjata*, 8 Oct. 1965. The word order of "Gerakan September 30" is not natural in Indonesian but it is in English, suggesting that foreigners may have been involved in coining the term.

events and sought to reverse the calls propagated by the Army and anti-communist civilian forces for the PKI to be banned. Speaking at a conference of provincial governors on 13 December, Sukarno mockingly questioned Armed Forces commander General Nasution about the timing of events on 1 October. "It was 3 a.m.," Nasution answered.

Sukarno pounced: "So it was already 1 October. So perhaps it is more accurate to say that it wasn't on 30 September, but on 1 October. G[erakan] 1 October. So, so how about it? G 1 October — so it should be Gestok. Not Gestapu, but Gestok. Okay, Gestok it is!"[2] Although Sukarno's intention in introducing the term "Gestok" was merely to counter the sinister connotations of "Gestapu", Indonesians began to use the term to refer to Suharto's counter-operations against both the September 30th Movement and the PKI. Deeply concerned by all challenges to its official version of events, the Army initiated a new media campaign to prevent such usage.[3] But the violence continued unabated, and by the end of December the death toll had risen to several hundred thousand.

Throughout the first half of 1966, as the Army's anti-communist witch-hunts and mass killings were initiated in new regions, Suharto consolidated his control over the central state apparatus and whittled away at Sukarno's authority. Yet Sukarno continued to speak out against the blatant lies and the propaganda inciting civilians to exact revenge, and the pogroms. His efforts to mobilise popular support faltered, his top aides were arrested, and he was prevented from leaving his palace in Bogor. At the special session of the Provisional People's Consultative Assembly (Majelis Permusyawaratan Rakyat Sementara, MPRS) held in June, Sukarno was called on to account for the September 30th Movement. In his speech, Sukarno explained

---

[2] Budi Setiyono and Bonnie Triyana, eds, *Revolusi Belum Selesai: Kumpulan Pidato Presiden Soekarno, 30 September 1965 — Pelengkap Nawaksara* (Semarang: Masyarakat Indonesia Sadar Sejarah, 2003), pp. 253–4. This speech prompted the first usage, and explanation, of the term in the press: "Bukan G-30-S Tapi G-1-0 [*sic*]", *Duta Masjarakat*, 14 Dec. 1965. The term "Gestok" has been the subject of much conjecture. See, for example, Arnold C. Brackman, *The Communist Collapse in Indonesia* (New York: W.W. Norton and Co., 1969), p. 96.

[3] M. Panggabean, *Berjuang dan Mengabdi* (Jakarta: Pustaka Sinar Harapan, 1993), pp. 339–40.

that he had no prior knowledge of Gestok (he refused to use the term "Gestapu" or "G30S"), which he blamed on "deviation of the leadership of the PKI, the machinations of neo-colonialist forces, and the criminal conspiracies of certain individuals".[4] The MPRS, which had been purged of leftists, rejected the accountability speech. Both time and the Army were against Sukarno. In March 1967 the Army-controlled MPRS stripped Sukarno of his presidency. By then half a million Indonesians had been massacred, and further killings would follow. Many more Indonesians were detained, some temporarily but others caught in the brutal tropical gulag. Shattered families were ostracised in their communities and faced institutional stigmatisation from the state.

This volume examines the mass violence against the Indonesian Communist Party, the Left more generally, and President Sukarno from 1965 until 1968. It makes the case for viewing the multiple forms of violence across a period of three years as a counter-revolution intended to curtail the mass mobilisation and popular participation unleashed by the national revolution; to destroy the social bases of Sukarno's left-leaning political system, called Guided Democracy; and to establish a new pro-Western military authoritarian regime. At the same time, this volume seeks to highlight the stages by which the attack proceeded and the corresponding shifts in the anti-communist coalition responsible for the violence. While the chapters provide in-depth analysis of the dynamics of violence in particular regions, the picture that emerges should also be of interest to a wider audience concerned with issues of mass violence, the Cold War, regime change and counter-revolution.

Problems and Approaches

One of the great ironies of scholarship on modern Indonesian history and politics is that the massive violence perpetrated against the Indonesian Left in the mid-1960s has been the subject of so little serious research; in fact, the bulk of the literature on this period skirts the violence itself. Scholars have produced excellent studies on the rise of the Indonesian Communist Party under Sukarno, but

---

[4] Sukarno, "Nawaksara", in Setiyono and Triyana, *Revolusi Belum Selesai*, pp. 128–38.

these works invariably end precisely when the tragedy begins.[5] Similarly, there are a host of competing "whodunnit" studies of the September 30th Movement, which shattered the uneasy balance of Sukarno's Guided Democracy and provided the pretext for the violent onslaught, but these typically focus exclusively on the events of early October and stop short of the cataclysm that was to come.[6] There is also a vast literature on the Indonesian military and Suharto's New Order regime (1966–98), but once again these works provide only abbreviated accounts of the violence out of which the regime emerged.[7] These general trends are replicated even in the best histories of modern Indonesia. M.C. Ricklefs' nearly 500-page history of modern Indonesia, for example, devotes less than a page to the mass killings, concluding simply that "[t]he killings came to an end in the first months of 1966, leaving a death toll which is never likely to be known with certainty".[8] Similarly, many of the finest regional histories treat the mass killings only in passing.[9] While there are several

---

[5] Notable works include Herbert Feith, "President Sukarno, the Army, and the Communists: The Triangle Changes", *Asian Survey* 4, 8 (Aug. 1964): 969–80; Donald Hindley, *The Communist Party of Indonesia (1961–1965)* (Berkeley: University of California Press, 1966); and Rex Mortimer, *Indonesian Communism under Sukarno: Ideology and Politics, 1959–1965* (Ithaca: Cornell University Press, 1974).

[6] Benedict R. Anderson and Ruth T. McVey, *A Preliminary Analysis of the October 1, 1965, Coup in Indonesia* (Ithaca: Modern Indonesia Project, Cornell University, 1971); Justus van der Kroef, "Gestapu in Indonesia", *Orbis* 9 (Summer 1966): 458–87; W.F. Wertheim, "Suharto and the Untung Coup: The Missing Link", *Journal of Contemporary Asia* 1, 2 (Winter 1970): 50–7; John Roosa, *Pretext for Mass Murder: The September 30th Movement and Suharto's Coup d'État in Indonesia* (Madison: University of Wisconsin Press, 2006). The one major exception that does treat the violence across time is Harold Crouch, *The Army and Politics in Indonesia* (Ithaca: Cornell University Press, 1978).

[7] See, for example, Ulf Sundhaussen, *The Road to Power: Indonesian Military Politics, 1945–1967* (Kuala Lumpur and New York: Oxford University Press, 1982); Julie Southwood and Patrick Flanagan, *Indonesia: Law, Propaganda and Terror* (London: Zed Press, 1983).

[8] M.C. Ricklefs, *A History of Modern Indonesia since c. 1200*, 3rd ed. (Hampshire: Palgrave, 2001), p. 347.

[9] For example, Ann Laura Stoler's superb study of a century of conflict in North Sumatra's plantation belt devotes less than two pages to the anti-communist violence: *Capitalism and Confrontation in Sumatra's Plantation Belt, 1870–1979* (New Haven: Yale University Press, 1985), pp. 163–4.

detailed works on the violence in specific locations in Indonesia,[10] to date there is not a single monograph on the overall contours of the violence against the Left, and only two serious edited volumes on the topic are available.[11]

There are many reasons for this scholarly lacuna. The most obvious of these are the lack of documentary evidence, difficulty in obtaining research permission during Suharto's 32-year rule, the reluctance of many Indonesians to speak about the violence, and genuine concern about the safety of informants.[12] Beyond these reasons for the scholarly lacuna is a more fundamental problem — defining the subject of study. Precisely because of the overall lack of serious research and our still sketchy understanding of the course of events, scholars have commonly resorted to shorthand terms — "the coup", "1965", "the mass killings". These may be convenient terms, but each conceals or obfuscates far more than it illuminates.

As our brief outline of the terms "G-30-S", "Gestapu" and "Gestok" illustrates, the notion of a "coup" is problematic because there are so many possible referents. Throughout mid-1965, rumours circulated widely in Jakarta that a right-wing Council of Generals was planning to stage a coup d'état against President Sukarno. In fact, senior officers around General Yani were not planning a putsch against Sukarno, though they were hoping that the Communist Party

---

[10] Geoffrey Robinson, *The Dark Side of Paradise; Political Violence in Bali* (Ithaca and London: Cornell University Press, 1995), Chapter 11; I Ngurah Suryawan, *Ladang Hitam di Pulau Dewa: Pembantaian Massal 1965 di Bali* (Yogyakarta: Galangpress, 2007); Hermawan Sulistyo, *Palu Arit di Ladang Tebu: Sejarah Pembantaian Massal yang Terlupakan (Jombang-Kediri 1965–1966)* (Jakarta: Kepustakaan Populer Gramedia, 2000).

[11] Robert Cribb, ed., *The Indonesian Killings of 1965–1966: Studies from Java and Bali* (Clayton: Centre of Southeast Asian Studies, Monash University, 1990); John Roosa, Ayu Ratih and Hilmar Farid, eds, *Tahun yang Tak Pernah Berakhir: Memahami Pengalaman Korban 65: Esai-Esai Sejarah Lisan* (Jakarta: Elsam, 2004).

[12] For a full discussion of such problems, see Robert Cribb, "Problems in the Historiography of the Killings in Indonesia", in *The Indonesian Killings*, ed. Robert Cribb (Clayton: Centre of Southeast Asian Studies, Monash University, 1990), pp. 3–14.

would launch an unsuccessful coup, thereby providing an opportunity for the Army to move against its enemies. The term "coup" is most commonly employed to refer to the actions of the September 30th Movement (G-30-S), though the movement's initial statements make it abundantly clear that the aim was not to seize state power from President Sukarno, but rather to protect him. This usage is often elided with a third, that being the claim (made by the Army in 1965, sustained by New Order propaganda, and uncritically repeated by a host of scholars) that the PKI masterminded Untung's movement (Gestapu-PKI) as a prelude to a communist takeover. And then there is the fourth referent: that in crushing the September 30th Movement and gradually whittling away at Sukarno's power, Major General Suharto and the Army carried out a "creeping coup". This confusion about the course of events led one author to throw up his hands and conclude: "Whatever happened was almost certainly too bizarre for a Western mind to conceive."[13] Other authors, more judicious, have insisted that the term "coup" should not be applied to the September 30th Movement, but that Suharto's actions be recognised for what they were — a seizure of state power (a coup d'etat).[14]

Another problem that has haunted the study of this period involves the multiple forms of violence. Mass killings were the most heinous aspect of the attack on the Left and have hence attracted the most media and scholarly attention. But it would be a mistake to treat killings, however massive the scale, in isolation from the other forms of violence. The attack also included the destruction and seizure of property, arrests, short-term detention, long-term imprisonment, torture, sexual violations and forced relocations. Furthermore, the term "massacre" has all too often reinforced the suggestion that the killings were carried out in a frenzy; the Malay term "amok" has been the subject of far more commentary than it ever warranted.[15] In fact, the vast majority of victims were detained for a period of days or weeks before being executed, strong prima facie evidence that the violence was coordinated and controlled. Many more detainees

---

13 Brian May, *The Indonesian Tragedy* (London: Routledge and Kegan Paul, 1978), p. 114.

14 Roosa, *Pretext for Mass Murder*, pp. 106, 200.

15 For a critique, see Cribb, "Problems in the Historiography", pp. 33–4.

were never killed but instead languished in makeshift detention centres. The lucky ones were released, though they may have subsequently fallen victim to the cold institutional violence of surveillance, summons and stigmatisation. In the last ten years scholars have begun to pay greater attention to the various forms of violence, and there are a growing number of local studies that examine detentions and imprisonment,[16] violence against women,[17] and ethnic and religious cleavages.[18]

The study of mass violence against the Indonesian Left in the 1960s has also been plagued by the problem of periodisation. While "1965" has served as a convenient shorthand, it was clearly only the starting point. It is often argued that what sets the pogroms against the Indonesian Left apart from mass killings in more advanced states is that they took place very rapidly and without the aid of a sophisticated bureaucracy to process and punish declared enemies (which would have left written records) or technology (such as gas chambers).[19] That is certainly true for the worst period of killings — October 1965 until April 1966 — but it fails to address a more fundamental question: What forces determined whether the violence began early (in Java, northern Sumatra and Bali), commenced only at the start of 1966 (as in southern Sumatra and the Lesser Sunda Islands) or not until quite late (as in West Kalimantan)? The answer to this question requires that we look beyond the victims and

---

[16] See the contributions in Roosa *et al.*, *Tahun yang tak Pernah Berakhir*; Taufik Ahmad, *Kamp Pengasingan Moncongloe* (Depok: Desantara, 2009).

[17] Saskia E. Wieringa, *Sexual Politics in Indonesia* (New York: Palgrave, 2002); Leslie Dwyer, "The Intimacy of Terror: Gender and the Violence of 1965–66 in Bali", *Intersections: Gender, History and Culture in the Asian Context* 10 (Aug. 2004).

[18] R.A.F. Paul Webb, "The Sickle and the Cross: Christian and Communist in Bali, Flores, Sumba and Timor, 1965–1967", *Journal of Southeast Asian Studies* 17, 1: 94–112; Steven Farram, "Revolution, Religion and Magic: The PKI in West Timor, 1924–1966", *Bijdragen tot de Taal-, Land- en Volkenkunde* 158, 1 (2002): 21–48; Jamie Davidson and Douglas Kammen, "Indonesia's Unknown War and the Lineages of Violence in West Kalimantan", *Indonesia* 73 (Apr. 2002): 53–87.

[19] Cribb, "Problems in the Historiography", pp. 15–8.

unravel the logic of the Army's attack on the social forces associated with Sukarno's Guided Democracy and explore the tensions within the brutal yet uneasy anti-communist alliance.

There are deep divisions among scholars concerning accountability and the death toll. One of the most commonly cited statements about the mass killings is a correction of fact allegedly made by Sarwo Edhie Wibowo, who in 1965 was the commander of the elite RPKAD. Shortly before his death, Sarwo Edhie told Permadi, a prominent psychic and later member of parliament: "Mr Permadi, three million were killed. Most of them on my orders."[20] The statement is remarkable for two reasons. The first of these concerns accountability. Some, typically those on the political Right, see the killings as primarily a horizontal conflict between competing social forces — communists on the one hand, and devout Muslims and "nationalists" on the other. Others, most commonly those on the Left, see the Army as the primary perpetrator, arguing that it planned the destruction of the PKI and played the leading role in the pogroms — pulling the trigger and organising, as well as arming and inciting, civilians.[21]

Sarwo Edhie's statement is also remarkable because his figure for the number of victims dwarfs all previous estimates. In early January 1966, a presidential Fact-Finding Commission presented a report to Sukarno in which it estimated that 78,500 individuals had been killed. In private, however, one of the commissioners told the President that in all probability the real figure was "five to six times higher, between 500,000 and 600,000".[22] At the time, of course, the killings were at fever pitch in East Java and Bali and were only just commencing elsewhere in the archipelago. In April 1966, a US

---

[20] Permadi SH, quoted in Coki Naipospos, ed., *50 Tahun Indonesia Merdeka Dan Problem Tapol/Napol* (Jakarta: Masyarakat Indonesia untuk Kemanusiaan, 1995), p. 59.

[21] See the translator's note in "Report from East Java", *Indonesia* 41 (Apr. 1986): 135.

[22] The report is reproduced in Oei Tjoe Tat, *Memoar Oei Tjoe Tat: Pembantu Presiden Sukarno* (Jakarta: Hasta Mitra, 1995), pp. 348–66; for Oei's conversation with Sukarno, see p. 192. John Hughes, based on conversations with an unnamed commissioner, cites a figure of 780,000 in *The End of Sukarno: A Coup that Misfired, a Purge that Ran Wild* (London: Angus and Robertson, 1968), p. 185.

Embassy official commented that "[e]ven the Indonesian Government probably has only a vague idea of the truth", though this did not prevent Ambassador Marshall Green from arriving at a figure of 300,000.[23] For now, suffice it to say that most scholars cite figures in the range of 500,000 deaths.[24] In the absence of state records — which have not come to light and most likely do not exist — we are unlikely to move beyond such guesses. The truth of the matter is that the precise death toll does not alter the nature of the crime: mass murder is mass murder.

But why mass murder? The question is far more complex than it would at first appear. The pogroms against the Left were neither an inevitable result of Sukarno's Guided Democracy nor a sudden, abhorrent deviation from Indonesia's natural development. On the one hand, it is all too easy, in retrospect, to identify multiple apparent causes: sharp ideological differences, intense Party competition, local factors ranging from disputes over land to the role of surviving aristocracies, a rapidly deteriorating economy with hyperinflation and food shortages, foreign policy adventures, and fears of foreign intervention. All these factors contributed to the palpable sense of crisis and fear, but neither singularly nor collectively do they explain why crisis and polarisation turned to mass killings (though they can help to explain some of the regional variations). On the other hand, it is important to avoid the suggestion, or perhaps more accurately the impression, emerging in some works that a happily independent Indonesia was suddenly burst asunder by the cruel machinations of the Army, foreign powers, or both. While it is clear that the Army, under the leadership of Major General Suharto, actively inflamed passions against the PKI and organised, encouraged and armed civilians, these anti-communist civilians were not mere dupes. As Ruth McVey observes, wide sections of society were all too eager

---

[23] See Airgram A661, US Embassy Jakarta to State Department, 15 Apr. 1966, Record Group 59, State Department Central Files 1964–1966, POL 2 INDON, National Archives and Records Administration [hereafter RG59 1964–66 documents referred to by file code and NARA]; and Marshall Green, *Indonesia: Crisis and Transformation, 1965–1968* (Washington, DC: Compass Press, 1990), p. 61.

[24] The death toll is discussed in Cribb, "Problems in the Historiography", pp. 7–14; and Cribb, "How Many Deaths? Problems in the Statistics of Massacre in Indonesia (1965–1966) and East Timor (1975–1980)", in *Violence in Indonesia*, ed. Ingrid Wessel and Georgia Wimhöfer (Hamburg: Abera, 2001).

to eliminate their enemies, to extirpate the evil they saw within the body politic.[23]

In another sense, however, the question "why mass murder" may be misleading. The question has led most authors to focus on the identities of the victims (the vast majority of whom were members of the PKI and its affiliated mass organisations) and, situating this within the context of the Cold War, to conclude that the violence was intended to destroy the PKI. But that is far too simplistic. In point of fact, the destruction of the PKI was only the first stage in a much broader attack against Sukarno and the Left, against Sukarnoism and the social bases of Guided Democracy. The destruction of the PKI — all but complete by December 1965 — removed the Army's only rival for power. At that stage, the Army set its sights on removing Sukarno, who was the lynchpin of Guided Democracy. But the attack went deeper still. Throughout 1966 the Army sought to undermine Sukarnoism, first by purging the civil service, then by targeting the Sukarnoist Indonesian National Party (Partai Nasional Indonesia, PNI), and finally by purging the ranks of the military itself of all leftist and Sukarnoist influences. Regions that, for one reason or another, had been spared violence in 1965–66 were then targeted, and the processing of detainees got into full swing. These clean-up operations were as much exemplary as they were instrumental. The conventional view that the attack on the PKI is best understood in the context of the Cold War is, paradoxically, insufficiently political. For this was not simply an attack on the Left, but a reorganisation of social forces and the reintegration of Indonesia into the capitalist world economy.[26] It was, in short, a counter-revolution.

Revolutions typically name that which they overthrow. François Furet begins his epic history by noting that the French Revolutionaries named their foe the *Ancien Régime*.[27] This was also the case in Indonesia. At an Army seminar in August 1966, the architects of the

[25] Ruth McVey, "The Great Fear in Indonesia", unpublished manuscript, n.d.

[26] See, for example, Hilmar Farid, "Indonesia's Original Sin", *Inter-Asia Cultural Studies* 6, 1 (2005): 3–16; Bradley Simpson, *Economists with Guns: Authoritarian Development and US-Indonesian Relations, 1960–1968* (Stanford: Stanford University Press, 2008).

[27] François Furet, *The French Revolution, 1770–1814*, trans. Antonia Nevill (Oxford and Cambridge, Mass.: Blackwell, 1996), p. 3.

violence introduced the label "Old Order" to refer to all that had come before 30 September 1965. They declared their aim to be the establishment of a "New Order"[28] that was to be based on law (the 1945 Constitution), religion (adherence to one of the officially recognised religions) and, predictably, capitalist development. This was a repudiation not just of Sukarno and his view that the "revolution was not yet complete", but more so a rejection of the popular mass participation that was unleashed during the Indonesian Revolution (1945–49) and which continued to thrive in the 1950s and early 1960s. While the Left was the most obvious victim of counter-revolutionary violence, the anti-communist alliance of "religious" and "nationalist" parties was also to fall victim to the Army, its leaders shunted aside and its rank and file of women's, peasants', workers' and teachers' organisations reduced to a depoliticised "floating mass".[29] With its actions, the Army began to consolidate a military-developmentalist regime based on an ideology of anti-communism.

This book seeks to enrich our understanding of the processes and key players involved in the destruction of the Indonesian Communist Party and the Indonesian Left more broadly. It argues for the need to treat all forms of violence across the archipelago over a period of roughly three years (October 1965 until the end of 1968) as a whole — a single attack not simply against the Indonesian Communist Party but also against the social forces and ideals associated with Sukarno and his Guided Democracy. The contributors cover a range of topics organised around four themes, with two chapters devoted to each: the September 30th Movement and the international environment; perpetrators of mass violence; regional dynamics of the violence, especially short- and long-term detention; and the experiences of those who sought to resist the onslaught and those who simply sought to survive. A concluding chapter examines the politics

[28] Apparently echoing Salazar's *Estado Novo*, Hitler's *Neue Ordnung* and the post-World War II fascist *Ordine Novo* in Italy.

[29] This doctrine, first propounded by General Ali Moertopo in 1971 and consolidated into law in 1975, held that the rural population should not be distracted by politics from the task of development. Ali Moertopo, *Akselerasi Modernisasi Pembanganun 25 Tahun*, 2nd ed. (Jakarta: Yayasan Proklamasi and Centre for Strategic and International Studies, 1973), pp. 95–6.

of investigating and commemorating mass graves. Rather than attempting to summarise the author's arguments, a task best left to the reader, we would like to provide an overview of the contours of the violence and indicate where each theme and chapter is situated within this larger framework.

The Contours of Counter-revolutionary Violence

The September 30th Movement caught many by surprise, but it did not come out of the blue. Ever since the end of parliamentary democracy and the declaration of Guided Democracy in 1959, President Sukarno had presided over a precarious political system and, by 1963, a rapidly deteriorating economy. One reason the Army had agreed to Sukarno's proposed system of Guided Democracy was to check the growth of the PKI. Paradoxically, the absence of elections drove the major political parties into ceaseless and fierce competition to recruit members and build up their affiliated mass organisations. The PKI proved particularly adept: by 1965 it claimed 3.5 million members in the Party and more than 20 million members in its affiliated organisations, including the Indonesian Farmers' Union (Barisan Tani Indonesia, BTI), the Federation of Indonesian Workers' Unions (SOBSI), the People's Youth movement (Pemuda Rakyat), the People's Cultural Institute (Lekra), and the Indonesian Women's Movement (Gerakan Wanita Indonesia, Gerwani).[30] Rex Mortimer argues that the reason the Party had a mass appeal to workers, peasants, teachers and low-level officials was that it was "the one significant political force displaying a devotion to their interests and seeking, under difficult circumstances, to give them an entrée onto a political stage dominated by neo-traditional elites and the swanky 'modern' suburbs of Djakarta, Bandung and Surabaya".[31] The Party's modernising vision and its emphasis on organisation and mass education also appealed to many.[32]

---

[30] Mortimer, *Indonesian Communism under Sukarno*, p. 366. As Mortimer suggests, these figures are probably inflated because one individual could belong to multiple PKI affiliates.

[31] Mortimer, *Indonesian Communism under Sukarno*, p. 11.

[32] Ruth McVey, "Teaching Modernity: The PKI as an Educational Institution", *Indonesia* 50 (Oct. 1990): 26.

The dramatic surge in membership and increasingly close relationship between the PKI and the President did not go uncontested, and each of the PKI's efforts to build support brought the Party into conflict with conservative forces. The PKI's focus on agrarian issues led to a wave of unilateral actions in 1963–64 to seize land from landlords who failed to abide by the 1959 Sharecropping Law and the 1960 Basic Agrarian Law. In Central and East Java, the BTI's actions met with fierce resistance, especially from Nahdlatul Ulama. In Bali, where Governor Suteja provided backing, the actions took place more smoothly, though they riled the landowning, PNI-affiliated aristocracy. The Party also supported Sukarno's military Confrontation campaign (1963–65), aimed at crushing the formation of Malaysia, which in his view was a "neo-colonialist" project. To support the case, the Party called for the arming of a fifth force, in addition to the four military services, to be made up of peasants and workers. The Army perceived this as a direct threat. The Party's rapid expansion beyond its core regions of popular support (Java, Bali and North Sumatra) brought it into conflict with local aristocrats, regional military commanders, former supporters of the Darul Islam and the 1957–58 PRRI/Permesta rebellions, and Western-oriented intellectuals.[33]

Religious groups and the Army struck back at the PKI. In East Java, Nahdlatul Ulama's youth wing (Ansor) and Multipurpose Brigade (Banser) launched widely reported attacks against the PKI. In early 1965, a combination of accurate news reports and wild rumours of PKI violence against Muslims in East Java prompted Islamic groups in Aceh to carry out attacks on newly established PKI offices in coastal towns. At the time, a US State Department official commented: "The PKI appears to be in real trouble in Atjeh, and there

---

[33] PRRI (Revolutionary Government of the Republic of Indonesia) in Sumatra and Permesta (Charter of Universal Struggle) in Sulawesi were regional rebellions led by military officers demanding greater regional autonomy. The Darul Islam rebellions, demanding the establishment of an Islamic state, were based in West Java, Aceh and South Sulawesi.

may very well be some blood spilt there."[34] There were also a growing number of violent incidents in neighbouring North Sumatra.[35] By September 1965, such incidents led a number of observers to note the consolidation of an anti-communist front and to suggest that violence was imminent. On 16 September, for example, a telegram from the US Consulate in Surabaya to the embassy in Jakarta reported: "Although the tensions between the PKI and the Moslems remained in a low key for some months, they erupted again during the month of August in a manner which seemed to confirm the feeling of some Indonesians that a civil war between the two groups will eventually be fought."[36] This poisoned atmosphere of fear and hatred also fuelled rumours of Sukarno's ill health and a coup planned by right-wing generals.

The September 30th Movement provided the trigger for the Army to take action against the PKI and, in doing so, to destroy Sukarno and Guided Democracy. The first pair of essays focuses on the September 30th Movement and the international context in which it occurred. In Chapter 2, John Roosa analyses the official constructions of the event by regime ideologues and argues that the inconsistencies help to reveal the true nature of what took place. Rubbing against the grain of accounts produced by those on the Left, he argues that the PKI's secretive Special Bureau (Biro Chusus) was involved in the conspiracy; countering accounts from the Right, he shows that with foreign support and encouragement the Army used the conspiracy as a pretext for carrying out the pogroms against the Left. The theme of foreign interests is further elaborated in Chapter 3, in which Bradley Simpson situates the violence within the context of the Cold War and US interests. He details US officials' concerns that the Indonesian military would not go far enough in destroying the Party, and the satisfaction they expressed when the violence eventually paved the way for greater control over the political and economic direction of Indonesia and for greater access to Indonesian resources and markets.

---

[34] Airgram A40, US Consulate Medan to US Embassy Jakarta, 15 Mar. 1965, POL 2 INDON, NARA.

[35] The most prominent of these was the killing of warrant officer Sudjono by BTI squatters and the subsequent revenge attack at Bandar Betsy in June 1965.

[36] Airgram A-5, US Consulate Surabaya to US Embassy Jakarta, 16 Sept. 1965, POL 18 INDON, NARA.

There was an essential unity to the destruction of the PKI and the regime that emerged out of the violence, but within this unity Suharto's counter-revolution was a complex process that lacked a simple schema or linear development. It required the formation and ongoing renegotiation of an Army-led anti-communist alliance. It entailed the horrific attack on members of the PKI and its affiliated organisations, as well as the consolidation of control over the provincial state apparatuses. Like other foundational acts of violence, the reign of terror was cloaked in the garb of legal procedures and consolidated through law. Although the timing and ordering of these processes varied widely, it is possible to identify four distinct phases.

The first phase, beginning with Suharto's counter-operations against the September 30th Movement and lasting until the end of 1965, saw the Army and the "religious" and "nationalist" anti-communist alliance unleash a horrific physical assault on the Communist Party and its supporters, dubbed "Gestapu-PKI". Party offices were ransacked, and Party members and sympathisers were detained, tortured and massacred. Curiously, the first massacres began in Aceh at the end of the first week of October. Although the PKI was a minor party in the province, the massacres were carried out with spectacular speed, and by December the regional military commander commented approvingly that "due to the quick and appropriate actions of the people, Aceh was the first region to be cleansed of counter-revolutionary G.30.S elements".[37] In Java, by contrast, the first two weeks of October were characterised by extreme uncertainty, vitriolic accusations, arrests and the destruction of Party headquarters in the capital, but not mass killings.

The turning point in Java was Suharto's appointment as commander of the Army on 16 October and his order for units from the Army Para-commando Regiment (RPKAD) to depart for Central Java. Ostensibly deployed to clean up remnants of the September 30th Movement, these troops spearheaded the attack on the PKI and the mobilisation of tens of thousands of civilians to form paramilitary killing squads. Mass killings began in East Java at the same time — though without the presence of RPKAD troops and without clear direction from the Regional Military Commander; much

---

[37] Quoted in Crouch, *Army and Politics in Indonesia*, p. 143.

depended on the initiative of lower-level military officers and civilian forces, in particular Nahdlatul Ulama. The killings most commonly proceeded in waves: first a murderous rampage by local members of the "religious" and "nationalist" groups, next mass arrests and short-term detention, and finally the turning over of prisoners by the military authorities to civilian killing squads to have them finished off. One of the most explicit descriptions comes from East Java: "... source described how a column of prisoners would be taken through villages and the commander would shout 'Do you want some?' and five or six prisoners would be pushed into the crowd where they would be killed on the spot."[38] By December, such public displays gave way to greater secrecy, and the executions were mostly carried out in isolated locations under cover of darkness.

By the end of 1965, perhaps as many as 100,000 people had been killed and 70,000 more remained under detention in Central Java, while some 200,000 people had been massacred and an estimated 25,000 were still under detention in East Java. The perpetrators of this violence in the Javanese heartland are the subject of the second pair of chapters. In Chapter 4, David Jenkins and Douglas Kammen explore the role of Colonel Sarwo Edhie's RPKAD troops in Central Java, as well as the mass mobilisation and coordination of anti-communist killing squads. The authors also seek to clarify long-standing confusion regarding RPKAD involvement in East Java and Bali. In Chapter 5, Greg Fealy and Katharine McGregor draw on Nahdlatul Ulama documents and interviews to examine why NU played a leading role in endorsing and overseeing the violence in East Java. The chapter analyses NU's coordination of the violence and the various roles of Islamic scholars, Ansor members, and regional and sub-regional military commanders in either encouraging or restraining the violence.

During the last quarter of 1965, large-scale massacres also commenced in West Java, North Sumatra and Bali. Killings on a smaller scale erupted in South Sulawesi and West Nusatenggara. The dynamics in these locations differed in key respects, however. Whereas the pogroms in Central and East Java started in mid-October, mass

---

38 Telegram A-391, US Embassy Jakarta to State Department, 9 Dec. 1965, POL 2 INDON, NARA.

killings did not begin in North Sumatra until the first week of November, and in Bali not until the first week of December.[39] The time lag was a function of a number of factors, the most important of which were the relative strength of the PKI, the attitude of regional military commanders and the legacies of regional rebellions. Where the PKI was particularly strong and the military command divided, as in North Sumatra and Bali, the Army first needed to consolidate its own ranks and rally an anti-communist alliance. In provinces where the Army had fought Darul Islam, as in West Java and South Sulawesi, regional commanders were apparently reluctant to arm civilians. In comparison with Central and East Java, the number of people detained and killed during the last quarter of 1965 in these provinces was far lower: in North Sumatra an estimated 15,000 were killed and another 15,000 detained;[40] in West Java, fewer than 10,000 were killed and 10,000 detained;[41] in South Sulawesi, a few thousand were killed. The one exception was Bali, where an estimated 45,000 people were massacred in December alone, with virtually none left in detention, and where the toll rose to an estimated 80,000 by mid-1966, making it the site of the highest rate of killings per capita.[42]

By mid-December 1965, Suharto and his allies were confident that the PKI had been destroyed as an organisation, and they made numerous statements about the need to "bring the killings under control". There is little evidence to suggest that they were serious about ending the massacres, though the statements did give rise to serious resentment on the part of particular anti-communist groups that rightfully feared a diminished role for themselves once the violence ended. While killings continued, Suharto and his allies now

---

[39] Little is known about the violence in West Java, and it has not been possible to determine precisely when the killings there began.

[40] Figures are from Telegram 1900, US Embassy Jakarta to State Department, 29 Dec. 1965, POL 23-9 INDON, NARA; and Telegram 924A, US Embassy Jakarta to State Department, 27 Dec. 1965, POL 23-9 INDON, NARA.

[41] The estimates are from Sundhaussen, *Road to Power*, p. 225; and Telegram 1566, US Embassy Jakarta to State Department, 26 Nov. 1965, POL 23-9 INDON, NARA.

[42] See Oei, *Memoar*, p. 187; and Robinson, *Dark Side of Paradise*, p. 373fn2.

trained their sights on the President. The first move was to force Sukarno to acquiesce to the appointment of a new triumvirate, composed of General Nasution, Sultan Hamengkubuwono IX of Yogyakarta and Ruslan Abdulgani, within the Supreme Operations Command (Komando Tertinggi, KOTI) — a move US sources described as "an elliptical procedure for assuming control of government".[43] As noted above, Sukarno responded by challenging the Army's propaganda, which he sought to counter with his own version of events — "Gestok".

During the second phase of violence, which can be dated from January until May 1966, the Army undermined President Sukarno's authority and personal prestige and sought to bring the political parties under control. In mid-January Sukarno and his loyal ministers tried to fight back, declaring the formation of a Sukarno Front (Barisan Sukarno), but without success. By March, stripped of key supporters, confined to his palace and with limited information, there was little the President could do. In mid-March, Sukarno was forced to transfer administrative authority to Suharto. As the high political drama played out in the capital, killings continued in Java and North Sumatra. This period also saw three crucial new developments. First, in the core regions of PKI strength (North Sumatra, Central Java and East Java), a struggle arose over the hundreds of thousands of detainees. Hard-line anti-communists and their allies within local military units sought to eliminate the detainees before they could be handed over to the Attorney-General's office for processing. Second, January 1966 saw the commencement of witch-hunts and mass killings in areas that had previously been spared the violence, most notably West Sumatra, Lampung and East Nusatenggara. Several thousand alleged communists were killed in each of these provinces. Third, during the first half of 1966 there were increasingly violent struggles within the anti-communist alliance between "religious" and "nationalist" groups, often paralleled and exacerbated by hostilities between the Army, on the one hand, and the police and Marines, on the other. There were very real differences within the anti-communist camp, but the Army also fuelled the violence — the counter-revolution was now destroying its children.

---

[43] Telegram 562A, US Embassy Jakarta to State Department, 15 Dec. 1965, POL 23-9 P, NARA.

The dynamics of detention and tensions within the anti-communist alliance provide the themes for our third pair of chapters. Chapter 6, by Yen-ling Tsai and Douglas Kammen, uses the experience of ethnic Chinese in Medan, North Sumatra, as a lens through which to explore the development of the anti-communist alliance and the tensions within, as well as the process of short-term detention. In Chapter 7, Taufik Ahmad provides an account of violence and longer-term detention in South Sulawesi, where the legacies of the Darul Islam rebellion strongly influenced the anti-communist assault. In contrast to the military justification that long-term detention camps were set up strictly for security purposes, Ahmad argues that the military exploited prison labour for the purpose of lucrative military businesses. Both chapters reflect on the role of the Indonesian military in the violence and the continuing processes of exploitation in these two locations.

During the short third phase of the violence, from June to October 1966, Suharto consolidated control over the central organs of state power. The key dynamics of this period were efforts to purge Sukarnoists from the civil service and the military, and to bring the political parties fully to heel. In June a special session of the People's Consultative Assembly was held; and under threat from the military, the delegates confirmed the powers Suharto had wrested from Sukarno in March. Outraged by Sukarno's unrepentant attitude, they also demanded that the President account for the causes of the September 30th Movement and his own actions. Over the course of several months, a pliant right-wing faction was installed to run the PNI. Leaders of NU and Masyumi (which had been banned by Sukarno) were told in no uncertain terms that their services in destroying the PKI had not earned them positions in the emerging new regime. Eager to demonstrate their own credentials to the Army and determined to bring down the President, the most radical anti-communist civilian militants waged another round of attacks on alleged communists and other political rivals.

By October 1966, however, Suharto made it clear that the emerging regime would not tolerate independent action and preferred to pursue a "constitutional" route in dealing with the President. High-ranking PKI officials and Sukarnoist ministers were put on trial, though, as Crouch has noted, these trials had less to do with the individuals in question than with "discrediting the President by proxy and demonstrating his lack of power to save his most loyal colleagues".[44] The confrontation between Sukarno and the Army finally came to an end in March 1967, when the MPRS declared that Sukarno had failed to carry out his "constitutional responsibilities", banned him from participation in politics and appointed Suharto as "Acting President".

The full consolidation of the new regime was accompanied by efforts to enforce the new social order, to right the economy and to complete the realignment of Indonesia's foreign policy, but the violence against the Left was far from over. The fourth and final phase of violence — 1967–68 — was marked by the legal processing and long-term imprisonment of hundreds of thousands of people, but also by "clean-up" operations against leftist remnants. The first of these operations was necessitated by an attack carried out against a small air force facility in West Kalimantan, not far from the Malaysian border. Although the military believed the attack to have been perpetrated by ethnic Chinese communists from Sarawak, it was in fact the work of the largely ethnic Chinese West Kalimantan branch of the PKI, together with "fellow travelers" from Sarawak. After several months of preparatory operations, again spearheaded by RPKAD, in November 1967 the Army once again turned to the use of civilian paramilitaries: ethnic Dayaks were mobilised to carry out an attack on ethnic Chinese in the interior, resulting in an estimated 3,000 deaths in the months of November and December alone. This was followed by the forced relocation of over 100,000 ethnic Chinese, many into makeshift concentration camps on the coast.[45] In 1968, the Indonesian military uncovered evidence of underground PKI activity and even small-scale rural bases in Java. This ranged all the way from Indramayu, in West Java, to the Merapi-Merbabu mountain complex and the greater Purwodadi area, in Central Java, and south Blitar and Mount Lawu, in East Java. The Army wasted no time in mobilising operations, first in south Blitar, then in Purwodadi and elsewhere.[46] Thousands of people were killed; many more were taken into custody and suffered long-term imprisonment and torture.

---

[44] Crouch, *Army and Politics*, p. 211.

[45] Davidson and Kammen, "Indonesia's Unknown War", pp. 67–8, 72–5.

[46] On Purwodadi, see Bonnie Triyana, "Peristiwa Purwodadi: Kasus Pembunuhan Massal Anggota dan Simpatisan Partai Komunis Indonesia di Kabupaten Grobogan Tahun 1965–1969", BA thesis, Universitas Diponegoro, 2003; a discussion of the PKI's alleged underground structure in Java is found on p. 129.

The fourth pair of chapters in this book examines the experience of PKI survivors who sought to reorganise, and the resilience and suffering of those who sought simply to survive and rebuild their lives. Vannessa Hearman, in Chapter 8, examines the response of the remaining PKI leaders to the violent repression and their attempts to engage in resistance. She analyses the operation of the south Blitar base and describes the experience of survivors under the brutal Trisula Operation conducted in mid-1968. She reveals how local people experienced the methods of coercion employed by the military to enlist support for the repression, mass evacuation of villagers, and patterns of forced marriage of women to military men and the removal of children. The following chapter, by Mary Ida Bagus, turns to the experience of survivors in Jembrana, the westernmost district in Bali, tracing the links between intricate political allegiances to either the PNI or the PKI across different aristocratic families, and the violence in 1965. Drawing on interviews, Ida Bagus analyses how people recall their experiences of — or participation in — many forms of violence. She traces the enduring effects of the violence showing a variety of coping strategies that include remarriage, transmigration and tending for the graves of both killers and their victims.

The final chapter, by Katharine McGregor, brings the story of counter-revolutionary mass violence up to the present by assessing the extent to which attitudes to such violence have shifted since the fall of Suharto in 1998. As Indonesia has democratised, the government and society have placed a stronger emphasis on human rights. Drawing on this new emphasis and on international precedents, survivors of the violence as well as non-governmental organisations have begun to collect evidence of the crimes of 1965 — for example, by documenting mass graves. Analysing the violent attack in 2001 on an attempted reburial of the remains of victims and the continuing controversy over mass grave documentation and exhumation, McGregor probes some of the specific barriers to addressing the past in post-Suharto Indonesia.

This Volume

Over the past decade, researchers, non-governmental organisations and the press have shown renewed interest in the mass violence against the Left in Indonesia during the 1960s. This resurgence is in large part a function of Suharto's resignation in 1998 and the country's democratisation, which have allowed for a much freer media, greater intellectual openness and calls for the country to redress the injustices of the past. Within Indonesia, former members of the PKI and other leftist organisations (many of whom were political prisoners during the New Order) have finally been able to publish memoirs and novels and produce documentary films, to begin to document the violence that they, their friends and their families experienced.[47] At the same time, the end of authoritarian rule has prompted a younger generation of Indonesians — students, scholars and activists alike — to challenge old orthodoxies, raise new questions and engage in fresh research. Outside of Indonesia, scholars have taken advantage of the end of the Cold War and the passage of time to lobby for the declassification of government documents in the United States, Great Britain, Australia and elsewhere that are beginning to provide a wealth of new information about the mass violence against the PKI, conflicts within the anti-communist front that waged the attack, Suharto's rise to power, and the interests and even involvement of foreign powers.

This book would not have been possible without this renewed interest, openness and access to new sources. The book originated out of a June 2009 conference on the 1965–68 Indonesian mass killings, hosted by the National University of Singapore and attended by more than 30 scholars and activists from Indonesia, Singapore, Taiwan, the Netherlands, Australia, Canada and the United States. The nine contributions in this volume draw on a wide range of material, both old and new. Although Indonesian military and intelligence archives have not been opened yet, official New Order histories and military publications — despite being intended to whitewash the violence, justify the new regime and indoctrinate the populace — provide a wealth of material. We are also fortunate that many people who directly experienced this period are still alive and willing to talk

[47] In the last ten years there have been many such films, memoirs and novels. Former political prisoner and poet Putu Oka Sukanta, who presented a paper and film at the 2009 conference, has written a semi-autobiographical novel about imprisonment (*Merajut Harkat*, Jakarta: Pustaka Pelajar, 1999) and has produced a number of documentary films on the 1965–66 violence.

about the past. Recently declassified materials in the US, Britain and Australia also provide abundant new information. Drawing on all of these sources, the contributors to this volume have produced vivid accounts of the actors, processes and forms of violence in localities across Indonesia, while also relating regional dynamics to central power and international actors and interests.

Needless to say, a volume of this sort cannot possibly be comprehensive, and there are many themes and regional dynamics that are not covered. The chapters in this volume, for example, probe in detail the specific roles and motives of several specific regional commands through to the elite RPKAD forces and non-military alliances in both priming and carrying out the violence, but to complete our understanding of the functions of different groups in this violence, we need further research on other commands and paramilitary forces across the regions of Indonesia. Further research on different regions of Indonesia could also reveal the extent to which class, ethnicity and local factors, such as earlier regional rebellions, also affected the patterns of violence. We hope that the conference and this collection will contribute to a more thoroughgoing examination of the political interests, social dynamics, experiences and enduring legacies of the tragedy.

2

The September 30th Movement: The Aporias of the Official Narratives

John Roosa

During the 32 years of the Suharto dictatorship, one history lesson drilled into all students, from the elementary grades to the university level, was that the Indonesian Communist Party (Partai Komunis Indonesia, PKI) had masterminded the September 30th Movement in 1965. Students were taught that the PKI was responsible for the murder of six Army generals in Jakarta, and that it had proven itself to be a dangerous and traitorous organisation which had to be thoroughly expelled from the body politic. The story about the September 30th Movement was told so often, in so many different ways, that it rivalled, if not overshadowed, the other all-important event of national history — the proclamation of Independence in 1945. After Major General Suharto seized state power from President Sukarno in the name of defending the state from PKI subversion, he constantly pointed to "the latent danger of the PKI", as if the Party was continuing to plot treacherous deeds. The regime used just about every method of propaganda to remind the populace of the September 30th Movement: textbooks, films, museums, statues, annual commemorations, street names, speeches, and radio and TV programmes. Whenever the regime wished to delegitimise its opponents, even as late as the mid-1990s, it labelled them "PKI". The story about the villainous PKI acting as the shadowy puppetmaster behind the September 30th Movement was familiar to every Indonesian, from Aceh to Papua.

Since the collapse of the Suharto dictatorship in May 1998, many books challenging the old orthodoxy about the September 30th Movement have been published.[1] Government officials, however, tend to remain committed to the version of history that they spent so many years forcing Indonesians to learn. Perhaps they fear that people will lose faith in the state if such a long-standing official narrative becomes discredited. Officialdom has invested much in this narrative and is loath to see it revised in any way. The Attorney-General's Office (AGO), uncertain of its authority to ban books in the wake of the post-1998 legal reforms, finally regained confidence in 2006. It began targeting books that did not state clearly that the PKI was responsible for the Movement. When the AGO banned 13 textbooks in 2007, it implicitly formulated a rule: every mention of the term "September 30th Movement" in a book had to be followed by "/PKI" to indicate the Party's responsibility for the Movement.

Many Indonesian readers have condemned this censorship and welcomed alternatives to what they call the "single narrative" (*narasi tunggal*) of Suharto-era propaganda.[2] The assumption has been that the Suharto regime presented only one version of the event. Certainly the regime's basic, unambiguous message for 32 years was that the PKI had masterminded the September 30th Movement. Nonetheless, the assumption of a single narrative is incorrect. The various publications sponsored by the regime actually presented different versions of the event.

This chapter argues that the Suharto regime presented three different versions of the event to the public and that the inconsistencies between these versions — and within each version — elucidate the reality of the event. My focus is on the moments when the official narratives become entangled in unresolved puzzles and compromise their own pretensions to objective truth. I am not looking so much for the silences or holes in the narratives, or even the outright lies, but rather the aporias, the knotted parts where the various claims

---

[1] For a comprehensive listing see the bibliography listed on the Indonesian Institute for Social History website: <http://www.sejarahsosial.org/2009/09/11/bibliography-on-the-events-of-1965-66-in-indonesia/>.

[2] "Meruntuhkan Narasi Tunggal Peristiwa 1965", *Kompas*, 24 July 2004.

become tangled up. The philosopher Nicholas Rescher has defined an aporia as "a collection of contentions that are individually plausible but collectively inconsistent".[3] This essay is meant as a qualification of the section in my book *Pretext for Mass Murder* that treats the Suharto regime's version as singular and consistent. Here I will argue that the Suharto regime could not consistently define three key elements of its storyline: the September 30th Movement, the PKI and the destruction of the PKI.[4] The essay concludes by considering why these aporias should exist in the first place. Ultimately, the reading becomes symptomatic, seeing, in Freudian fashion, the aporias as traces of a repressed reality.[5]

The Event

The September 30th Movement was a one-day affair that took place in Jakarta. Army troops under the command of several junior officers abducted six generals from their homes on 1 October 1965 around 4 a.m. They trucked the generals to a secluded rubber grove south of the city, where they killed the ones who were not already dead from injuries sustained during the abduction. Among the dead unceremoniously dumped down a well was Lieutenant General Achmad Yani. Elsewhere in the city, hundreds of troops gathered in front of

---

[3] Nicholas Rescher, "Aporetic Method in Philosophy", *Review of Metaphysics* 41, 2 (Dec. 1987): 283. The word "aporia" originated in ancient Greece, where its literal meaning was "without passage" and its extended meaning concerned "puzzlement". Dominic Scott, *Plato's Meno* (Cambridge: Cambridge University Press, 2006). The aporetic experience has been an abiding theme for deconstruction that does not assume there is always a passage out of the puzzlement. Jacques Derrida, *Aporias*, trans. Thomas Dutoit (Stanford: Stanford University Press, 1993).

[4] John Roosa, *Pretext for Mass Murder: The September 30th Movement and Suharto's Coup d'État in Indonesia* (Madison: University of Wisconsin Press, 2006), pp. 62–9.

[5] An example of a symptomatic reading of an aporia is Freud's joke about a man accused of having returned a borrowed kettle to its owner in a damaged condition. He gave a succession of mutually contradictory excuses. The excess of excuses is a symptom stemming from the repression of the fact that he broke the kettle. Sigmund Freud, *The Interpretation of Dreams* (London: Vintage, 2001), p. 120.

the presidential palace and other strategic sites around the city's Independence Square (Medan Merdeka). One platoon took over the national radio station and forced an announcement to be read on air. Thus listeners learned that the Movement was led by Lieutenant Colonel Untung, a commander of the Presidential Guard who wished to protect President Sukarno from an imminent coup by right-wing Army generals. In the early afternoon, the Movement announced that it was decommissioning Sukarno's cabinet and creating a 45-member Indonesian Revolutionary Council that would temporarily hold all state power. Thus, what appeared in the morning to be an internal Army mutiny meant to protect the President by the afternoon seemed to have become a coup d'état.[6]

Before it could clarify its intentions and reveal the identity of its other leaders, the Movement had disappeared. By early evening, the troops around the radio station and adjacent square had either fled or surrendered to the senior surviving Army general, Major General Suharto. The other troops located south of the city in the swampy rubber grove called Lubang Buaya (Crocodile Hole) scattered in all directions the next morning as Suharto's troops approached. At the same time, Untung and his fellow junior officers abandoned their headquarters — a small, inconspicuous house in the Halim Perdanakusuma Air Force Base complex. They did not organise any resistance to Suharto's attack. Most Indonesians, not owning radios, became aware of the Movement only after it had collapsed.

The only place in the country outside Jakarta where troops took significant action in support of the Movement was Central Java. Some senior officers were abducted in the cities of Solo, Salatiga and Yogyakarta. After just two days of poorly coordinated, largely ineffectual actions, the insurgent troops disbanded and either returned to their posts or went into hiding. There was little incentive to continue when the action in Jakarta had failed and further instructions from Untung's group were not forthcoming. The Movement in Central Java ended on its own by 3 October. Troops in Solo and Salatiga released their prisoners unharmed, while those in Yogyakarta killed two of their prisoners: Colonel Katamso and Lieutenant Colonel Soegijono.

---

[6] See Editors, "Selected Documents Relating to the 'September 30th Movement' and Its Epilogue", *Indonesia* 1 (Apr. 1966): 134–9.

After the collapse of the Movement, Major General Suharto and his allies in the Army high command took control of the radio and newspapers. They immediately closed down pro-PKI and pro-Sukarno newspapers and strictly censored the newspapers that were allowed to continue. Information in the Indonesian press about the Movement from 2 October onward was thus entirely one-sided. Under Suharto's command, the Army decided to blame the PKI for the Movement and use the press as a weapon in its attack on the Party. Editors were told in early October that the Army was starting a campaign against the PKI and anyone printing information critical of that campaign would be considered an ally of the PKI.[7] No neutrality was permitted.

Three Official Narratives

The first official narrative about the September 30th Movement was one of sensational journalism, much of it composed by Army psychological warfare specialists, with pieces of the story accumulating day after day, leading readers to conclude that the PKI, as an organisation, was responsible for events that were nationwide, brutal and treasonous.[8] There was no fact-finding commission to determine precisely what had happened on 1 October, just a steady building up of hysteria in the mass media.[9] Every day for several weeks, headlines

---

[7] Personal communication, Aristides Katoppo (editor of the newspaper *Sinar Harapan*), June 2008, Jakarta.

[8] The first accusation that the PKI "masterminded" the Movement appears to have been levelled by the Action Front to Crush September 30th Movement (later abbreviated as KAP-Gestapu) on 4 October 1965: *Berita Yudha*, 5 Oct. 1965. The US Embassy called KAP-Gestapu an "Army-inspired but civilian-staffed action group" and secretly funnelled money to it: US Embassy Jakarta to Department of State, 2 Dec. 1965; US Department of State, *Foreign Relations of the United States, 1964–1968*, vol. 26 (Washington, DC: United States Government Printing Office, 2001), pp. 379–80.

[9] President Sukarno ordered a fact-finding commission to investigate the mass arrests and mass murders in Central Java, East Java, Bali and North Sumatra; the commission did not investigate the September 30th Movement itself. The commission's hastily composed report entirely whitewashed the Army's own role in the killings and grossly underestimated the number of deaths. It was not released to the public. See Anonymous, "Laporan tentang Hasil Fact Finding Commission KOTI", 10 Jan. 1966.

blared that the Movement was "counter-revolutionary" and "barbarous". The Army newspapers *Berita Yudha* and *Angkatan Bersendjata* led the propaganda campaign with calls for the PKI to be outlawed, its offices ransacked and burnt down, its members "eliminated", and all its supporters purged from government agencies, businesses and professional associations. The newspapers printed a variety of false stories alleging that Colonel Katamso's wife and children had been chopped into little pieces, that a man had been ordered to assassinate President Sukarno, that eye-gouging instruments were to be used on enemies spared death, that PKI members had prepared 200 wells in which to dump corpses in Klaten District, and so on.[10]

The most sensational lies centred on female members of the PKI-affiliated Indonesian Women's Movement (Gerakan Wanita Indonesia, Gerwani). Women were alleged to have danced naked in front of captured generals, cut their bodies a thousand times with razor blades, gouged out their eyeballs, and sliced off their genitals.[11] The entire story was fabricated. Autopsies performed on 4–5 October revealed that the generals had died of gunshots and had not been mutilated.[12] President Sukarno's protests about the black propaganda were rarely reported.[13]

The second official narrative came from the director of the Armed Forces History Centre, Nugroho Notosusanto. In the midst of the repression of the PKI and Major General Suharto's undermining of Sukarno's presidency in late 1965, he quickly synthesised the various stories in the Army's files to produce a comprehensive

---

[10] These stories appeared in *Berita Yudha*: "Biadab: Seluruh keluarga Dan Rem 72 ditjintjang" (6 Oct. 1965); "Saja mendapat tugas untuk bunuh presiden" (13 Oct. 1965); "Kebiadaban terror kontra revolusi 'G30S': Bagi jang tidak perlu dibunuh, oleh mereka disediakan alat pentjukil mata" (13 Oct. 1965); and "Di Klaten 'G30S' sediakan 200 'Lubang Buaja'" (9 Dec. 1965).

[11] The core of this story began with a *Berita Yudha* article on 11 October 1965, and further details were added over the following weeks. Saskia E. Wieringa, "The Birth of the New Order State in Indonesia: Sexual Politics and Nationalism", *Journal of Women's History* 15, 1 (Spring 2003): 79–81.

[12] Benedict Anderson, "How did the Generals Die?" *Indonesia* 43 (Apr. 1987): 109–34.

[13] Budi Setiyono and Bonnie Triyana, eds, *Revolusi Belum Selesai: Kumpulan Pidato Presiden Sukarno 30 September 1965 — Pelengkap Nawaksara*, 2 vols. (Semarang: MESIASS, 2003).

narrative: *The 40-Day Debacle of the September 30th Movement.*[14] Some of what he wrote in this book reappeared two years later in an English-language publication that he co-wrote with a military prosecutor, Lieutenant Colonel Ismail Saleh: *The Coup Attempt of the "September 30th Movement" in Indonesia* (1967). This book was intended to convince sceptical foreign observers that the PKI had indeed, as the Army had contended from early October 1965, masterminded the September 30th Movement.[15] Notosusanto penned yet another account of the Movement when he served as editor for the government's massive six-volume history of the nation from ancient times to the present: *Sejarah Nasional Indonesia* (*SNI*).[16] The sixth volume, which covers the Japanese Occupation and the post-1945 period, contains his version of the Movement. It was a shortened and repackaged version of the *SNI* account of the Movement that usually appeared in primary school textbooks. This chapter refers to only one of Notosusanto's three very similar publications: *The Coup Attempt of the "September 30 Movement" in Indonesia.*

The third official narrative was the "White Book" published by the State Secretariat's office in 1994: *The September 30th Movement: The Attempted Coup of the Communist Party of Indonesia: Its Background, Actions and Eradication.*[17] English and Indonesian versions were issued simultaneously to target both domestic and foreign audiences. The book was designed to represent the objective, depersonalised voice of officialdom: the authors were left anonymous; the book's cover was plain white with a red band across the middle,

---

[14] Pusat Penerangan Angkatan Darat, *40 Hari Kegagalan "G-30-S" 1 Oktober–10 November*, 2nd ed. (Jakarta: Staf Pertahanan Keamanan, 1966).

[15] Nugroho Notosusanto and Ismail Saleh, *The Coup Attempt of the 'September 30 Movement' in Indonesia* (Jakarta: Pembimbing Masa, August 1968). The preface is dated 12 April 1967. A translation of the book for the Indonesian public was not issued until 1989: Nugroho Notosusanto and Ismail Saleh, *Tragedi Nasional Percobaan Kup G30S/PKI di Indonesia* (Jakarta: Intermasa, 1989). On the drafting of this book as a response to the "Cornell Paper", see Benedict Anderson, "Scholarship and Raison d'État: Personal Experience", *Indonesia* 62 (Oct. 1996): 1–3.

[16] Sartono Kartodirdjo, Marwati Djoened Poesponegoro and Nugroho Notosusanto, eds, *Sejarah Nasional Indonesia* (Jakarta: Departemen Pendidikan dan Kebudayaan, 1975).

[17] Sekretariat Negara Republik Indonesia, *Gerakan 30 September: Pemberontakan Partai Komunis Indonesia: Latar Belakang, Aksi, dan Penumpasannya* (Jakarta: 1994).

evoking the national flag; the text was divided into numerous sections and sub-sections, each carefully itemised in an eight-page table of contents; the language strived to be wholly literal. The Suharto regime intended for this book to put to rest once and for all debate about the Movement and to provide the one true, complete and final account. No claims were referenced to primary sources, and they did not need to be — if they were in the official book, they must be true.

I have identified these three separate narratives issued under the imprimatur of Suharto in his capacity as either Army Commander or President: the anti-PKI propaganda in the newspapers in late 1965 and early 1966, Notosusanto's writings, and the State Secretariat's White Book.[18] All three affirm that the PKI was responsible for the September 30th Movement, but do they present the same description of how it was responsible? All three affirm that the Movement was treasonous and had to be suppressed, but do they define the nature of the Movement in the same way? All three mention that the PKI was "destroyed" because of its leadership of the Movement, but do they tell the same story about the manner in which the Party was "destroyed"?

First Aporia: How Was the PKI Responsible?

According to press reports of late 1965 and early 1966, the September 30th Movement represented much more than a purge of the Army high command. It was a social revolt led by the PKI that would, if not stopped, lead to many more murders of non-communists throughout the country. The newspapers presented the Movement as a prodigious combination of three different kinds of events: a mutiny against the Army generals, a coup against the President and a mass revolt against all decent patriotic Indonesians. PKI members across the country, from big cities to inaccessible villages, were part of one vast conspiracy to overthrow the state and establish a communist dictatorship. They were allegedly digging mass graves to hold

[18] I consider other official narratives that have emerged since as largely derivative of these three. See, for instance, the 1984 film *Pengkhianatan G30S/PKI*, which was turned into a "novel": Arswendo Atmowiloto, *Pengkhianatan G30S/PKI* (Jakarta: Sinar Harapan, 1986).

their intended victims, stockpiling weapons from China and typing up lists of names of their enemies to be killed. The sadistic tortures inflicted on the generals in Jakarta were to be repeated on all of the Party's opponents around the country. Suharto assured the country that the Movement itself had been defeated within a week after 1 October, but suggested that the countless individuals who had been plotting it were still at large, ready to cause further trouble.[19] Everyone had to be alert and vigilant. Since the September 30th Movement was a nascent social revolt, it was argued, the violence had to be directed against all Party members, not just the top leaders. As Suharto put it in November 1965, the Movement had to be "destroyed down to its roots".[20] Press reports provided justification for the violence against PKI members and sympathisers from late 1965 to mid-1966, and helped generate an atmosphere of "kill or be killed".

Notosusanto and Saleh, writing in 1967, presented a remarkably different version. They claimed that the PKI Politburo "entrusted" Chairman Aidit with the task of working with a group of progressive military officers to prevent a coup by right-wing generals. Aidit, on his own, organised the officers through a clandestine wing of the Party, the Special Bureau (Biro Khusus).[21] The implication was that the PKI leadership and nearly all of the rank-and-file members did not know about this covert action. The book did not prove that everyone in the Party was responsible for the action. Likewise, it did not claim that the action amounted to a social revolt. The unstated conclusion was that Aidit and the Special Bureau had led an action that was supposed to benefit the Party, but Party members could not be held collectively responsible for it. A reader of the book might wonder why the Party had to be "destroyed down to its roots" for a small-scale conspiratorial action organised by a few of its leaders.

The anonymous authors of the 1994 White Book must have recognised this weakness in the Notosusanto and Saleh book on the

[19] "Dalam waktu seminggu kontra revolusi terror 'G30S' gagal total mengkup Negara RI", *Berita Yudha*, 14 Oct. 1965; "G30S tlh. Menodai dan indjak2 martabat ABRI: Menjeleweng dari relnja Revolusi — Semua pelaku dan dalang2nja harus dihantjurkan", *Berita Yudha*, 12 Nov. 1965.

[20] Alex Dinuth, *Dokumen Terpilih Sekitar G-30-S/PKI* (Jakarta: Intermasa, 1997), p. 137.

[21] Notosusanto and Saleh, *The Coup Attempt*, pp. 8–13.

issue of defining the PKI's responsibility, for they did not portray Aidit and the Special Bureau as the only perpetrators. They claimed that the Central Committee, consisting of about 85 people, decided to launch this movement to seize state power. The Politburo implemented the Central Committee's decision by ordering the Special Bureau to carry out the September 30th Movement. Thus, the Party was institutionally responsible for the Movement. In accordance with the book's protocols, no evidence was adduced to support this novel claim of a Central Committee decision. Indeed, the claim appears only as a subheading: the body of the text contains no mention of the decision.[22]

Of the three official narratives, only the newspaper propaganda justified the mass violence against all members and sympathisers of the PKI, all of whom were supposedly still skulking about, plotting attacks on their political rivals throughout the country. Even if we follow the White Book and believe that the Central Committee had approved of the Movement, we have to wonder why more than a million people had to be detained and hundreds of thousands summarily executed for a decision they never had the chance to act upon. Why should everyone affiliated to the PKI have been judged guilty for the September 30th Movement?

The regime's public statements did not address these questions, but its internal documents did. The National Resilience Institute (Lembaga Pertahanan Nasional, Lemhanas), which indoctrinated top officials in the correct version of the "state ideology", prepared a book in 1969 about the events of 1965–66.[23] This book was classified and not meant for public distribution. It raised the question that many officials must have been pondering: Was every member of the PKI necessarily involved in the September 30th Movement/PKI? The answer in the book was a definite "yes": "All members of the PKI can be considered to have been involved either directly or indirectly." The reasoning for such a judgement followed in parentheses: "Each person is required to report to the authorities if he knows of a crime

[22] The subheading reads: "The CC PKI decision to launch a movement to seize state power". Sekretariat Negara, *Gerakan 30 September*, pp. 66–73.

[23] Lembaga Ketahanan Nasional, *Bahan-Bahan Pokok G-30-S/PKI dan Penhancurannya* (1969), pp. 17–8.

that is about to take place and also, according to the PKI's organising principle, all decisions of the Party leadership become binding on all members." According to this argument, many Party members had been informed about the action beforehand and remained silent. They were guilty of not reporting a criminal conspiracy. Even if they had not been informed beforehand and had done nothing to support the action, they were still guilty simply by being members of the Party. Even if they had disagreed with the Party leadership's decision, they were, to use an old Stalinist term, "objectively guilty". The elasticity of the term "indirectly involved" allowed the regime to consider someone who had not participated in the Movement as being "involved".

The fact that this Lemhanas justification for mass violence was not part of the public record, where the term "the PKI" was never disaggregated, suggests that the regime did not want the public to think about the details of the story. Even the classified Lemhanas document did not go into detail. It presented no information about how ordinary Party members had been informed beforehand of the Movement and did not elaborate on the reasoning that condemned all Party members to suffer imprisonment and death for the actions of a handful of leaders.

Given that the official narratives are so inconclusive, let us consider again the question of PKI responsibility. According to the September 30th Movement's first radio announcement around 7:15 a.m. on 1 October 1965, the Movement was "an internal Army affair" led by one of the commanders of the Presidential Guard, Lieutenant Colonel Untung. The official newspaper of the PKI, *Harian Rakjat*, ran an editorial the next day supporting the Movement as "an internal Army affair". These statements disavowing the involvement of any political party did not convince Suharto's Army officers or various anti-communist organisations. Within just three days after the collapse of the Movement, they began claiming that the PKI had been the hidden mastermind. At the time, they had no evidence to support the claim. Their memoirs speak of hunches and intuitions.[24]

[24] Soeharto, *My Thoughts, Words, and Deeds: An Autobiography* (Jakarta: Citra Lamtoro Gung Persada, 1991), p. 100; Yoga Sugama, *Memori Jenderal Yoga* (Jakarta: Bina Rena Pariwara, 1990), pp. 148, 152–3.

They did know that the PKI had something to do with the Movement given that Suharto's troops encountered armed PKI-affiliated youths on the afternoon of 1 October.[25] But they could not point to anything demonstrating PKI leadership of the Movement.

The Army first offered evidence of PKI leadership of the September 30th Movement in November 1965, when it issued reports citing the interrogation transcripts of Lieutenant Colonel Untung (captured in Central Java on 11 October) and his co-conspirator Colonel Latief (captured in Jakarta on 11 October).[26] Both men had supposedly confessed to taking orders from the PKI. For contemporary historians — as for duly constituted courts — confessions extracted in secret interrogation rooms are worthless as evidence, especially as, in this case, both men contradicted the interrogation reports once they were put on trial (in Latief's case, 13 years later).[27]

The only admissible evidence that the Suharto regime obtained in respect to the PKI's leadership of Untung's movement was the courtroom testimony of Sjam, the leader of the Special Bureau, the PKI's covert agency for communicating with active-duty military personnel. Sjam testified in July 1967 as a witness at the trial of the Party's general secretary, Sudisman.[28] Sjam claimed he was the main leader of the September 30th Movement and that he had acted on orders from the Party chairman, D.N. Aidit. Sjam testified that he, as head of the Special Bureau, had recruited Untung, Latief and the other military personnel to carry out the action against Army

---

[25] *Berita Yudha* reported that 20 members of the PKI's youth group, Pemuda Rakyat, were found with guns behind Hotel Indonesia on 2 October, and 15 more were found at the telecommunications building. "Dalam waktu seminggu kontra revolusi terror G30S gagal total mengkup Negara RI", 14 Oct. 1965.

[26] "Penerbitan Chusus No. 2, Tg. 5 Nopember 1965", reprinted in Pusat Penerangan Angkatan Darat, *Fakta2 Persoalan Sekitar 'Gerakan 30 September'* (Jakarta: P.N. Balai Pustaka, 1966). Notosusanto's book *The 40-Day Debacle*, published in December 1965, quotes extensively from the Untung interrogation report to substantiate the claim that the PKI masterminded the Movement (*40 Hari Kegagalan "G-30-S" 1 Oktober–10 November*, pp. 11–6).

[27] On the misuse of these interrogation reports, see John Roosa, "President Sukarno and the September 30th Movement", *Critical Asian Studies* 40, 1 (2008): 143–59.

[28] For excerpts of Sjam's testimony, see Roosa, *Pretext for Mass Murder*, appendix 2. Reports of the Kopkamtib interrogations of Sjam in November 1967 are available at the Guy Pauker Papers, Hoover Institution Archives, Stanford University.

generals suspected of being part of the right-wing General's Council. According to Sjam, the Movement had two components: the military and the political. Untung was in charge of the military side and Sjam of the political side. The two sides, however, were not equal. Sjam claimed that the military side was subordinate to the political side and thus he had overall responsibility for the Movement.

Sjam's courtroom testimony in 1967 and his secret interrogation report of the same year were the main sources of information for Notosusanto and Saleh's book about the central role of the Special Bureau. Many scholars (such as Benedict Anderson, Ruth McVey and W.F. Wertheim) were not convinced that Sjam's story was reliable. He was a previously unknown person claiming to have had great powers inside the PKI, someone with no military experience claiming to be in charge of the PKI's covert relations with military personnel. Many of his fellow political prisoners reported that he enjoyed friendly relations with Army interrogators after his capture. Perhaps he was an Army loyalist planted inside the Party. Harold Crouch, an Australian political scientist analysing the Movement in the 1970s, discounted Sjam's story and concluded that the PKI leadership was at most an equal partner in a joint action with some left-leaning military personnel who had their own agenda.[29]

More reliable information about the relationship between the Special Bureau and the military officers inside the Movement has appeared recently. The highest-ranking military officer inside the Movement, Brigadier General Supardjo, wrote an analysis of the event sometime in 1966 for the benefit of the surviving PKI leaders. While this document has been known since the late 1960s, it was ignored by most scholars. My book *Pretext for Mass Murder* (2006) offered the first detailed, critical analysis of it. Supardjo claimed that an unnamed PKI member working with military officers had been in charge of the Movement, and that was precisely the reason for its failure — leadership by a civilian who did not understand basic military matters, such as the need for a clear chain of command (rather than an informal partnership between a political and a military side)

[29] Harold Crouch, "Another Look at the Indonesian 'Coup'", *Indonesia* 15 (Apr. 1973): 1–20; *The Army and Politics in Indonesia* (Ithaca: Cornell University Press, 1978).

and a carefully designed plan of action, complete with contingency planning.[30]

Supardjo did not name this PKI member, but he was clearly referring to Sjam. Someone who knew Sjam, Asep Suryaman, acknowledged in interviews with me that Sjam was indeed the head of the Special Bureau and that this covert agency of the PKI maintained connections with military personnel.[31] Suryaman worked under Sjam for about one year (1964–65) as one of the five members of the central leadership of the Special Bureau. He regarded Sjam as someone completely loyal to Aidit. He affirmed that Sjam was the main organiser of the September 30th Movement, the person who brought military officers together for planning sessions and insisted that they go through with the plan.

Another important recently discovered document was written by a Politburo member, Iskander Subekti, in 1986. From inside Jakarta's Cipinang prison, Subekti smuggled out the handwritten document page by page. He claimed that Aidit had informed the Politburo in late August 1965 that a group of left-wing military officers wished to foil an upcoming coup attempt by right-wing Army generals: "there was a movement of junior officers opposed to the plan of the Generals Council to stage a coup."[32] Aidit recommended that the Party assist those officers. The Politburo agreed: "In that meeting of the Politburo, the decision was taken to provide political support to the movement. There wasn't any idea of the Party planning the movement." How that "political support" was to be given was left up to Aidit, who selected a handful of Politburo members to secretly discuss the issue over the month of September. Subekti, as part of that small team, knew that Aidit was communicating with the left-wing officers through Sjam. Subekti and the other members of the team were under the impression that the officers were indeed organising the action on their own and relying on Aidit (via Sjam) for political guidance.

---

[30] Roosa, *Pretext for Mass Murder*, Chapter 3.

[31] Asep Suryaman passed away on 30 October 2009. In *Pretext for Mass Murder*, I used the pseudonym Hasan to refer to him.

[32] Iskandar Subekti, "G-30-S Bukan Buatan PKI", Indonesian Exiles of the Left Collection, International Institute of Social History in Amsterdam, the Netherlands.

Subekti insisted in his document that "the PKI" as an organisation was not responsible for the September 30th Movement. Most members of the Politburo did not know about the Movement, and even the members of Aidit's hand-picked special team did not think they were in charge of the Movement: "if the movement originated from the PKI, or was 'masterminded' by the PKI, it had to have been discussed and decided upon by the highest organ of the Party leadership: the Central Committee." But the Central Committee "never discussed the matter, or much less made a decision about it". Subekti's claim here must be correct, and the White Book's claim about a Central Committee decision must be incorrect. Central Committee discussions were not secret. With about 85 members, the Committee could not hope to keep its deliberations confidential. Moreover, Army intelligence had spies inside the top levels of the Party leadership and knew the substance of all its discussions. If the Movement had been discussed in the Central Committee, the Head of Army Intelligence, Major General Parman, would have known about it and would have been able to avoid being killed by the Movement.

Whereas the Subekti document shows that Party leaders thought that the military officers were in charge of the Movement, the Supardjo document reveals that those military officers (Untung, Latief, Supardjo and others) believed that the Party was in charge, and that they were just following orders. Supardjo regretfully admitted that he had trusted the PKI too much: he knew Sjam's plan by itself "did not add up" but assumed that Sjam's superiors, leading such a large, well-organised and well-informed organisation, must have possessed some larger plan within which this night-time abduction of the generals would make strategic sense. Sjam, the middleman between the military officers and the Party leaders, unwittingly bamboozled both sides, dragging them into an action that neither had properly planned.

On the day of the action, the Movement collapsed from the weight of its own mistakes before Suharto's attack in the evening. President Sukarno, meeting Supardjo on the morning of 1 October, ordered that the Movement be called off; and Supardjo agreed to follow the President's order. Untung and Latief also agreed. The group of conspirators took no further action, even though Sjam tried to keep the Movement going by issuing more inflammatory radio announcements in the early afternoon.

In the days after the action, President Sukarno repeatedly urged calm, arguing that the Movement was just a "ripple in the ocean of the Indonesian revolution", one of a long line of violent incidents since Independence was declared in 1945, including several assassination attempts on his own life.[33] He argued that there was no need to round up all PKI members and sympathisers in response to the Movement. Some Army officers loyal to Sukarno tried to prevent indiscriminate repression. The CIA, reporting to the White House on 7 October, was worried that these officers might succeed: "President Sukarno seems to be making progress in his efforts to play down the 30 September Movement and prevent any effective anti-communist action. The US embassy comments that there is danger the Army may settle for action against those directly involved in the murder of the generals and permit Sukarno to get much of his power back."[34] The legally correct response to the Movement was, of course, to identify and prosecute "those directly involved in the murder of the generals". However, the US government and Suharto's clique wanted to use the Movement as a pretext to break the power of both the PKI and Sukarno. And so they ensured that the repression would become indiscriminate. Hundreds of thousands of people who had nothing to do with the event were accused of being "indirectly" involved and then imprisoned without charge or killed. Over the following years, the Suharto regime never ordered an investigation into the details. The ambiguity over the meaning of "the PKI" was necessary in order to implicate everyone in or associated with the Party for a small, covert action that had involved only a handful of the top Politburo leaders.

Second Aporia: What Was the September 30th Movement?

Besides their differences in locating the PKI's responsibility for the Movement, the three official narratives presented to the public could not define the Movement in a precise way. The propaganda in the press generated an atmosphere of fear, claiming that everyone belonging to the PKI was secretly plotting more atrocities in the wake

---

[33] Setiyono and Triyana, *Revolusi Belum Selesai*, vol. 1, pp. 22–3, 38.

[34] US Department of State, "CIA Operations Center to White House Situation Room," 7 Oct. 1965, *Declassified Documents Quarterly* 1, 2 (1975): 53.

of the murder of the six generals. The Movement was not just a purge of the Army leadership or an attempted coup; it was nothing less than a nationwide uprising of demon-possessed atheists bent on bringing murder and mayhem to devout, peace-loving Indonesians.

The second official version, curiously enough, did not repeat these propaganda stories about an imminent PKI terror campaign. Notosusanto and Saleh's book portrays the PKI as passive after the collapse of the Movement on 2 October. They affirmed the correctness of the information that was already on public record: PKI leaders stated in early October that the Party had nothing to do with the Movement and recommended that President Sukarno be allowed to proceed with his own method of resolving the crisis. According to Notosusanto and Saleh, the PKI did not begin to take up arms until 19 October, when its leaders realised that they were going to be attacked in Central Java. The Party leaders reacted to the Army-led repression by authorising the use of weapons: they "belatedly threw off their camouflage of innocence and began to organise for their defense".[35] When planning the Movement, they had not called for ordinary Party members to take up arms. Even after 19 October, their self-defence was limited to some minor actions. Notosusanto and Saleh mention only the erection of roadblocks to stop the RPKAD trucks in Central Java.

The 1994 White Book also did not repeat all the claims in the psy-war propaganda about the PKI digging mass graves, stockpiling eyeball gougers, and so on. It called the Movement both an attempted "seizure of power" and a "revolt", combining the two terms with a backslash (*perebutan kekuasaan/pemberontakan*). The anonymous authors were not concerned about the difference between the two terms. The Indonesian-language title uses the term "revolt" (*pemberontakan*), while the English-language title uses "attempted coup". The latter term accords better with the book's narrative of events, but even that term is not quite accurate. The Movement, according to one passage in the book, did not intend to overthrow President Sukarno, only to force him to grant the PKI more power.[36] It is hard to see from the

[35] Notosusanto and Saleh, *The Coup Attempt*, p. 74. Notosusanto presented a different story in *The 40-Day Debacle*, claiming that the PKI in Central Java had been conducting a campaign of terror since 1 October. See *40 Hari Kegagalan "G-30-S" 1 Oktober–10 November*.

[36] Sekretariat Negara, *Gerakan 30 September*, p. 117.

material presented how the Movement constituted a coup, much less a revolt. There is no mention of PKI uprisings across the country and no mention of civilians being killed by the PKI. In the section on "armed actions" after the Movement had collapsed, the book mentions only an unarmed strike of railway workers and unspecified "attacks" in Solo in October 1965. That is the sum total of the armed revolt prior to the PKI's real attempt at armed struggle in West Kalimantan in 1967 and in south Blitar and the mountains of Central Java in 1968.

So what was the Movement? How should it be categorised? It is clear from the factual record that the September 30th Movement was a mutiny of some sort; it was a purge of the Army's high command by lower-ranking military personnel. The intended victims of the Movement in Jakarta were all senior officers with positions in the General Staff.[37]

But did the Movement extend beyond a purge of the Army high command? The Movement is often called "an attempted coup". Both adherents and detractors of the Suharto regime's versions of the Movement agree on this designation. Going by the Movement's own radio announcements on 1 October, the name would certainly seem to be correct. One announcement "decommissioned" Sukarno's cabinet and stated that "all power" had fallen into the hands of the Movement's Revolutionary Council. But at the time of the announcement in the early afternoon, the Movement's emissary, Brigadier General Supardjo, had already met with Sukarno and had agreed to follow his order to call off the Movement. The radio announcement bore no relation to the actions of the Movement. Supardjo made no attempt to abduct Sukarno or force him to support the Movement. The Movement did not attempt to install any one of its own members as the new Army commander: it left that decision up to Sukarno. If the Movement had intended to overthrow Sukarno, why did it leave the decision on Army caretaker to Sukarno? Untung, Latief and Supardjo could have easily made the decision themselves and insisted that the President endorse their choice.

---

[37] There were four accidental casualties: General Nasution's aide (Lieutenant Tendean), Nasution's five-year-old daughter, a security guard at the house next door, and a nephew of Brigadier General Panjaitan.

The radio announcement on the "decommissioning" of the cabinet should be seen as a last-ditch effort by Sjam to redirect a Movement that had failed to gain Sukarno's support. The Revolutionary Council that the Movement called for on the afternoon of 1 October was originally designed to exert pressure on Sukarno, so that he would appoint more left-wing and PKI ministers, not as a replacement to his cabinet.

Sukarno himself did not believe that the Movement wished to overthrow him. He saw Supardjo as an emissary of a movement that was patriotic and loyal to the President, if misguided. He consulted the Movement on the morning of 1 October as to whom he should appoint as the caretaker Army commander. He took their recommendations into consideration before appointing Major General Pranoto, an appointment that Major General Suharto countermanded. In his later speeches, Sukarno denounced the Movement for that radio announcement stripping his power to appoint ministers, but he stopped short of calling the Movement a coup attempt.[38]

So the Movement was — and was not — a coup attempt. Was it a social revolt? Here the answer is largely "no". By itself, the September 30th Movement did not involve the mobilisation of masses of people. It was a strictly military action. Yet it does appear to have been intended as the starting point for a wider mobilisation, a "lighting of the firecrackers", as Supardjo put it. The Movement's radio announcements on the morning of 1 October called on all people to come out in support of the military personnel who were supposed to be establishing "revolutionary councils" in various towns throughout the country. Aidit had told other Party leaders to listen to the radio for instructions. Party members were not ordered before 1 October to organise demonstrations. Aidit must have expected that demonstrations would come out on the streets once Party members heard the call over the radio. If the Movement had not collapsed, the Party would soon have organised mass demonstrations.

Aidit was not planning on an immediate seizure of power, because he knew that the PKI did not have enough popular support to run the state on its own. He saw the Movement as a step

---

[38] The *Far Eastern Economic Review* complained in an editorial that Sukarno "persists in referring to the *coup* as a 'movement'", 28 Oct. 1965: 147 (italics in original).

towards a coalition government in which the PKI would have greater power. Sukarno would remain the president, and all of his principles (Nationalism-Religion-Communism [Nasakom], the Political Manifesto [Manipol], etc.) would remain the guidelines for state policy. With the right-wing generals out of the way and the Army under a more "progressive" commander, the PKI would have greater room to manoeuvre. Sukarno, always trying to balance competing political forces, would lean more to the left and have the confidence to dismiss some right-wing ministers. Mass demonstrations would show that the Movement had popular support. A violent, wide-ranging revolt, however, had to be avoided because it would endanger the "popular front" upon which the PKI built its political position. The PKI was not ready yet to transcend the nationalist, populist, pro-Sukarnoist position that it had been following since the early 1950s.[39]

The quick collapse of the Movement meant that there were no further actions from the PKI. It was completely passive in the aftermath of the Movement. No revolt was under way when Suharto's shock troops, the RPKAD, started the mass arrests and mass killings in Central Java in late October. The troops met virtually no resistance. Party members, having no prior knowledge of the Movement and having done nothing to support it, did not expect that they would be imprisoned without trial for years or be summarily executed. Some voluntarily presented themselves to police and Army posts, believing they would be briefly held for questioning and then released.[40] The Army was not suppressing a social revolt or engaged in a war; it was attacking unsuspecting, unarmed civilians.

Third Aporia: How Was the PKI "Destroyed"?

The third aporia in official narratives of the Movement concerns the mass killings of people accused of being PKI members or sympathisers. The Suharto regime was never sure how to narrate those killings, whether to exclude them altogether or to make excuses for

[39] On Aidit and the PKI's strategies, see Roosa, *Pretext for Mass Murder*, Chapter 5.

[40] Rinto Tri Hasworo, "Pengangkapan dan Pembunuhan di Jawa Tengah Setelah G-30-S", in *Tahun yang tak Pernah Berakhir: Memahami Pengalaman Korban 65: Esai-Esai Sejarah Lisan*, ed. John Roosa, Ayu Ratih and Hilmar Farid (Jakarta: Elsam, 2004), pp. 25–60.

them. And if excuses were to be made, which ones would work best? The newspapers from October 1965–68 did not carry any reports about the mass killings. According to the press coverage, the "destruction" of the PKI "down to its roots" was an almost bloodless affair. Articles that appeared in the newspapers were about Party chapters disbanding themselves, Party members being fired from government institutions, and mass rallies demanding that President Sukarno ban the PKI. A few reported on the RPKAD killing individual PKI members who resisted them, but none reported on *massacres*.[41]

Notosusanto and Saleh, out of step with Army propaganda in the press, admitted that mass killings had occurred. The killings were supposedly spontaneous acts by overly emotional patriots who wished to take revenge against the PKI for its treasonous coup attempt. The person to blame was President Sukarno, who had not immediately put the PKI leaders on trial and banned the Party. "Seeing justice neglected," they wrote, the people "decided to act as judges themselves, which resulted in the mass killings in Central and East Java and other parts of Indonesia."[42] The killings were "deplorable" but understandable, given popular anger against the PKI for its aggressive actions during the previous six years of Sukarno's Guided Democracy. Local tensions, they wrote, "exploded into communal clashes resulting in bloodbaths".[43] Notice that the authors did not claim that the killings occurred because the PKI had begun a mass social revolt. The killings were presented as acts of revenge for previous PKI actions, not self-defence against an imminent PKI aggression. President Suharto himself, when giving a speech in 1971, endorsed this line of argument. He noted in passing that mass killings had occurred in the countryside in 1965–66 as a result of pre-existing political tensions.[44]

---

[41] The first press reports about massacres of suspected PKI supporters appeared in February–March 1969, when three newspapers in Jakarta (*Harian KAMI*, *Sinar Harapan* and *Indonesia Raya*) ran stories about Army-organised killings in Purwodadi District of Central Java that began in November 1968. See Maskun Iskandar, "Purwodadi: Area of Death" and Jopie Lasut, "Report from Purwodadi", in *The Indonesian Killings of 1965–66*, ed. Robert Cribb (Clayton: Centre of Southeast Asian Studies, Monash University, 1990), pp. 203–26.

[42] Notosusanto and Saleh, *The Coup Attempt*, p. 88.

[43] Notosusanto and Saleh, *The Coup Attempt*, p. 77.

[44] "Surat Perintah 11 Maret Untuk Mengatasi Situasi Konflik Ketika Itu", *Kompas*, 11 Mar. 1971.

The third official narrative, the White Book, remained silent about the mass killings. The killings went unmentioned, as if they had never occurred. The "eradication" of the PKI mentioned in the title referred only to administrative measures to bring PKI members to justice. People suspected of being involved in the September 30th Movement were arrested, interrogated, classified into one of three categories (according to their degree of involvement), and then either released or further detained. It was an entirely rational, bureaucratic and transparent process. The section of the book titled "Spontaneous Mass Actions against the PKI" did not mention any acts of violence. It only mentioned a mass rally and some attacks on PKI-owned buildings in Jakarta on 8 October, and the formation of various anti-communist organisations (Pancasila Front, KAMI, KAPPI and KASI).[45]

Thus, in all these official narratives, a great silence surrounds the Army's actions, decisions and motivations. The Suharto regime presented the Army as the innocent victim of the September 30th Movement. Busy carrying out its patriotic duties of national defence, the Army was suddenly "stabbed in the back". What is most intriguing in these narratives is that the hero, the Army, is not the main character. The focus is almost exclusively on the villain: the PKI. The plot centres on the villain's treacherous actions, starting from the Madiun revolt in 1948. No wonder that some schoolchildren, after watching the regime's film about the September 30th Movement, wanted to take on the roles of PKI characters in their daily games of play-acting, since those roles were of tough guys — unlike the Army generals, who were depicted as genteel family men who could not defend themselves.[46]

In the film, after being victimised the hero counter-attacks — but that violence is nowhere narrated; the actual events of PKI members being beaten up and killed are left unnarrated. The story centres on the victimisation of the hero, not on the hero's righteous vengeance. The violence is referred to only in abstract terms such as "crushing", "destroying", "eliminating" or "purging". Why should

[45] Sekretariat Negara, *Gerakan 30 September*, pp. 134–6.

[46] Anecdote related by Ariel Heryanto, "Where Communism Never Dies: Violence, Trauma, and Narration in the Last Cold War Capitalist Authoritarian State", *International Journal of Cultural Studies* 2, 2 (1999): 162.

violence that is lauded in the abstract not be narrated in its specifics? If that violence were heroic, like the violence against the Dutch troops during the years of the Revolution (1945–49), then one would expect it to be narrated in celebratory terms. The lack of any description of the anti-PKI violence and the casting of men who consider themselves great warriors as victims suggests something amiss in this narrative. It is at the moments of incoherence in the emplotment that the narrative appears false.

The narrative of the PKI's villainy displaces the narrative about the drive to state power by the Army leadership before 1 October 1965, the Army's alliance with the CIA to provoke the PKI into taking some sort of rash action, and its orchestration of the executions of unarmed civilians after the event — all those quite real "stabs in the back". The regime's narrative taken as a whole, with its incoherent emplotment, finds its truth as a diversionary tactic. The narrative is false, and not merely because it is silent about something important — every narrative, given its finiteness, has to pass over many events. The falsity derives from the very way the narrative tries to create coherence out of the events that it includes.

The Suharto regime could not narrate the killings, because they were a crime. There is nothing heroic about mass murder. The Army was not facing another army: it was facing unarmed civilians who were not resisting. From hundreds of oral interviews conducted over the past ten years by researchers at the Indonesian Institute of Social History as well as myself, I have come to the conclusion that the typical pattern was for the victims to be detained first, taken out at night, trucked to an isolated spot in the countryside, shot, stabbed or bludgeoned to death, and then left in unmarked mass graves or dumped in a river.[47] Much more research needs to be done, especially on the relationship between the Army and civilian militias, but it is clear from what is already known that cold-blooded executions, not frenzied mob attacks, accounted for most of the deaths.

The difficulty of turning such actions into a heroic story is revealed in the case of Abdul Rahman Lubis, the pseudonymous executioner in North Sumatra profiled by the filmmaker Joshua Oppenheimer. Unlike so many executioners, Lubis wants to recount

[47] The oral interviews are archived at the Indonesian Institute of Social History in Jakarta.

his deeds and wants to be proud of them. He tries to cast himself as a great warrior, even though he killed bound detainees handed to him by the Army and then dumped their bodies in a river. His actions were as heroic as a machine killing cows in a slaughterhouse — as a civilian, he was just a labour-saving device for the Army. In a paper, Oppenheimer and his co-author, Michael Uwemedimo, comment on Lubis's re-enactments and recounting of the some 32 executions he committed:

> Clichéd invocations of massacre as 'heroic' and 'historic' frame the killing as part of an epochal battle against an enemy of mythic proportions ... Abdul Rahman empowers his victim as a mythic power to be conquered, allowing Abdul and Iwan [another executioner] to claim that power at the moment of slaughter, transforming themselves into heroes rather than people who committed the cowardly deed of executing those with no power to resist.[48]

Most perpetrators have recognised the advantage of keeping the whole story about the "destruction" of the PKI at an abstract level so that their shameful deeds do not have to be described. The aporia must be present for the narrative to be heroic.

Conclusion

During its 32 years in power, the Suharto regime obsessively issued all manner of propaganda about the September 30th Movement. Yet it could never arrive at a narrative with which it could be satisfied, and it could never compose narratives that were not crude, vague and undeveloped. Even the State Secretariat's White Book, issued nearly 30 years after the event, by which time all the evidence should have been carefully amassed and analysed, was entirely unpersuasive: it did not reference any of its claims and was inconsistent about the claims it made. The story about the PKI's responsibility for the Movement constituted the regime's raison d'être. While fit for vulgar indoctrination, it could not be substantiated with detailed, sustained

---

[48] Joshua Oppenheimer and Michael Uwemedimo, "Show of Force: A Cinema-Séance of Power and Violence in Sumatra's Plantation Belt", *Critical Quarterly* 51, 1 (2009): 94.

analysis. The regime assiduously suppressed alternative versions of the event, yet was never consistent in its own telling of the event.

If one puts the three official narratives together, one finds a consistency on the basic claims that "the PKI" was responsible for the September 30th Movement and that the PKI was "destroyed" because of its responsibility for the Movement. But there are three questions for which the official narratives' answers are inconsistent: Who in the PKI was responsible (only Aidit and the Special Bureau, the Central Committee, or every single member)? What kind of event was the September 30th Movement (a purge of the Army high command, a coup attempt, a social revolt, or all three)? And how was the PKI "destroyed" after the Movement had collapsed (by bloodless administrative measures or widespread mass killings)?

Having so thoroughly indoctrinated the populace during and after the Suharto reign, officialdom was stuck in a trap: it wanted to continue the same propaganda as before but also wanted to prevent any detailed investigations about what happened in 1965–66. In December 2009, the Attorney General's Office (AGO), invoking an archaic and draconian law from Sukarno's period of authoritarian rule, banned the Indonesian translation of my book *Pretext for Mass Murder*. When pressed by journalists to explain the reason for the ban, the AGO spokesman claimed that his office had conducted a thorough review of the book and compiled a report cataloguing 143 objectionable passages. The report, however, could not be released to the public. There was to be no public discussion about the errors in the book; having been banned, the volume should simply be forgotten: "We won't go into the details on the reasons because the public, especially at the lower levels, may react in a way that could open the way for conflicts."[49] "We won't go into the details": That could be the motto of all state propaganda about the September 30th Movement — we will not because we cannot; we cannot go into the details without ruining the very narrative we wish to keep as an essential, eternal element of Indonesia's national identity.

---

[49] Dicky Christanto, "AGO Defends Banning of Five Books", *Jakarta Post*, 6 Jan. 2010. In October 2010, in response to a petition by the publisher of my book in Jakarta, the Constitutional Court struck down the 47-year-old law allowing the AGO to unilaterally ban books. The court's decision is a significant step forward for freedom of expression in Indonesia. For more information about the case, see <http://lawanpelaranganbuku.blogspot.com/> (accessed 26 Feb. 2012).

3

International Dimensions of the 1965–68 Violence in Indonesia

*Bradley Simpson**

On the morning of 1 October 1965, US President Lyndon Johnson received a terse situation report at the White House from the Central Intelligence Agency: "A power move which may have far reaching implications is underway in Jakarta."[1] Within 24 hours of the still murky events taking place on the other side of the globe, efforts were under way in Washington and London. In Washington, National Security Advisor McGeorge Bundy and his staff began planning for the resumption of US aid to Indonesia, which had been gradually cut off over the preceding 18 months as relations with President Sukarno soured. The White House also began planning for the possible provision of covert assistance to Indonesia's Armed Forces, hoping to exploit the political possibilities of what officials assumed to be a failed coup attempt by the Indonesian Communist Party (Partai Komunis Indonesia, PKI).[2] Across the Atlantic, British officials who had spent

---

* Adapted from *Economists with Guns: Authoritarian Development and U.S.-Indonesian Relations, 1960–1968* by Bradley Simpson. Copyright (c) 2008 by the Board of Trustees of the Leland Stanford Jr. University. All rights reserved. Used with the permission of Stanford University Press, www.sup.org.

[1] Memo for President Johnson, 1 Oct. 1965, US Department of State, *Foreign Relations of the United States, 1964–1968* [hereafter *FRUS, 1964–68*], vol. 26 (Washington, DC: US Government Printing Office, 2001), pp. 300–1.

[2] Memo from Bundy and Rostow to Ball, 2 Oct. 1965, Record Group 59, Policy Planning Staff Subject and Country Files, 1965–1969, Box 319, National Archives and Records Administration [hereafter NARA]; CIA Intel Memo OCI No. 2330/65, 3 Oct. 1965, NSF CO File, Indonesia, vol. 5, Memos, 10/65–11/65, NARA.

the previous two years conducting covert operations in response to Indonesia's policy of Confrontation with Malaysia immediately sent Norman Reddaway, the Coordinator of Political Warfare against Indonesia, to his new post in Singapore in order to take advantage of the changed circumstances in Jakarta.[3] Over the next three months the US and UK, supported by other nations in the region, conducted wide-ranging secret operations aimed at supporting and encouraging the Army-led slaughter of alleged PKI supporters and the eventual ouster of Indonesian President Sukarno, building on programmes geared to this end and under way for the better part of a year.

Historians and political scientists writing about the September 30th Movement and the ensuing slaughter have rightly stressed their internal roots and dynamics. But these could also be considered as international events of profound importance for all of the Asian powers in the global Cold War. The mass killings in Indonesia were a form of efficacious terror, an indispensable prerequisite to the overthrow of Sukarno, to Indonesia's reintegration into the regional political economy and international system, and to the ascendance of a modernising military regime. The mass violence against the Indonesian Left, in other words, had a political and economic logic apparent to officials in London, Washington, Tokyo, Kuala Lumpur, Moscow and elsewhere.[4]

The Western commitment to an authoritarian regime in Indonesia had deep roots. Following the collapse of the regional PRRI (Pemerintah Revolusioner Republik Indonesia, Revolutionary Government of the Indonesian Republic) and Permesta rebellions in the late 1950s, successive US Administrations encouraged the emergence of a military-led regime in Indonesia committed to modernisation and anti-communism. They worked with elements of the Indonesian Armed Forces and Western-oriented intellectuals who had become

---

[3] Top Secret Telegram from the Political Adviser to CinCFE Singapore, 1 Oct. 1965, FO 1011-2, United Kingdom National Archives [hereafter UKNA]; David Easter, "British Intelligence and Propaganda during the 'Confrontation', 1963–66", *Intelligence and National Security* 16, 2 (Summer 2001): 83–102.

[4] Memo of Conversation, 14 Feb. 1966, Record Group 59, State Department Central Files 1964–1966, POL 2 INDON, National Archives and Records Administration [hereafter RG59 1964–66 documents referred to by file code and NARA].

disillusioned with the perceived failures of parliamentary democracy to facilitate political stability and promote economic development. The US and other Western governments provided these domestic forces with military and economic assistance; philanthropic foundations trained economists and military officers in management and administration; international financial institutions such as the International Monetary Fund and the World Bank promoted early variants of "structural adjustment"; and social scientists deployed theory to account for and legitimise the growing political and economic role of the military in the development process. Their goal was not only the containment of communism but also the reversal of Indonesia's non-aligned position and ramshackle state-led development plans.

US officials in the 1960s believed that integrated technical, military and economic assistance programmes would stabilise and modernise the Indonesian economy while plugging holes in the containment dyke being breached by PKI activists and Soviet and Chinese officials. But this was a contested strategy, vulnerable to domestic critics in the US, dependent upon Western-oriented technocrats in Indonesia and Sukarno's willingness to adopt policies urged upon it by the US and the IMF, and contingent upon Washington's allies playing roles that complemented its regional policies. Chief among these unforeseen contingencies was Britain's formation of Malaysia out of the remnants of its Southeast Asian empire in the early 1960s. Indonesia's opposition to Malaysia's creation in late 1963 would lead over the next two years to a low-level military confrontation with Malaysia (Konfrontasi), Britain and, indirectly, the United States. Konfrontasi also accelerated Indonesia's gravitation towards China and away from the USSR, and accelerated political polarisation and economic collapse in Indonesia. By the time of the September 30th Movement, the US and many of its allies viewed the wholesale annihilation of the PKI and its mass base as an indispensable prerequisite to Indonesia's reintegration into the international political system, and supported the establishment of a modernising military regime as the logical means of achieving this aim.

The Collapse of US-Indonesian Relations

Konfrontasi transformed Indonesia's foreign relations and the regional strategies of the US, Britain, China and the USSR, at a time when the U.S was deepening its commitment to the war in Vietnam and thus unable to respond with great attention or resources. Accordingly, the US gradually reduced economic and military assistance to Indonesia, while seeking to protect US investments and maintain contacts with sympathetic military officers. In August 1964 the US adopted a covert strategy aimed at ousting Sukarno from power and sparking a violent conflict between the Armed Forces and the PKI. US intelligence concluded that President Sukarno's grip on power was unlikely to be challenged during his lifetime, US Ambassador-at-large Averell Harriman argued, "unless, of course, some [of] our friends wished to try to overthrow him".[5] Commonwealth governments had already arrived at such a position, having adopted a covert warfare approach in 1963 to frustrate Indonesia's ability to wage Confrontation and, if possible, to provoke "a prolonged struggle for power leading to civil war or anarchy".[6] Nevertheless, British and US officials agreed that the PKI was unlikely to come to power in the immediate future, and that the Army was reluctant to crush the PKI unless first provoked. Edward Peck, Assistant Secretary of State in the British Foreign Office, suggested "there might be much to be said for encouraging a premature PKI coup during Sukarno's lifetime" — provided, of course, the coup failed.[7]

Indonesia's relations with the West neared collapse in early 1965, following Sukarno's withdrawal of Indonesia from the United Nations in anger over the Netherlands' refusal to return West Papua, the continuation of Confrontation, and accelerating economic deterioration — trends which all worked to the benefit of the PKI.[8] Jakarta's diplomatic realignment away from the Soviet Union and towards China — which expressed its support for PKI militants and

---

[5] National Intelligence Estimate 55-63, "The Malaysia-Indonesia Conflict", 30 Oct. 1963, NSF, NIE Box 55, Indonesia, Lyndon B. Johnson Library [hereafter LBJL].

[6] John Subritzky, *Confronting Sukarno: British, American, Australian and New Zealand Diplomacy in the Malaysian-Indonesian Confrontation, 1961–1965* (New York: St. Martin's Press, 1999), pp. 97–102; David Easter, "British and Malaysian Covert Support for Rebel Movements in Indonesia during the 'Confrontation,' 1963–66", *Intelligence and National Security* 14, 4 (Winter 1999), p. 202.

[7] "The Succession Problem in Indonesia", DOS/INR Research Memo RFE-16, 9 Mar. 1964, NSF CO Files Indonesia, vol. 1, LBJL; Memo from Templeton to Peck, 19 Dec. 1964, FO General Correspondence Files FO 371/15251, DH 1015/112, UKNA.

[8] CIA Special Memo, Office of National Estimates, 26 Jan. 1965, NSF, NIE 55, Box 7, LBJL.

began calling for the formation of an armed "fifth force" of workers and peasants — bolstered this perception.[9] While continuing to meet with PKI officials and maintaining cordial public relations with Sukarno, the Brezhnev government responded to Indonesia's tilt towards Beijing by seeking counterweights to the increasingly pro-China PKI, turning towards the Armed Forces, PNI and even Nahdlatul Ulama. Soviet officials approvingly quoted Nahdlatul Ulama officials who argued that the "PKI is working against the Soviet Union and the Soviet Union is a friend of Indonesia. Therefore [the] PKI should be taken care of."[10]

The PKI threw down an even greater challenge to Western interests in Indonesia in February 1965 when estate workers in the Party-affiliated Plantation Workers' Union of the Republic of Indonesia (Sarekat Buruh Perkebunan Republik Indonesia) attempted to seize plantations owned by US Rubber Company in North Sumatra. As demonstrators stormed the US Consulate in Medan in February 1965, Estates Minister Frans Seda, Third Deputy Foreign Minister Chaerul Saleh and President Sukarno called in US Rubber and Goodyear representatives to announce that the government was taking temporary "administrative control" of foreign-owned rubber estates and endorsed the takeover of Western properties more generally, a prospect that greatly alarmed Caltex, Stanvac and Shell Oil, the major oil companies still operating in Indonesia.[11] "It's been made clear to Sukarno and key military commanders," US officials in Jakarta warned, "that the moment anything happens indicating interference with control of Caltex ... [the] lift of oil from Indonesia will be halted", which would cause the economy to implode.[12] Even the *Indonesian Herald* editorialised on the need to ensure the flow of oil,

[9] CIA Intelligence Information Cable 314/00496-65, 13 Jan. 1965, NSF CO Files Indonesia, vol. 3, LBJL; Subritzky, *Confronting Sukarno*, p. 132.

[10] Stephen P. Gilbert, "Wars of Liberation and Soviet Military Aid Policy", *Orbis* 10, 2 (Fall 1966): 830–46, quoted in Odd Arne Westad, *The Global Cold War: Third World Interventions and the Making of Our Time* (New York: Cambridge University Press, 2005), p. 187.

[11] Telegram 1642, US Embassy Jakarta to State Department, 22 Feb. 1965, NSF CO File Indonesia, Box 246, vol. 3, LBJL; Memo from James C. Thomson to McGeorge Bundy, 1 Mar. 1965, James C. Thomson Papers, Box 12, John F. Kennedy Library.

[12] Telegram 1718, US Embassy Jakarta to State Department, 3 Mar. 1965, PET INDON-US, NARA.

while Julius Tahija of Caltex predicted that Army leaders would move against First Deputy Prime Minister Subandrio and the PKI if company takeovers halted production, a move that would immediately cripple the Armed Forces, which relied heavily upon air and sea transport.[13] "In the long run," George Ball fretted to McGeorge Bundy, "this may be more important than South Vietnam."[14] This was neither the first nor the last time that US officials made such comments in internal documents regarding the position of Western capital in Indonesia.

The political and economic crisis created the essential preconditions for the conflagration that erupted on 1 October and continued in the months that followed. US, British and other Western policymakers were now convinced that even if Sukarno could be overthrown, Armed Forces disunity and the continued existence of the PKI were the main source of their troubles in Indonesia.[15] British fears that Indonesia intended to continue Confrontation indefinitely and US concerns about the PKI's growing strength also prompted discussions in both London and Washington about the possibility of dismembering Indonesia.[16] The Foreign and Commonwealth Relations Offices concluded in September 1965 that Britain should consider "making a determined effort to break up Indonesia because, however chaotic and unstable the consequences, this would be preferable to a strong and menacing communist state of 100 million people".[17] There is no doubt that the Johnson Administration and its British counterparts, far from being resigned to failure, were actively considering not only ways to oust Sukarno from power, but also, should that fail, contingency plans to break up Indonesia.

---

[13] Telegram 1844, US Embassy Jakarta to State Department, 13 Mar. 1965, PET INDON-US, NARA; Editorial, "Ensuring Oil Flow", *Indonesian Herald*, 23 Mar. 1965.

[14] Transcript of telephone conversation between Ball and Bundy, 15 Mar. 1965, George Ball Papers, Box 4, LBJL.

[15] Guidance No. 7, "Indonesia: The Coming Struggle for Power", 6 Jan. 1965, FO 371-180311, UKNA.

[16] Matthew Jones, *Conflict and Confrontation in Southeast Asia, 1961–1965: Britain, the United States and the Creation of Malaysia* (Cambridge and New York: Cambridge University Press, 2001), pp. 128, 212, 227–8, 231, 263; Telegram 1161, State Department to US Embassy Jakarta, 15 Apr. 1964, POL 23-9 INDON, Box 2317, NARA; Easter, "British and Malaysian Covert Support", p. 205.

[17] Easter, "British and Malaysian Covert Support", p. 205.

The continued deterioration of relations with Jakarta convinced the State Department to "reduce [the] American presence in Indonesia" while attempting to create "conditions which will give the elements of potential strength the most favorable conditions for confrontation" between the Army and PKI.[18] In late February, the CIA reviewed the progress of its covert operations in Indonesia and proposed an operational programme for future activities, including "covert liaison with and support for existing anti-Communist groups, black letter operations, media operations, including [the] possibility [of] black radio and political action within existing Indonesian institutions and organisations" aimed at "exploiting PKI factionalism".[19] At the Baguio Chiefs of Mission Conference a few days later, US Ambassador to Indonesia Howard Jones mused that "from our viewpoint, of course, an unsuccessful coup attempt by the PKI might be the most effective development to start a reversal of political trends in Indonesia".[20] Declassified British files reveal that in the winter of 1965, the UK also decided to expand its military and covert political operations directed against Indonesia, creating a "director of political warfare against Indonesia" to be based at the Information Research Department in Singapore.[21]

The September 30th Movement and the Destruction of the PKI

US and British worries became moot once the September 30th Movement occurred. More important than the September 30th Movement itself, as John Roosa has argued, was the way that Major General

[18] Telegram 795, State Department to US Embassy Jakarta, 5 Mar. 1965, NSF CO Files Indonesia, vol. 4, LBJL; Memo for the President from Ball, undated, NSF Indonesia, vol. 4, LBJL; Frederick Bunnell, "American 'Low Posture' Policy toward Indonesia in the Months Leading up to 1965 'Coup'", *Indonesia* 50 (Oct. 1990): 40.
[19] Memo prepared for the 303 Committee, 23 Feb. 1965, *FRUS, 1964–1968*, p. 234.
[20] Presentation by Howard Jones at the 1965 Chief of Mission Conference, n.d., Howard Jones Papers, Box 22, Hoover Institution Archives, Stanford University.
[21] Memo from E.H. Peck to Lord Walston, "Political Preparations for Proposed Military Action", 6 Jan. 1965, FO 371-181490, UKNA; Memo, "War of Nerves — Indonesia", 23 Sept. 1965, FO 1011-1, UKNA.

Suharto, the Indonesian Army and their supporters in the international community used the Movement to justify the annihilation of the PKI.[22] The emergence of the Indonesian Army as the dominant political force and the military's pressing need to address the country's economic crisis provided the United States and other Western powers with unusual leverage to shape the conditions under which the Army would consolidate its power and legitimise its role in a modernising military regime. Washington was confident that "the next few days, weeks, and months may offer unprecedented opportunities for us to begin to influence people and events, as the military begin to understand problems and dilemmas in which they find themselves".[23]

The US, British, Japanese, Soviet and other embassies initially reacted to the events of 1 October 1965 with surprise and confusion. Speculation about responsibility for the September 30th Movement centred quickly on the PKI, although the US Embassy admitted that "the situation in Jakarta is far from clear".[24] Soviet officials offered no public comment until nearly two weeks after the Movement had collapsed; the scant documents that have been made available to researchers suggest their genuine uncertainty about what had happened.

In Washington, officials assembled an ad hoc Indonesia working group, recognising that the opportunity to crush the PKI was at hand but fearing the Army might not go all the way.[25] The CIA warned of the danger that the Army might "settle for action against those directly involved in the murder of the generals and permit Sukarno to get much of his power back". The Army's destruction of the PKI, the Ambassador cabled Washington, "will not be successful unless it is willing to attack communism as such", which meant going after

[22] John Roosa, *Pretext for Mass Murder: The September 30th Movement and Suharto's Coup d'État in Indonesia* (Madison: University of Wisconsin Press, 2006).

[23] Telegram 545, State Department to US Embassy Jakarta, 29 Oct. 1965, POL 23-9 INDON, NARA.

[24] Transcript of telephone conversation between Ball and McNamara, 1 Oct. 1965, Ball Papers, Box 4, Indonesia 4/64–11/65, LBJL; Cabinet Joint Intelligence Committee, Special Assessment 796/65, Indonesia, 4 Oct. 1965, PREM 13, 2718, UKNA.

[25] CIA Intel Memo OCI No. 2330/65, "The Upheaval in Indonesia", 3 Oct. 1965, NSF CO File, Indonesia, vol. 5, Memos, 10/65–11/65, LBJL; Ragna Boden, "The 'Gestapu' Events of 1965 in Indonesia: New Evidence from Russian and German Archives", *Bijdragen tot de Taal-, Land- en Volkenkunde* 163, 4 (2007): 519.

Sukarno and the entire PKI apparatus, including unarmed rank-and-file members and affiliates.[26] The British Embassy agreed that the Army might be "letting this opportunity slip through their fingers as Sukarno attempts to exercise restraint".[27]

Since no Western intelligence agencies argued that PKI involvement in the September 30th Movement extended to the rank and file, one can only conclude that their greatest fear was that the Army might *refrain* from mass violence against the Party's unarmed members and supporters. UK Ambassador Andrew Gilchrist called for "early and carefully [planned] propaganda and psywar activity to exacerbate internal strife" and ensure the "destruction and putting to flight of the PKI by the Indonesian Army".[28] The US and Britain, joined by Australia, offered their support to the Indonesian Army by creating and distributing propaganda about "the PKI's guilt, treachery and brutality" and alleged ties between the September 30th Movement and China.[29]

On 13 October, US Secretary of State Dean Rusk cabled the US Embassy in Jakarta that the time had come to "give some indication to military of our attitudes toward recent and current developments". Noting that the Army's campaign against the PKI was picking up steam, Rusk continued: "If [the] army's willingness to follow through against the PKI is in any way contingent upon or subject to influence by US, we do not wish miss opportunity for US action."[30] General Nasution provided an opportunity when his aide approached US Ambassador Marshall Green, who had replaced Ambassador Jones in July 1965, to request portable communications equipment for use by the Army high command. The move towards covert US assistance

---

[26] CIA Information cable, OCI 13114, 17 Oct. 1965, NSF CO File, Indonesia, vol. 5, LBJL.

[27] Telegram 671, Singapore to Foreign Office, 5 Oct. 1965, FO 371-180313, UKNA.

[28] Telegram 264 from the Political Adviser to CinCFE Singapore, 5 Oct. 1965, FO 1011-2, UKNA.

[29] Telegram 868, US Embassy Jakarta to State Department, 5 Oct. 1965, POL 23-9 INDON, NARA; Drew Cottle and Narim Najjarine, "The Department of External Affairs, the ABC and Reporting of the Indonesian Crisis, 1965–1969", *Australian Journal of Politics and History* 49, 1 (2003): 48–60.

[30] Telegram 452, State Department to US Embassy Jakarta, 13 Oct. 1965, NSF CO File Indonesia, vol. 5, LBJL.

for the Indonesian Army signalled Washington's tacit withdrawal of recognition of Sukarno as the legitimate leader of Indonesia. Other embassies in Jakarta were of the same view. Japanese Ambassador Saito Shizuo, who called for Western governments to provide economic aid to the Indonesian military, told British officials: "An Army dominated government is so much better than any other prospect that we cannot allow it to be ruined in public esteem by an accumulation of public misery in the form of a rice famine."[31]

Over the next few weeks, Western embassies in Jakarta fed on a steady diet of gruesome reports about the massacres then under way. At the end of October, reports reached the US Embassy of mass attacks against PKI supporters in East, Central and West Java. A military adviser just returned from Bandung reported that villagers were "clearing out PKI members and affiliates and turning them over to Army" for arrest or execution.[32] On 4 November the Embassy cabled the State Department that RPKAD forces in Central Java under Colonel Sarwo Edhie's command were "providing Muslim youth with training and arms" and "will keep them out in front against PKI". While Army leaders arrested higher-level PKI leaders for interrogation, "smaller fry" were "being systematically arrested and jailed or executed".[33] In North Sumatra and Aceh a few days later: "IP-KI Youth Organisation, and other anti-Com elements" were engaged in a "systematic drive to destroy PKI ... with wholesale killings reported"; the "specific message" from the Army "is that it is seeking to 'finish off' the PKI".[34]

---

[31] Saito quoted in Telegram 1238, US Embassy Jakarta to State Department, 28 Oct. 1965, AID 1 INDON, NARA; John Welfield, *An Empire in Eclipse: Japan in the Postwar American Alliance System* (London and Atlantic Highlands: Athlone Press, 1988), p. 219; Telegram 2543, British Embassy Jakarta to Foreign Office, 27 Oct. 1965, FO 371-181519, UKNA.

[32] Telegram 545, State Department to US Embassy Jakarta, 29 Oct. 1965, *FRUS, 1964–1968*, pp. 340–43; Telegram 1255, US Embassy Jakarta to State Department, 28 Oct. 1965, POL 23-9 INDON, NARA.

[33] Telegram 1326, US Embassy Jakarta to State Department, 4 Nov. 1965, POL 23-9 INDON, NARA.

[34] Telegram 1374, US Embassy Jakarta to State Department, 8 Nov. 1965, NSF CO File, Indonesia, vol. 5, LBJL; Telegram 1401, US Embassy Jakarta to State Department, 10 Nov. 1965, POL 23-9 INDON, NARA. IPKI (Ikatan Pendukung Kemerdekaan Indonesia or League of Upholders of Indonesian Independence) was an Army-affiliated party.

US officials were quick to publicly praise Major General Suharto and the military for taking action and sought to absolve the good anti-communists from wrongdoing. On 20 October, for example, a US Airgram with biographical information about Major General Suharto informed Washington that he was known for "his smart appearance" and "has a good reputation as incorruptible and lives modestly".[35] On 1 December, despite the overwhelming evidence to the contrary, Ambassador Green noted that the "East Java mass killings are perpetrated by irresponsible elements, whereas political parties and others are cooperating with military to stop this rampage".[36] In a more sober communiqué, the Political Affairs Officer at the US Embassy cautioned:

> The present struggle between Sukarno and military leaders has led many Western observers to cast Nasution and other key Army Generals not only as determined opponents of communism (which they are) but as sincere proponents of democracy (which they are not). There is in fact every reason to believe that the Indonesian military leadership is dedicated to a totalitarian form of government.[37]

The gathering reports that a campaign of detentions and mass murder might be under way did not give pause to US or other Western officials. Instead, as the scope and intensity of the Army's campaign against the PKI became apparent, US officials began considering greater covert assistance to the Army in the form of military and economic aid. At the end of October, White House officials began plans to provide covert aid to the Indonesian military, which would need food, raw materials, access to credit and "small weapons and equipment ... to deal with the PKI". Ambassador Green recommended that the US move forward with assistance in the form of communications equipment, medicine and, later, small arms, noting approvingly that the Army was "moving relentlessly to exterminate the

---

[35] Airgram A-286, US Embassy Jakarta to State Department, 20 Oct. 1965, POL 6 INDON, NARA.
[36] Telegram 33A, US Embassy Jakarta to State Department, 1 Dec. 1965, POL 23-9 INDON, NARA.
[37] Airgram A-489, US Embassy Jakarta to State Department, 1 Feb. 1966, POL 23-9 INDON, NARA.

PKI". Washington agreed with the embassy that aid was warranted, but the Administration was split over whether to tie the provision of short-term, covert aid to the resumption of overt economic and military assistance.[38] Although the US was "generally sympathetic with and admiring of what [the] army [is] doing", US Political Consul Francis Galbraith told an aide to General Nasution that serious disagreements between the two countries remained, especially with regard to US oil interests, which, if not resolved, could preclude the extension of aid.[39] Over the next few months, however, a small but politically significant stream of aid, including small arms and cash, was delivered to Army officers. While some historians and US officials have suggested that the US stance in Vietnam emboldened the Indonesian Army in its efforts to destroy the PKI, far more important were the concrete expressions of support and the unmistakable signals that such support conveyed about the wishes of Washington and its allies.[40]

US officials were reasonably well informed about the mass violence that was under way. The US Consulate in Medan reported that a "widespread slaughter" was taking place.[41] On 13 November, Police Information Chief Colonel Budi Juwono reported that "50–100 PKI members are being killed every night in east and central Java by civilian anti-communist groups with blessing of Army". Three days later "bloodthirsty" Pemuda Pancasila members informed the consulate in Medan that the organisation "intends to kill every PKI

---

[38] Telegram 1304, US Embassy Jakarta to State Department, 2 Nov. 1965, NSF CO File Indonesia, vol. 5, LBJL; Memo from Assistant for Indonesia to Deputy Assistant Secretary of Defense for ISA, 30 Oct. 1965, *FRUS, 1964–1968*, pp. 351–3.

[39] Telegram 1326, US Embassy Jakarta to State Department, 4 Nov. 1965, POL 23-9 INDON, NARA.

[40] Telegram 1090, US Embassy Jakarta to State Department, 20 Oct. 1965, POL 12 INDON, NARA; Memo from Assistant for Indonesia to Deputy Assistant Secretary of Defense for ISA, 30 Oct. 1965; Memo from Assistant for Indonesia to Deputy Assistant Secretary of Defense for ISA, 30 Oct. 1965, *FRUS, 1964–1968*, pp. 343–5; Telegram 1288, US Embassy Jakarta to State Department, 1 Nov. 1965, POL 23-9 INDON, NARA.

[41] Telegram 32, US Consulate Surabaya to State Department, 14 Nov. 1965, NSF CO File, Indonesia, vol. 5, LBJL.

member they can get their hands on".[42] Other sources told the consulate that "much indiscriminate killing is taking place". Consular officials concluded that, even accounting for exaggeration, there was a "real reign of terror".[43] The CIA reported late in the month that former PKI members in Central Java were being "shot on sight by Army". Missionaries in East Java told the US Consulate in Surabaya that 15,000 communists had reportedly been killed in the East Java district of Tulungagung alone. In Pasuruan, East Java, a British engineer named Ross Taylor described the massacres of workers at the Nebritex textile factory. Using lists of known or suspected members of the PKI, the Indonesian Workers' Union (Sentral Organisasi Buruh Seluruh Indonesia) or PKI-affiliate groups, the local Army commander placed victims in one of five categories, killing those in the first three and arresting the rest. Taylor estimated that 2,000 people had been killed in the vicinity of the factory (and at least 200 from the factory itself) since late November, with Army units working from the main roads and radiating outwards.[44]

The US response to mass murder in Indonesia was enthusiastic. Washington began giving aid to the Army just as the mass killings started. It continued to do so long after it was clear that atrocities on a truly massive scale were being committed — and in the expectation that US assistance would contribute to this end. Not a single official ever expressed concern in public or private about the slaughter. "Our policy was silence," US National Security Advisor Walt Rostow later wrote to President Johnson, which he deemed a good thing "in light of the wholesale killings that have accompanied the transition" from Sukarno to Suharto.[45] The CIA argued that "we should avoid being too cynical about [the Army's] motives and its self interest, or too hesitant about the propriety of extending ... assistance *provided* we can do so covertly" and without being embarrassed. "No one

[42] Telegram 1438, US Embassy Jakarta to State Department, 13 Nov. 1965, POL 23-9 INDON, NARA.
[43] Telegram 65, US Consulate Medan to State Department, 16 Nov. 1965, POL 23-9 INDON, NARA.
[44] Letter from British Embassy Jakarta to Foreign Office, 16 Dec. 1965, FO 371-181323, UKNA.
[45] Memo from Walt Rostow to President Johnson, 8 June 1966, NSF CO Files Indonesia vol. 7, 5/66-6/67, LBJL.

cared," recalled Howard Federspiel, the State Department's Department of Intelligence and Research staffer for Indonesia in 1965, "as long as they were Communists, that they were being butchered."[46]

The US was hardly alone in displaying this callous attitude. The Soviets continued to ship weapons throughout the period in an effort to maintain relations with the military and further undermine Chinese influence, "letting it be known to the Generals that if it comes down to a choice between the PKI or no PKI, the USSR would prefer the latter". Thailand offered rice to the Indonesian Army as a means of encouraging it both to destroy the PKI and to oust Sukarno.[47] Historians still lack access to sufficient Soviet and Chinese archival materials to come to firm conclusions about these countries' knowledge of the September 30th Movement or their internal deliberations in the weeks that followed. It is clear, nevertheless, that the Soviet Union, while condemning the massacres and persecution of "progressive" elements in Indonesia, kept its distance from the PKI. Soviet officials accused the Party of adventurism, lax membership policies and recruitment policies, and insufficient discipline — in effect suggesting that the PKI was getting what it deserved. Before long, Soviet officials were privately blaming the September 30th Movement and the destruction of the PKI on Chinese-inspired adventurism, having long since abandoned the Party to its fate.[48] China's leadership, having spent the previous three years cultivating closer ties to the PKI and urging the Party to greater militancy, was reportedly "shocked" by the turnaround in Indonesia. Far from chastening the PKI, however, many Chinese officials were convinced that "they should concentrate on supporting indigenous left-

---

[46] CIA Memo, 9 Nov. 1965, *FRUS, 1964–1968*, pp. 361–3; Federspiel quoted in Kathy Kadane, "Ex-Agents Say CIA Compiled Death Lists for Indonesians", *States News Service*, 19 May 1990; Kai Bird, *The Color of Truth. McGeorge Bundy and William Bundy: Brothers in Arms* (New York: Simon & Schuster, 1998), p. 353.

[47] Memo for Mr. Bundy from Chet Cooper, 16 Oct. 1965, NSF Name File, Box 2, Chet Cooper folder, LBJL; Letter from British Embassy Moscow to Foreign Office, 12 Nov. 1965, FO 371 180334, UKNA.

[48] Boden, "The 'Gestapu' Events of 1965 in Indonesia": 515–20; Cablegram 2960 from Canberra to Washington, 13 Oct. 1965, File 3034/2/1/8, ANA; Cablegram 420 from Australian Embassy Moscow to Canberra, 16 Oct. 1965, ANA.

wing revolutionary movements", helping to inaugurate a Maoist turn among surviving PKI cadres.[49]

US officials, like their counterparts in the Indonesian Army, viewed the campaign to eliminate the PKI leadership and destroy its infrastructure in strategic terms, as "a power struggle" with a rival power centre, "not an ideological struggle". The British Consul at Medan framed the Army-PKI struggle in Sumatra over control of local ports and rubber and tin estates as one "for the commanding heights of the Indonesian economy", and for the foreign exchange reserves and access to resources which such control conveyed. Not surprisingly, the tin and rubber estates in North Sumatra were the scene of some of the bloodiest attacks against PKI supporters, with the Army "arresting, converting or otherwise disposing of some 3000 PKI members a week".[50]

The Price of Aid

The Johnson Administration remained deeply ambivalent about the Indonesian military, even as it supported the Army's efforts to annihilate the PKI and seize control of the country. This ambivalence stemmed partly from the Army's wavering stance throughout late 1965 on removing President Sukarno, and partly from concern that it would resist Western demands for a restructuring of Indonesia's economy and foreign policy. Officials in Washington, London and other capitals were aghast at the prospect of any accommodation and insisted that the military must not only destroy the PKI but also get rid of Sukarno and his supporters.[51] They agreed that so long as Sukarno remained in power, it would be difficult to resume assistance or for the Indonesian Army to begin making the drastic changes necessary to restore political and economic stability under conditions

[49] Cablegram 371, Australian Trade Commission, Hong Kong, to Department of External Affairs, 13 Nov. 1965, File 3034/11/87, ANA.

[50] See Airgram A-512 from Jakarta to State Department, 11 Feb. 1966, DEF 6 INDON, NARA; Dispatch from British Consulate Medan to Foreign Office, 3 Jan. 1966, FO 371-186027, UKNA.

[51] Telegram 1304, US Embassy Jakarta to State Department, 2 Nov. 1965, NSF CO Files Indonesia, vol. 5, LBJL.

acceptable in Washington and other capitals.[52] More important, as one official noted, the Army was "still strongly nationalistic and crushing the PKI won't change this".[53]

Within hours of the September 30th Movement, the White House began cataloguing the Army's need for short-term credit and commodity assistance if it took power.[54] A week later, Army generals began approaching the US Embassy to seek assistance in procuring weapons, spare parts, cotton, rice and other supplies. State Department officials argued that the US "should be in no hurry to get such aid, and when we do there should be definite strings attached to it".[55] As covert aid began to flow and the massacre of PKI supporters commenced, Washington began detailed discussions with allies to clarify the conditions under which they might resume economic assistance to Indonesia and the broader policy goals to which aid would be tied.[56] Merely smashing the PKI was not enough. Sukarno would have to go, Confrontation would have to end, and attacks on US and Western policy and investments would have to cease before significant aid would be resumed. Once resumed, the US Embassy argued, aid would be tied to Indonesia's willingness to "tackle some of the structural problems which have prevented economic development". Aid would also be directly linked to US- and IMF-approved economic plans, and would be disbursed on a multilateral basis, preferably with the Japanese taking the lead.[57]

US officials expressed frustration that Suharto and other military officers wanted to put off these issues and "treat [the] aid question in isolation from [the] broader politico-economic context [of]

---

[52] "Short-term Policy toward Indonesia, Summary of Pointers", from discussions on 1–2 Dec. 1965 amongst Australian, British, New Zealand and US officials, n.d., Averell Harriman Papers, Box 451, Library of Congress Manuscript Division.
[53] Memo from Cuthell to Bundy, 3 Nov. 1965, *FRUS, 1964–1968*, pp. 348–51.
[54] Memo from Bundy and Rostow to Ball, 2 Oct. 1965, PPS Subject and CO Files, 1965–1969, Box 319, NARA.
[55] Telegram 1113, US Embassy Jakarta to State Department, 22 Oct. 1965, POL 23-9 INDON, NARA.
[56] Telegram 1712, US Embassy Jakarta to State Department, 10 Dec. 1965, POL 23-9 INDON, NARA; Top Secret Telegram 9645, Foreign Office to Washington, 3 Dec. 1965, PREM 13, 2718, UKNA.
[57] Airgram A-317, US Embassy Jakarta to State Department, 9 Nov. 1965, AID (US) INDON, NARA.

US-Indo relations". All that the Army leaders seemed to want to know, as one group of them put it to Ambassador Green, was "how much is it worth to us that PKI be smashed and the trend here reversed, thereby saving big part SEA from communism?"[58] Nevertheless, US frustration was misplaced. Army leaders had a clear strategy: to extort as much Western assistance as they could in order to consolidate power, while avoiding the conditions Washington hoped to impose as the price of support for military rule.[59]

The position of Western oil companies in Indonesia was unquestionably the most important of these broader concerns. In September Sukarno had instructed Third Deputy Prime Minister Chaerul Saleh to complete the management takeover of US oil operations and accelerate the purchase of their refining assets by the end of the year. A month later the government's position had not changed even though the Armed Forces were in effective control. It would "take time to develop [a] meaningful dialogue on oil matters with [the] Army", the Embassy concluded, and applying pressure carried real political risks.[60] Time, however, was running short. Stanvac executives warned that the company was cornered and might withdraw from Indonesia if negotiations failed. "This would be a disaster and destroy chances of being able [to] aid Indo Army," Rusk wrote to the Embassy, instructing Ambassador Green to do "anything which can be done to get into heads of new Indo leadership" the dire consequences of forcing the oil companies out.

US officials bluntly and repeatedly warned the emerging Indonesian leadership that Washington's support and their own grip on power were at stake, suggesting how inseparable the wider position of foreign capital was in the White House's considerations. The

---

[58] Telegram 741, State Department to US Embassy Jakarta, 8 Dec. 1965, POL 23-9 INDON, NARA; Telegram 1605, US Embassy Jakarta to State Department, 1 Dec. 1965, POL 23-9 INDON, NARA.

[59] Telegram 1509, US Embassy Jakarta to State Department, 19 Nov. 1965, NSF CO Files Indonesia, vol. 5, LBJL; Telegram 1542 from US Embassy Jakarta to State Department, 23 Nov. 1965, POL 23-9 INDON, NARA.

[60] Telegram 696, US Embassy Jakarta to State Department, 20 Sept. 1965, PET 15-2 INDON, NARA; Telegram 1358, US Embassy Jakarta to State Department, 6 Nov. 1965, PET 15-2 INDON, NARA.

problem, as the Embassy crudely put it, was that "even most anti-Communist Army leadership are strongly imbued with [the] conviction that Indonesians must control their own natural resources" and have "control over [their] own affairs". A precipitous move against the oil companies, Galbraith told an aide to General Nasution, would "profoundly affect both US-Indo future relations and [the] Indo economic situation", crippling not just the economy but also the Armed Forces. Australian and Japanese officials, who were also worried about the wider implications of Indonesia's actions, apparently decided to intervene as well, indirectly warning that they would refuse future aid if Indonesia took over the oil companies. These blunt threats had their intended effect. On 16 December, Suharto told a group of high-level Indonesian officials that "[the] military would not stand for precipitous moves against oil companies", thereby averting a serious crisis.[61] Never before reported, this episode highlights the broader economic concerns through which Washington and other Western governments filtered their considerations of Indonesia's future, even at the moment of the Army's greatest political vulnerability.

During the first three months of 1966, the Indonesian economy neared collapse as Army officials put increasing public pressure on Sukarno. In mid-January Indonesia notified Washington and other governments that it was defaulting on its commercial loans, crossing "the great divide", as the Embassy put it, and "completing the ruin of its international credit standing".[62] Now Army leaders sought to distance themselves from Sukarno's economic policies, sending word to Western embassies that they "should give no rpt [repeat] no econ assistance to Indonesia, including to [the] Indonesian Army".[63] Perhaps more important, however, Army leaders worked to promote

---

[61] Telegram 546, State Department to US Embassy Jakarta, 29 Oct. 1965, PET 15-2 INDON, NARA; Telegram 1401, US Embassy Jakarta to State Department, 10 Nov. 1965, POL 23-9 INDON, NARA; Telegram 1720, US Embassy Jakarta to State Department, 10 Dec. 1965, PET 15-2 INDON, NARA; Telegram 1787, US Embassy Jakarta to State Department, 16 Dec. 1965, PET 15-2 INDON, NARA.

[62] Airgram A-528, US Embassy Jakarta to State Department, 22 Feb. 1966, E 2-2 INDON, NARA.

[63] Letter from British Embassy Jakarta to Foreign Office, 9 Nov. 1965, FO 371 181519, UKNA.

Indonesia's economic collapse by diverting funds from the government and Central Bank in order to create a parallel government, with US and British support.[64] In early February, General Suharto and Ibnu Sutowo told Julius Tahija of Caltex that the military "desperately needed funds" to import basic commodities and supplies for its own needs — in other words, a separate budget and income. They instructed Caltex to begin paying Indonesia's oil revenues "into an unnamed bank account in Holland rather than to the Indonesian central bank". Plantation Minister Frans Seda made similar arrangements with Goodyear and US Rubber and explored doing so for tin as well. "Indonesia's need for foreign exchange," US Embassy officer David Cuthell wrote approvingly, "is now a greater influence than the G[overnment] O[f] I[ndonesia]'s desire to nationalize."[65] The diversion of Indonesia's three largest sources of foreign exchange fatally wounded Sukarno, effectively stripping the government of access to hard currency and demonstrating its powerlessness to feed and clothe the populace.

On 11 March 1966, amid mounting political pressure from the Army, Sukarno handed over power to General Suharto.[66] US officials could hardly conceal their delight. The annihilation of the PKI and the steady diminution of Sukarno's power radically altered the dynamics of US-Indonesian relations. Having realised its most important short-term goals, Washington shifted its attention from anti-communism to helping the Army consolidate a "moderate, responsible, and economic-minded regime" in Jakarta.[67] For General Suharto and his military allies, the most important tasks were political: purging Sukarnoists from the government, ending Confrontation with Malaysia, continuing the attack against the remnants of

[64] Memo from J.O. Moreton to Minister of State, 16 Feb. 1966, DO 169 416, UKNA; Telegram 235, British Embassy Jakarta to London, 10 Feb. 1966, DO 169 416, UKNA; Telegram 88, US Consulate Medan to State Department, 14 Feb. 1966, DEF 6 INDON, NARA.

[65] Telegram 2255, US Embassy Jakarta to State Department, 6 Feb. 1966, PET 15-2 INDON, NARA; Memo from Cuthell to Berger, 28 Mar. 1966, PET 15-2 INDON, NARA.

[66] Tovar letter to Pauker, 28 Mar. 1966, Guy Pauker Papers, Box 1, Correspondence, Hoover Institution Archives, Stanford University.

[67] Telegram 1182, State Department to Jakarta, 22 Mar. 1966, POL 1 INDON, NARA.

the PKI, and solidifying the Army's hold on power. US officials, on the other hand, contended that Indonesia's crucial tasks were now primarily economic, that is, resuming aid; rescuing, stabilising and rehabilitating the Indonesian economy; regaining creditor and investor confidence; and re-enmeshing Indonesia in webs of Western influence. These priorities starkly underlined the intimate connections between Western anti-communism and the broader political and economic structures whose imperatives gave it meaning.

Suharto and his advisers quickly recognised the need to secure international backing for the new regime, both to consolidate their power and to gain access to aid that could help rescue the economy and restore a modicum of stability, thereby preventing a leftist resurgence. But Indonesia had "offered no signs of being willing to talk to creditors as a group or to demonstrate it is prepared to tackle its problems in a rational manner to induce capital exporting countries to be able to be of any assistance". The US Embassy drove this point home to officials in Jakarta at every opportunity, making it clear that aid would march in tandem with Indonesia's efforts to reverse Sukarno's policies, restore its economic credibility, and stabilise the economy in accordance with policies approved by Western creditors and international institutions.[68]

In 1966, Indonesian military officers and the technocrats with whom they were allied had few options: the country was virtually bankrupt, inflation was running at 600 per cent, industrial production had ground to a halt, and the government had limited access to desperately needed hard currency. The international community, particularly the US and Japan, was thus in an unusually strong position to press the government to undertake the far-reaching economic reforms it considered essential to Indonesia's recovery, and to steer the military-technocratic alliance it expected to dominate the political and economic landscape. Over the next two years Jakarta drafted a new foreign investment law and acceded to a harsh structural adjustment programme demanded by the IMF and the Inter-Governmental Group on Indonesia, which consisted of the US, Japan and European governments. In exchange, Indonesia had its external debt renegotiated and received more than $450 million annually in economic

---

[68] Memo of conversation, 14 Feb. 1966, POL 2 INDON, NARA.

assistance. The World Bank as well as various UN agencies, NGOs and foundations would provide tens of millions more, accounting for the vast proportion of government spending on development from 1966 to 1974, by which time a massive expansion in oil revenues lessened Indonesia's relative dependence on foreign aid.[69] Indonesia was "a pioneer case", Rostow told the National Security Council, an opportunity to "establish a new pattern of multilateral help in Asia" linked to the Asian Development Bank and patterned on the US experience in Latin America and elsewhere.[70]

The return of foreign investors to Indonesia was central to US planning for Indonesia's post-Sukarno future. As Suharto took power, US Embassy officials told their Indonesian counterparts that Jakarta needed to restore the confidence not just of creditor nations but also of foreign investors. The case of the New Orleans-based mining company Freeport Sulphur illustrates the extent to which the delicate situation was exploited. Between 1959 and 1965 Freeport had worked to reach an arrangement with the Indonesian Ministry of Mining to explore for copper and nickel in West Irian, only to watch Sukarno close the door on foreign investment.[71] Within days of Sukarno's 11 March transfer of power, however, Freeport technicians were tramping through the jungles of West Irian, 96 kilometres from its southern coast, hoping to be the first to reach Ertsberg, a "copper mountain" rising 183 metres from the jungle floor.[72]

Freeport was a crucial test of the regime's intentions. The US Embassy characterised the start of talks between Freeport and Indonesian officials in mid-June as the "initial posing of the important question of whether Indonesia's negative attitude toward foreign

---

[69] Telegram 1444, US Embassy Jakarta to State Department, 23 Sept. 1966, FN 9 INDON, NARA; Background Paper, "Economic and Military Assistance", Bilateral Briefing Book for Deputy Secretary's Trip to East Asia, 25 Mar. 1974, RG 59, Lot Files 75091, Office of the Executive Secretary, Box 186, Briefing Books 1958–1976, NARA.

[70] Notes of the 563rd Meeting of the NSC, "NSF, NSC Meetings", vol. 4, Tab 4, 8/4/66, LBJL.

[71] Telegram 4096, US Embassy Jakarta to State Department, 15 Apr. 1965, INCO MINING INDON, NARA.

[72] Telegram 2771, US Embassy Jakarta to State Department, 29 Mar. 1966, INCO MINING INDON, NARA; Forbes Wilson, *Conquest of Copper Mountain* (New York: Atheneum, 1981), pp. 1–157.

investment is undergoing a change", or whether the annihilation of the PKI had only removed one symptom of a deeper anti-Western, anti-capitalist animus.[73] Ali Budiardjo, an Indonesian official who later went to work for Freeport, recalled that "no one had any idea of how to proceed. There was no foreign investment office and ... no foreign investment law."[74] "This seems [an] excellent opportunity," the Embassy wrote back to Washington, "especially in light [of the] current visit by Freeport Sulphur reps ... to influence GOI thinking on foreign investment."[75]

Two months after the visit by Freeport officials, Minister of Foreign Affairs Adam Malik told Ambassador Green that economic ministers had begun working on a new foreign investment law and were prepared to start talks on an investment guarantee agreement with Washington.[76] During 1966 the US heavily influenced the drafting of Indonesia's foreign investment law. A consultant from the Denver-based Van Sickle Associates helped the economist Widjojo Nitisastro write the bill, which Indonesian officials gave to the Embassy, asking for comments on "possible improvements from [the] standpoint [of] US investors". State Department lawyers complained that the proposed legislation reserved for the state "a large area private foreign enterprises would want to enter", primarily in extractive enterprises. Widjojo revised the bill "in accordance with US suggestions", seeking language that would ensure the "maximum liberalisation" he also favoured while placating economic nationalists on the lookout for signs that Jakarta was bowing to Western pressure.[77]

---

[73] Airgram A-769, US Embassy Jakarta to State Department, 15 June 1966, E 2-2 INDON, NARA.

[74] Jeffrey Winters, *Power in Motion: Capital Mobility and the Indonesian State* (Ithaca: Cornell University Press, 1996), p. 75; "The End for Sukarno", *The Economist*, 28 Jan. 1967.

[75] Telegram 3390, US Embassy Jakarta to State Department, 9 June 1966, FN 9 INDON, NARA.

[76] Telegram 749, US Embassy Jakarta to State Department, 13 Aug. 1966, AID (US) INDON, NARA; Telegram 509, US Embassy Jakarta to State Department, 26 Aug. 1966, AID (US) INDON, NARA.

[77] Telegram 1444, US Embassy Jakarta to State Department, 23 Sept. 1966, FN 9 INDON, NARA; on Van Sickle, see Airgram A-269, US Consulate Medan to State Department, 21 Sept. 1966, FN 9 INDON, NARA.

Following the lead of Freeport Sulphur, a steady stream of prospective foreign investors descended upon Indonesia, many involved in raw materials extraction and production: mining, timber, independent oil, chemical and fertilizer companies, as well as the banks that financed them. From early 1967 Indonesian officials fanned out across the US, Japan and Western Europe, speaking at business forums and seeking to spread the word about the new opportunities for foreign capital. At an American Indonesian Chamber of Commerce meeting in New York, Indonesian Ambassador Suwito Kusumowidagdo insisted that the Suharto government had abandoned "rigid state control of the economy" for a greater reliance on market forces and stressed the opportunities for investors to "cooperate with Indo under favorable terms in developing the nation's rich natural resources ... now exploited at only one-tenth of their potential capacity".[78] The arrival of trade missions from Belgium, the Netherlands, Australia, France and South Korea prompted the Dutch newspaper *De Volksrant* to observe that "a fierce international competitive struggle for a favorable position in the Indonesian market has broken out".[79] In a series of international meetings attended by hundreds of corporate representatives, Indonesian officials outlined the steps the Suharto regime was taking to attract foreign capital. The US Embassy approvingly noted the speech of Manpower Minister Dr Awaluddin Djamin at one such meeting, describing the new regime's repressive labour policies in a manner "designed to allay any fears prospective investors may harbour about possible trouble with trade unions".[80] By the end of 1967, Jakarta's main hotel was "crowded with businessmen from the US, Western Europe, Japan, and neighboring Asian countries" seeking investment opportunities.[81] *Fortune* observed that

---

[78] "International envoy stresses nation's needs, chances for private firms to aid development effort profitably", *International Commerce*, 17 Apr. 1967; "Post-Sukarno Welcome Mat: Indonesia Courts Firms It Earlier Ousted in Bids to Improve Deteriorating Economy", *Wall Street Journal*, 18 Apr. 1967.

[79] Airgram 806, US Embassy The Hague to State Department, 26 May 1967, RG 59 1967–1969, T7 INDON NETH, NARA; Winters, *Power in Motion*, p. 57.

[80] Airgram A-100, US Embassy Jakarta to State Department, 23 Aug. 1967, RG 59 1967–1969, LAB 1 INDON, NARA.

[81] Memo from James Linen to Burke Knapp, Vice-President of the World Bank, 5 July 1978, "Indonesian Investment Conference: Confidential Report", Accession A1995-164, Indonesia General Correspondence, vol. 2, Folder 1786834, World Bank Archives.

Indonesia "is putting on trial what many observers have long considered to be model rules of behavior for backward nations". If successful, Indonesia could "point the way for many a floundering country in Asia, Africa and Latin America".[82]

Conclusion

By 1968, US officials viewed the Suharto regime as one of the great successes of American foreign policy. Sukarno and the PKI had been destroyed, political parties had been neutralised, the regime had committed to pro-Western economic reform and was open to foreign capital, and the Army was beyond effective political challenge. Moreover, Indonesia was playing a moderate, responsible political role in the region through its participation in the new Association of Southeast Asian Nations. While Indonesia resolutely maintained its non-alignment in public, the government's utter dependence on foreign aid and investment and the military's bitter anti-communism lent Indonesian neutralism a decidedly pro-Western cast.

The September 30th Movement, and the ensuing mass murder of PKI supporters that paved the way for Suharto's ascendancy, made US officials appear prescient as well as lucky. The liquidation of the PKI in Indonesia was "perhaps the greatest setback for Communism in the Third World in the 1960s" and an event with enormous implications for each of the Great Powers, particularly with regard to Vietnam.[83] For the US, the PKI's destruction changed the political calculus of the Vietnam War and significantly reduced the possible regional consequences of victory by Hanoi and the National Liberation Front, though ironically too late to affect the course of the Johnson Administration's escalation of the war. For the Soviet Union and China, the destruction of the Left in Indonesia increased the importance each attached to holding firm in Vietnam lest their credibility as revolutionary powers in the region be further undermined. Britain viewed the ousting of President Sukarno and the demise of the PKI as the first steps towards ending Confrontation and beginning its gradual retrenchment from Southeast Asia, a policy to which

---

[82] "Indonesia's Potholed Road Back", *Fortune*, 1 June 1968.

[83] Westad, *The Global Cold War*, p. 185.

Washington was deeply opposed as its military commitment to the region intensified.[84]

Bundy wrote to President Johnson that the dramatic turnaround in Jakarta was "a striking vindication of our policy … of keeping our hand in the game for the long-term stakes despite recurrent pressures to pull out".[85] This policy was also a reflection of Washington's persistent conviction — one shared by the British, Japanese and other Western governments — that Indonesia would be unable to solve its manifold economic and political problems until the PKI was destroyed. The evidence is both voluminous and persuasive that the US, British and other governments appreciated that the continued existence of a radical, mass-based alternative to Army rule posed irreducible obstacles to Indonesia's firm integration into the regional and world economy and the associated institutions of liberal order. Their enthusiastic support for the Army-led slaughter was thus a predictable, if damnable, result of the United States' persistent linking of its own global credibility with the fortunes of indigenous radicalism and local military forces — a pattern repeated in Guatemala, Brazil, Chile and countless other countries during the Cold War, and one magnified in importance by the escalation of the war in Vietnam. The US and Western response to the events of 1965–66, however, was inseparable from the broader challenge posed by Sukarno and the PKI to the position of Western capital in Indonesia and by the Sukarnoist regime's gradual severing of ties with the West. That challenge was both political and economic, a function of the "problem" of Indonesian nationalism only partially solved by the annihilation of the PKI and Sukarno's ouster.

---

[84] Telegram 868, US Embassy Jakarta to State Department, 5 Oct. 1965, *FRUS, 1964–1968*, p. 307.

[85] Memo from McGeorge Bundy to President Johnson, 22 Oct. 1965, *FRUS, 1964–1968*, pp. 334–5.

4

The Army Para-commando Regiment and the Reign of Terror in Central Java and Bali

David Jenkins and Douglas Kammen[1]

The September 30th Movement's actions in Jakarta on the morning of 1 October 1965 were followed just hours later by dramatic developments in Central Java. In Semarang, a coterie of middle-ranking officers declared their leadership of the Diponegoro regional military command and, according to radio broadcasts from Jakarta, prepared to set up regional Revolutionary Councils. While the Movement in Jakarta collapsed within a day and its counterpart in Central Java dissolved three days later, these events were a major challenge — but also an opportunity — for Major General Suharto, the commander of the Army Strategic Reserve (Kostrad), who had assumed control of the Army. It was essential for Suharto to regain the political, military and psychological initiative in Central Java as soon as possible. He had to act swiftly and decisively, at the same time showing great circumspection. The situation in Central Java, a densely settled, largely rural province, was tense and volatile, with a complex pattern of political allegiances. The Indonesian Communist Party (Partai Komunis Indonesia, PKI) enjoyed strong support. The Indonesian National Party (Partai Nasional Indonesia, PNI) leadership was largely

[1] The authors would like to thank Ben Anderson, Bob Elson, Ruth McVey, Jamie Mackie, Greg Rooney and Ken Ward for their comments on early drafts of this chapter.

hostile to the PKI, as was the Nahdlatul Ulama. Provincial Army units were divided in their loyalties, and some of the more dependable battalions were serving outside the province.

In analysing those events, this chapter attempts to resolve some of the enduring mysteries that surround the deployment and operational methods of Indonesia's elite red beret Army Para-commando Regiment (Resimen Para Komando Angkatan Darat, RPKAD), which played a central role in organising and inciting the wave of anti-communist mass killing in this province and perhaps Bali too; provide new information about the scope of the killings; and clarify some matters that were previously misunderstood. Focusing on RPKAD actions in Central Java and Bali, the chapter will examine the political loyalties of various military units, the movement of troops, military operations against both the September 30th Movement and the PKI and its sympathisers, and the mobilisation of anti-communist civilians into roaming Army-trained militias that helped round up and kill hundreds of thousands of people. The focus of this study is restricted to the last three months of 1965, when the killings were at their height.

The Military Situation in Jakarta and Central Java, 1–15 October

In the early hours of 1 October 1965, a self-proclaimed September 30th Movement kidnapped and killed six of the Indonesian Army's most senior officers, including Lieutenant General Achmad Yani, the minister/commander of the Army, and dumped their bodies in an unused well not far from Halim Perdanakusuma Air Force Base. Members of the coup group also tried to kidnap the Minister of Defence, General A.H. Nasution, but he managed to escape. At 7 a.m. the putative leader of the Movement, Lieutenant Colonel Untung, the commander of a battalion in the elite Tjakrabirawa Presidential Guard, announced over Radio Republik Indonesia the formation of a Revolutionary Council intended to safeguard President Sukarno from a coup planned by a CIA-backed council led by the six kidnapped generals and Nasution.[2] Oddly, the plotters made

---

[2] Benedict R. Anderson and Ruth T. McVey, *A Preliminary Analysis of the October 1, 1965 Coup in Indonesia* (Ithaca: Modern Indonesia Project, Cornell University, 1971), pp. 12–28.

no attempt to kidnap or otherwise sideline Major General Suharto, although he had routinely deputised for Yani when the latter was out of the country. Nor did they take effective steps to sideline the RPKAD, the obvious spearhead for any counter-attack against the coup forces. Although some of his officers and soldiers were sympathetic to the September 30th Movement, the RPKAD commander, Colonel Sarwo Edhie Wibowo, promptly put his troops at the disposal of Suharto and the anti-coup group.[3]

The failure to make allowance for a possible counter-attack by Suharto and other important officers proved costly. On the evening of 1 October, after remnants of the rebel force had withdrawn to Halim, Suharto ordered Sarwo Edhie to secure the radio station studio and the telecommunications building in Central Jakarta, which had been left in the hands of a few lightly armed members of the PKI-affiliated Pemuda Rakyat (People's Youth) movement.[4] On 2 October, four RPKAD companies, supported by a Kostrad unit and nearly two dozen armoured vehicles, recaptured Halim.[5] Following the discovery of the bodies of the generals, Suharto and his supporters in the Army skilfully used the media to demand that the PKI be disbanded and encouraged mass rallies at which similar demands were made. Starting on 8 October, the Army and anti-communist forces began to attack PKI offices and homes in Jakarta; mass detentions soon followed. Before long, the Army was calling on the public to help it destroy the G30S/PKI "down to its roots".

The situation in Central Java was considerably more complex. On 1 October, while the commander of the Central Java Regional Military Command (Kodam VII/Diponegoro), Brigadier General Surjosumpeno, was away from Semarang — the provincial capital — his Assistant I (Intelligence) Colonel Sahirman, acting in close collaboration with Assistant III (Personnel) Lieutenant Colonel Maryono, proclaimed himself the leader of the September 30th Movement in

---

[3] Sarwo Edhie's son-in-law, retired General Susilo Bambang Yudhoyono, was elected President of Indonesia in 2004 and re-elected to a second term in 2009.

[4] The attack on the Radio Republik Indonesia studio was made by companies D and I; the attack on the telecommunications building was made by Company B.

[5] The companies were B, C and D, with E in a reserve role. See Hendro Subroto, *Sintong Panjaitan: Perjalanan Seorang Prajurit Para Komando* (Jakarta: Kompas, 2009), p. 120; and Ken Conboy, *Kopassus: Inside Indonesia's Special Forces* (Jakarta: Equinox, 2003), p. 138.

Central Java. Lieutenant Colonel Usman Sastrodibroto, the Assistant V (Territorial Affairs), was placed in command of the Diponegoro command. Elsewhere in the province, two of the three Sub-regional Military (Korem) commanders were deposed by subordinates. By the evening of 1 October, five of the seven infantry battalions then in Central Java were under rebel command.[6] All but one of the key cities of Central Java were also in rebel hands, however insecurely, and all had come out in support of Colonel Untung's Revolutionary Council.[7]

Faced with this dramatic challenge to his authority and not knowing initially which units he could trust, Surjosumpeno made his way to the garrison town of Magelang, where he joined forces with Lieutenant Colonel Soeprapto, his Solonese Assistant II (Operations and Training). The Central Java commander was in an invidious position. For more than a year, General Yani and the members of his inner circle had been concerned that the deployment of troops to Sumatra and Kalimantan as part of Indonesia's "Confrontation" with Malaysia was denuding Java of forces that might be needed to curb possible PKI unrest. The problem was especially acute in Central Java.[8] Colonel Jasir Hadibroto's Fourth Infantry Brigade, which included three of Central Java's most dependable battalions, was in North Sumatra, and two battalions from the Fifth Infantry Brigade were in Kalimantan.[9] That left the Sixth Infantry Brigade (Battalions K, L and M), which had come out in support of the September 30th Movement, and not much else. The only forces Surjosumpeno had close at hand were his Magelang-based cavalry, engineer and artillery units, and the RPKAD's new and under-strength Battalion II. The officers who commanded these units, convinced that the PKI was behind the coup, remained loyal to the central Army leadership.

---

[6] See Harold Crouch, *The Army and Politics in Indonesia* (Ithaca: Cornell University Press, 1978), pp. 100–1, 143–51; and Anderson and McVey, *Preliminary Analysis*, pp. 46–63.

[7] Anderson and McVey, *Preliminary Analysis*, p. 49.

[8] The Army faced a similar problem in East Java, where more than half of the 16 Brawijaya battalions were serving outside of Java. See Telegram 29, US Consulate Surabaya to US Embassy Jakarta, 7 Nov. 1965, Record Group 59, State Department Central Files 1964–1966, POL [illegible] INDON, National Archives and Records Administration [hereafter RG59 1964–66 documents referred to by file code and NARA].

[9] Crouch, *Army and Politics*, pp. 143–4.

But, as one officer put it, "it was very difficult to know who was friend and who was foe".[10]

In a meeting that is said to have begun at 9 p.m. on 1 October and lasted until 4 a.m., Soeprapto briefed the loyalist officers. Surjosumpeno, who arrived at midnight, ordered Colonel Jasin Husein, the commander of the Second Cavalry Battalion, to spearhead a counter-attack on Semarang.[11] As it happened, the collapse of the September 30th Movement in Jakarta, announced by Suharto in a 9 p.m. radio broadcast on 1 October, had shattered the morale of the coup leaders in Semarang.[12] They decided during the night to flee to the barren upper slopes of Mount Merapi. Surjosumpeno's force retook Semarang unopposed on 2 October. By the morning of 5 October, overt military resistance to Surjosumpeno had ceased. Across Central Java, "a watchful and tense stillness" now reigned.[13] But the balance of power in the province remained "extremely precarious" because of the uncertain loyalty of the five battalions that had supported the coup movement. Above all, Surjosumpeno needed to neutralise the three battalions of the Sixth Infantry Brigade. In a ruse aimed at defusing the situation without his troops losing face, the Central Java commander ordered these units to prepare for transfer to the Outer Islands as part of Confrontation.[14]

As preparations were being made to ship the unreliable battalions out, Suharto ordered Jasir Hadibroto to bring his Fourth Infantry Brigade back from Confrontation duties in Sumatra.[15] The brigade was not expected, however, before mid-October at the earliest,

---

[10] Personal communication, Lieutenant General Purbo Suwondo, 24 Sept. 2009, by telephone with David Jenkins.

[11] *Minggu Pagi*, 19 Dec. 1965, cited in Ruth McVey, "A Preliminary Excursion through the Small World of Lt. Col. Untung", unpublished manuscript, pp. 120–1; Personal communication, Lieutenant General Purbo Suwondo, 29 Sept. 2009.

[12] Crouch, *Army and Politics*, p. 145.

[13] Anderson and McVey, *Preliminary Analysis*, pp. 52, 58–9.

[14] Crouch, *Army and Politics*, pp. 147–8.

[15] See Yasir Hadibroto, "Tangguh dan Berbobot", in *Diantara Para Sahabat: Pak Harto 70 Tahun*, ed. G. Dwipayana and Nazaruddin Sjamsuddin (Jakarta: Citra Lamtoro Gung Persada, 1991), pp. 955–6.

and would not be available for operations until early November.[16] Nor was it clear that the arrival of Jasir's brigade would tip the balance sufficiently in Jakarta's favour. In theory, Suharto could have sent elements from the West Java Regional Military Command (Kodam VI/Siliwangi) to help restore order in Central Java;[17] however, Suharto knew that the Siliwangi command was deeply unpopular in Central Java, where it had been relocated in 1948 and used by the Hatta government to crush left-leaning forces at Madiun. Its arrival might have exacerbated an already tense political and military standoff. Given all this, Surjosumpeno was in no position to move decisively against all those Army elements of doubtful loyalty and communist groups sympathetic to the September 30th Movement.[18]

On 16 October, immediately after he was installed as commander of the Army, Suharto moved to crush the September 30th Movement and the PKI in Central Java. Faced with a critical situation in the province, concerned about the loyalty of local Army units and knowing it would take some time for Jasir to re-establish himself, he ordered Sarwo Edhie to lead an RPKAD force to Central Java to deal with what Suharto and his fellow officers saw as the dual threat of the September 30th Movement mutineers and the PKI, on which all blame for the Movement had been laid. In the months ahead, at the behest of Suharto, Sarwo Edhie was to instigate a reign of terror and mass murder in Central Java, crushing both the September 30th Movement and the PKI, and tipping the uncertain political balance decisively in the Army's favour.

There are five salient points that need to be borne in mind about the RPKAD. First, it was commanded by a man who had been both a friend and a loyal subordinate of Yani for more than two

---

[16] *Sejarah Rumpun Diponegoro dan Pengabdiannya* (Semarang: Dinas Sejarah Militer Kodam VII/Diponegoro and C.V. Borobudur Megah, 1977), pp. 588–91.

[17] On 1 November 1965, Siliwangi commander Major General Ibrahim Adjie told *Los Angeles Times* correspondent Arthur Dommen that no Siliwangi troops were sent to Central Java. See Airgram A-329, US Embassy Jakarta to State Department, 15 Nov. 1965, POL 23-9 INDON, NARA.

[18] See Hamish McDonald, *Suharto's Indonesia* (Blackburn: Fontana/Collins, 1980), p. 51; and Ulf Sundhaussen, *The Road to Power: Indonesian Military Politics 1945–1967* (Kuala Lumpur and New York: Oxford University Press, 1982), p. 215.

decades and who had been shocked and angered by Yani's murder.[19] In the months after 1 October 1965, Sarwo Edhie seems to have given full vent to his fury at Yani's death. Referring to the RPKAD commander's harsh actions against the PKI in 1965, Major General Sukotjo Tjokroatmodjo, the Military Police Corps commander in Jakarta at that time, said, "whatever Sarwo did, it was just like a vengeance. Personal!"[20] Second, the RPKAD was a relatively small force. It consisted of one full-strength battalion (Battalion I, based in Cijantung, south of Jakarta) and two under-strength battalions (Battalions II and III) in Central Java. The battalions were subdivided into 11 companies, with about 75 men in each company.[21]

RPKAD Units and Commanders[22]

Battalion I (Jakarta)	Major C.I. Santoso
Company A/Alpha	1st Lieutenant Edi Sudradjat
Company B/Ben Hur	Captain Urip Sucipto
Company C/Cobra	1st Lieutenant Kentot Harseno
Company D/Dracula	Captain Heru Sisnodo
Company E	Kayat
Battalion II (Magelang)	Major Soegianto
Company F	Sembiring or Tedjo
Company G	Captain C. Salim
Company H	Sembiring or Tedjo
Battalion III (Semarang/Kartosuro)	Major R.A. Kosasih
Company I/India	1st Lieutenant Feisal Tanjung
Company J	1st Lieutenant Ramelan?
Company K	Muchadi
Army Para-commando School (Batujajar)	Singungkarya

[19] Sarwo Edhie was born in 1927 in Purworejo, Central Java, where Yani had been born five years earlier. Sarwo Edhie trained with Yani in the Japanese-sponsored self-defence force (PETA) and served under him during the Revolution.
[20] Major General Sukotjo Tjokroatmodjo, interviewed by David Jenkins, 4 Mar. 2009, Jakarta. Sukotjo was in almost daily contact with Suharto and Sarwo Edhie in the first few days after the coup.
[21] Hendro Subroto, interviewed by David Jenkins, 11 Sept. 1998, Jakarta.
[22] Compiled from various sources. Some sources provide alternative names (Muchadi [Company C], Muchtar, Saridho), which refer to previous commanders or subordinates.

Third, the RPKAD was a disproportionately Javanese force, and Central Javanese at that. Sarwo Edhie was from Central Java, although by now closely associated with the Army high command in Jakarta. So, too, was Major C.I. Santoso, the commander of the regiment's most effective unit, Battalion I. The two newest RPKAD battalions were former Central Java "Raider" battalions. Although some of the new company commanders were non-Javanese, many — if not most — of the officers and men were operating in familiar surroundings in Central Java.

Fourth, the RPKAD had, like a number of other units, been influenced to some extent by the September 30th Movement and the PKI. On the morning of 1 October, it has been claimed, several officers tried to persuade Sarwo Edhie to "support the Revolutionary Council and oppose the Council of Generals".[23] More than two dozen members of the RPKAD airborne and commando school at Batujajar, near Bandung, "openly sided" with the September 30th Movement.[24] In Jakarta, Sarwo Edhie's adjutant was arrested on account of his communist sympathies,[25] and two of the best company commanders in Battalion I — Urip Sucipto and Heru Sisnodo — were later found to have had links with the communists.[26] RPKAD Battalions II and III in Central Java were found to have a number of Party members. In striking contrast to those on the Left who were to fall victim to the RPKAD-led purges in Central Java and Bali, left-leaning red beret officers do not seem to have been treated at all harshly: some were dismissed, others simply chastised.

Finally, although the RPKAD had a less distinguished combat record than was commonly supposed, it had enough weaponry, enough swagger and enough of a reputation as an elite force to instil a degree of fear in the much larger infantry units it came up against in 1965. This was to prove decisive. What is more, it was to have no compunction about using violence against civilians.

---

[23] Hendro Subroto, *Perjalanan Seorang Wartawan Perang* (Jakarta: Pustaka Sinar Harapan, 1998), p. 184.

[24] See Conboy, *Kopassus*, pp. 154, 163, on which this paragraph draws.

[25] Major General Sukotjo Tjokroatmodjo, telephone interview with David Jenkins, 30 Oct. 2009.

[26] Urip Suripto was a member of the PKI during the Revolution and had participated in some post-revolutionary reunions. Heru Sisnodo was a member of a secret PKI cell.

The RPKAD Commences Operations

On 17 October 1965, Sarwo Edhie sent three RPKAD companies, under Major Santoso, by road from Jakarta to Semarang.[27] These units, which were joined by one company of armoured vehicles from the First Cavalry Brigade and a tough combat company from the military police, arrived in the city early the next afternoon. This force was hardly sufficient to tip the numerical balance in Surjosumpeno's favour. Nevertheless, Suharto was hoping that the presence of the red beret forces would "overawe" the rebel forces and encourage them to comply with Surjosumpeno's order to leave the province, as indeed happened.[28] On the afternoon of 19 October, Sarwo Edhie joined his troops in Semarang, which was calm but tense.[29] The red beret units then took part in what was described as a "show of force". That night, Surjosumpeno and Santoso detained more than 1,000 people and encouraged youths from "religious" (that is, Nahdlatul Ulama, Muhammadiyah and the Catholic Party) and "nationalist" (that is, PNI) groups to attack communist and Chinese buildings in Semarang.[30] This pattern — RPKAD operations, mass detentions, and rioting by anti-communist groups against the PKI and ethnic Chinese — was soon to be repeated in towns throughout Central Java.

By 21 October or thereabouts, as the Army crackdown destroyed the PKI's structure and command system, Army newspapers began to report that Party supporters in the Yogyakarta-Surakarta region, hitherto passive, were taking initiatives of their own.[31] Reports came in that they were setting up regional commands in villages, initiating strikes and disrupting communications by felling trees across roads

---

[27] *Sejarah Rumpun Diponegoro*, p. 574; Conboy, *Kopassus*, p. 147. Hendro Subroto (*Sintong Panjaitan*, p. 138) claims there were four companies, namely, those commanded by Urip, Kayat, Ramelan and Tanjung.

[28] Crouch, *Army and Politics*, p. 148.

[29] *Sedjarah Rumpun Diponegoro*, p. 575; Hendro Subroto, *Wartawan Perang*, p. 202.

[30] Anderson and McVey, *Preliminary Analysis*, pp. 61–2; *Fakta2 Persoalan Sekitar 'Gerakan 30 September'* (Jakarta: P.N. Balai Pustaka, 1966), pp. 191, 205; Crouch, *Army and Politics*, p. 148.

[31] Anderson and McVey, *Preliminary Analysis*, p. 62.

and cutting telephone lines.[32] In a highly charged atmosphere of fear and distrust, some communists are alleged to have begun kidnapping and killing their opponents.[33] Some non-communists, fearing for their lives, chose to flee, while others began to mobilise, turning to the Army for support. The most serious unrest was reported in the districts of Boyolali, Klaten and Wonogiri. In Boyolali, a tense stand-off developed between PKI youths, on the one hand, and members of Ansor, the youth organisation of the conservative, rural-based Nahdlatul Ulama association, and the PNI-linked Marhaenis youth group, on the other.[34] On 21 October 1965, the local police and Army commanders, having received reports that PKI supporters were planning to attack Boyolali, distributed about 60 weapons to members of anti-communist youth movements. The anti-communists, supported by four RPKAD soldiers who had been sent as reinforcements from Solo, succeeded in driving off "thousands" of attackers armed with traditional weapons.

On the same day, with the situation in Semarang under control, Sarwo Edhie sent companies E/Kayat and I/Tanjung south to Magelang, where they linked up with Lieutenant Tedjo's company from the RPKAD's undermanned Battalion II.[35] Here, after another show of force, anti-communists burned the home of the PKI mayor, Argo Ismoyo, and destroyed buildings belonging to the PKI and the Consultative Body for Indonesian Citizenship (Badan Permusyawaratan Kewarganegaraan Indonesia, Baperki), an association of Indonesian Chinese that had close PKI links, as well as those of "their lackeys".[36] Later, as the RPKAD companies that had stayed on in

[32] For PKI preparations and actions, see press reports from the military dailies in *Fakta2*, pp. 204–11, 276–7; Crouch, *Army and Politics*, pp. 149–50; and Arnold C. Brackman, *The Communist Collapse in Indonesia* (New York: W.W. Norton and Co., 1969), p. 109.

[33] Sarwo Edhie's own estimate in early November was that 200 anti-communists had been killed in the Surakarta region. See Crouch, *Army and Politics*, p. 150fn34.

[34] See "September 30 Movement and Its Crushing", an eyewitness report by Mohammad Dimyathi Saleh, a resident of Boyolali and an informant of *Washington Post* correspondent Stanley Karnow. Dimyathi's report, dated 3 April 1966, is attached to Airgram A-25, US Consulate Surabaya to US Embassy Jakarta, 14 Apr. 1966, POL 12 INDON, NARA.

[35] See Conboy, *Kopassus*, p. 147; and *Sejarah Rumpun Diponegoro*, p. 575.

[36] *Sejarah Rumpun Diponegoro*, p. 575.

Semarang moved south to Yogyakarta, the task force in Magelang headed east, in a rapid night-time sweep via Yogyakarta and on to the RPKAD base at Kartosuro, 11 kilometres west of Solo. From there, Company E/Kayat peeled off to Boyolali, where it launched "arrest and clean-up operations" in the wake of the abortive mass attack on the town by PKI supporters.[37] The other companies (Tedjo and I/Tanjung), under the command of Sarwo Edhie, continued to Solo on 22 October, where members of the PKI-affiliated railway union, Serikat Buruh Kereta Api, had gone on strike at the Balapan railway station the day before, halting trains from Yogya, Semarang and Madiun.[38] Members of Gerwani, the PKI-affiliated Indonesian Women's Movement, made what seems to have been a symbolic attempt to prevent the RPKAD from entering the city. According to a report from the US Embassy in Jakarta, citing the Indonesian Army Information Centre:

> ... para-commandos (RPKAD) in armored vehicles entering city of Surakarta [no date given] were blocked in village at outskirts by nine 'witches' from ... Gerwani, who insulted them and refused to let them pass. After asking them quietly to give way, and firing into air, para-commandos were 'forced by their intransigence to terminate breathing of these nine Gerwani witches'.[39]

Two weeks later, a despatch from the Australian Embassy noted what appeared to be a new Army tactic: "[I]t has apparently become the practice in factories and other workplaces for the army to assemble the labour force and ask them whether they wish to continue work as usual or not. Those who decline are asked again, and, unless they change their mind, summarily shot."[40] These were the tactics that

---

[37] Markas Besar Angkatan Bersenjata Republik Indonesia, Pusat Sejarah dan Tradisi ABRI, *Bahaya Laten Komunisme di Indonesia, vol. 4: Pemberontakan G30S/PKI dan Penumpasannya* (Jakarta: Yayasan Telapak, 1995), p. 251.

[38] The striking railway workers were probably trying to make it impossible for Battalions K and M of the Sixth Infantry Brigade to leave Solo in accordance with Surjosumpeno's order. See Crouch, *Army and Politics*, pp. 149–50.

[39] Telegram 1360, US Embassy Jakarta to State Department, 6 Nov. 1965, POL 23-9 INDON, NARA; see also "14 Orang anak tanggung didjagal dan dilempar kelobang kuburan andjing", *Angkatan Bersendjata*, 6 Nov. 1965 — this article places the incident on 22 October.

[40] "Political Savingram No. 58", Australian Embassy, Jakarta, 19 Nov. 1965, p. 6. A1838/280. 3034/2/1. Part 48, National Archives of Australia [henceforth NAA].

Sarwo Edhie employed in Solo. Proceeding directly to the railway station, wearing dark glasses, carrying a swagger stick given to him by General Yani and accompanied by heavily armed troops, he delivered an ultimatum to the striking rail workers. "Those who wish to strike should gather on my left," he told them. "Those who don't want to strike should gather on my right. I will give you five minutes." Those present seemed to have understood clearly what might happen if they made the wrong choice. Before the five minutes had elapsed, all the unionists had assembled on his right. "Oh," said Sarwo Edhie, in mock surprise, "it seems that nobody wants to strike. If so, start the trains!" In a little more than an hour, the trains were running normally.[41]

That afternoon, the Army staged a now routine show of force in Solo. A convoy of military vehicles, including British-made Ferret scout cars, six-wheeled Saladin armoured cars and 14-ton Saracen armoured personnel carriers, followed by 90 trucks packed with troops, made its way through the streets of Solo. The arrival of the RPKAD shattered the eerie calm of the previous weeks. According to an Indonesian journalist with close RPKAD links, the mood changed when the onlookers heard the message of an Information Department loudspeaker unit and "saw the friendly troops who waved their hands".[42] The loudspeaker truck called on the people to join with the armed forces in resisting the "G-30-S/PKI" that had betrayed the state. Immediately behind the loudspeaker unit came a succession of jeeps, led by the one belonging to Sarwo Edhie. The red beret commander seemed, however, to have been taking no chances that day. During the show of force, he travelled in the third jeep, having ordered a sergeant major who resembled him to travel in the first jeep, "so if [the pro-G30S forces] shoot, they kill the sergeant major".[43] Most PKI supporters are said to have remained indoors. Anti-communists, growing increasingly confident, gave the troops a tumultuous reception.

The Sixth Infantry Brigade, which had come out in support of the September 30th Movement only three weeks earlier, made no

[41] Subroto, *Wartawan Perang*, pp. 203–4.
[42] Subroto, *Wartawan Perang*, p. 204.
[43] Subroto, interviewed by David Jenkins, 14 Sept. 1998, Jakarta; Hendro Subroto, *Wartawan Perang*, p. 204.

attempt to oppose the RPKAD convoy. However, "the anti-Communist demonstration met with some resistance when a parade was fired on and six people were killed and twenty-nine wounded".[44] That evening, a group of KI youths are alleged to have lured 14 young men, who were returning home after participating in the RPKAD convoy, into a trap and murdered them on the outskirts of the city.[45] The "show of force" was followed by the now familiar pattern of arrests and anti-PKI mob violence, leaving houses and offices destroyed.

On 26 October, concerned about the reports he was receiving about PKI violence and believing that he had insufficient troops, Diponegoro commander Brigadier General Surjosumpeno declared a "state of war" in Central Java and Yogyakarta. That same day, Sarwo Edhie presided at a meeting of the new "Surakarta Joint Security Staff" and a new division of territorial responsibilities was established.[46] Reviewing the situation on 29 October, the US Embassy noted that the security situation was deteriorating in several important areas: "Most serious region is Central Java (Yogya-Solo-Madiun) where Army has announced state of war, and PKI, feeling time running out for regrouping and strike, may be [words missing] to move against army. Air forces [*sic*] [words missing] ferrying [RPKAD] paratroopers to meet security threat there ..."[47]

Over the following days, Sarwo Edhie directed the onslaught against the PKI from his new forward headquarters at the RPKAD's Battalion III base in Kartosuro. He met local military and police commanders, and presided over ceremonies formally dissolving local PKI branches. Speaking at mass meetings in Semarang, Yogya, Solo, Boyolali, Kudus, Demak and Purwokerto, Sarwo Edhie warned his listeners about the dangers of communism and stressed the need to

---

[44] Crouch, *Army and Politics*, p. 149, citing *Fakta2*, pp. 304–5.
[45] "Gerombolan PR sembelih 14 anak2", *Duta Masjarakat*, 6 Nov. 1965; M. Hari Mulyadi *et al.*, *Runtuhnya Kekuasaan "Kraton Alit": Studi Radikalisasi Sosial "Song Sala" dan Kerusuhan Mei 1998 di Surakarta* (Solo: Lembaga Pengembangan Teknologi Pedesaan, 1999), p. 300.
[46] A Kodam VII/Diponegoro document dated 27 October states that RPKAD was responsible for the old Surakarta Residency. See *Fakta2*, p. 214. A conflicting account is provided in *Sejarah Rumpun Diponegoro*, pp. 588–91.
[47] A "sanitised" copy of this document, which was prepared by the "country team", seems to have been passed to the Australian government. A copy is in A1838/280 3034/2/1/8, Part 4, NAA.

exterminate the PKI and its supporters, justifying the use of violence on the morning of 1 October against the Army generals.[48] In his speeches, he announced the discovery of documents which, he claimed, revealed communist plans to massacre members of "nationalist" and "religious" groups.

Mobilising Civilians, Late October–November 1965

Although Colonel Sarwo Edhie was in control of Solo, he believed he had too few troops to establish his authority in the surrounding rural areas, many of which enjoyed strong PKI support. When he contacted Suharto to ask for reinforcements, he was told that additional troops would not be available until the end of the month.[49] He then requested permission to "arm and train youths from the religious and nationalist organisations". After a delay, Sarwo Edhie was given the green light, presumably by Suharto. This was a pivotal moment. "We decided," Sarwo Edhie recalled, "to encourage the anti-communist civilians to help with the job. In Solo we gathered together the youth, the nationalist groups, the religious organisations. We gave them two or three days' training, then sent them out to kill the communists."[50]

Before long, the RPKAD was training youths in many other places as well. In a later despatch from Yogyakarta, R.E. Stannard Jr, the Jakarta bureau chief for United Press International, wrote that when "Communist youth terrorist gangs" began roving the countryside after the coup, "shooting, burning and torturing almost at will", some young Muslims and nationalists armed themselves with primitive weapons — bamboo spears, farm implements, swords, daggers, slingshots, and bows and arrows — to defend their villages: "They moved in vigilante groups that sought to stave off communist raiders. Sometimes they themselves launched raids on neighbouring Communist villages they feared."[51] Now the Army was training and arming

[48] Amir, interviewed by Theodora Erlijna, 23 Aug. 2007, Solo.
[49] Crouch, *Army and Politics*, p. 150.
[50] John Hughes, *The End of Sukarno: A Coup that Misfired, a Purge that Ran Wild* (London: Angus and Robertson, 1968), p. 151.
[51] See R.E. Stannard Jr, dispatch from Yogyakarta, 24 Nov. 1965, in Series A1838/280, item 3034/2/1/8, part 6, p. 111, NAA.

these bands, "seeking to weld this amorphous, potentially dangerous element into a disciplined home guard". Firearms were being issued to the anti-communist civil militia. The new village vigilante groups, Stannard noted, retained their political identity and organisation.

> The army simply picks out four or five young men it trusts from the local nationalist party youth organisation or Moslem party group and authorizes them to mobilize their comrades. That way it becomes virtually impossible for fugitive Communist elements to infiltrate back into recognized forces and it spares the army the problems of screening and selection that could damage its own popularity at the grass roots.[52]

These units were organised along regular military lines, with companies, platoons and squads. Members wore no uniforms and received no payment. But their militancy showed. Young Muslim fighters wore kerchiefs around their foreheads with the Islamic affirmation "God is great!" Young nationalists often wore headgear in the national red-and-white colours. Once the militia members had completed their rudimentary courses in killing, RPKAD units led them into the villages to root out communists.

In each village, members of communist organisations were rounded up and taken away. After quick interrogation, those considered to be activists were killed; passive supporters were placed under detention in camps and jails. Over the following weeks, similar operations were conducted throughout Central Java.[53] At the end of October, the US Embassy began to receive reports of "killings and atrocities" against PKI members, "which were generally reported upon in the context of continued armed PKI resistance".[54] On 4 November US Ambassador in Jakarta Marshall Green reported that Deputy Chief of Mission Francis Galbraith had been informed that

---

52 Ibid.

53 Crouch, *Army and Politics*, p. 151, based on an interview, 5 Sept. 1970 with Sarwo Edhie.

54 See Document 162, "Editorial Note", US Department of State, *Foreign Relations of the United States, 1964–1968*, vol. 26 (Washington, DC: United States Government Printing Office, 2001), p. 338 [hereafter FRUS, 1964–1968].

Suharto, not Nasution, was the one who was giving orders in Indonesia, conceiving his own strategy and confronting Sukarno directly.[55] In Central Java, the source had added, "Army (RPKAD) is training Moslem youth and supplying them with weapons and will keep them out in front against PKI. Army will try to avoid as much as it can safely do so direct confrontation with PKI." According to this source, "Smaller fry [are] being systematically arrested and jailed or executed." The Army was confident it could "break the back of PKI attempted insurgency before it gets too serious". On 13 November, Green reported that "from 50 to 100 PKI members are being killed every night in East and Central Java by civilian anti-Communist troops with blessing of the army".[56] According to Sudjatmoko, a liberal intellectual, in East and Central Java, "pro and anti-Communist forces are evenly balanced, and there is a paralysing sense of fear and uncertainty". But, he added, "the whole of the rest of the country outside Java is delighted with recent events".[57]

During the first half of November 1965, B.K. Tiwari, an Indian journalist who had made a number of earlier visits to Indonesia, spent 11 days in Central Java as a guest of Sarwo Edhie. The RPKAD commander, two Australian diplomats reported after an interview with Tiwari, "had been very cooperative and had permitted him to accompany army patrols in the Solo-Yogyakarta area".[58] It was during one of these patrols, on 10 November, that Tiwari saw "action" while accompanying an RPKAD unit in the vicinity of Boyolali.

On this occasion the patrol numbered 400 men, and at about 6.30 a.m. it fired "test shots" into the air, as was its usual practice from time to time. Between 100 and 200 people, including many women and children, appeared at the side of the road and advanced

---

[55] Telegram 1326, Ambassador Green to State Department, 4 Nov. 1965, POL 23–9, Indonesia, NARA. For a slightly different version of this cable, see Document 169, *FRUS, 1964–1968*, vol. 26, pp. 353–6.

[56] Telegram 1438, US Embassy Jakarta to State Department, 13 Nov. 1965, POL 23-9, Indonesia, NARA.

[57] Cablegram from Shann, Australian Embassy Jakarta, 12 Nov. 1965, A 1838/280, 3034/2/1/8, Part 5, NAA.

[58] An account of his visit and the situation in Central Java can be found in "Record of Conversation with Mr Tiwari, of the 'Indian Express' on 16th November, 1965", Australian Embassy, Jakarta, A1838, 3034/2/1/8, Part 6, NAA.

on the troops with cries of "Nekolim" (a Sukarno-era slogan meaning "neo-colonialism and imperialism"). They were variously armed with bamboo spears, knives and one or two guns. Shots fired over their heads by the patrol failed to deter them, and the Army was obliged to shoot, killing seven and wounding 17.[59]

This rather matter-of-fact account of a morning's slaughter in Central Java is followed by confirmation that the Indonesian Army was training civilian death squads:

> Tiwari said that Colonel Eddy [*sic*] estimated that before the coup about seventy-five per cent of the population in the Solo-Yogyakarta area were Communist. He now believed that forty per cent of the people were on his side and that this percentage would increase. The Colonel had also spoken of the training he was giving Muslim groups (as yet no arms had been issued) and of his belief that mass movement should be fought by mass movement. To ensure that no Communists were inadvertently given training army units were instructed to select five known anti-Communist Muslims who would then be responsible for all further recruiting. Muslim youths were acting as the ears and eyes of the Army in the region, guiding patrols and generally informing ... On the whole Tiwari had been impressed by the sense and restraint shown by the Army in their operations.[60]

Tiwari's belief that the Army was showing impressive restraint was, at best, naïve. In late 1965, determined to destroy the Communist Party once and for all, Suharto and his fellow Army officers were going out of their way to inflame communal tensions in what was already a deeply and dangerously polarised society, provoking pious Muslims (and, in some places, Hindus and Christians) to turn without mercy on their generally poorer, PKI-voting *abangan* (nominal Muslim) neighbours.

"Fifteen Hundred Assassinations per Day"

The mobilisation of civilian militias expanded dramatically throughout November 1965. On 13 November, the US Embassy reported that in the Solo area the Army was "training and equipping some

---

[59] "Record of Conversation with Mr Tiwari".
[60] Ibid.

24 thousand Moslem youth for action against communists".[61] Elaborating on this development two days later, the Army newspaper claimed that in Solo the RPKAD had trained 17 platoons of young men from Ansor, Pelajar Islam Indonesia (PII, the high school student affiliate of the banned Masyumi Party) and Muhammadiyah; thousands more were trained in Boyolali.[62] A week later, following an alleged PKI massacre of civilians in Cilacap, RPKAD troops began training youths there as well.[63] An Indonesian journalist who accompanied the RPKAD on their operations provided the following description:

> Each day, wherever there are RPKAD posts, religious and Marhaenis youth from all over the place arrive and ask to be trained. This is a request that the RPKAD leader cannot refuse just like that. So, everyday the RPKAD ... go from kampung to kampung to provide information and training. Returning to the kampungs, these youths guard their villages with exuberant spirits. In the face of these signs, one no longer hears of evil deeds such as arson, kidnappings and murders.[64]

The most detailed descriptions of RPKAD training of civilian militias are from the strongly Islamic belt in the north-eastern part of the province, from Demak through Kudus to Pati. Operations in this region were conducted by 1st Lieutenant Feisal Tanjung's company from the RPKAD's Battalion III.[65] An ethnic Chinese member of the Catholic Party in Pati told US officials that RPKAD troops "solicited the assistance of the Catholic, [the Army-backed] IP-KI and Nahdlatul Ulama Party organisations in rooting out the PKI".[66]

---

[61] Telegram 1435, US Embassy Jakarta to State Department, 13 Nov. 1965, POL 23-9 INDON, NARA. Eleven days later, Sarwo Edhie gave a similar figure; the RPKAD, he estimated, had trained nearly 25,000 young anti-communists. See R.E. Stannard Jr, dispatch from Yogyakarta, 24 Nov. 1965.

[62] See "Brimob dan RPKAD latih pemuda progresif", *Berita Yudha*, 15 Nov. 1965; and Nurinwa Ki S. Hendrowinoto *et al.*, *Jenderal Sarwo Edhie Wibowo*, p. 161fn189.

[63] "G30S di Tjilatjap bunuh 40 orang penduduk", *Berita Yudha*, 22 Nov. 1965.

[64] *Berita Yudha*, late 1965.

[65] See Aziz Ahmadi, ed., *Feisal Tanjung: Terbaik untuk Rakyat, Terbaik bagi ABRI* (Jakarta: Dharmapena, 1999), p. 211.

[66] Airgram A-386, US Embassy Jakarta to State Department, 10 Dec. 1965, POL 23-9 INDON, NARA.

In Demak, where anti-communist youth were "taught and trained by the RPKAD", a *Berita Yudha* journalist noted their distinctive dress: "Entirely black. Black shirts, black pants and caps. They are the progressive revolutionary youth...." The article explained that when the training came to a close, "265 platoons of civil guards [Hansip] and peoples' guards [Hanra] had been formed. Each village had one platoon of peoples' guards, consisting of 100 members ... In addition to these forces, forces consisting of elementary school students from class six and up were also formed."[67]

These operations were monitored closely by Major General Suharto, who visited Central Java in mid-November, travelling to Semarang, Solo and Yogya to see for himself what was going on.[68] Shortly after, on 18 November, Sarwo Edhie flew to Jakarta to report to Suharto. The following day, Sarwo Edhie commented that the situation was "entirely under the military's control", while cautioning that the "cleansing down to the roots" was still incomplete. On 19 November, Ambassador Green reported that the embassy had been told that "General Suharto has ordered military commander[s] in East and Central Java to shoot without further investigation PKI members not involved in September 30 Movement and to hold for interrogation those involved".[69]

For six weeks, a CIA study noted on 22 November, the Indonesian Army was engaged in a major campaign against the PKI. Party members and sympathisers "are being rounded up and interned by the military; others are being purged from local government positions", and in Central Java PKI adherents were reportedly shot on sight by the Army. "The army has risked much of its prestige and political future on this campaign."[70] On 18 November, Green advised Washington that "RPKAD is not taking prisoners. (I gather this

---

[67] "Mengikuti Operasi RPKAD: Barisan Seragam Hitam", *Berita Yudha*, 30 Dec. 1965.

[68] "Men/Pangab diam-diam sudah nengok Semarang, Jogjakarta dan Solo", *Berita Yudha*, 18 Nov. 1965. Suharto may have made more than one visit to Central Java at around this time. See *Tempo*, 7 Oct. 2007.

[69] Telegram 736A, Ambassador Green to State Department, 19 Nov. 1965, POL 23-9 INDON, NARA.

[70] See "Intelligence Memorandum", OCI No. 2943/65, Washington, 22 Nov. 1965, Johnson Library, National Security File, Country File Indonesia, vol. VI, 11/65–5/66, Document 178, US Department of State, *FRUS, 1964–1968*, vol. 26.

means they are shooting the PKI on sight.).”[71] This may have been the case during the initial operations in the greater Surakarta region and later against Army personnel who had led the September 30th Movement in the province, but it was clearly not the norm. The most common procedure was for civilian paramilitaries operating under the direction of a small RPKAD post to arrest suspected communists and then take them to designated detention centres. The detainees were interrogated, however briefly, to separate PKI cadres from ordinary Party members, sympathisers, and relatives. Cadres were taken to isolated locations and killed. But this left large numbers of detainees, whom the military was neither interested in nor capable of feeding and housing. The solution was for military personnel to “move” detainees at night and en route hand them over to designated civilian death squads.[72]

On 1 December, Sarwo Edhie took command of Operation Merapi Command, aimed at tracking down and destroying key Central Java Army plotters, including Sahirman, Maryono and Usman, who had fled to the slopes of Mount Merapi.[73] Usman was found and shot on 9 December.[74] Sahirman and Maryono (who had broken his spectacles while on the run, rendering him quite helpless) fared no better. With their food supplies exhausted, they hid in a pine forest for four days. RPKAD troops captured them on 13 December and shot them the following day.[75] On the day of Sahirman and Maryono’s capture, Suharto announced that the “physical” situation in Central and East Java was good but the economic situation needed special attention.[76]

---

[71] Telegram 674A, US Embassy Jakarta to State Department, 18 Nov. 1965, POL 23-9 INDON, NARA.

[72] Airgram A-353, US Embassy Jakarta to State Department, 30 Nov. 1965, POL 2-1 INDON, NARA.

[73] The force consisted of four RPKAD companies (Urip, Kayat, Tedjo and Sembiring), two Diponegoro battalions (E and F), a platoon of cavalry, three Soviet-made Mi-4 helicopters and “young men who had received training”. See Hendro Subroto, *Sintong Panjaitan*, p. 141.

[74] *Pikiran Rakyat*, 20 Dec. 1965, cited in McVey, “Small World”, p. 119; *Sejarah Rumpun Diponegoro*, p. 592.

[75] *Pikiran Rakyat*, 18 Nov. 1965; and *Kedaulatan Rakyat*, 16 Dec. 1965, cited in McVey, “Small World”, p. 119. Soepardio, interviewed by David Jenkins, 10 Sept. 1998, Jakarta.

[76] Letter from S.J.G. Cambridge, British Embassy Jakarta, to Foreign Office, 16 Dec. 1965, FCO 371/180325.

The elimination of the September 30th Movement leaders in Central Java did not end the mass killing of those associated with the Left. In mid-December, Trade Minister Adam Malik, a member of the small "national-Communist" (but fiercely anti-PKI) Murba Party and a man who was to serve as Suharto's foreign minister from 1968 to 1977, told the US Ambassador it was better that "the people should suffer somewhat longer in the interest of [an] adequately complete purge than leave Sukarno with sufficient power so as to stage a comeback". When Green asked if this was the way Nasution and Suharto viewed the situation, Malik said it was.[77] Three months after the coup, the Indonesian death toll was of staggering proportions, even by conservative estimates. On 23 December, the Australian Embassy reported:

> Estimates of the number of people killed vary between 100,000 and 200,000, the latter being the figure accepted by the American and West German embassies. The West Germans have heard that 70,000 people have been killed in East Java alone. Without having any firm basis for making an estimate we would if we had to name a figure put it at between 100,000 and 150,000. This works out at about 1,500 assassinations per day since September 30th.[78]

The destruction of the September 30th Movement, the elimination of the PKI and the massacres may have been a "success", but other tensions had begun to emerge. The situation was particularly acute in East Java, where the Marines, who were staunch supporters of President Sukarno, soon came into conflict with regional Army commanders and the Nahdlatul Ulama. Although less severe, similar problems developed in Central Java. Many soldiers were upset to see friends and relatives being victimised for their political affiliations, and outraged by the callous disrespect shown by the RPKAD for

[77] Green cable, 15 Dec. 1965. In 1965, it has been claimed, Adam Malik was on the CIA payroll; he was, according to former CIA covert operator Clyde McAvoy, "the highest-ranking Indonesian we ever recruited". See Tim Weiner, *Legacy of Ashes: The History of the CIA* (London and New York: Allen Lane, 2007), pp. 259–61.

[78] Savingram 64, Australian Embassy Jakarta to Canberra, 23 Dec. 1965, A1838/280, 3034/2/1, Part 48, NAA.

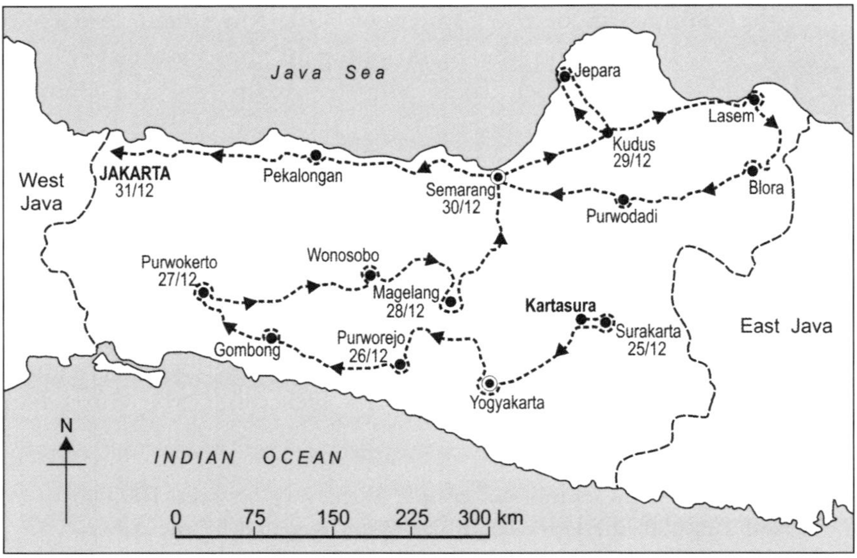

Planned route of military "victory" convoy through Central Java (redrawn from map published in *Berita Yudha*, 25 December 1965)

Diponegoro units, including the ransacking of barracks and facilities. These tensions exploded on 24 December in the town of Gombong, in Kebumen District, where a "bloody clash" occurred between RPKAD and Diponegoro troops. A US Embassy telegram reported that the withdrawal of RPKAD units was "publicly heralded as due to pacification of area", but commented "this obviously not the case is given by rapid replacement of RPKAD by KKO (Marines) in Central Java which now underway".[79]

With Central Java officially "safe", the Army announced that the RPKAD troops that had been operating there would take part in a week-long convoy through the province before returning home to Jakarta.[80] Five RPKAD companies (those of Kayat, Tedjo, Sembiring, Ramelan and Tanjung) were to participate, supported by tanks and

[79] Telegram 176A, US Embassy Jakarta to State Department, 6 Jan. 1966, POL 1 CENTRALCAW, NA; see also Airgram A-444, US Embassy Jakarta to State Department, 11 Jan. 1966, POL 2-1 INDON, NARA, citing a senior Army officer.

[80] See "Mengikuti Operasi RPKAD: Pulang kekandang", *Berita Yudha*, 20 Dec. 1965.

armoured cars. Rolling out of Kartosuro, which had served as Sarwo Edhie's forward headquarters for the previous two months, the 65-vehicle convoy took the southern road from Yogyakarta to Purwokerto, doubled back on the mountain road through Wonosobo and Salatiga to Semarang, and toured the north-eastern towns of Jepara, Kudus, Blora and Purwodadi before returning to Semarang. From Semarang, the convoy took the north coast road back to Jakarta.

The route appears to have been selected so as to "visit" the primary areas in which RPKAD had operated: the Surakarta region (where the largest military operations had centred on Solo, Klaten and Boyolali); the Banyumas region (the RPKAD had been particularly active in Cilacap); Semarang, where the convoy made two stops; and the Demak-Kudus-Pati-Purwodadi region (the first two places being centres of paramilitary training, the latter two sites of extensive arrests and killings). The convoy was scheduled to arrive back in Jakarta on 31 December because, in the words of a US Embassy informant, of "Army expectations of trouble in Jakarta on New Year's Day".[81] Trouble did not materialise. On 5 January the military daily *Angkatan Bersendjata* reported that Major General Suharto, wearing an RPKAD uniform, addressed the RPKAD troops that had just returned to Jakarta from Central Java.[82]

The RPKAD in East Java

While it is clear that the RPKAD played the leading role in organising anti-PKI violence in Central Java, much less is known about the situation in East Java, where the Regional Military Command (Kodam VIII/Brawijaya) was also seriously under-manned until well into November and where equally horrific massacres took place. Several scholars have suggested that the killings and detentions on Java spread eastward in lockstep with the movement of RPKAD troops from Central Java through East Java and finally to Bali. Peter Dale Scott, for example, has argued that the worst killings occurred in "staggered stages" as RPKAD troops travelled east.[83] In a similar

[81] Telegram 137A, US Embassy Jakarta to State Department, 5 Jan. 1966, POL INDO [no.?], NARA.

[82] "RPKAD sewaktu2 dpt dikerahkan untuk hadapi Malaysia", *Angkatan Besendjata*, 5 Jan. 1966.

[83] Peter Dale Scott, "The United States and the Overthrow of Sukarno", *Pacific Affairs* 58 (Summer 1985): 239–64.

vein, historian Geoffrey Robinson has written that Siliwangi and RPKAD troops "were deployed through Central and East Java with the explicit objective of helping to wipe out the PKI".[84] Robinson claims that "RPKAD troops wound up their campaign of terror in East Java" during the first week of December and landed in Bali on 7 or 8 December.[85]

The suggestion that RPKAD troops moved from Central to East Java and then crossed the narrow strait to Bali does not bear close scrutiny. The Indonesian press and official military publications, which provide extensive reporting about the location and activities of RPKAD companies throughout Central Java, do not provide a single reference to an RPKAD presence in East Java during the last three months of 1965. The only primary source that mentions RPKAD troops in the Brawijaya region during late 1965 is a leaked Indonesian military intelligence report, but this mentions only a single RPKAD "task force" and fails to provide the location.[86] It is true that at least one RPKAD unit made a foray into East Java, but it apparently went no farther than Madiun, which is only 40 kilometres across the border from Central Java.[87] No red beret units were despatched at this time to Surabaya, or indeed to any other part of the province, and there was no relentless overland advance to the east.

Why was East Java different? There were two reasons. First, as we have seen, in Central Java pro-September 30th Movement officers had seized control of the regional military command and many subunits had also come out in support of the Movement. It was essential for Suharto to regain the initiative as soon as possible. He did this by sending the RPKAD, backed by armoured vehicles and military police reinforcements, to shock and awe the dissident forces, which were far more numerous than the arriving forces. In East Java, by contrast, despite considerable intra-military tension, the Brawijaya command had not come under the control of September 30th Movement forces. On the contrary, it had remained loyal and had responded with enthusiasm to a detailed order by Suharto in November

[84] Geoffrey Robinson, *The Dark Side of Paradise: Political Violence in Bali* (Ithaca and London: Cornell University Press, 1995), p. 281.
[85] Robinson, *Dark Side of Paradise*, pp. 285, 295–7.
[86] "Report from East Java", *Indonesia* 41 (Apr. 1986): 147.
[87] Major General Sukotjo Tjokroatmodjo, telephone interview with David Jenkins, 30 Oct. 2009.

that called for the destruction of the PKI. In 1966, the new Brawijaya commander, Major General Soemitro, told a *New York Times* correspondent that "most local commanders did their utmost to kill as many cadres as possible".[88] Second, the RPKAD lacked the resources to mount a substantive intervention in East Java. A declassified US document from early December reports that, according to police and military sources, the Army was indeed considering deploying Siliwangi and RPKAD units to East Java but was concerned about "whether they [RPKAD] could be spared from Central Java".[89] That observation ties in with what is known about the disposition of the 11 RPKAD companies at that time. In fact, it was only in June 1966 that RPKAD troops were sent to East Java.[90]

The RPKAD in Bali, December 1965

In early December 1965, after two months of rising political competition at the local level and what appears to have been a military campaign aimed at inflaming passions against the PKI, a wave of mass killing erupted in Bali. By mid-1966, this had claimed the lives of an estimated 80,000 people.[91] In the course of these events, two RPKAD companies were sent to Bali to assist the forces of the local military command, Kodam XVI/Udayana. When did the RPKAD companies arrive in Bali, and what role did they play during their time on the island?

There is considerable confusion over the date on which RPKAD units arrived in Bali. As noted above, Robinson has suggested that RPKAD units entered Bali from East Java on 7 or 8 December, and that their arrival precipitated the mass killings. Other sources have

---

[88] Seymour Topping, "Slaughter of Reds Gives Indonesia a Grim Legacy", *New York Times*, 24 Aug. 1966.

[89] Telegram 47, US Consulate Surabaya to Jakarta and State, 6 Dec. 1965, POL 23-8 INDON, NARA.

[90] Telegram 3562, US Embassy Jakarta to State Department, 30 June 1966, POL 2 INDON, NARA; see also Pipit Rochijat, "Am I PKI or non-PKI", trans. Benedict Anderson, *Indonesia* 40 (Oct. 1985): 38.

[91] For an excellent account of the forces at work in Bali, see Robinson, *Dark Side of Paradise*, pp. 273–303. The figure of 80,000 victims can be traced to the wife of Deputy Foreign Minister Anak Agung Gedé Agung; see Airgram A-527, US Embassy Jakarta to State Department, 25 Feb. 1966, POL 23-9 INDON, NARA.

suggested that these units arrived in mid- or even late December.[92] The available evidence shows that at least one RPKAD company did arrive on 7 December.[93] A second RPKAD company may have followed a week or so later.[94] However, these units did not arrive across the Bali Strait from Java but were rather, according to the Air Force Information Centre, transported aboard Antonov-12 transport aircraft directly from Jakarta.[95] On 8 December the commander of the Udayana military region presided over a ceremony to address troops that had arrived in Bali the previous day. Curiously, however, these units are identified as the "Paracommando Regiment's Parga Company" and "one Platoon of Civilian Combat Engineering Tanks from the Brawijaya [East Java] Division".[96] It is entirely possible, though unproven, that the Udayana commander addressed *both* RPKAD troops who had arrived by plane from Jakarta *and* Brawijaya troops, accompanied by Ansor civilian paramilitaries, who may have crossed the strait from East Java to west Bali.[97]

By that time, however, mass killing was well under way in Bali. In a memo dated 9 December, a US Embassy officer produced a memorandum of a conversation with an informant who said that "approximately 6000 people have been killed in Bali, including 3000

---

[92] For claims of a mid-December arrival, see Subroto, *Wartawan Perang*, p. 208; and Nurinwa Ki S. Hendrowinoto *et al.*, *Jenderal Sarwo Edhie Wibowo*, p. 162. For late December, see Robert Cribb, *The Indonesian Killings of 1965–1966: Studies from Java and Bali* (Clayton: Centre of Southeast Asian Studies, Monash University, 1990), p. 243.

[93] Personal communication, Gianyar, 3 Jan. 2010, with eyewitness who saw RPKAD troops on Diponegoro Street in Denpasar at midday on 7 December; "Panglima Brigdjen Sjafiudin: 'G 30 S' harus dipatahkan", *Suara Indonesia*, 10 Dec. 1965. This was most probably Company E/Kayat.

[94] This was Company B/Ben Hur. RPKAD troops in Bali were under the command of Major Djasmin. See *Berita Yudha*, 29 Dec. 1965.

[95] "RPKAD bantu penerbitan [*sic*] di Bali", *Suara Indonesia*, 11 Dec. 1965.

[96] "Panglima Brigdjen Sjafiudin: 'G 30 S' harus dipatahkan", *Suara Indonesia*, 10 Dec. 1965. "Parga" is not among the names of RPKAD units. Similarly, the word "Warga" (member, citizen) seems out of place in the name of a Brawijaya Combat Engineer Tank platoon. It seems possible, therefore, that these were not in fact RPKAD and Brawijaya units at all, but rather civilian (warga, pasukan warga = parga) paramilitary units that had received military training and then were either given or adopted names reflecting their mentors.

[97] Cribb, *Indonesian Killings*, p. 247.

members of the PKI in West Bali".[98] This is not to say that the RPKAD played no part in the killing in Bali. On the contrary, the evidence suggests that the force was sent to the island to lead the pogrom against the PKI and to ensure a requisite degree of order and predictability to the killing, which had quickly become indiscriminate, sweeping up many non-communists.[99] In a time of turmoil and intense fear, the Army and the police, working with the civilian authorities, were expected to control and channel the violence, ensuring that only the "right" kind of people were killed. The RPKAD, it would appear, wasted no time in doing just that. By one account, on 16 December RPKAD troops organised and carried out the public massacre of about 30 men in the village of Kapal, southern Bali.[100] During their deployment in Bali, it has been claimed, RPKAD units distributed blacklists of PKI members marked for liquidation and trained gangs of youths, generally called Tameng Marhaenis, in the basic techniques of killing.[101]

A few days after his troops landed, Sarwo Edhie flew to Bali on an inspection tour. During his visit, he went to Denpasar, Klungkung, Gianyar and Jembrana. All along the road, in an atmosphere gripped by fear, houses lay in ruins, having been destroyed or burnt by "the masses".[102] What exactly did the two RPKAD companies do during their stay on Bali, which seems to have lasted between five and eight weeks?[103] Forty-five years after these events took place, we still have very few answers to that question. We do know, however, that their arrival coincided with the rapid intensification of the killings in mid-December 1965.[104]

In seeking to explain the difference between the situations in Central Java and Bali, Sarwo Edhie is alleged to have told a leading

---

[98] "Confidential Memorandum of Conversation", dated 9 Dec. 1965, in Telegram A-391, US Embassy Jakarta to State Department, 13 Dec. 1965, POL 2 INDON, NARA.

[99] Hughes, *End of Sukarno*, p. 181; see also Robinson, *Dark Side of Paradise*, p. 297.

[100] Roosa, *Pretext for Mass Murder*, p. 29.

[101] Cribb, *Indonesian Killings*, p. 241.

[102] Subroto, *Wartawan Perang*, pp. 208–9.

[103] A US Embassy report in early January 1966 suggested that the two RPKAD companies were to pull out in mid-January. See Telegram 137-A, Jakarta Embassy to State Department, 5 Jan. 1966, POL INDO [no.?], NARA.

[104] Robinson, *Dark Side of Paradise*, pp. 295–7.

Balinese, "In Java we had to egg the people on to kill Communists. In Bali we have to restrain them, make sure they don't go too far."[105] It seems clear that Sarwo Edhie did indeed say something along those lines, and the observation has been widely quoted.[106] However, the reported remarks do not capture with sufficient clarity the distinction between the situations in Central Java and Bali —because either the red beret commander was misquoted, he expressed himself badly or he was seeking to obfuscate. The evidence suggests that in Bali the Army was quite ready to egg the people on in their killing, so long as they were killing alleged communists.

Conclusion

In the early years of the New Order, Sarwo Edhie was frequently portrayed as a hero, a man whose red beret force had helped save the nation from unimaginable horrors. Few Indonesians seemed interested — or were unwise enough — to question that view. Not long before he died in 1989, however, Sarwo Edhie was said to have been "full of regret" over the number of people RPKAD had killed in 1965. Having spoken to the families of some of the victims, he expressed concern that so many had been killed and that "they were killed as soon as his troops came into that area. They began the killing when Sarwo came into the villages and the towns."[107]

Whatever the truth of that claim, Suharto showed not the slightest sign of remorse or regret over the mass killing, for which he, more than anyone else, was responsible. On the contrary, he seems to have felt that a purge of this kind was necessary in order to rid the nation of the communist threat. Suharto, the evidence suggests, was not only well pleased with the work of the RPKAD in Jakarta, Central Java and Bali in 1965–66 (though careful not to leave incriminating evidence of his own sponsorship of and support for a vast network of civilian death squads); he also learned a useful lesson about the usages of exemplary terror.

---

[105] Hughes, *End of Sukarno*, p. 181.

[106] In an interview (14 Sept. 1998), Hendro Subroto said that Sarwo Edhie had told him the same thing: "It was terrible in Bali at that time. If there was one Communist in a house, they [local people] killed everyone in the house."

[107] Major General Sukotjo Tjokroatmodjo, personal communication with David Jenkins, 30 Oct. 2009.

During the New Order, the RPKAD, later renamed Kopassus (Komando Operasi Khusus, Special Forces Command), became a larger and more professionally competent force. However, it was still dogged by allegations of human rights violations, including kidnapping, torture, murder, and the sponsorship from time to time of brutal civilian militias, not unlike those it created in 1965. The RPKAD/Kopassus was deployed not only in what were ostensibly military operations in places such as East Timor and Aceh, but in actions against civilian "targets", as was the case when, in the 1980s, it garrotted and shot, on Suharto's orders, some 5,000 alleged criminals, or when it kidnapped and tortured (and in some cases apparently killed) political opponents of the regime. In this context, it is worth noting that a number of the young company and platoon commanders who were "blooded" in the violent RPKAD crackdown in 1965 went on to hold powerful positions in the Army during Suharto's presidency, helping to perpetuate a system in which violence was used routinely against those who were seen as a threat to the state and/or the regime.

5

East Java and the Role of Nahdlatul Ulama in the 1965–66 Anti-communist Violence

*Greg Fealy and Katharine McGregor**

In each province of Indonesia the military cooperated with different coalitions of anti-communist organisations to attack supporters of the Indonesian Communist Party (Partai Komunis Indonesia, PKI). In East Java, the most important player in the anti-PKI alliance was the Islamic organisation and political party Nahdlatul Ulama (Revival of the Islamic Scholars, NU). At the national, provincial and local levels, NU leaders endorsed hostilities against the PKI and encouraged NU youth to participate in killing communists and eliminating the PKI.

Throughout the Cold War, religious organisations were often strong opponents of communism, partly because of the assumption that communism rejected religious belief and partly because its class critique threatened the power and privilege of religious elites and their wealthy patrons. In Southeast Asia, the Catholic Church was a bulwark against communism in the Philippines and Vietnam, the Buddhist clergy (*sangha*) played a similar role in Thailand, and Islamic leaders were key sources of opposition to the Malayan Communist Party. In Indonesia these broad factors contributed to hostilities, but in East Java there were specific sources of antagonism between NU and the PKI.

During the independence struggle of 1945–49 and again from the late 1950s, East Java had seen fierce conflict between NU and

---

* Some sections of this chapter appeared in earlier form in "Nahdlatul Ulama and the Killings of 1965–66: Religion, Politics, and Remembrance" by Greg Fealy and Katharine McGregor, *Indonesia* 89 (Apr. 2010): 37–60.

the PKI. A major clash occurred following the Madiun uprising of September 1948 in which soldiers took over local government in the East Javanese town of Madiun in objection to the proposed rationalisation of leftist troops from the Army. As the Republican troops pursued them, the rebels attacked and killed NU members deemed to be supporters of the main Islamic party, Masyumi.[1] The PKI endorsed the uprising, and this led to an enduring suspicion of the PKI within both the Army and NU.

To understand why NU leaders supported the violence in 1965–66 and why the organisation played such a pivotal role in East Java, we need to grasp the interests at stake and the dynamics of power within NU, including the influence of *kiai* (religious scholars) on their followers.[2] NU was founded in East Java in 1926 to protect and foster traditional Islam and underpin the authority of the kiai. The majority of its founders were East Javanese, and until today NU's most powerful clans of religious scholars (*ulama*) and its biggest and most influential Islamic schools are still located in that province. East Java was therefore the location of NU's most valuable assets, including large landholdings. It was also a critical source of financial and political support for the organisation. Many NU leaders were concerned over the PKI's rapidly growing support, as evidenced by the Party's strong performance in the 1955 national and 1957 regional elections. Besides its electoral success, the PKI's sharp critiques of class and religious elites and its calls for direct action against them clearly threatened the standing and interests of NU leaders.

This chapter examines the dynamics of the Army-NU coalition in the anti-communist campaign in East Java. In recent years, there has been much debate within NU and scholarly circles about the extent to which NU acted at the direction of the Army. Some old NU leaders active in the 1960s have argued that NU was subservient to the military and that primary responsibility for the slaughter lies

---

[1] George Kahin, *Nationalism and Revolution in Indonesia* (Ithaca and London: Cornell University Press, 1970), p. 300.

[2] This chapter extends on our previous analysis of the role of NU as an organisation in endorsing and defending the violence to examine why NU's role in this province was so prominent. Greg Fealy and Katharine McGregor, "Nahdlatul Ulama and the Killings of 1965–66: Religion, Politics and Remembrance", *Indonesia* 89 (Apr. 2010): 37–60.

with Army leaders.[3] We argue that while the Army encouraged and coordinated the killings, NU leaders, especially in East Java, were determined to move against the PKI and readily sanctioned the participation of NU members in the killing squads. Though there are no accurate figures on the death toll, it is likely that more people died in East Java than in any other province. There is good evidence that members of the NU youth organisation, Ansor, were directly involved in the majority of these killings. Across the province, the level of support provided by the Army to NU varied according to the loyalties of the regional and sub-regional commanders. Some were loyal to Sukarno, the PKI or Suharto. The Army toughened its attitude towards NU as the former sought to curtail the violence.

The chapter draws on primary source materials including branch communiqués, internal NU documents, recently declassified US State Department telegrams and interviews with those who supported the killings. We focus on official NU pronouncements about the PKI and the actions recommended to NU members to crush the PKI along with accounts of the role of ulama in inciting and supporting violence. Drawing on State Department telegrams, we chart the complex tensions in East Java between sections of the military and Ansor and between Ansor and the Indonesian National Party (Partai Nasional Indonesia, PNI). Interviews with NU members provide insights into how the killings were carried out.

Kiai, NU and Power

Muslims in East Java have always been more traditional than Muslims of Central Java, the other province dominated by ethnic Javanese. For centuries, Muslims in East Java have been educated and organised through *pesantren* (Islamic boarding schools). These schools are led by kiai, who are often charismatic figures as well as experts in Islamic law and sciences. Large pesantren can have thousands of students (*santri*) and extensive networks of alumni, many of whom

[3] Yusuf Hasyim and Chalid Mawardi were two NU leaders who, on occasion, asserted that the Army, rather than NU, was responsible for the killings, though neither man was consistent about this. Yusuf Hasyim, interviewed by Greg Fealy, 26 Oct. 1991, Jombang, East Java; Chalid Mawardi, interviewed by Greg Fealy, 25 Feb. 1992, Jakarta.

retain a lifelong connection to their school. Intense dyadic relationships between kiai and santri are common. Kiai are not just teachers but also trusted moral guides, patrons, sources of capital and contacts, seers, and mediators with the spiritual world. A kiai famous for his erudition and/or supernatural powers can draw santri from across Java and Indonesia, and more serious santri study at various pesantren to broaden their knowledge and networks in the hope of eventually establishing themselves as kiai. Until recent decades, a kiai's word was writ among his students and supporters. A santri's voting behaviour, attitudes towards other community groups, and responses to major social issues were more often than not shaped by their kiai.[4]

The leaders of Nahdlatul Ulama founded the organisation in Surabaya in January 1926 to serve the interests of kiai and their traditional Islamic communities. At that time, traditionalist ulama were under growing pressure from the rapidly expanding modernist Islamic movement. The traditionalists based their ritual and jurisprudential practices on the four main Sunni law schools, whose origins trace back to ninth- and tenth-century efforts to codify and establish a broad consensus among scholars about how Islam should be practised. In the early twentieth century, reformist or modernist thinking spread from the Middle East to Indonesia. Reformists questioned the relevance of much of the medieval law school teachings and sought to purify Islam by returning to the unimpeachable sources of law: the Qur'an and the example of the Prophet Muhammad. They criticised the role of kiai and the culture of deference that surrounded them. As modernist organisations such as Muhammadiyah and al-Irsyad were established in the 1910s and 1920s and encroached into former traditionalist communities, kiai responded by forming NU in order to better represent and defend their interests. Thus, right from its inception, NU was reactive and defensive. Without the threat of expanding modernism, traditionalist ulama might never have formed NU given that their attention was focused on their own individual pesantren, not collective action. During the late 1920s and early

---

[4] For a good introduction to the culture surrounding kiai, santri and pesantren, see Zamakhsyari Dhofier, *The Pesantren Tradition: The Role of the Kiai in the Maintenance of Traditional Islam in Java* (Tempe: Monograph Series Press, Program for Southeast Asian Studies, Arizona State University, 1999).

1930s, rivalry and rancour between NU and its modernist counterparts were commonplace, occasionally resulting in violence. Only from the mid-1930s did relations between traditionalist and modernist Muslims improve, due in part to growing common opposition to perceived anti-Islam Dutch policies.[5]

Upon Indonesia's declaration of independence in August 1945, NU joined other prominent Islamic organisations to form a single Muslim political party, Masyumi (Majelis Suryo Muslimin Indonesia). However, in 1952, perceived domination of Masyumi by modernist factions drove NU to form its own political party of the same name. NU emerged in the 1955 general elections as Indonesia's third-largest party, with 18.4 per cent of the national vote, only 2 per cent behind that of Masyumi.[6] NU viewed politics primarily as a means of securing the interests of traditionalist Islam and its ulama elite. Its main focus was on gaining positions of influence within government in order to provide resources and opportunities to its members and supporters. NU held seats in all cabinets from 1953 to 1971, one of the few parties to do so, and its ministers and bureaucrats ensured that NU cadres received trading licences, government contracts, positions of status and privilege, and state funding for pesantren and other educational and welfare activities. Control of the Department of Religious Affairs was the main prize. By the mid-1950s, it was NU's main bastion in the bureaucracy, employing thousands of NU kiai and lay members at the national and local levels. During this time, many NU leaders enjoyed not only rising prominence but also wealth. In their minds, this was religiously valid because Islamic doctrine held that politics and faith were inseparable: increasing their prosperity and power would help to strengthen traditional Islam and protect it from the predations of its modernist Muslim and non-Muslim rivals.[7]

---

[5] Choirul Anam, *Pertumbuhan dan Perkembangan Nahdlatul Ulama*, Jatayu, Solo, 1985; Deliar Noer, *The Modernist Muslim Movement in Indonesia, 1900–1942* (Kuala Lumpur: Oxford University Press, 1973).

[6] Greg Fealy, "Ulama and Politics in Indonesia: A History of Nahdlatul Ulama, 1952–1967", PhD dissertation, Monash University, 1998, pp. 158–63.

[7] For a detailed study of NU and politics in the 1950s, see Fealy, "Ulama and Politics in Indonesia".

By the mid-1950s NU claimed, with some justification, to be the country's largest Muslim organisation. The deeper its engagement in politics, the more it sought to recruit and mobilise traditionalist Muslims. Despite NU's growing national membership, East Java remained the organisation's heartland. In the 1955 general elections, for example, NU gained almost half (47 per cent) of its total seven million votes from East Java, a figure repeated in the 1971 election. When, in the early 1960s, NU had to provide data to the government on its membership in order to retain party registration, the party's report showed East Java to have the most branches and by far the most members.[8]

Relations between NU and the PKI

NU leaders often express the view that their organisation has always been implacably anti-communist. They point to the late 1920s and early 1930s, when traditionalist ulama opposed close relations between the PKI and the main mass Muslim organisation of the time, the Sarekat Islam, in which many NU members were active. Then in the 1940s and the 1950s, NU consistently opposed communists holding seats in any of the many cabinets or being appointed to senior bureaucratic or military positions. They referred to the violence between Muslim and communist fighters during the 1945–49 Revolution, particularly the communists' killing of numerous kiai and their santri after the Madiun uprising.[9]

This view probably overstates the intensity of NU's anti-communism. While there were episodes of hostility towards the PKI, especially after the Madiun uprising, during much of the 1940s and 1950s NU was more pragmatic in its stance than Masyumi and other modernist Muslim organisations. NU agreed to join cabinets that had leftist members, whereas Masyumi refused to do so. NU participated willingly in Sukarno's Guided Democracy regime, which

---

[8] Fealy, "Ulama and Politics in Indonesia", p. 160.

[9] Tim Penyusun Jawa Pos, *Lubang-Lubang Pembantaian Petualangan PKI di Madiun* (Jakarta: Grafiti Press, 1990). George Kahin estimated the number of Masyumi people who died at several hundred, but he relied strongly on Masyumi sources, so there is reason for some scepticism concerning this figure. From 1945 to 1952 NU was, with Muhammadiyah, one of the two main pillars of Masyumi. Kahin, *Nationalism and Revolution in Indonesia*, p. 300.

required the party to not only work together with communists but also to subscribe to an official ideology that asserted the compatibility of communism and religion. In the 1955 election campaign, NU regarded Masyumi, not the PKI, as its greatest threat because Masyumi was seen as a direct competitor for devout Muslim votes. Like many other parties, NU underestimated the level of support enjoyed by the communists and did not anticipate that the PKI would emerge as the fourth-largest party, with 16 per cent of the national vote.[10]

Only in the late 1950s did NU begin to see the PKI as posing a serious threat. The regional elections in 1957 showed a sharp increase in the communist vote, particularly in Java — where it averaged 27 per cent — suggesting that at the next scheduled general election in 1959 the PKI would emerge as the largest party. In the East Java regional elections held in July 1957, NU retained its top ranking but its vote dropped by 11 per cent from the 1955 result. By contrast, the PKI's vote rose 17 per cent, giving it second ranking, while the Party gained control of eight district parliaments in the city of Surabaya and the south and west of the province.[11]

The PKI was the chief beneficiary of the shift from parliamentary to Guided Democracy, which President Sukarno and the Army engineered between 1957 and 1959 (see Chapter 1). Sukarno insisted that the PKI become an integral part of the new regime, and all parties participating in Guided Democracy had to agree to work with the PKI. As a result, Sukarno appointed communist and other leftist ministers to Cabinet and the boards of influential state institutions, brought communist and PKI-sympathising officers into senior military positions, and increased the number of PKI-affiliated members of Parliament to 35 per cent (Muslim party MPs were reduced from 40 per cent to 25 per cent).[12]

These developments caused great unease within NU and by the early 1960s had led to deep divisions within the party's leadership over how to respond. The two factions are most aptly described as

[10] Robin Bush, *Nahdlatul Ulama and the Struggle for Power within Islam and Politics in Indonesia* (Singapore: Institute of Southeast Asian Studies, 2009), pp. 24–65; Fealy, "Ulama and Politics in Indonesia", pp. 78–141.
[11] Fealy, "Ulama and Politics in Indonesia", p. 188.
[12] Fealy, "Ulama and Politics in Indonesia", p. 218.

"accommodationist" and "militant". The accommodationists strongly disliked communism but on pragmatic grounds held that it was too risky for NU and the Islamic community to directly oppose Guided Democracy or, above all, to resist Sukarno's inclusion of the PKI in government. They argued that Sukarno and the Army were too powerful and that Islamic organisations could be excluded from Guided Democracy altogether, or even proscribed, if seen to be openly dissenting. They pointed to the example of Masyumi, which had trenchantly objected to Guided Democracy and which had been banned by the government in 1960 after some of its leading members had in 1958 backed the rebellions in Sumatra and Sulawesi.[13] Until October 1965 the accommodationists dominated NU's central leadership. Key figures in this group included Kiai Wahab Chasbullah (NU's long-serving president), Idham Chalid (NU chairman), Saifuddin Zuhri, Masykur, Djamaluddin Malik and Muhammad Ilyas. Many of these leaders had close personal relations with Sukarno and, like the President, had been raised in East Java and shared many of his cultural views.

The militants, by contrast, were intensely anti-communist. They disapproved of Guided Democracy for its authoritarianism but above all because it enabled the PKI to be represented in the government. The militants saw the PKI as atheistic, even though some communists were at least nominally Muslim, and regarded it as an affront to both Islam and Indonesia's formal acknowledgement of "Belief in Almighty God" as a foundation principle of the state. In the 1950s and 1960s, the greatest division within the broader Muslim community was that between santri (devout Muslims) and *abangan* (nominal Muslims). Many of the Muslims in the communist movement were abangan in orientation — meaning they either seldom, if ever, attended Islamic devotions or they blended their Islamic beliefs with other spiritual and religious observances, including beliefs with Hindu and Buddhist origins.[14]

[13] Fealy, "Ulama and Politics in Indonesia", pp. 219–24.

[14] For a discussion of the historical differences between abangan and santri Muslims in East Java, see Merle Ricklefs, *Mystic Synthesis in Java: A History of Islamisation from the Fourteenth to the Early Nineteenth Centuries* (Norwalk: EastBridge, 2006), Chapters 3 and 4. On divisions in the 1960s, see Clifford Geertz, *The Religion of Java* (Chicago and London: University of Chicago Press, 1976), Chapter 10.

For its part, the PKI was wary of attacking rival parties such as NU on religious grounds and instead, using President Sukarno's parlance, emphasised the categories of "revolutionary" or "non-revolutionary" and promoted the idea that religion should be a personal choice.[15] NU, however, viewed communists as a direct political, economic and physical threat to Muslims. Party leaders referred constantly to earlier communist violence towards Muslims, particularly the 1948 Madiun uprising.[16] Many of the militants were former soldiers, conservative kiai and younger intellectuals. Leading figures within their ranks included Yusuf Hasyim and Munasir Ali, two ex-Army officers; the wealthy entrepreneur Subchan; and senior East Java ulama such as Kiai Bisri Syamsuri, Kiai Ahmad Siddiq and Kiai Machrus Ali. The militants cultivated good relations with anti-communist figures and groups within other political parties and especially the Army.

Hostility between NU and the PKI reached dangerous levels in 1963–64, when the communists launched their "unilateral action" (*aksi sepihak*) campaign, aimed at expropriating land from large landholders and turning it over to poor peasants. These actions stemmed from the failure of the government to implement the land reforms outlined in the 1959 Crop Sharing Law and the 1960 Basic Agrarian Law. In the NU-dominated areas of East Java, pesantren, kiai families and their supporters were big landowners and thus were targeted by PKI-affiliated groups. By early 1964, clashes between NU and communist groups became frequent and more severe, often involving injuries and occasionally fatalities. The worst violence occurred in districts such as Kediri, Banyuwangi, Ponorogo, Jember and Jombang. In most cases, NU groups proved superior in discipline and strength, and were able to drive off the communists with little or no loss of land. In order to mobilise their members against the communists, NU leaders used religious symbols and justifications for opposing the communists, claiming that they threatened religion.[17] This resulted

---

[15] Budiawan Purwadi, *Mematahkan Pewarisan Ingatan: Wacana Anti-komunis dan Politik Rekonsiliasi Pasca Soeharto* (Jakarta: Elsam, 2003), p. 111; Muslich, interviewed by Greg Fealy, 26 Sept. 1991, Jakarta.

[16] Fealy, "Ulama and Politics in Indonesia", pp. 250–1.

[17] Margo L. Lyon, *Bases of Conflict in Rural Java* (Berkeley: Center for South and Southeast Asia Studies, University of California, 1976), pp. 62–4.

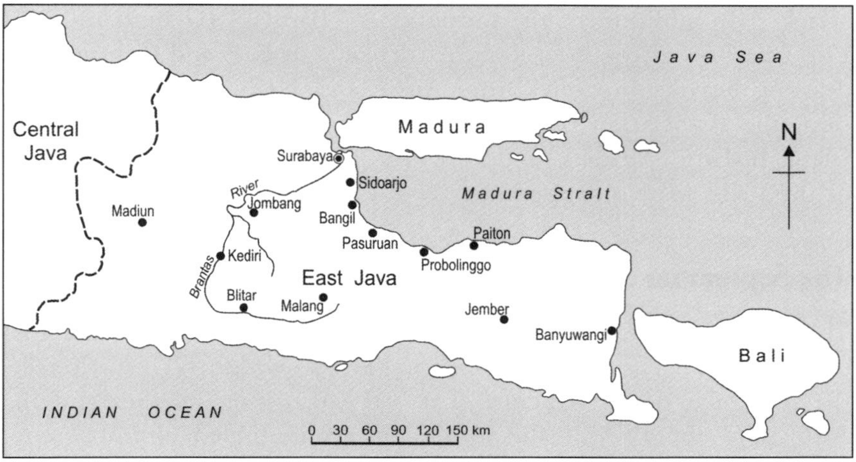

Map of East Java

in a lasting impression amongst people within NU that the clashes were the result of the PKI attacking Islam as a religion. Indeed, NU militants regarded the unilateral action campaign as proof of the PKI's malign intent towards the devout Muslim community and its leaders.

NU leaders believed the unilateral action vindicated their decision to form a paramilitary corps known as Banser within NU's young men's wing, Ansor, for the purpose of protecting NU from PKI attack.[18] Banser was formed in Kediri, East Java, in 1962, and its squads soon established a reputation during the unilateral actions for unflinching defence of NU leaders and assets. This pressure forced the PKI leadership to halt the faltering land reform campaign in early 1965. Although NU had humbled the communists in this confrontation, NU leaders remained convinced that the PKI continued to pose a threat. Rumours of the PKI receiving arms from China and of forming a secret military force were taken seriously by the militants, causing them to boost NU preparedness for a possible PKI

[18] "Banser" is a contraction of Barisan Ansor Serba Guna (Ansor Multi-Purpose Brigade). Its origins can be traced back to 1938, when Ansor formed Barisan Nahdlatoel Oelama (Banoe) to provide physical training for and instill discipline into NU youth. See <http://www.gp-ansor.org/banser/sejarah-banser> (accessed 15 Feb. 2012).

attack.[19] In addition to the formation of Banser, NU built up anti-PKI networks at the local level, particularly in East and Central Java, drawing heavily on cadres from Ansor and NU's veterans' organisation, the Association of Muslim Ex-Fighters (Ikatan Bekas Pejuang Islam, Ikabepi). Leaders used NU mass organisations to counter each of the PKI's mass organisations.[20]

The September 30th Movement

The actions of the September 30th Movement shifted the balance of political power not only in Indonesia but also within NU. Nationally, the triangular power structure that had Sukarno at its apex and the Army and the PKI at the lower corners crumbled almost immediately. From 1 October 1965, the position of the anti-communists within the Army was greatly strengthened and Sukarno and the PKI were very much undermined and thrown on the defensive. Anti-communist sections of the Army, under the leadership of Major General Suharto, quickly put down the Movement and immediately began asserting their authority. The Army was suspicious of Sukarno due to his cautious reaction to the Movement, as typified by his decision to travel to meet the leaders of the Movement at Halim Perdanakusuma Air Force Base. The PKI stood accused of plotting the kidnapping and murder of the generals after some of its leaders and sections of its youth and women's wings were revealed to have been implicated in the events of 30 September. Although Sukarno strived to reassert his authority after 1 October, particularly to protect the PKI and other Indonesians from violence and eventual banning, effective power now lay in the hands of the Army and Suharto.

Within NU the impact of the Movement was to break the accommodationists' dominance and allow the militants to take over the Party's decision making. The Army's political ascendancy favoured

---

[19] Harold Crouch, *The Army and Politics in Indonesia* (Ithaca: Cornell University Press, 1978), pp. 94–6; Munasir, interviewed by Greg Fealy, 14 Sept. 1991, Mojokerto, East Java.

[20] Some examples are the NU peasants' organisation Petanu (Pertanian Nahdlatul Ulama) and the NU labour organisation Sarbumsi (Sarekat Buruh Muslimin). See Slamet Effendy Yusuf, Mohamad Ichwan Syam and Masdar Farid Mas'udi, *Dinamika Kaum Santri: Menelusuri Jejak and Pergolakan Internal NU* (Jakarta: Rajawali, 1983), p. 48.

the militants, as they were much closer to anti-communist officers than the accommodationists. While few in NU had good ties with Major General Suharto, the militants had good relations with numerous officers within his inner circle. By contrast, the accommodationists were uncertain whether their patron, President Sukarno, could recover from the political setback that the Movement had created. The accommodationists had always argued that NU's best interests were served by avoiding political risk and that compliant participation in Sukarno's Guided Democracy was the safest course. Now militants could argue that their military and non-communist civilian allies held the best prospect of safeguarding NU. The alleged involvement of the PKI in the September 30th Movement was taken as a vindication of militant concerns about the threat posed by communism and the need to prepare for physical confrontation. Those arguing for compromise and cooperation with the PKI were seen as having misjudged the situation. When NU accommodationists argued for a cautious response to the September 30th Movement, militants responded that such policies had helped to create the current crisis and that only resolute action could rectify matters.

The absence of key accommodationists from Jakarta around the time of these events made it easier for the militants to assume control of NU decision making. Wahab Chasbullah, the most formidable of the accommodationists, was in East Java and did not return to the capital for several weeks. Idham Chalid reportedly went into hiding, apparently fearing that he may have been a PKI target, and played no role in any of the immediate NU leadership meetings. In Wahab's and Idham's absence, militants such as Munasir, Yusuf Hasyim, Subchan and Ahmad Syaichu took the initiative to issue directives to branches and statements to the media. More than a few official documents issued in the name of the NU Central Board (Pengurus Besar Nahdlatul Ulama, PBNU) contained signatures of senior officeholders forged by the militants.[21]

The militants were determined that NU use the failed Movement to strike emphatically against the PKI. Even before being presented with evidence from the Army of communist involvement in the Movement, many militants were convinced that it was the work

[21] Chalid Mawardi, interviewed by Greg Fealy, 14 Aug. 1991, Jakarta; Hamid Baidowi, interviewed by Greg Fealy, 5 Aug. 1991, Jakarta.

of the PKI. They had long discussed with other anti-communist groups the imperative of destroying the PKI as a political and social force. The September 30th Movement appeared to provide an opportunity to do this. Within hours of the Movement's collapse late on 1 October 1965, NU militants began meeting with their military contacts. They sought information about the plot and indications of what response the Army was planning. They received briefings on PKI complicity and tacit approval for preparing to mobilise against communists. Some NU leaders were even given guns for personal protection. Couriers were sent out to branches across Indonesia, especially in Java, reporting information about the Movement and giving instructions as to how to respond.[22] While the militants wanted to prepare NU's branches for anti-PKI actions, they were fearful that local groups might launch spontaneous or premature attacks that could lead to retaliation from the Army. Before unleashing NU's members, NU leaders wanted to be sure of military approval. To ensure coordination at the grass roots, a special team known as the NU Organisation Security Coordinating Body (Badan Koordinasi Keamanan Jamiah Nahdlatul Ulama, BKKJNU) was established under the chairmanship of Munasir. A group of militants led by Subchan gained permission from Major General Suharto to broadcast on 5 October the first message on national radio to claim that the PKI was behind the September 30th Movement and call for the Party to be banned.[23] Subchan played a leading role, with a number of Catholic student leaders, in forming the Action Front to Crush the September 30th Movement (Kesatuan Aksi Pengganyangan Gestapu, KAP-Gestapu), the first anti-PKI "action front". It was to play a pivotal role over the following months in mobilising student groups against the PKI.[24]

---

[22] Fealy, "Ulama and Politics in Indonesia", p. 250.

[23] PBNU, "Pernjataan Pengurus Besar Partai 'Nahdlatul Ulama' Beserta Segenap Ormas-Ormasnja", 5 Oct. 1965, Pamphlet Collection, Monash ASRL; PP GP Ansor, "Instruksi", 1st/02/PP/1965, 3 Oct. 1965, File 172, Koleksi Nahdlatul Ulama, Arsip Nasional Republik Indonesia [hereafter NU-AN].

[24] Harry Tjan Silalahi, interviewed by Greg Fealy, 12 May 1992, Jakarta; Eki Syachruddin, interviewed by Greg Fealy, 13 Mar. 1992, Jakarta; Subchan, interviewed by Harold Crouch, 16 Apr. 1970. Also Ulf Sundhaussen, *The Road to Power: Indonesian Military Politics, 1945–1967* (Kuala Lumpur and New York: Oxford University Press, 1982), p. 211; and Crouch, *Army and Politics*, p. 141.

The tone of NU Board communications with branches during October and November 1965 was designed to feed anti-communist animus, while stopping short of formally endorsing violence. Central Board instructions to the regions made frequent reference to the communist slaughter of Muslims during the Madiun uprising, and used terms such as *menumpas* (eradicate), *menghabiskan* (finish off), *mengganyang* (crush, gobble up) and *mengikis habis* (eliminate) in describing what should be done to the PKI.[25] Branches were also told that any member "killed in the battle" would die a martyr. NU leaders must have been in little doubt as to the effect these communiqués would have on the party's grass roots. Hostility towards the communists was intense, and the board's instructions effectively sanctioned physical action against the PKI.

NU-Army Cooperation and Local Actions

Most of the violence against the PKI and members of affiliated organisations occurred in the provinces. At the national level NU leaders endorsed the killings, but in rural towns and villages there were also instructions from local NU leaders directing their members to assist in the destruction of the Communist Party. NU leaders and Ansor men coordinated to carry out the violence. NU branches from around Indonesia quickly sent expressions of support to NU headquarters in Jakarta for its strong anti-PKI stance. Following NU's 5 October national radio broadcast condemning the September 30th Movement and calling for the proscription of the PKI, on 10 October the Religious Council (*Syuriah*) of NU's Surabaya branch denounced the plotters of the Movement and called for a quick and total cleansing of "counter-revolutionary elements".[26] In the provinces there were additional layers of authority among regional NU leaders, heads of pesantren and leaders of Ansor. These men played important roles in endorsing and coordinating the killings.

NU leaders in East Java received varying degrees of support from Sub-regional Military commanders. The East Java Regional Military Command (Kodam VIII/Brawijaya) was for the most part

[25] PBNU, "Instruksi" [no number], 9 Oct. 1965, File 172, NU-AN.
[26] "Pernyataan Pimpinan Sjuriajah Partai NU (Tjabang Surabaja)", Bubutan VI/2, Surabaya, 10 Oct. 1965, File 182, NU-AN.

anti-communist, but some officers had supported the September 30th Movement.[27] The main split within the Brawijaya Command, however, was between those who supported the anti-communist Armed Forces Chief of Staff General Nasution and those who were pro-PNI and loyal to President Sukarno. Because Sukarno had refused to condemn the September 30th Movement, the pro-PNI sections of Brawijaya were less hostile to the PKI and reluctant to move against the Party.

Mass violence involving NU members began in mid-October. Around 10 October, East Java Ansor leaders drew up plans, with the Army's approval, for a series of mass rallies to be held on 13 October in cities across the province. These were to be followed by attacks on PKI buildings and the killing of Party supporters.[28] The best-documented instance of events surrounding these rallies was in Kediri. After a large rally of anti-communist organisations, a section of the crowd, including local Banser units, descended on the PKI office and killed 11 Party members as they tried to defend the building. The round-up of PKI members and suspected sympathisers began soon afterwards.[29]

Despite some Army support for these anti-communist rallies, the officer corps in East Java did not initially approve of NU-led violence and was instead focused on preserving order.[30] On 16 October, following attacks on PKI offices in Surabaya, the military detained some 200 anti-communist Muslims. On 18 October Brawijaya Commander Brigadier General Basuki Rahmat and Chief of Staff Colonel Widjaja Sukardanu publicly warned against excesses, including actions that might cause the loss of life or property. Elsewhere in East Java, a policeman shot dead an Ansor member near

---

[27] Crouch, *Army and Politics*, p. 143.

[28] Crouch, *Army and Politics*, p. 147; Notes from a confidential interview with an Ansor leader by Harold Crouch, Oct. 1970. See also Sundhaussen, *Road to Power*, p. 216.

[29] Kenneth R. Young, "Local and National Influences in the Violence of 1965", in *The Indonesian Killings of 1965–66: Studies from Java and Bali*, ed. Robert Cribb (Clayton: Centre of Southeast Asian Studies, Monash University, 1990), p. 80; Crouch, *Army and Politics*, p. 147.

[30] Crouch, *Army and Politics*, p. 146. Incoming Telegram 22R, US State Department, received from US Consulate Surabaya, 30 Nov. 1965, Record Group 59, State Department Central Files 1964–1966, POL 23-8 INDON, National Archives and Records Administration [hereafter RG59 1964–66 documents referred to by file code and NARA].

Bangil on 13 October.[31] In response to the shooting, the Bangil NU branch noted that considering the need to channel Muslim community anger and avoid any further NU victims, they would seek the Brawijaya commander's approval to disband the PKI and all affiliated organisations in East Java.[32]

Despite the East Java Army commander's warnings, NU-led violence continued across the province. For example, there were clashes between NU and PKI groups in the Banyuwangi region on 18 October, the same day that a mass grave containing the bodies of 35 NU supporters was discovered. Several thousand PKI members would lose their lives over the next few days.[33] Ansor managed to gain support from local Army officers and some sub-regional military commanders such as Colonel Sumardi in Malang.[34] When Brigadier General Sunariyadi replaced Basuki Rahmat as Brawijaya commander in November 1965, NU hoped that the Brawijaya command would more strongly support the anti-PKI repression.[35] Anti-communist violence escalated after Sunariyadi's appointment, but sections of the Brawijaya command still hesitated in leading the campaign against the communists. Clashes between soldiers and Ansor continued, sometimes resulting in deaths of NU members. There were reports of soldiers attacking Madurese Muslims, possibly NU members, in November 1965.[36] In December 1965, the US Consulate in Surabaya reported that there were nightly killings by Muslims on the outskirts of the city and continued rounding-up of PKI members.[37]

Across East Java, violence was generally more severe in areas where the PKI's unilateral actions had been most intense. These included districts such as Kediri, Banyuwangi, Ponorogo, Jember, Blitar

---

[31] Crouch, *Army and Politics*, p. 146.

[32] "Pernjataan Bersama Partai Nahdlatul Ulama Tjabang Bangil Dengan Seluruh Ormasnja", Bangil, 19 Oct. 1965, File 182, NU-AN.

[33] Centre for Village Studies, Gadjah Mada University, "Rural Violence in Klaten and Banyuwangi", in *The Indonesian Killings*, ed. Cribb, pp. 154–7; Crouch, *Army and Politics*, p. 147.

[34] Crouch, *Army and Politics*, pp. 147, 152.

[35] Telegram 183, US Consulate Surabaya to US Embassy Jakarta, 26 Nov. 1965, POL 23 [-9 INDON], NARA.

[36] Incoming Telegram 189, US Embassy Jakarta, received from US Consulate Surabaya, 30 Nov. 1965, POL 23-9 [INDON], NARA.

[37] Incoming Telegram 05RA, US State Department, received from US Consulate Surabaya, 16 Dec. 1965, POL 23-8 INDON, NARA.

and Sidoarjo. NU's role varied across districts. In some districts NU members, together with Army officers and other non-communist groups, compiled lists of local PKI members, participated in their apprehension, and sat on ad hoc "tribunals" that decided whether or not the captives were to be executed before carrying out the killings. In other districts the military carried out the rounding-up of detainees and assessment of their involvement in communist organisations, leaving NU and other civilian groups, such as Muhammadiyah, al-Irsyad and the Islamic Students' Association (Himpunan Mahasiswa Islam), to conduct the executions. In January 1966, for example, the US Consulate in Surabaya reported that in Pasuruan the Army was delivering ten PKI members every night for Muslims to slaughter.[38] In this case, and many others, the Army organised transportation for the PKI members to be taken away and killed. In 1991 in Kertosono, a former Banser member recalled:

> In our area the military would capture the Communists and deliver them to a particular location — usually a secluded place beside a river. The Banser commander would then be told to assemble [his unit] there to do the killings. That was all Banser was allowed to do.[39]

Thus, accounts differ as to the level of autonomy exercised by Ansor/ Banser members and by kiai in relation to the military.

There is evidence of support for the violence at different levels of NU. An NU preacher in Bangil recalled that NU leader Subchan came to the district and declared at a large public rally of mostly NU supporters that the PKI must be banned.[40] This rally was a trigger for NU members to act. A number of kiai played central roles in overseeing the anti-PKI violence and liaising with local military officers. In East Java, these included Kiai As'ad Syamsul Arifin of Situbondo, Kiai Machrus Ali and Kiai Syafi'i Marzuki in Kediri, Kiai Achmad and Kiai Abdullah Siddiq in Jember, Kiai Djufri in Pasuruan, Kiai Zaini in Paiton, and Kiai Bisri Syamsuri in Jombang.[41]

---

[38] Incoming Telegram 15R, US State Department, received from US Consulate Surabaya, 19 Jan. 1966, POL 23-8 INDON, NARA.
[39] AA, interviewed by Greg Fealy, 18 Oct. 1991, Gresik, East Java.
[40] AB, interviewed by Vannessa Hearman, 11 Feb. 2009, Bangil, East Java.
[41] AC, interviewed by Greg Fealy, n.d.; "Report from East Java", *Indonesia* 41 (Apr. 1986): 142–3.

In order to steel NU members in their responses, the more militant kiai drew upon Islamic concepts to instill a sense that eradication of the PKI was a religious duty. For example, NU's Surabaya branch issued a statement on 10 October 1965 declaring that based on chapter 2 (The Cow), verse 191, of the Qur'an, the appropriate response to the September 30th Movement attempt was to "eradicate those who had disrupted the order wherever they are, and remove them from their positions as they have done, because disorder is worse than this".[42] Some kiai issued a religious edict (*fatwa*) declaring that the PKI were "unbelievers" (*kafir harbi*) belligerent towards Islam and rebels against the "legitimate government" (*bughat*), against whom it was obligatory for Muslims to wage war.[43] Such rulings were usually conveyed to santri in closed meetings and then spread by word of mouth to other Muslims. The fatwa gave religious licence to the work of the killing squads. One group of NU santri at the Tanwirul pesantren in Bangil, for example, was instructed by Kiai H. Abdul Muchdi that PKI members should be killed because they had insulted Islam and revolted against the government. Moreover, local ulama in Bangil issued instructions to carefully identify and kill members of the PKI. One source said, "Ansor members regarded these ulama as members of the local Syuriah council, such that whatever they said they accepted".[44] This comment reflects the high authority enjoyed by NU's religious leaders. A December 1965 report from the US Consulate in Surabaya notes that one anti-communist informed the writer that Muslim leaders were ignoring pleas from both civilians and the military to stop the violence.[45] In addition, the report detailed that an NU source felt that the NU leadership was not acting firmly enough against the communists and that they should also be killing PKI supporters in Jakarta.

---

[42] Pimpinan Sjurijah Partai NU, Tjabang Surabaja, Bubutan VI/2 Surabaja, 10 Oct. 1965, File 182 NU-AN. This is our translation of the Indonesian explanation of verse 191 provided in the declaration, which paraphrases rather than directly quotes from chapter 2 of the Qur'an.

[43] K.H. Aziz Masyhuri, interviewed by Greg Fealy, 26 June 1992, Jakarta; Syafi'i Sulaiman, interviewed by Greg Fealy, 1 July 1992, Surabaya, East Java.

[44] AB, interviewed by Vannessa Hearman, 11 Feb. 2009, Bangil, East Java.

[45] Incoming Telegram 05RA, US State Department, received from US Consulate Surabaya, 16 Dec. 1965, POL 23-8 INDON, NARA.

In his detailed study of the violence in Jombang and Kediri, Hermawan Sulistyo also highlights the central role of kiai in mobilising NU members. For example, he notes that in the case of the initial anti-PKI rally in Kediri, which led to the first killings, the head of NU in Kediri had to first gain approval from a leading kiai in Lirboyo pesantren. The NU leader admitted to recruiting people to participate in "night patrols" (*ronda malam*), less euphemistically known as "killing squads". When necessary, NU leaders would summon people from other areas to join operations. The head of NU in Kediri also sent his men to help with nearby killings, such as in Malang. Several national NU leaders, for instance Yusuf Hasyim, who had contacts throughout the region, went back and forth between Kediri and Jombang assisting with the organisation of these activities.[46]

In Jombang, the house of a prominent kiai became a gathering point for anti-communists. This kiai, who is not identified by Sulistyo, instructed members of both the NU labour union (Sarbumusi) and Ansor to take preliminary actions and to kill if necessary.[47] The kiai received visits from NU leaders in other East Java towns and districts, such as Pasuruan, Bangil, Bojonegoro and Madiun, seeking assistance to destroy the PKI in their areas. This was part of a wider pattern of organising people from one region to kill people in another region, possibly because outsiders may have had less compunction in executing people they did not know.

The son of a prominent anti-communist kiai in East Java stated that his father was asked to help the military to crush the PKI and thus ordered his santri to comply.[48] He recalls that his father had close ties with the local battalion commander, even before 1 October. Because the father had opposed and fought the communists, the military protected his pesantren and supplied the kiai there with weapons to safeguard the pesantren. On the question of who directed the killings, the kiai's son stated: "The orders [to kill] came from kiai,

---

[46] Hermawan Sulistyo, *Palu Arit di Ladang Tebu: Sejarah Pembantaian Massal yang Terlupakan (Jombang-Kediri 1965–1966)* (Jakarta: Kepustakaan Populer Gramedia, 2000), p. 185.

[47] Sulistyo, *Palu Arit di Ladang Tebu*, p. 159.

[48] AD, interviewed by Katharine McGregor, 29 Feb. 2008, undisclosed location.

especially those in the NU." He noted that members of Ansor were not forced to kill PKI members; rather, "they were full of spirit because the PKI was the enemy of Islam and they needed to be exterminated".[49] The above comments suggest that although the military provided direct encouragement and weapons, NU members were enthusiastic participants in the violence.

Sulistyo argues that the Army was cautious in backing anti-PKI actions, taking care to avoid too conspicuous a role. The District Military Commander in Kediri, for example, supported the first anti-communist rally and promised to send soldiers in civilian garb. Following the rally, Brawijaya troops who joined Ansor as executioners again dispensed with their uniforms.[50] There were regular meetings and exchanges of information between Ansor leaders and the local military commander, who visited Ansor sub-branches in Kediri.

The extent of the massacres perpetrated by NU shows the influence of a number of factors. Most important was the prevalence of a virtual war psychology in which santri believed they had but two options: kill or be killed. The phrase "kill or be killed" (*membunuh atau dibunuh*) was the most commonly encountered comment in interviews with NU members involved in the killings. One interviewee said, with some emotion, "If I didn't get rid of (*menghabisi*) them [the PKI], then I'm convinced they would have got rid of me, and perhaps my family and kiai as well. That's what happened at Madiun."[51] For many Muslims, the lessons of Madiun and unilateral actions were that the Muslim community would never be safe until communism was annihilated. NU militants promoted the idea that Muslims must use the opportunity to strike first: any hesitation or weakness would allow the initiative to shift to the communists. Years of vilifying and dehumanising the PKI made the task easier. Army-inspired accounts of mutilation of the murdered generals confirmed fears about the wickedness of communists. In general, however, there were very few instances of PKI violence against members of the NU after 30 September (see Chapter 8).

---

[49] AD, interviewed by Katharine McGregor, 29 Feb. 2008, undisclosed location.
[50] Sulistyo, *Palu Arit di Ladang Tebu*, p. 173.
[51] AE, interviewed by Greg Fealy, 15 Oct. 1991, Mojokerto.

Accounts of the Killings

For the most part, the killings were carried out in a systematic and orderly manner: accounts of frenzied or anarchical massacres were rare. Victims' throats were usually cut with knives, sickles or machetes; less commonly, and apparently only when civilians were reluctant to cooperate, the condemned persons were shot by the military. Dozens of people could be killed at a given site each evening. Ansor execution squads usually acted with the approval of senior local NU leaders and the Army before proceeding with each new round of killings.[52]

Kiai Ichsan was 15 years old in 1965, when he witnessed some killings in Kediri. On several occasions, he had joined fellow santri and the military to arrest PKI members in their homes.[53] In the round-ups, between two and ten people were usually taken in. The houses of PKI members were often used as temporary detention centres. The PKI members were commonly held for three to four days and then handed over to the local military command for processing. Ichsan believes that PKI members were arrested with the approval of Ansor and the military, and they were killed directly after verifying their "guilt" with military escorts. They were killed in the forests, and usually it was Ansor men who did the killing. Many Ansor members experienced trauma after killing people, and some suffered prolonged mental disturbance as a result. Kiai were often involved in "healing" traumatised executioners.[54]

In Jombang, the largest-scale operation occurred on 25 October in Mlancu, an isolated mountain area on the border between Jombang and Kediri: 700 people were killed. A battalion of soldiers in civilian clothes was supplied, headed by a local captain, to give protection to those involved in the killing, although the soldiers did not themselves kill. A local kiai pointed out who was to be killed, then the victims were executed and buried. Disturbed by the level of violence, another kiai from nearby Mojowarno tried to stop the killings. He told the head of the killing squad that the communists should be tried, but few people listened. Some workers and teachers

---

[52] Confidential interviews; Young, "Local and National Influences in the Violence of 1965", pp. 79–85; Crouch, *Army and Politics*, p. 270; Pipit Rochijat, "Am I PKI or non-PKI", trans. Benedict Anderson, *Indonesia* 40 (Oct. 1985): 37–52.

[53] AF, interviewed by Katharine McGregor, 29 Feb. 2008, undisclosed location.

[54] Ibid.

who were afraid of being labelled "communist" took shelter in the kiai's house.[55]

Another example of a kiai who opposed violence against the PKI was Mohammad Cholil Bisri, the head of Ansor in Rembang. According to his obituarist, Cholil forbade his branch members from persecuting communists. He felt that differences in ideology did not justify such violence and that communists were still neighbours and sometimes separated by only a wall. He himself was a neighbour of the Rembang PKI head. In his view, if PKI members were wrong it was better to put them on trial.[56] Such cases were exceptions; in most cases kiai provided an important source of support for the killings. In addition, Ansor men were at the forefront of most campaigns in East Java.

The Last Phase of the Killings

By December 1965, the Army leadership in Jakarta had become concerned that the killings needed to be reined in. The great majority of PKI members had, by then, been either detained or killed. Reports from killing sites told of growing incidents of score-settling and killing squads turning on victims with only a tenuous or no connection to the PKI. Military commanders in Central and East Java began warning NU leaders that if they did not halt the bloodshed, NU members would be arrested. In early 1966, they threatened that those who persisted with executions would be summarily shot.[57]

Alarmed at the prospect of confrontation with the Army, the NU Central Board acted to halt the killings. In early January 1966, branches were ordered to "assist all Government Officials in their efforts to create a calm environment within the community in order to hasten a political settlement". NU accused the PKI of "trying to lure its enemies into illegal and criminal actions".[58] Yet these warnings from the centre were not sufficient to prevent NU-military clashes.

---

[55] Sulistyo, *Palu Arit di Ladang Tebu*, pp. 175–6.

[56] Obituary for K.H Mohammad Cholil Bisri posted on Ansor website, <http://www.gp-ansor.org/page_id+121> (accessed 13 June 2007).

[57] Crouch, *Army and Politics*, pp. 153–4.

[58] PBNU, "Instruksi P.B.N.U. untuk Turut Mentjiptakan Suasana Tenang" (3542/Tanf/C/I-66), 6 Jan. 1966, File 117, NU-AN.

One aspect of the killings in East Java that has not been canvassed much is the rivalries between different factions of anti-communists. US consular reports from East Java suggest that from late 1965, rivalries between anti-communist forces intensified and nationalists from the PNI and leftist elements from the armed forces, who may not have been directly linked to the PKI, were killed. In January, February and March 1966, for example, the US Consulate in Surabaya reported military personnel and Ansor members clashing and sometimes killing each other.[59] In March 1966 the consulate reported that leftist Brawijaya troops at the port of Surabaya had picked up 25 Ansor members who had executed PKI members, and the Brawijaya troops had killed them in retribution.[60] There were reports of retributions led by Navy personnel for the murder of their relatives.[61] These reports suggest more complex political cleavages between Ansor and different political forces, including sections of the military. The alleged confrontation between NU and the military was not, however, mentioned in interviews until long after the violence. This could mean either that the clashes were incorrectly reported by the consulate, or that they were not recounted so as to avoid contradicting the long-held narrative of the military and NU jointly defending the nation against the communist threat. There is a misconception that the military and NU consistently stood on the same side (see Chapter 8).

Political friction between NU and PNI members escalated from late 1965. After NU and PKI, the PNI was the most significant political force in East Java. In the 1955 election, for example, NU gained 35 per cent of the vote, the PKI 24 per cent and the PNI 23 per cent. Although we cannot verify this information, a report from an intelligence officer to his superiors written in November 1965 suggests growing tensions between the PNI and NU, and the possibility

---

[59] Incoming Telegram 15R, US State Department, received from US Consulate Surabaya, 19 Jan. 1966, POL 23-8 INDON, NARA; Incoming Telegram 04R, US State Department, received from US Consulate Surabaya, 9 Feb. 1966, POL 23-9 INDON, NARA; Incoming Telegram 014, US State Department, received from US Consulate Surabaya, 11 Mar. 1966, POL 23-8 INDON, NARA.

[60] Incoming Telegram 014, US State Department, received from US Consulate Surabaya, 11 Mar. 1966, POL 23-8 INDON, NARA.

[61] Incoming Telegram 03R, US State Department, received from US Consulate Surabaya, 2 Feb. 1966, POL 23-8 INDON, NARA.

that some PKI members were being sheltered by supporters from the left-wing or Ali-Surachman faction of the PNI.[62] Anticipating a showdown, an NU source reported to the US Consulate in December 1965 that it might be necessary to kill "PKI followers of Ali".[63] By early 1966, most PKI leaders had been killed or arrested. The second target of the purges was the left-wing or the Ali-Surachman faction of the PNI, which was staunchly behind President Sukarno and was widely supported by the Marines.[64]

In February 1966 PNI leader Sartono arrived in East Java, and this precipitated a PNI show of force in Surabaya, Pasuruan and Malang. Sartono criticised what he called NU's "wild actions" and accused NU of not supporting Sukarno.[65] PNI members were also resentful that NU's prestige had been boosted by its role in crushing the PKI and that PNI followers had been killed by NU members. American diplomats reported rumours that the Navy, whose main base was in Surabaya, was siding with the PNI to pre-empt retaliation by NU to the PNI's show of strength. The Marines were angry over NU-led murders of their relatives in November and December 1965.[66] Henry Heymann, the consular official who lodged many of these reports in Surabaya, recalled in an interview in 1993 that in Surabaya the left wing of the PNI was "infiltrated by Communists" and "remained a formidable force". He believed that "[w]ith the

[62] "Report from East Java", p. 144.

[63] The expression "PKI followers of Ali" alludes to the broader meaning of the term PKI to include those who were also pro-Sukarno or supportive of the left wing of the PNI. Incoming Telegram 05RA, US State Department, received from US Consulate Surabaya, 16 Dec. 1965, POL 23-8 INDON, NARA.

[64] For more on the split in the PNI, see Joel Rocamora, "Nationalism in Search of Ideology: The Indonesian Nationalist Party, 1946–1965", PhD dissertation, Cornell University, 1974, pp. 531–54. For a description of Surabaya politics at this time, refer to Jacob Walkin, "The Moslem-Communist Confrontation in East Java, 1964–1965", *Orbis* 13, 3 (1969), pp. 822–47.

[65] Incoming Telegram 04R, US State Department, received from US Consulate Surabaya, 9 Feb. 1966, POL 23-9 INDON, NARA.

[66] Incoming Telegram 04R, US State Department, received from US Consulate Surabaya, 9 Feb. 1966, POL 23-9 INDON, NARA. In February, the consulate reported that Muslims had killed two PNI men in Pasuruan and that 230 *haji* (people who have made the Islamic pilgrimage to Mecca) had been arrested in Malang as a preventive measure against anti-PNI actions. Incoming Telegram 03R, US State Department, received from US Consulate Surabaya, 2 Feb. 1966, POL 23-8 INDON, NARA.

assistance of the local police and Marines they were seeking to gain political supremacy". He claimed that the situation was reversed only after the arrival of the new regional commander.[67] Consistent with this observation, Major General Soemitro, who in June 1966 became the new regional commander for the Army in East Java, noted in his biography that he was appointed because his family links to both NU and the PNI were seen as useful in helping to bridge differences between these two groups.[68] Soemitro claimed that he was sent to East Java to halt the killings and to prevent ulama from taking political advantage of the situation.[69]

NU support for the violence extended to its women's divisions, Muslimat and Fatayat, which enlisted older and younger female activists respectively. The divisions had previously tried to counter the influence of the PKI-aligned women's organisation, the Indonesian Women's Movement (Gerakan Wanita Indonesia, Gerwani). In 1964 members of Muslimat and Fatayat underwent military training in several cities, including Jakarta, Solo, Banjarmasin and Lampung, in order to match the military training Gerwani was undergoing in the Confrontation campaign against Malaysia. After the September 30th Movement, Muslimat leader Asmah Sjahruni recommended that the Indonesian Women's Congress (Kongres Wanita Indonesia, Kowani) make a declaration to ban Gerwani and the children's kindergartens and crèches it ran. She was also Muslimat's representative on the KAP-Gestapu committee and coordinator of the women protestors in the anti-communist demonstrations in Jakarta involving NU, Muhammadiyah and PNI.[70] There are no reports of NU women being directly involved in the killings,[71] but Sidney Jones noted in

---

[67] "Interview with Henry L. Heymann", by Charles Stuart Kennedy, 15 July 1993. The Foreign Affairs Oral History Project of the Association for Diplomatic Studies and Training. Available at <http://memory.loc.gov/cgi-bin/query/D?mfdip:1:./temp/~ammem_mMF4> (accessed 18 May 2010).

[68] Ramadhan K.H., *Soemitro: Former Commander of Indonesian Security Apparatus* (Jakarta: Pustaka Sinar Harapan, 1996), p. 99.

[69] Ramadhan K.H., *Soemitro*, p. 114.

[70] Asmah Sjahruni, interviewed by Vannessa Hearman, 27 July 2007, Jakarta.

[71] For a broader discussion of the ways in which women participated in the destruction of the Party and attacks on alleged communists, see Anne Pohlman, "Ashes in My Mouth: Women, Testimony and Violence during the 1965–1966 Massacres in Indonesia", PhD dissertation, University of Queensland, 2011.

some preliminary research on the violence in Kediri that women and girls sometimes chanted the *takbir* (Allahu Akbar, or God is Most Great) before a victim's throat was to be cut, suggesting they were at least witnesses to some killings.[72]

Although most of the anti-communist killings had been halted by February, systematic purging of the civil service and the Brawijaya command commenced only in mid-1966.[73] NU members also participated in the final military-led campaign against surviving members of the Communist Party in Blitar, East Java, in 1966–68. As explained in Chapter 8, the PKI reprisals against Ansor members were the trigger for the discovery of the new PKI base at Blitar.

Conclusion

In East Java although the Army played a key role in sanctioning and overseeing the killings, as well as in providing logistical support and sometimes weapons, much of the violence was carried out by NU members under the direction of local ulama and pesantren leaders. This was in contrast to the other two main locations of anti-communist bloodshed: Central Java and Bali. In Central Java most of the killings appear to have been directed by soldiers with assistance from Muslim and Christian groups (Chapter 4), while in Bali PNI supporters conducted most of the slaughter — although in west Bali NU members were also active in the killings (Chapter 9).

In East Java, military support for the destruction of the PKI was more tenuous, at least initially, due to splits within the Brawijaya command and enduring loyalty to President Sukarno. Early on in the violence, the Brawijaya commander was reluctant to act against the PKI. At the lower levels of the military, those officers siding with prominent anti-communist generals such as Nasution and Suharto cooperated closely with NU. Some surviving documents suggest that the divisions between NU and sections of the Army may have been greater than previously thought, while there were also clashes between NU and the PNI.

We dispute the version put forward by some within NU that the organisation played a subservient or subsidiary role in the killings

---

[72] Sidney Jones, unpublished manuscript provided to the authors.

[73] Crouch, *Army and Politics*, pp. 153–4.

and that the violence was locally driven and uncoordinated. It is clear from the PBNU communiqués cited in this chapter that NU's central leadership had a critical role in unleashing and endorsing the violence, and that it was kept well-informed by local leaders of the detentions and killings taking place across the country. Under regime pressure, the Central Board acted in early 1966 to halt the killings.

Amongst followers of NU, religion is often deemed a central justification for the violence. We have argued, however, that political and socio-economic factors were more important than religion as such. The rapidly growing electoral popularity of the PKI as well as its perceived hostility towards Islam caused alarm within NU's East Java branch — not least because this was the province that NU saw as its political bastion. Loss of dominance within Indonesia's most populated province would have been a huge blow to NU's influence at the national level. Moreover, the PKI posed a big threat to the socio-economic standing of NU's ulama elite. The communists' ridiculing and condemnation of economically privileged groups — such as ulama — created much anxiety among NU leaders, because in many areas they were prominent landowners or affluent traders within poor and deprived communities. Thus, the motivation to retain power and privilege was critical in explaining the killings and attests to the counter-revolutionary aspect of the repression.

6

Anti-communist Violence and the Ethnic Chinese in Medan, North Sumatra

Yen-ling Tsai and Douglas Kammen

The story of the three million ethnic Chinese in Indonesia in the aftermath of the September 30th Movement remains largely untold. Among the few publications that do consider the plight of the Chinese during those tumultuous years, many refer incorrectly to massacres.[1] The fact is, of course, that victims of the pogroms were overwhelmingly members of the Indonesian Communist Party (Partai Komunis Indonesia, PKI) and its affiliated mass organisations. In their critical appraisal of this myth of a Chinese massacre, Robert Cribb and Charles Coppel call the popular misrepresentation of the Chinese experiences in 1965–66 a "genocide that never was".[2] They argue that the ongoing currency of this myth can be attributed to the trope equating the social position of Chinese in Indonesia to that of Jews in Europe and claiming that their mobilising power lies in combating past and present discrimination against Chinese Indonesians. The myth has also persisted because so little is known about what happened to the Chinese during this period. Most of the news

[1] Examples are discussed in Robert Cribb and Charles A. Coppel, "A Genocide that Never Was: Explaining the Myth of Anti-Chinese Massacres in Indonesia, 1965–1966", *Journal of Genocide Research* 11, 4 (Dec. 2009), especially pp. 451–4.
[2] Cribb and Coppel, "A Genocide".

accounts of violence against ethnic Chinese in 1965–66 originated from either Antara, the Indonesian state news agency, or Xin Hua (and the associated China News Agency). Xin Hua, in particular, had a strong tendency to perceive individual incidents of violence as "local" manifestations of a "national" wave of anti-Sinicism. Such decontextualised reporting made it difficult for contemporary and later observers to understand those incidents in their local context.

This chapter examines the experience of the ethnic Chinese in the multi-ethnic city of Medan from October 1965 until early 1967. It does so by drawing on declassified US diplomatic telegrams, newspaper archives and oral interviews with a dozen Medan Chinese informants. While the US reports provide a wealth of local information through which a chronology of regional events regarding the 1965–66 violence can be reconstructed, the interviews show how people experienced those fateful months. Most of the people whose stories we retell here were members of the left-leaning Consultative Body for Indonesian Citizenship (Badan Permusyawaratan Kewarganegaraan Indonesia, Baperki), whose branches proliferated in North Sumatra before 1965, only to be crushed shortly afterwards. The combination of sources reveals a complex network of political identification and affiliation within the Chinese community and an economy of violence that connected the Medan Chinese to the local Army and the various youth forces that spearheaded the mass killings. The chapter concurs with Coppel and J.A.C. Mackie's conclusion that ethnic Chinese were not the target of extensive massacres,[3] though it shows that at three key moments (October 1965, December 1965 and March–May 1966) the building and renegotiation of an anti-communist coalition in North Sumatra resulted in attacks against and the long-term detention of ethnic Chinese in Medan.

The Ethnic Chinese and Baperki

In the late colonial era, North Sumatra was dominated by a mode of production involving North Atlantic capital, agricultural plantations

---

[3] J.A.C. Mackie, "Anti-Chinese Outbreaks in Indonesia, 1959–1968", in *The Chinese in Indonesia: Five Essays*, ed. J.A.C. Mackie (Honolulu: University Press of Hawaii, 1976), pp. 117–8; Charles Coppel, *Indonesian Chinese in Crisis* (Kuala Lumpur: Oxford University Press, 1983).

and indentured labour from southern China and Java.[4] After Indonesia's declaration of independence in 1945, parts of the East Coast plantation belt as well as neighbouring Aceh saw the outbreak of social revolution against the old aristocracy, though by 1947 Republican forces had restored a semblance of order. The PKI built large constituencies, particularly among Javanese estate workers and Batak peasants, by means of the plantation and peasant labour unions (Sarekat Buruh Perkebunan Republik Indonesia, SARBUPRI, and Barisan Tani Indonesia, BTI).[5] However, the PKI's growing influence in North Sumatra did not go unchallenged. Taking advantage of the declaration of martial law in March 1957 and Sukarno's order to seize Dutch-owned enterprises late the same year, the Army took over the big estates in the region. This brought the Army and the PKI into increasingly direct conflict.[6]

During the early 1960s, the PKI in North Sumatra moved well beyond its traditional base in labour and the peasantry. The Party enjoyed growing support from the upper echelons of North Sumatran society, including Governor Ulung Sitepu and large segments of the provincial bureaucracy. It also developed strong influence over the press, the state news bureau (Antara), radio, youth organisations and schools. According to one estimate, by 1965 the PKI in North Sumatra had 120,000 members, making it the largest PKI branch outside Java.[7] Expressing deep concern, a US diplomatic telegram in 1965 characterised North Sumatra as a communist stronghold where the PKI and its affiliated organisations had "most levers of political power in or near its hands".[8]

---

[4] See Karl J. Pelzer, *Planter and Peasant: Colonial Practice and the Agrarian Struggle in East Sumatra, 1863–1947* ('s-Gravenhage: Martinus Nijhoff, 1978); and Ann Laura Stoler, *Capitalism and Confrontation in Sumatra's Plantation Belt, 1870–1979* (New Haven: Yale University Press, 1985).

[5] This was particularly true of the Karo Batak. Mary Steedly, *Hanging without a Rope: Narrative Experience in Colonial and Post-colonial Karoland* (Princeton: Princeton University Press, 1993), p. 267.

[6] Karl J. Pelzer, "The Agrarian Conflict in East Sumatra", *Pacific Affairs* 30, 2 (1957), pp. 151–9.

[7] Audrey Kahin, *Rebellion to Integration: West Sumatra and the Indonesian Polity, 1926–1998* (Amsterdam: Amsterdam University Press, 1999), p. 244.

[8] Airgram A-912, US Embassy Jakarta to State Department, 28 May 1965, Record Group 59, State Department Central Files 1964–1966, POL 2 INDON, National Archives and Records Administration [hereafter RG59 1964–66 documents referred to by file code and NARA].

The arrival of Major General Mokoginta, the new interregional commander for Sumatra, in November 1964 led to a further deterioration in Army-PKI relations.[9] A devout Muslim, Mokoginta seconded Army personnel to the big estates, established pro-Muslim and pro-Army newspapers,[10] cultivated militant youth groups by enlisting the services of local toughs and, in the context of Indonesia's policy of Confrontation with Malaysia, even began arming members of the Army's own unions.[11] There were a growing number of violent incidents in the first half of 1965, most notably the killing of warrant officer Sudjono by BTI squatters and the subsequent revenge attack at the Bandar Betsy plantation in Simalungun District in June.[12] In short, North Sumatra was a region with a strong PKI support base and a growing military-Muslim alliance waiting to strike back.

Where did the ethnic Chinese stand in this delicate political milieu? North Sumatra has had a strong Chinese presence since the late nineteenth century. The census of 1930 showed that ethnic Chinese accounted for one-third of Medan's population and that more than 10 per cent of the population of the entire Residency (then called Sumatra's East Coast) was Chinese; by 1943 there were 280,000 ethnic Chinese in the Residency.[13] In the post-war years Malay, Batak and Javanese migrants poured into the city, but the ethnic Chinese continued to dominate small-scale industry and the retail sector and were a prominent part of the multi-ethnic mosaic.

Although few ethnic Chinese joined the PKI, like other Indonesians many sought to articulate their political aspirations via the leftist programme and vocabulary of the day. Many also took pride in the establishment of the People's Republic of China and were its ardent supporters. Most of all, the Chinese found themselves increasingly disadvantaged by policies intended to benefit "indigenous" Indonesians by curtailing the economic position of those categorised

---

[9] He was subsequently installed as the Authority for the Execution of Dwikora in Sumatra (Pepelrada/Sumatra).

[10] Muhamad T.W.H., *Perlawanan Pers Sumatera Utara terhadap Gerakan PKI* (Medan: Yayasan Pelestarian Fakta Perjuangan Kemerdekaan RI, 1996), pp. 195–6.

[11] Kahin, *Rebellion to Integration*, p. 239. See also Airgram A43, US Consulate Medan to US Embassy Jakarta, 15 Mar. 1965, POL 2 INDON, NARA.

[12] Harold Crouch, *The Army and Politics in Indonesia* (Ithaca: Cornell University Press, 1978), pp. 87–96.

[13] Pelzer, *Planter and Peasant*, p. 126.

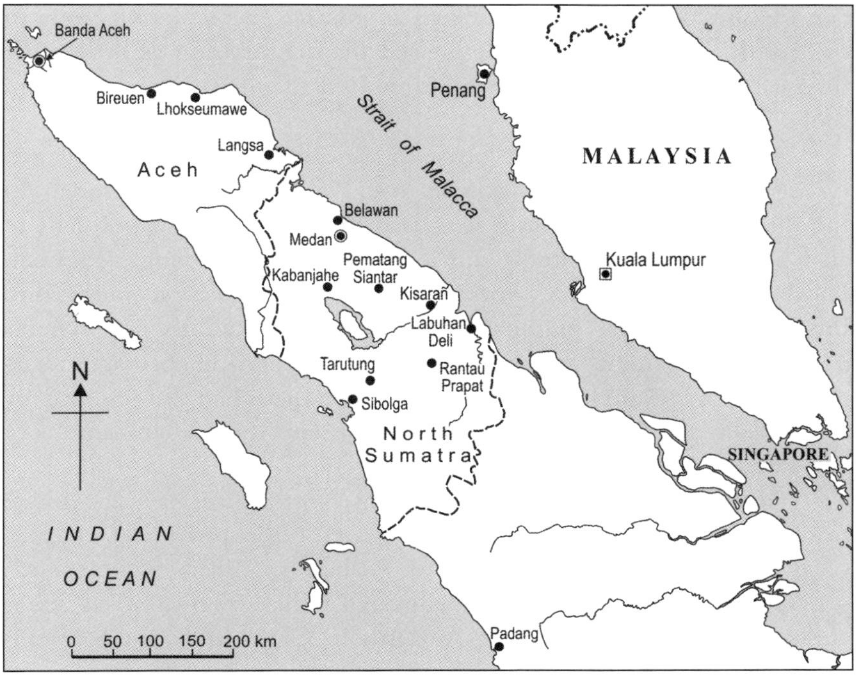

Map of North Sumatra and Aceh

as "alien" (that is, those without Indonesian citizenship), which led to bureaucratic discrimination against *all* ethnic Chinese, including those with Indonesian citizenship. In North Sumatra, as elsewhere, nationalised Chinese found Baperki the best defender of their interests.

Baperki, the brainchild of journalist-cum-parliamentarian Siauw Giok Tjhan, was the first and largest Chinese mass organisation in Indonesia after Independence. Founded in 1954 in response to surging debates over the dual nationality issue, the organisation quickly expanded and worked to defend Chinese Indonesians against official and unofficial forms of racial discrimination.[14] Its activities involved policy campaigns as well as practical efforts to assist those Chinese applying for citizenship and licences. In North Sumatra, such tasks often included translation for the region's largely Hokkien- and Mandarin-speaking Chinese. A successful businessman who became

[14] Coppel, *Indonesian Chinese in Crisis*, pp. 44–63.

the Treasurer of the Baperki branch in Kisaran, a plantation town in the South, commented that he viewed the organisation as little more than a "service bureau" for its hundred-odd members, most of whom spoke very little Indonesian.[15]

Baperki also became involved in education. The 1957 "Djuanda Order" resulted in tight controls over "alien schools" throughout Indonesia; in North Sumatra it caused the closure of 80 per cent of all Chinese-language schools and a sharp drop in student enrolment. Local Baperki branches worked to convert "alien schools" into Indonesian-language "national schools" and to establish new schools under their organisational umbrella.[16] Ten Baperki schools were registered in North Sumatra in 1961; by 1965, these had been joined by the Andalas primary and secondary schools and the Medan campus of Res Publica University (URECA).[17]

The leaders of Baperki branches in North Sumatra were drawn from diverse backgrounds. The chairman of the provincial chapter, Chang Hsi Sek [張希石], born in Asahan in 1909, was a third-generation Sumatran and Peking-educated radical who survived persecution from both Kuomintang warlords in China and Dutch intelligence in the Netherlands Indies. After returning to Medan in the 1950s, he became active in publishing, journalism and education and belonged to a dozen other organisations in addition to Baperki.[18] Yoe Sim Boen, born in Tarutung in 1924, was a mestizo former revolutionary guerilla fighter who served as chairman of Baperki Medan from 1954 until 1965 and was an advocate for lower-class Chinese residents of Medan.[19] Tan Ho Lan [陳荷蘭], who was born

---

[15] BA, interviewed 27 May 2009, Jakarta, by Cindy Tan, who kindly provided access to the transcript.

[16] See Lee Kam Hing, *Education and Politics in Indonesia, 1945–1965* (Kuala Lumpur: University of Malaya Press, 1995), pp. 151–2; and Mary Somers Heidhues, *Chinese Politics in Indonesia* (Ithaca: Modern Indonesia Project, Southeast Asia Program, Cornell University, 1964), pp. 20–2.

[17] G.T. Siauw, *Lima Jaman: Perwujudan Integrasi Wajar* (Jakarta: Yayasan Teratai, 1981).

[18] Information obtained from an unpublished manuscript written by Chang Hsi Sek, accessed on 4 June 2009, Hong Kong, kindly provided by Zheng Guanghuan [鄭光煌].

[19] After being imprisoned in 1965–74 and again in 1975–78, Yoe died in obscurity in 2006. Yoe Sim Boen, interviewed by Dirk Buiskool, 21 Aug. 1994 and 17 Sept. 1994, Medan; transcripts kindly provided by Buiskool.

in Kabanjahe and became the treasurer of Baperki Medan, had connections with the local military command as well as both the pro-Kuomintang/Taiwan and the pro-communist/Beijing camps in Medan's Chinese community. Unlike the Indonesian-speaking professionals who typically dominated Baperki leadership in Java, these men and other Baperki branch leaders in North Sumatra were transcultural figures whose life trajectories resist the conventional dichotomy between foreign-born (*totok*) and locally born/assimilated (*peranakan*).

The early 1960s witnessed a sharp leftward turn of the Baperki leadership in both Jakarta and North Sumatra. After the May 1963 anti-Chinese riots in West Java, the general apprehension pushed Baperki to prove its loyalty to Indonesia.[20] This meant aligning with Sukarno and, to the extent that Sukarno seemed to protect the PKI, the Left as well.[21] This move to the left was particularly dramatic in North Sumatra in mid-1965. During this period, the PKI experienced a dramatic increase in membership in North Sumatra. In concert with this, new Baperki branch offices were established in district towns throughout the province.[22] As the PKI aligned itself more closely with the Chinese Communist Party after the split of the international communist movement, Baperki in North Sumatra also moved closer to the Association of Overseas Chinese (Huaqiao Zhonghui [華僑總會], hereafter Hua Zhong, the umbrella organisation of alien Chinese in Indonesia) through organisational activities and political alliance. Andalas school students, for example, banded together with students from the Hua Zhong schools to celebrate International Labour Day. *Harian Harapan*, the news organ of both Baperki and the PKI in North Sumatra campaigned against three pro-Taiwan secondary schools in Medan until their forced closure in mid-1965 on charges of being "anti-communist nests" (*sarang anti-Komunis*).[23]

---

[20] On anti-Chinese riots in the early 1960s, see Mackie, "Anti-Chinese Outbreaks in Indonesia," pp. 93–4, 97–110.

[21] Airgram A-7, US Consulate Medan to US Embassy Jakarta, "Fearful Mood of Chinese in Java Pushed Them Leftwards", 2 Sept. 1965, POL 12 INDON, NARA.

[22] Airgram A-59, American Consul Medan to US Embassy Jakarta and State Department, 2 June 1965, POL 2 INDON, NARA.

[23] *Harian Harapan* was published by Chang Hsi Sek and edited by Tan Fhu Kiong [陳富強], a Java-born Chinese who was a PKI member, secretary of Baperki North Sumatra, and head of the provincial branch of the Indonesian Journalists' Association. Muhamad T.W.H., *Perlawanan Pers Sumatera Utara*, p. 192.

Within just a few months, Baperki and Hua Zhong were to become a convenient target of anti-communist attacks.

The September 30th Movement and the First Wave of Violence

When news of the September 30th Movement reached Medan on the morning of 1 October, regional officials were initially in the dark about the course and meaning of the events in Jakarta. Recognising, however, that the Movement provided an opportunity for the Army to move against the PKI, that night the American Consul in Medan sent a cable to the embassy in Jakarta requesting permission to provide "non-sensitive information" to Major General Mokoginta, commander of the Sumatra Interregional Command (Komando Antar Daerah 1, abbreviated Koanda 1), in order to "help Anti-Communist elements here make right decisions".[24] By the next morning the senior military officers in Koanda 1, together with Kostrad deputy commander Brigadier General Kemal Idris, had concluded that the September 30th Movement was a leftist plot engineered by Foreign Minister Subandrio, who happened to be in Medan at the time, and set about mobilising anti-communist forces.

That afternoon the newly formed North Sumatra Youth Action Command (Komando Aksi Pemuda), spearheaded by Pemuda Pancasila, the youth wing of the Army-backed League of Upholders of Indonesian Freedom (Ikatan Penerus Kemerdekaan Indonesia, IPKI), held a mass rally in downtown Medan to oppose the PKI.[25] On 5 October Mokoginta issued an "order of the day", declaring that the September 30th Movement was a tool of foreign powers intent on destroying the Indonesian revolution.[26] In conjunction with this statement the Youth Action Command staged a second mass rally, this time demanding that the PKI be banned. The crowd turned violent, smashing windows and looting the provincial PKI headquarters, but reportedly took sufficient care to collect documents containing

---

[24] Telegram 219, US Consulate Medan to US Embassy Jakarta, 1 Oct. 1965, POL 23 INDO[N?], NARA.

[25] Telegram 813, US Embassy Jakarta to State Department, 2 Oct. 1965, POL 23-9 INDO[N?], NARA.

[26] Telegram 877, US Embassy Jakarta to State Department, 6 Oct. 1965, POL 23-9 INDO[N?], NARA.

membership information. In the subsequent days the Youth Action Command widened the attack to include houses owned by PKI leaders as well as Baperki and Hua Zhong schools.[27]

The course of anti-communist violence in the city of Medan cannot be understood in isolation from the course of developments throughout northern Sumatra. Closely following cues from Jakarta and Medan, and with direct encouragement from the regional military commander, on 6 October anti-communist forces in Aceh held mass rallies and began to round up hundreds of PKI members and sympathisers and turn them over to the Army, which, over the following days, released them back into the hands of civilians to be executed.[28] Although the PKI was a minor party in devoutly Muslim Aceh,[29] the mass killings there — the first anywhere in Indonesia — proceeded at an extraordinary pace: they were over by mid-November, and the press carried cryptic reports that the province was "calm".[30] In a cable, the American Consul in Medan wrote: "General Mokoginta on 25 December told me there are only 120 PKI left in Atjeh, and a [word deleted] source on Mokoginta's staff reported 6000 have been killed there."[31]

---

[27] Telegram 956, US Embassy Jakarta to State Department, 11 Oct. 1965, POL 23-9 INDON, NARA; S.B. Nasution, *Kisah Nyata Aksi Massa Pemuda Sumatera Utara Dalam Penumpasan Gerakan 30 September/PKI di Sumatera Utara* (Medan: Yayasan Pembaharuan Pemuda Indonesia, 1992), pp. 102–28.

[28] On events in Aceh during the first week of October, see Jessica Melvin, "A Silent Massacre: The Indonesian Communist Party and the Mass Killings in Aceh", BA Honours thesis, University of Melbourne, 2009.

[29] Siegel estimates that the Aceh branch of the PKI had 2,000–3,000 members. James Siegel, *Rope of God* (Berkeley: University of California Press, 1969), p. 408. The PKI's affiliates certainly had more members.

[30] "Atjeh Tenang", *Berita Yudha*, and "Atjeh kembali tenang", *Angkatan Bersendjata*, both 11 Nov. 1965.

[31] Source on General Mokoginta's staff, quoted in Telegram 924A, US Consulate Medan to US Embassy Jakarta, 27 Dec. 1965, POL 23-9 P [INDON?], NARA. An Army publication from Aceh states that 1,941 members of the PKI, its affiliates and Baperki were "kidnapped/arrested". See Kodam-1, "Laporan Tahunan Lengkap Kodam-1/Kohanda Atjeh, Tahun 1965", n.d., pp. 6–7. David Mozingo reports that "several hundred" ethnic Chinese were killed in Aceh but does not provide a source or specify whether this was during the October–November 1965 anti-PKI pogrom or during the March–April 1966 second-wave attack on ethnic Chinese. David Mozingo, *Chinese Policy toward Indonesia, 1949–1967* (Ithaca: Cornell University Press, 1976), p. 251.

The situation in North Sumatra was far more complex. The PKI and its affiliates had a huge following in the province, and Governor Ulung Sitepu, though not a Party member, was on the Left. Rumours circulated that Party members were gathering in the southern part of the plantation belt, in the Karo region west of Medan, and near Sibolga on the west coast in preparation for an offensive. On 13 October, a US diplomatic cable warned that "fighting was expected"; it had not yet commenced.[32] The key factor was that the Army was divided sharply along institutional and ideological lines. Koanda I commander Major General Mokoginta was a staunch anti-communist but had few troops under his direct command. During the second week of October, Army units from Java that had been posted to North Sumatra in the context of Confrontation were ordered to return home, leaving a vacuum in key areas south of Medan. The commander of the North Sumatra Regional Military Command (Kodam II/Bukit Barisan), Brigadier General Darjatmo, had leftist sympathies, as did many within the officer corps and large numbers of troops.[33]

Concerned that he was not in a strong enough position to carry out an anti-communist drive, Mokoginta moved cautiously to appoint new officers to key posts, purge the strongly PKI civil defence forces, and provide weapons to anti-communist plantation workers.[34] He and his staff also encouraged the Youth Action Command and other anti-communist elements in Medan to step up their own militancy. One target of this was the PRC Consulate, which refused to fly its flag at half-mast as requested by the Army.[35] This stoked racial

---

[32] Telegram 994, US Embassy Jakarta to State Department, 13 Oct. 1965, POL 23-9 INDON, NARA. The notion that mass killings in North Sumatra began in early October seems to originate from the hyperbolic account in John Hughes, *The End of Sukarno: A Coup that Misfired, A Purge that Ran Wild* (London: Angus and Robertson, 1968), pp. 19, 141.

[33] US sources estimated that 30 per cent of troops in Kodam II/Bukit Barisan were pro-communist. Telegram 1098, US Embassy Jakarta to State Department, 20 Oct. 1965, POL 18 INDON, NARA. This is the same as estimates for Central Java.

[34] Telegram 994, US Embassy Jakarta to State Department, 13 Oct. 1965, POL 23-9 INDON, NARA. This began in March 1965.

[35] *Huaqiao Ribao*, 24 Oct. 1965, citing Radio Malaysia as its source.

tensions and led to further attacks on Baperki property.[36] Rising anti-communist militancy also provoked street fighting between rival youth groups, which resulted in the murder of two anti-communist university students by members of the PKI's People's Youth (Pemuda Rakyat) organisation on 25 October. The fact that this case became a *cause célèbre* suggests that large-scale killings had not yet begun. Indeed, as late as 28 October, a US Embassy telegram noted that "there are as yet no reports of trouble in North Sumatra".[37]

The turning point came the next day. On 29 October, Bukit Barisan commander Brigadier General Darjatmo was replaced by Brigadier General Sobiran, whom US officials described as being "violently anti-Communist".[38] Confident that it had consolidated control over its own ranks, the Army wasted no time initiating mass demonstrations. On 2 November, an estimated 100,000 people rallied in downtown Medan to demand that the PKI be disbanded, Governor Sitepu be removed from office, diplomatic ties with the PRC be severed, and Baperki be disbanded and its property confiscated. This demonstration was the cue for the assault on the PKI and its affiliated organisations. On 8 November, the US Embassy reported a "systematic drive to destroy PKI in northern Sumatra and wholesale killings".[39] Two weeks later, according to US officials, a "Sumatra military officer reported that Army, while counseling public restraint, is actually encouraging Moslems to kill all PKI cadres, and that hundreds are presently being killed every day in North Sumatra".[40]

---

[36] For an extensive list of attacks on property, see Pusat Penerangan Angkatan Darat, *Fakta2 Persoalan Sekitar "Gerakan 30 September"* (Jakarta: P.N. Balai Pustaka, 1966), pp. 181–6.

[37] Telegram 1317A, US Embassy Jakarta to State Department, 28 Oct. 1965, POL 23-9 [INDON?], NARA. See also Airgram A-15, US Consulate Medan to US Embassy Jakarta, 18 Nov. 1965, POL 2 INDON, NARA.

[38] "Brigdjen P. Sobiran Pangdam II/BB", *Berita Yudha*, 2 Nov. 1965; the quote is from Airgram A-15, US Consulate Medan to US Embassy Jakarta, 18 Nov. 1965, POL 2 INDON, NARA.

[39] Telegram 309A, US Embassy Jakarta to State Department, 8 Nov. 1965, POL 23-9 [INDON?], NARA; repeated in Telegram 798A, 22 Nov. 1965, POL 23-9 [INDON?], NARA.

[40] Airgram A-16, US Consulate Medan to US Embassy Jakarta, 6 Dec. 1965, POL 2 INDON, NARA.

Meanwhile, the Army and its allies in North Sumatra intensified the attack on Baperki, which, the Army argued, had financed the September 30th Movement. On 12 November, Brigadier General Sobiran ordered the seizure of all Baperki and Partindo property and the suspension of both organisations' bank accounts.[41] Ten days later, all members of Baperki and its affiliates were ordered to report to the military authorities.[42] Nevertheless, violence against the ethnic Chinese community was confined to attacks on Baperki and Hua Zhong schools and the confiscation of their property. While several informants noted the murders of particular individuals, such as Tan Fhu Kiong, the secretary of the provincial Baperki branch and editor of the PKI daily *Harian Harapan*, no one recalled any systematic effort to arrest or kill ethnic Chinese.

The Army was sending mixed signals: while it supported the violence, it was clear that some officers were serious about bringing the violence under control. At the same time, rising tensions within the anti-communist civilian alliance led to the Ansor having violent clashes with Pemuda Pancasila radicals, on the one hand, and the pro-Sukarno Indonesian National Party (Partai Nasional Indonesia, PNI), which was accused of harbouring communists, on the other.[43] On 30 November, the US Consul in Medan reported on a meeting during which he learnt about the formation of a secret organisation that, despite the Army's order for a "slowdown", planned to continue the "silent killings". This informant insisted that he was "not under direction of Army, which he regarded as too slow and too uncertain", and stated that he had been detained by the Army for a week because of his involvement in "unauthorised killings". He claimed to have recruited 4,000 men, mostly from Pemuda Pancasila in Medan, and planned to extend the killings to other areas of North Sumatra.[44] Mass killings were now well under way, but there was also growing friction within the anti-communist alliance. The resolution would

[41] Partai Indonesia (Partindo) was a left-leaning, nationalist party.

[42] Telegram 838A, US Consulate Medan to US Embassy Jakarta, 23 Nov. 1965, POL 23-9 [INDON?], NARA.

[43] Airgram A-15, US Consulate Medan to US Embassy Jakarta, 18 Nov. 1965, POL 2 INDON, NARA.

[44] Cable 1037A, US Consulate Medan to US Embassy Jakarta, 30 Nov. 1965, POL 23-9 [INDON?], NARA.

take place on the streets of Medan and involve attacks against Baperki in particular, and the ethnic Chinese more generally.

The 10 December Killings

The combination of mixed signals from Army commanders and competition between anti-communist civilian groups made for a volatile situation. While the Army's public calls for a "slowdown" may have dissuaded some within IPKI, it pushed the most radical members of Pemuda Pancasila to adopt ever more violent aims. The Army also encouraged the entry of other anti-communist umbrella groups. Splits within the PNI led to the establishment of a right-wing Democratic Youth Front that took to the streets of Medan. The Islamic Students' Association (Himpunan Mahasiswa Islam) was also busy expanding its membership, claiming on 4 December that it had just admitted 1,900 new members. At the same time, Mokoginta spoke at the inauguration of the new North Sumatra Muslim Joint Committee, which was heeding calls issued by religious leaders for holy war. On 9 December, Mokoginta again addressed this group, urging his audience to extend their organisation down to the district and even village level in order to "undertake an Islamic offensive" against the PKI.[45] The intense competition between anti-communist forces and their respective, often competing patrons within the Army set the stage for the next wave of violence in Medan.

On the morning of 10 December 1965, the Pemuda Action Command, "[s]pearheaded by Muslim youth from Atjeh and extremist elements of the Medan Pemuda Pancasila", held a mass rally in front of the PRC Consulate in southeast Medan.[46] Protesting against the pro-communist views aired by Radio Beijing, the crowd bombarded the consulate with stones and bricks, wounding three members of the consulate staff. When Indonesian police fired shots into the crowd, killing at least one demonstrator, hundreds of incensed demonstrators ran from the scene yelling "Kill Chinese" and brandishing weapons. The crowd "rampaged through the city, pulling Chinese off pedicabs

[45] The previous three sentences are based on Airgram A-19, US Consulate Medan to State Department, 20 Dec. 1965, POL 2 INDON, NARA.
[46] Airgram A-19, US Consulate Medan to State Department, 20 Dec. 1965, POL 2 INDON, NARA.

and motor scooters, hacking them with long knives, ransacking their stalls in the Central market, killing or wounding all who resisted".[47] A US Embassy telegram noted: "According to [the] official estimate, Chinese casualties numbered four dead and 161 wounded while [US] Consulate sources in Chinese community place death toll at 20 and [name of source deleted] reported 100 dead."[48]

News accounts of what happened in Medan on 10 December 1965 provide a simple master narrative: sparked by a clash in front of the Chinese Consulate, the violence spread to the city centre and then dispersed to the outskirts and other towns in the region. This narrative suggests that the violence was the work of an agitated crowd gone wild. Yet interviews with a dozen ethnic Chinese residents who experienced the day first-hand suggest a more complex picture. For example, an informant who taught at the nationalised Sutomo school and was in his sixties at the time of the interview remembered 10 December as a partially premeditated event with selected targets ranging from Baperki leaders to teachers of the Andalas school and staff of Hua Zhong. Leaving school on his motorcycle, he witnessed a small crowd attacking the shop of a Baperki member; but when he arrived home, he found that his family shop was still open. A friend telephoned around 2 p.m. to inform him of outbreaks of "Chinese beating" [Hokkien: *pa denlan*, 打唐人] in the outskirts of Medan. Soon afterwards, a crowd turned up on his street to attack the radio shop that belonged to Chang Hsi Sek, the chairman of North Sumatra Baperki. The crowd looted the expensive radios and burned the remaining merchandise in the street.[49]

This informant's recollection highlights the selective nature of the 10 December attack as it took place in downtown Medan. Even though the man witnessed the looting of shops belonging to Baperki

---

[47] Quoted in Coppel, *Indonesian Chinese in Crisis*, pp. 60–1. The attack is all the more remarkable because two days earlier the Supreme Operations Command (Komando Tertinggi) had assigned the Institute for the Promotion of National Unity the task of "mend[ing] the problem of the Chinese community organisation Baperki". See Airgram A-390, US Embassy Jakarta to State Department, 13 Dec. 1965, POL 13-3 INDON, NARA.

[48] Telegram 451A, US Embassy Jakarta to State Department, 13 Dec. 1965, POL [illegible] 2 [INDON?], NARA; Airgram A-19, US Consulate Medan to State Department, 20 Dec. 1965, POL 2 INDON, NARA.

[49] BB, interviewed by Yen-ling Tsai, 21 Dec. 2008, Medan.

members on two occasions in one day, he did not perceive an imminent threat to his own security — as he did when he heard of instances of *pa denlan* in the city outskirts. He was quite certain at that time that violence against Baperki members was of a different nature from *pa denlan*. Other interviewees suggested that outbreaks of *pa denlan* in Medan outskirts such as Tembung, Belawan and Labuhan Deli on 10 December victimised the Chinese in a more arbitrary fashion.[50]

Declassified US documents provide an extraordinary picture of the motivations behind the 10 December violence. A US Consulate source "high in the all-Sumatra army command" noted that the Youth Action Command planned the riot and that the plan was condoned by the Army. However, this source quoted Major General Mokoginta "saying that he does not care if the entire Chinese quarter is burned, but he will not permit physical injury to Chinese persons". Although Army troops were not sent to protect the PRC Consulate, on the afternoon of 10 December "troops were out in force throughout the threatened areas of the city, and for several hours Medan echoed with gunfire as troops repeatedly broke up attacks on Chinese persons and Chinese establishments".[51] Over the ensuing days the violence spread to smaller towns surrounding Medan. There are numerous reports of attacks on Chinese-owned shops and even the rape of Chinese women. The spread of anti-Chinese violence gave rise to higher casualty estimates, ranging from 30 killed and hundreds injured to as many as 200 killed.[52]

It appears that the violence was only partly "anti-Chinese" in nature; it also involved the Army opening fire on rioting youths and taking many into custody. Furthermore, there are remarkable reports about the involvement of Acehnese youths. According to a cable from American Consul Theodor Heavner, "the rioters were in fact led by the Medan Pemuda Pancasila and the Pemuda Tanah Rentjong from Atjeh". The same cable noted that a week later the Army "stopped five truckloads of Atjehnese youth bent on attacking the Chinese and

[50] BC, interviewed by Yen-ling Tsai, 3 Jan. 2009, Medan; BD, interviewed by Yen-ling Tsai, 2 Jan. 2009, Medan.

[51] Airgram A-19, US Consulate Medan to State Department, 20 Dec. 1965, POL 2 INDON, NARA.

[52] Coppel, *Indonesian Chinese in Crisis*, p. 191fn36. The riot was never reported in the Jakarta press.

forced them to return to Atjeh".[53] Despite the crackdown, inflamed exchanges between the Army and the PRC government continued. On 29 December General Mokoginta was reported to have warned the PRC to drop what he saw as an "anti-Indonesian campaign", while urging Indonesian citizens of Chinese descent to "show clearly whether or not they are loyal to Indonesia".[54]

Meanwhile, the onslaught against the Left in North Sumatra was in full swing. By the end of 1965, there were reports about widespread killings throughout the East Coast plantation belt, the PKI stronghold among the Karo Batak, and beyond. In Rantau Prapat, the district military commander stated that 400 people had been killed and another 800 remained in detention; he set a nightly "quota" of victims. In neighbouring Asahan District, it was estimated that 2,500 people had been killed. A plantation manager noted that "at least 100 headless corpses [had been] left on his estate in recent weeks".[55] In contrast with Java and Bali, there is very little information about the overall number of people killed in North Sumatra. In late December, an IPKI activist told an embassy officer that 15,000 people had been killed across the province;[56] three months later, extrapolating from the death toll on a single plantation, the British Consul estimated that between 27,000 and 40,000 people had been massacred.[57] Despite the scale of the savagery, and belying the degree of Army direction, on 29 December US Ambassador Green cabled Washington: "North Sumatra still bloody but situation never really out of control there except perhaps in certain districts."[58]

---

[53] Airgram A-19, US Consulate Medan to State Department, 20 Dec. 1965, POL 2 INDON, NARA.

[54] 蘇島司令製造反華藉口, 大公報 ["Sudao siling zhizhao fanhua jiekou", *Da Gong Bao*], 29 Dec. 1965.

[55] All cases reported in Airgram A-19, US Consulate Medan to US Embassy Jakarta, 20 Dec. 1965, POL 2 INDON, NARA.

[56] Telegram 991A, US Embassy Jakarta to State Department, 29 Dec. 1965, POL 23-9 INDON, NARA. Curiously, a 1966 Army publication claims that the September 30th Movement had plans to kill 15,000 people in North Sumatra; see *40 Hari Kegagalan "G-30-S" 1 Oktober–10 November*, 2nd ed. (Jakarta: Staf Pertahanan Keamanan, 1966), pp. 112–3.

[57] Cited in Kahin, *Rebellion to Integration*, p. 244. See also Stoler, *Capitalism and Confrontation*, pp. 163–4.

[58] Telegram 991A, US Embassy Jakarta to State Department, 29 Dec. 1965, POL 23-9 INDON, NARA.

Detention

The large number of detainees presented a very real problem for the military. In early December, Brigadier General Sobiran "revealed that the Army is holding 11,000 PKI prisoners in the province of North Sumatra"; then in late December 1965, General Mokoginta said that there were 15,000 communists under detention.[59] The vast majority of the detainees, being members of PKI-affiliated peasant and plantation worker unions, were held in rural areas. Some sources noted that the Army had allocated a budget to deal with the huge number of detainees and was busy building detention centres, suggesting that not all detainees would be killed. The largest of these centres, intended to hold up to 3,000 detainees, was to be built on a rubber estate owned by American company Goodyear.[60] There were, however, persistent rumours that the budget allocated for detention centres was insufficient and so the Army intended to kill many of the prisoners, perhaps even transporting them to Aceh for execution.[61]

In contrast with the plight of peasants and plantation workers, detainees in urban areas were far less likely to be killed. This is particularly true of the ethnic Chinese members of Baperki. Although there is little documentation about detention, interviews provide a glimpse into the experience of ethnic Chinese under detention in Medan. In North Sumatra, as was the case elsewhere in Indonesia, many detention camps or "rehabilitation centres" were set up in large buildings that had been confiscated from civilians accused of being pro-PKI. Torture was commonplace in the detention camps, murder not infrequent. One of the most notorious detention centres in Medan was housed in the clubhouse of the North Sumatran Teochiu Association, known as the Teochiu Huikuan [潮州會館]. For more than a decade after 1965, the Operations Command to Restore Security and Order (Kopkamtib) and its much-feared Special Task Force (Laksus Kopkamtib, established circa 1967) used the building to incarcerate, interrogate and torture political prisoners. Among those

[59] Telegram 924A, US Embassy Jakarta to State Department, 27 Dec. 1965, POL 23-9 [INDON?], NARA.

[60] Airgram A-16, US Consulate Medan to US Embassy Jakarta, 6 Dec. 1965, POL 2 INDON, NARA.

[61] J.B. Wright to British Embassy, 8 Feb. 1966, Records of the Foreign Office, 810–25, 1966, United Kingdom National Archive.

known to have been held at the Teochiu Huikuan from 1967 to 1970 were four members of the Kisaran Baperki: two died of wounds soon after their release, and the other two are still very apprehensive about recounting their ordeal.[62]

The experience of ethnic Chinese detainees in Medan is aptly illustrated by another ethnic Chinese informant. On 20 December 1965, he was told to report to the detention centre that had been set up in the clubhouse of the Association of the Xinghua Chinese in Medan, known as the Xingan Huikuan [興安會館]. He was in a mixed batch of 108 detainees, most of whom were Baperki members from Medan, with the remainder coming from other ethnic groups and organisational affiliations. He remembered particularly that several female teachers from the Andalas school were in the camp with their children. Although he was taken into detention in December 1965, his case was not "processed" until May 1966. The interrogations were conducted by a team from the regional military command, led by a man known as "As Rangkuti".[63] Each detainee was required to state his/her political affiliations and whereabouts on 30 September/1 October 1965.[64] After wrapping up their investigations at the Xingan Huikuan, the team of military officers moved on to the former Teochiu Huikuan, where they dealt with the PKI members.

For many Baperki members the experience at the Xingan Huikuan was not particularly traumatic, and in one sense the detention centre provided Baperki members with protection from hostile anti-Chinese youth groups. Detainees were allowed to organise amongst themselves for food, cleaning, purchasing, security and sports activities, while Baperki members who were not detained supported those in the camps.[65] With a special permit, the detainees were even allowed to go home during the day. These recollections correspond with that of Oei Tjoe Tat, a Minister of State under Soekarno and a Baperki member who visited Medan as part of the Presidential

---

[62] BE, interviewed by Cindy Tan, 27 May 2009, Jakarta; transcript kindly provided by Tan. For an account of the Teochiu Huikuan building, see Yen-ling Tsai, "Through a Building Darkly", *Inside Indonesia* 95 (2009).

[63] Most likely an ethnic Batak "assistant" on the Kodam I/Bukit Barisan staff.

[64] BF, interviewed by Yen-ling Tsai, 23 Oct. and 24 Dec. 2004, Medan.

[65] BG, interviewed by Yen-ling Tsai, 6 Jan. 2009, Medan.

Fact-Finding Mission in late December 1965. At a Chinese school, he observed about 300–400 prisoners who were mostly members of Baperki and the Indonesia Party (Partai Indonesia, Partindo).[66] Having already seen the abuse of Baperki leaders in camps in East Java, Oei was impressed by the cooperativeness of the commander of the detention camp, who readily provided information and allowed Oei unhampered access to the detainees. Before leaving the camp, Oei later wrote:

> ... the former Chinese school reverberated with the sound of hundreds of detainees, both men and women, dutifully singing [the national anthem] Indonesia Raya. They did not seem too oppressed and were full of certainty in Bung Karno's policies. I was moved hearing the national anthem sung by people in such adverse circumstances and it was difficult for me to hold back tears ....[67]

The rather benign situation inside the Xingan Huikuan partly reflected the wealth and social connections of the Baperki detainees. One of these detainees was Tan Ho Lan. In the years before 1965, Tan had befriended the regional military command through his active participation in the local football scene, resulting in the commander granting Tan a lucrative concession to import bulk steel from the USSR to North Sumatra. The relationship between Tan's family and the military remained strong despite Tan's detention. The commander continued to grant licensing privileges to Tan's son and held shares in his glass factory, while Tan's father, having fled to Singapore after spending three months in detention, became the overseas supplier to the family business.[68] Others, however, came to understand their detention as part of an ongoing process of victimisation. Yoe Sim Boen, the chairman of the Medan branch of Baperki, who was transferred from one camp to another over the course of 13 years, noted that detention allowed the Army not only to keep him away from local politics but also to blackmail anyone the Army chose to accuse

[66] Oei Tjoe Tat, *Memoar Oei Tjoe Tat: Pembantu Presiden Soekarno*, ed. Pramoedya Ananta Toer and Stanley Adi Prasetyo (Jakarta: Hasta Mitra, 1995), pp. 189–90.
[67] Oei, *Memoar Oei Tjoe Tat*, p. 190. Bung Karno is the affectionate nickname for President Sukarno.
[68] BH, interviewed by Yen-ling Tsai, 10 Oct. 2004, Medan.

of being his acquaintance or a Baperki member, or anyone who had simply sought assistance from Baperki when applying for Indonesian citizenship.[69]

The Third Wave, 1966

The first two-and-a-half months of 1966 were marked by intense political manoeuvrings between Sukarno and Suharto's forces in Jakarta. Sukarno attempted to reassert his authority, first by encouraging the formation of a mass-based "Sukarno Front" to challenge the Army's Action Front to Crush the September 30th Movement (KAP-Gestapu), then by reshuffling his cabinet and dismissing Army Chief of Staff General Nasution. These efforts energised the PNI and Sukarnoists, but only served to sharpen the focus of the Army and its allies. On 11 March 1966, under intimidation and threat, Sukarno was forced to sign the "Order of 11 March" (Surat Perintah 11 Maret, abbreviated Supersemar), authorising Lieutenant General Suharto to "take all measures considered necessary to guarantee security, calm, and stability of the government and the revolution".[70] The next day Suharto used his new powers to ban the PKI. Suharto's victory in Jakarta provided a trigger for a new round of demonstrations and violence in Medan and other parts of northern Sumatra.

Once again, Baperki and ethnic Chinese provided a convenient target for the most radical anti-communist factions. Between 26 and 31 March 1966, hundreds of youths took over buildings and schools belonging to 13 Chinese organisations in Medan. Similar takeovers occurred in towns all over North Sumatra into April.[71] These actions prompted Major General Mokoginta to issue a "stiff order [on] April 21 forbidding acts of racialism or disturbances of peace" and "specifically forbade pillaging or burning of shops and stores and promised stiff actions against any who disturbed normal life of 'certain layers of

---

69 Yoe Sim Boen, interviewed by Dirk Buiskool, 21 Aug. 1994 and 17 Sept. 1994, Medan.

70 Crouch, *Army and Politics*, p. 189.

71 印尼反動派對華僑進行瘋狂迫害與掠奪，人民日報 ["Yinni fandongpai dui huaqiao jinxing fongkuang puohai yu lueduo", *Renmin Ribao*], 2 May 1966.

our society' (i.e. Chinese)".[72] By then, however, 31 Chinese schools had been seized.[73]

The attack on ethnic Chinese was even more severe in neighbouring Aceh. In April there were anti-Chinese riots in Lhokseumawe, Bireuen and other towns, and the Hua Zhong buildings in Banda Aceh and Langsa were taken over.[74] Ironically, in late April the police barred the Chinese from leaving Langsa,[75] but two weeks later the military authority ordered the Chinese leaders to leave the province by June and all "alien Chinese" to leave by 17 August. The campaign to purify Aceh of all alien Chinese influence was so intense that the same authority also barred cohabitation of alien Chinese with those who held Indonesian citizenship, even if they belonged to the same family.[76] Thousands of ethnic Chinese fled south to Medan, joining the estimated 10,000 who had already poured into the city in late 1965. The North Sumatra Military Command ordered all pro-PRC Chinese to report their property holdings,[77] required all "ex-PKI, ex-Baperki and all Indonesian citizens of foreign descent" to attend a Pancasila Indoctrination programme,[78] and in mid-May banned the Hua Zhong.[79]

The anti-Chinese violence in North Sumatra was widely seen as part of a nationwide campaign in which various student action fronts

[72] Incoming Telegram 615, Department of State received from US Consulate Medan, 22 Apr. 1966, POL 23-8 INDON, NARA.

[73] 文匯報 [*Wen Hui Bao*], 1 Apr. 1966. See also "Nasution Calls for Settlement of 'Chinese Issue'", *South China Morning Post*, 30 May 1966.

[74] Incoming Telegram 646, US State Department received from US Consulate Medan, 4 May 1966, POL 23-8 INDON, NARA.

[75] 印尼反動派對華僑進行瘋狂迫害與掠奪, 人民日報 ["Yinni fandongpai dui huaqiao jinxing fongkuang puohai yu lueduo", *Renmin Ribao*], 2 May 1966.

[76] 印尼反動派反華排華暴行日益猖狂, 人民日報 ["Yinni fandongpai fanhua paihua baoxing riyi changkuang, *Renmin Ribao*], 24 May 1966.

[77] 印尼棉蘭親中共華人奉令需登記財產, 工商日報，人民日報 ["Yinni mianlan qing zhonggong huaren fongling shu dengji caichan", *Gongshang Ribao*], 1 May 1966.

[78] Reported in "Indoktrinasi di Kota Madya Medan", *Sinar Harapan*, 3 July 1966, and "WNI Turunan Asing dan Exanggota PKI Selesai Diindoktrinasi", *Sinar Harapan*, 2 Aug. 1966.

[79] 印尼反動派反華排華暴行日益猖狂, 人民日報 ["Yinni fandongpai fanhua paihua baoxing riyi changkuang", *Renmin Ribao*], 24 May 1966.

that had earlier demonstrated against Sukarno and PKI-related organisations redirected their attacks to target Chinese-owned property.[80] But while demonstrations of a similar kind had gradually died down in other places by May 1966, anti-Chinese militancy in North Sumatra and Aceh escalated. The exodus of ethnic Chinese from Aceh set the stage for a third wave of violence, targeting not property but refugees housed in 14 makeshift refugee camps scattered throughout the city and its outskirts. Living conditions inside the camps were dire, and conflicts often arose between refugees and youth groups. A US diplomatic telegram noted that many ethnic Chinese were desperate to leave the country altogether:

> Chinese in Medan are extremely nervous. Talk of departure is widespread. If ships were to be provided right now for repatriation to mainland China several estimates indicate that as many as 20 or 30 thousand might go from this area. On [a] smaller scale, those with money are seeking to immigrate to Europe or anywhere else.[81]

In May 1966, the PRC announced that it would send ships to pick up its "nationals" who wished to be repatriated.[82] Only four voyages were made, repatriating only a few thousand people.[83] The arrival of each ship provided an occasion for further violence. The largest unrest occurred on 9 November 1966, three days after the Chinese-flag

---

[80] Coppel, *Indonesian Chinese in Crisis*, pp. 63–6; Mackie, "Anti-Chinese Outbreaks in Indonesia", p. 116.

[81] Incoming Telegram 768A, Department of State received from US Consulate Medan, 22 Apr. 1966, POL 2-1 INDON, NARA.

[82] Mozingo, *Chinese Policy toward Indonesia*, p. 250.

[83] The first ship arrived at the Belawan port on 26 September 1966 (中共輪船抵棉蘭港, 工商日報 ["Zhonggong Lunchuan di Mianlanggan", *Gongshang Ribao*], 27 Sept. 1966); the second ship called on 6 November 1966 (第二批受害僑胞乘光華輪離印尼回國, 人民日報 ["Dierpi shouhai qiaobao cheng kuanghualun huiguo", *Renmin Ribao*], 25 Nov. 1966) and left on 20 November 1966 (在棉蘭陸軍監獄中英勇鬥爭四十天的四十一名難僑青少年, 中國新聞 ["Zai Mianlang lujunjianyu zhong yingyong douzheng sishitiang de sishiyiming nanqiao qingshaonian", *Zhongguo Xinwen*], 27 Nov. 1966); the third ship arrived back in China on 5 February 1967, and the fourth and final ship called at Belawan on 14 April 1967 (光華輪駛抵棉蘭港外五日印尼政府仍無理阻撓我國接僑, 中國新聞 ["Guanghualun shili Mianlang ganwai wuri Yinni zhengfu ren wuli zurao woguo jieqiao", *Zhongguo Xinwen*], 20 Apr. 1967).

liner *Guang Hua* had made its second call at Belawan and one day after an official representing the Bukit Barisan Military Command had guaranteed the safety of the refugees in a meeting with PRC diplomats from Jakarta. According to Chinese sources, two crowds, numbering over 400 and 100 respectively, launched attacks and hurled rocks at the refugees outside the camp.[84] Meanwhile, the youth groups continued to pressure the municipal and North Sumatran provincial authorities,[85] demanding the expulsion of all alien Chinese by the end of the year as well as a nationwide withdrawal by the Ministry of Trade of the trading licences of all alien Chinese. None of these demands were met.

Like the 10 December 1965 riot, the conflicts between radical youth groups and displaced refugees from Aceh revealed a discord between the local Army command and the youth groups. "Throughout the second half of 1966," Mackie explains, "the authorities seem to have been very much on the defensive against the student militias of the ethnically heterogeneous and hard-boiled city of Medan."[86] Indeed, on 9 November 1966 Mokoginta again issued a stern threat of action against "actions aimed at disturbing society", insisting that "demands for the repatriation of foreign Chinese should be made through legal channels".[87] The warning did not seem to have had much effect, and anti-Chinese incidents in Medan occurred well into 1967.

One of the main sources of friction between the regional Army command and radical IPKI, KAMI and KAPPI youths in Medan was control over property confiscated from the PKI, Baperki and other leftist organisations. While authorities in Jakarta regularised the takeovers in May 1966 by banning all alien schools, they did not stipulate the future of the properties, thereby leaving the decision to the discretion of the regional military command. The authority of local military commanders was not always honoured by the youth groups, for whom "the school buildings were part of the spoils of victory of

---

84 印尼反動派又在棉蘭迫害華僑, 人民日報 ["Yinni fandongpai youzai Mianlan pohai huaqiao", *Renmin Ribao*], 11 Nov. 1966.

85 See the Introduction in this volume for youth demands regarding Sukarno and his use of the term "Gestok".

86 Mackie, "Anti-Chinese Outbreaks in Indonesia, 1959–1968", p. 117.

87 Quoted in Mackie, "Anti-Chinese Outbreaks in Indonesia, 1959–1968", p. 118.

the New Order".[88] One such instance involved a stand-off at the North Sumatra headquarters of Hua Zhong in Medan. Having occupied the building in early 1966, the Youth Action Command barricaded the building in order to resist the Army's taking over. Several youths were subsequently detained, but the Youth Action Command was eventually allowed to keep the building collectively with several other youth organisations for two years. When Brigadier General Sarwo Edhie Wibowo was appointed commander of the Bukit Barisan Regional Military Command in June 1967, he banned the PNI and sought to address the problem of seized properties.[89] Eventually the Youth Action Command surrendered the Hua Zhong building to the Army, though in exchange it received the Xingan Huikuan building, which to this day is the headquarters of the Communication Forum of the Sons and Daughters of Military Retirees.[90]

Conclusion

Aceh and North Sumatra are recognised to have been the regions where the Chinese suffered most heavily during 1965–66,[91] but it does not necessarily follow that the general populace, the Youth Action Commands or the Army there were any more "anti-Chinese" than elsewhere in Indonesia. That anti-Chinese violence occurred in a particular place because people there were anti-Chinese is just a tautology. Instead, this chapter has looked into the local condition of violence, where discord within the anti-communist camp in North Sumatra developed before it manifested itself in a series of anti-Chinese outbreaks. The particular constellation of Party, ethnic and Army cleavages made it necessary for the Army to solidify the anti-communist alliance in urban areas before venturing to eliminate PKI strongholds in the East Coast plantation belt and other rural areas.

---

[88] Coppel, *Indonesian Chinese in Crisis*, p. 66.

[89] Crouch, *Army and Politics*, pp. 234–6.

[90] See Nasution, *Kisah Nyata Aksi Massa Pemuda Sumatera Utara*, p. 134.

[91] See Mackie, "Anti-Chinese Outbreaks in Indonesia, 1959–1968", pp. 117–8.

[92] Joshua Oppenheimer, "Freemen: When Killers Make Movies", www.final-cut.dk; Joshua Oppenheimer and Michael Uwemedimo, "Show of Force: A Cinema-Séance of Power and Violence in Sumatra's Plantation Belt", *Critical Quarterly* 51, 1 (2009): 84–110.

This chapter has shown that violence against ethnic Chinese occurred in distinct phases that corresponded to shifts in the anti-communist alliance in North Sumatra. Throughout October 1965, the coalition-building mass actions in Medan were directed against not only PKI offices and select leaders but also the PRC Consulate and property belonging to Baperki and other ethnic Chinese organisations. Mass killings began in early November but were not directed against the ethnic Chinese per se. By early December, as factions emerged within the anti-communist coalition, the ethnic Chinese community, now swollen with newcomers fleeing the bloodbath in Aceh and rising tensions in district towns, again provided a convenient target for the Youth Action Commands looking for new enemies and new ways to remain active. The result was the 10 December 1965 anti-Chinese riot and killings. During 1966, as the Army sought to bring the hardliners under greater control and repress Sukarnoism, a third wave of attacks targeted ethnic Chinese, this time threatening the large number of displaced ethnic Chinese huddled in camps and seeking to gain control over property. For ethnic Chinese with Indonesian citizenship, the brutal detention process was paradoxically also a form of protection; for those without citizenship, life in makeshift camps was a prelude to further attacks and the icy institutional violence of the new regime.

Far from being forgotten, the anti-communist violence in North Sumatra has been commemorated in a bizarre way and from the most unlikely of sources. A British filmmaker has produced a documentary about several members of the civilian killing squads in North Sumatra, who at the time of writing were prominent and feared public figures in Medan. They themselves were making a movie about the mass executions they had carried out four decades ago.[92] In the documentary, one of the characters speaks cheerfully of how, on 10 December 1965, he stabbed every Chinese person he met between the PRC Consulate and the heart of the Chinese quarter, where he and his friends looted and burned Chinese property.

7

South Sulawesi: The Military, Prison Camps and Forced Labour

Taufik Ahmad[1]

In the forest located about 30 kilometres from Makassar, the capital city of South Sulawesi, the Hasanuddin Military Regional Command (Kodam XIV) established a camp for prisoners accused of involvement in the September 30th Movement and/or association with the Indonesian Communist Party (Partai Komunis Indonesia, PKI).[2] More than 900 prisoners were detained in this camp between 1969 and 1977. Moncongloe was one of many such prison camps throughout the archipelago.

Short- and long-term detention were key elements of the post-September 30th repression. From 1965 prisoners were classified into three categories. Category A was for prisoners involved in the September 30th Movement, Category B was for those who were members of the PKI or leaders of associated mass organisations, and Category C was for members of mass organisations affiliated with

[1] This chapter was translated from Indonesian to English by Vannessa Hearman.
[2] Under government regulation No. 5 of 1960, South and Southeast Sulawesi were one province (Sulawesi Selatan and Tenggara, abbreviated Sulsera). From 1964, Sulsera was divided into two provinces, though both were under the jurisdiction of the Hasanuddin Regional Military Command (Kodam XIV/Hasanuddin).

the PKI.[3] Category C prisoners were generally detained for less than ten years. Category A prisoners were detained for longer periods — they were either awaiting trial, serving sentences, or on death row. It was mostly Category B prisoners who were sent to prison camps. The military set up the camps because was there was not enough evidence to prosecute these prisoners. While there are several written accounts about the notorious prison camp on Buru Island in Maluku, including an account by former prisoner Pramoedya Ananta Toer,[4] little is known about other prison camps throughout Indonesia.

Drawing on interviews and local archives, this chapter examines the repression in South Sulawesi, from the initial outbreak of violence to long-term imprisonment in Moncongloe. South Sulawesi's ethnic make-up and the aristocratic background of some military officers influenced the patterns of violence. Antagonisms that had emerged between Muslims and the PKI during the Darul Islam rebellion reverberated in the post-September 30th period when the anti-communist Hasanuddin military commander unified a coalition of anti-communist forces against the PKI. The military justification for the prison camps was the need to provide security for the population and guidance to the ideologically misdirected prisoners. By detailing the patterns of life, work and deprivation in the prison camps, I argue that these prisons were not just a means of isolating the prisoners from society. The military also used the prisoners in Moncongloe as forced labour for its own economic gains, including the building of lucrative military businesses. Drawing on accounts of former political prisoners, I examine their experiences of imprisonment and how they engaged in acts of resistance and solidarity.

The Prelude to Violence: Sources of Tension in South Sulawesi

The violence in South Sulawesi cut across religious, class and ethnic divisions. The four main ethnic groups in this province are the

[3] See Greg Fealy, "The Release of Indonesia's Political Prisoners: Domestic Versus Foreign Policy, 1975–1979" (Clayton: Working paper, Monash University, 1995), pp. 6–8.

[4] Pramoedya Ananta Toer, *Nyanyi Sunyi Seorang Bisu*: *Catatan-catatan dari P. Buru* (Jakarta: Hasta Mitra, 2000).

Buginese, the Makassarese, the Mandarese — all devout Muslims — and the predominantly Christian Torajans from the highlands.[5] There are also significant migrant populations, including Javanese and ethnic Chinese. In the 1960s the aristocracy controlled the great majority of all land and was the dominant class.[6] The nobility was well represented in the officer corps.[7]

Across these ethnic and class groups, the PKI had the greatest appeal for those working in agriculture and fishing — for them, the PKI became their most supportive advocates. In marked contrast with the situation in other countries, the PKI enjoyed strong support amongst the Christian Torajans, who felt devalued by the Buginese and Makassarese. The Torajans were also committed to eliminating the feudal aspects of government administration.[8]

In the two decades between Independence and the violence of the mid-1960s, the PKI clashed with a variety of political groups. The first of these was the political movement of Kahar Muzakkar, which began in 1950. The revolt was in part a reaction to the lack of official recognition of soldiers from the area in the national Army, but it was also in reaction to perceived favouritism towards the Javanese in civilian and military posts.[9] As the movement progressed, it turned to Islam as an ideological basis for the struggle, this being the best way of garnering widespread support amongst the people.[10] The movement then became part of the larger House of Islam (Darul Islam, DI) movement that was most powerful in West Java. The

---

[5] Suratman and Patrick Guinness, *Transmigration in South Kalimantan and South Sulawesi* (Yogyakarta: Working paper, Population Institute, Universitas Gadjah Mada, 1977), pp. 26–7.

[6] Barbara Sillars Harvey, *Tradition, Islam, and Rebellion: South Sulawesi, 1950–1965*, PhD dissertation, Cornell University, 1974, p. 234.

[7] Abdul Rasyid Asba, *Kopra Makassar Perebutan Pusat dan Daerah: Kajian Sejarah Ekonomi Politik Regional di Indonesia* (Jakarta: Yayasan Obor Indonesia, 2007), pp. 215–47.

[8] Ichlasul Amal, *Hubungan Pusat-Daerah: Kasus Sumatera Barat dan Sulawesi 1949–1979* (Yogyakarta: PAU-Studi Universitas Gadjah Mada, 1988), p. 101.

[9] Barbara Sillars Harvey, *Permesta Pemberontakan Setengah Hati* (Jakarta: Grafiti Press, 1983), p. 15.

[10] Esther Velthoen, "Hutan and Kota: Contested Visions of the Nation-State in Southern Sulawesi in the 1950s", in *Indonesia in Transition: Rethinking "Civil Society", "Region", and "Crisis"*, ed. Samuel Hanneman and Henk Schulte Nordholt (Yogyakarta: Pustaka Pelajar, 2004), p. 156.

ulama (Islamic scholars), several military officers and some members of the nobility supported the movement.[11]

Darul Islam was built on a strong anti-Javanese platform. In South Sulawesi, the Javanese had become associated with communism. In 1950, the military leadership had sent left-leaning Brawijaya and Diponegoro battalions to South Sulawesi to crush the Andi Aziz rebellion. Their shooting of two former guerilla leaders led to local resentment.[12] In 1951 or 1952, Diponegoro Batallion 422, which had been involved in the Madiun uprising of 1948, was sent to Toraja, where it provided moral and sometimes military support for the development of the Indonesian Peasants' Union (Barisan Tani Indonesia, BTI) and for its land reform programme.[13] Muzakkar used the term "Communist Javanese Army" (*tentara Djawa komunis*) to refer to the Indonesian Armed Forces fighting against him. Barbara Harvey suggests that this term emphasised the *abangan* (nominal Islamic) practices of the Javanese in contrast to the stricter version of Islam practised in South Sulawesi. She also claims that in using the term "communist", Darul Islam sought to cause alarm among the aristocracy, whose position could be under threat from the communists.[14] Such hostility towards the PKI and the Javanese left an imprint on the thinking of the local community, especially those who were Muslim.

The second big clash was between the PKI and the followers of another regional rebellion. In 1957, several military officers, including Lieutenant Colonels Herman Nicolas Ventje Sumual, Jacob Frederick Warouw and Muhammad Saleh Lahade, proclaimed the Universal Struggle Charter (Piagam Perjuangan Semesta, Permesta), a movement aiming to restore the rights of the regions and to increase their financial and political independence. These officers proclaimed martial law in eastern Indonesia and tried to attract support by campaigning for regional autonomy and founding a youth organisation.[15]

---

[11] Mustari Bosra, *Tuang Guru, Anrong Guru dan Daeng Guru: Gerakan Islam di Sulawesi Selatan 1914–1942* (Makassar: La Galigo Press, 2008), pp. 270–1.

[12] Velthoen, "Hutan and Kota", p. 169.

[13] Terance William Bigalke, *Tana Toraja: A Social History of an Indonesian People* (Singapore: Singapore University Press, 2005), p. 241.

[14] Harvey, *Tradition, Islam and Rebellion*, p. 262.

[15] Amal, *Hubungan Pusat-Daerah*, pp. 74–5.

The PKI opposed both Darul Islam and Permesta. The Party attacked the Permesta officers as anti-nationalist and criticised the Islamic parties as Darul Islam supporters.[16] On 6 March 1956, the PKI newspaper *Harian Rakjat* published an article headlined "The Poison of Regionalism", attacking Masyumi and the Indonesian Socialist Party (Partai Sosialis Indonesia, PSI) for supporting separatist movements.[17] Similarly, the PKI was the most aggressive party in demanding that the government disband Masyumi, an Islamic political party, for its support of Darul Islam.[18]

After the military had successfully put down the Darul Islam and Permesta rebellions and Masyumi had been disbanded, there were more political opportunities for the PKI. The PKI held political courses for its own members as well as members of its mass organisations.[19] It also conducted literacy programmes for the peasantry in each district.[20] In the Cenrana sub-district of Bone, for example, PKI activists supported the distribution of agricultural and fishing equipment and organised local communities to speed up post-DI recovery. Fishing folk and farmers welcomed the programme and began to see the PKI as struggling on their behalf and for their interests.

The development of the PKI could also be seen in the rapid increase in mass organisations in each district in South Sulawesi. From 1959 all districts had a BTI branch, which held activities right through to the sub-district level. In South and Southeast Sulawesi, the PKI-aligned People's Cultural Institute (Lembaga Kebudayaan Rakyat, Lekra), led by Mahmud Yusmanor, had around 300 members by 1960; amongst the members were literary critics, writers and painters.[21] Ichlasul Amal estimates that by 1965, across the province

---

[16] Mahmud Yusmanor, interviewed by Taufik Ahmad, 8 Aug. 2009, Polewali Mandar, West Sulawesi.

[17] "Ratjun Daerahisme", *Harian Rakjat*, 6 Mar. 1957.

[18] See Anhar Gonggong, *Abdul Kahar Muzakar: Dari Patriot Hingga Pemberontak* (Yogyakarta: Ombak, 2004), pp. 366–70.

[19] "Surat menyurat 1960–964 tentang masalah yang berhubungan dengan Partai Komunis Indonesia (PKI) di Tana Toraja, Buton, dan Makassar", Reg. 33, Arsip Propinisi Sulawesi Selatan dan Sulawesi Tenggara.

[20] "Surat-Surat Masuk/Keluar tahun 1950–1957 tentang masalah berhubungan dengan PKI di Sulawesi Selatan dan Tengara", Reg. 344, Arsip Propinisi Sulawesi Selatan dan Sulawesi Tenggara 1946–1960.

[21] Mahmud Yusmanor, interviewed by Taufik Ahmad, 8 Aug. 2009, Polewali Mandar, West Sulawesi.

there were approximately 10,000 rank-and-file members of PKI-affiliated organisations.[22]

Nevertheless, the PKI continued to experience military obstruction. The Hasanuddin Regional Military Commander, Colonel Andi Muhammad Yusuf, encouraged Islamic organisations, specifically the Islamic Students' Association (Himpunan Mahasiswa Islam, HMI), to wage a propaganda war against the PKI. He even tried to get members of banned parties such as Masyumi to re-engage in politics. Not only was Yusuf very anti-leftist, he also favoured the Buginese and Makassarese. This fuelled ethnic resentment and resulted in increased support from other ethnic groups for the PKI, which was seen as being more inclusive and a growing political force.[23] Yusuf also strengthened support for anti-communism by removing pro-Left troops and sending more battalions from the anti-communist Siliwangi Command to the region and appointing Lieutenant Colonel Solichin as his chief of staff.[24] During the period after the banning of Masyumi in 1960, the aristocrats directed their allegiances to the Army, largely due to its anti-PKI stance.[25]

Amidst strong pressure from the military, the PKI continued to try to build networks with the peasantry through land reform. The central government sought to reform the highly unequal landownership structure in South Sulawesi through the Basic Agrarian Law of 1960.[26] The implementation of this law was chaotic.[27] The modus operandi of the communist-led BTI was to occupy lands owned by absentee landlords. Land reform thereby polarised villagers into two opposing classes — landlords (dubbed "village devils") and landless farmers. It also strengthened alliances based on political parties.

In the months before the September 30th Movement, Kiai Haji Abdul Rahman Ambo Dalle, a prominent ulama in South Sulawesi

---

[22] Amal, *Hubungan Pusat-Daerah*, cited in Bigalke, *Tana Toraja*, p. 267.

[23] Amal, *Hubungan Pusat-Daerah*, pp. 101, 171.

[24] Bigalke, *Tana Toraja*, p. 266.

[25] Amal, *Hubungan Pusat-Daerah*, p. 99.

[26] See "Pidato Menteri Agraria RI Sadjarwo pada sidang Dewan Pertimbangan Agung pada tanggal 13 Januari 1960", Reg. 541, Arsip Muhammad Saleh Lahade, Badan Arsip dan Perpustakaan Daerah Provinsi Sulawesi Selatan.

[27] Hermawan Sulistyo, *Palu Arit di Ladang Tebu: Sejarah Pembantaian Massal yang Telupakan 1965–1966* (Jakarta: Kepustakaan Populer Gramedia, 2000), p. 134.

who was previously a strong supporter of Darul Islam under Kahar Muzakkar,[28] expressed his disappointment and anger at the PKI: it was they who, in his view, had encouraged conflict in society.[29] His *pesantren* (Islamic boarding school), Darul Dakwah wal Irsyad, conducted physical training exercises to retaliate against PKI actions and made it compulsory for pesantren residents to fight against the PKI.[30] This resembled the armed training that Ansor members were undertaking in the pre-1965 period (Chapter 5). In the middle of September 1965 the boarding school held its tenth conference in Makassar and announced the decision to urge the national government to ban the PKI and its mass organisations.[31] When the conference was interrupted by intimidation and stone-throwing from outside the venue, the school leadership immediately assumed that the PKI had masterminded this action, thus strengthening the conviction that the PKI was anti-religious.[32]

The Outbreak of Violence in South Sulawesi

Most of my interviewees held that anti-PKI aggression was driven by the view that the PKI was hostile to religion and that the Party was responsible for the cruel murder of the generals. Political rumour-mongering, the history of past rebellions (such as Darul Islam and Permesta), political discord, anti-DI actions by the PKI, as well as an economic crisis also played a part in the anti-PKI violence. Nonetheless, as in other areas of Indonesia, the role of the military in encouraging anti-PKI mass organisations to carry out the violence cannot be discounted.

In South Sulawesi the anti-communist coalition comprised the Army, ex-DI supporters, ex-Masyumi members united within Pancasila Youth (Pemuda Pancasila), Ansor and HMI. These anti-PKI groups acted as judge, jury and executor, deciding whether a captured

---

[28] Gonggong, *Abdul Kahar Muzakar*, p. 96.

[29] Taufik Adnan Amal, "Gurutta K.H. Abdul Rahman Ambo Dalle (c. 1900–1996) Ulama Besar dari Tanah Bugis", in *Transformasi Otoritas Keagamaan: Pengalaman Islam di Indonesia*, ed. Jajat Burhanuddin and Ahmad Baedowi (Jakarta: Gramedia Pustaka, 2003), p. 213.

[30] "Gurutta Seabad Lebih", *Gatra*, 24 Feb. 1996.

[31] Abdul Muis Karby, *Sejarah Kebangkitan dan Perkembangan Darul Dakwah wal Irsyad [DDI]* (Pare-pare: Pondok Pesantren Putri Ujung Lare, 1989), p. 127.

[32] Amal, "*Gurutta K.H. Abdul Rahman Ambo Dalle*", p. 213.

person was from the PKI or not. The military carried out formal arrests under the jurisdiction of the Operations Command to Restore Order and Security (Komando Operasi Pemulihan Keamanan dan Ketertiban, Kopkamtib). The Regional Investigation Team (Team Periksa Daerah, Teperda) was then authorised to screen all those accused of being communist. My research suggests that sometimes the military offered shelter to PKI supporters but did not protect them from killing squads. Killings also occurred in the District Military Command complexes, suggesting the military allowed anti-communists to come and take those they wanted to kill from detention. The military also used the mass killings as a pretext for the arrest, exile and exploitation of political prisoners.

Unlike other regional military histories, the official history of the Hasanuddin Command does not detail its role in suppressing the PKI during the period of late 1965 to early 1966.[33] The following account of the violence is based on the limited secondary literature available on this topic and on interviews with survivors of this period.

On 1 October 1965, the government functioned as usual and economic activity continued. Local newspapers did not report the September 30th Movement in Jakarta. There was a perception that the kidnapping of the generals in Jakarta was a political issue with many unanswered questions. Several days later, in some sub-districts in the city of Makassar, people began to conduct night watches and patrols because they were worried about political developments.[34] They took the initiative to protect their environment and ensure that their area was clear from any "elements" of the September 30th Movement.

On 2 October 1965, local newspapers began to mention the September 30th Movement. Two days later, in Makassar, anxious members of the PKI-affiliated People's Youth (Pemuda Rakyat) gathered at the home of Aminuddin Muchlis (one of the PKI leaders) on Kancil Street, the home of Paiso (also a PKI leader) and the PKI headquarters on Badak/Onta Baru Street, in order to prepare themselves.[35] Reporting on the PKI's involvement in the kidnapping of the

---

[33] See Tim Jarah Dam XIV Hasanuddin, *25 Tahun Kodam XIV Hasanuddin 1957–1982* (Makassar: Angkasa, 1982).

[34] Tj. Kadullah, interviewed by Taufik Ahmad, 26 Aug. 2008, Makassar, South Sulawesi.

[35] Anwar Abbas, interviewed by Taufik Ahmad, 14 June 2008, Makassar, South Sulawesi.

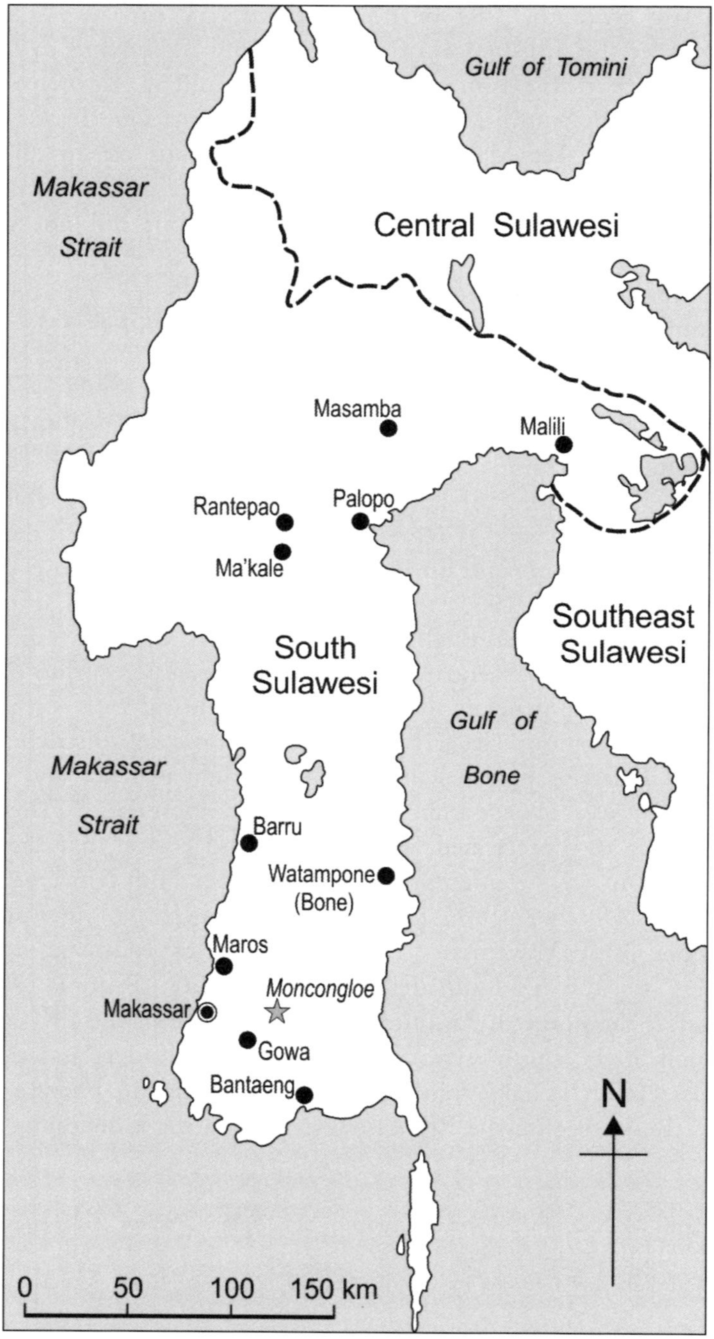

Map of South and Southeast Sulawesi

generals in military newspapers such as *Berita Yudha* and *Angkatan Bersendjata* (echoed by local papers such as *Pedoman Rakyat*) increased the anti-PKI sentiment encouraged by Kahar Muzakkar, Commander Yusuf and a range of Islamic organisations. On 5 October 1965 Dr Soenarso, a member of the PKI-linked Indonesian Graduates' Association (Himpunan Sarjana Indonesia), was attacked and killed at his surgery by a mass of "unknowns" after he had been accused of supporting PKI activities.[36] After that incident, there were demonstrations against the PKI and its mass organisations and sympathisers. On 15 October 1965 some 22 mass organisations demonstrated at the Karebosi Square in Makassar, calling for the PKI to be disbanded.[37] This demonstration was one of many nationwide actions against the PKI, motivated by media reports about the generals' deaths and alleged PKI responsibility.

On Major General Suharto's instructions, on 18 October 1965 Colonel Solichin Gautama Poerwanegara ordered district commanders to begin taking actions against the PKI and its mass organisations.[38] In December 1965 Solichin was appointed commander of the Hasanuddin Division, replacing Colonel Yusuf. During this period Siliwangi troops were under the control of Solichin, and they focused on purging the civilian administration. Meanwhile, the District Military Commands provided backing and advice to local anti-communist youth groups.[39]

In the early 1960s, after the Darul Islam rebellion had been put down and Masyumi banned, a section of former DI supporters went back into the military, where they bolstered anti-communist sentiment. Ex-Masyumi members joined other Islamic organisations, such as the NU youth organisation, Ansor, and an organisation created by Colonel Yusuf. With the support of the military men from Ansor, Pancasila Youth, Muhammadiyah and student organisations (such as HMI) as well as former Masyumi activists (who previously supported

---

[36] Dr Soenarso helped many poor people obtain medical help. Anwar Abbas, interviewed by Taufik Ahmad, 14 June 2008, Makassar, South Sulawesi; Tj. Kadulah, interviewed by Taufik Ahmad, 26 Aug. 2008, Makassar, South Sulawesi.

[37] Tim Jarah Dam XIV Hasanuddin, *25 Tahun Kodam XIV Hasanuddin 1957–1982*, p. 354.

[38] Bigalke, *Tana Toraja*, p. 267.

[39] Bigalke, *Tana Toraja*, p. 269.

the DI) stood together against the PKI.[40] Members of NU and Ansor, already very influential in South Sulawesi, became even stronger after the ban on Masyumi. Commander Yusuf also prepared members of the Muslim student organisation HMI for a showdown with the PKI.

Attacks on PKI property and arrests of PKI members continued into November 1965. The houses of PKI leaders along with the offices of PKI and other organisations were attacked. Hundreds of members of the PKI and its mass organisations, as well as those who surrendered voluntarily, were held in the District Military Command buildings and the Makassar police station.[41] The people arrested outnumbered those who surrendered voluntarily, but all were detained in the same buildings.

In addition to the violence against the PKI and its affiliated organisations, Chinese homes and shops, mostly concentrated in the cities, were also ransacked and destroyed.[42] This might have occurred because of pre-existing anti-Chinese sentiments, due to the ethnic Chinese domination of the local economy as well as the presumption that ethnic Chinese were supporting the communists (Chapter 6).

Some Javanese were also targeted because they were thought to be left-leaning. The destruction of these people's houses occurred at the end of November 1965 in Balang Boddong, Makassar.[43] One Javanese, Kasman, led a traditional Javanese musical group.[44] The group developed rapidly in the 1960s and often held traditional Javanese performances such as *ketoprak* and *ludruk*, accompanied by the gamelan on Saturday nights and on special occasions such as

[40] Pemuda Pancasila originated in 1959 as a wing of A.H. Nasution's anti-communist veterans' party League of the Supporters of Indonesian Independence (Ikatan Penerus Pelajar Indonesia, IPKI). Loren Ryter, "Pemuda Pancasila: The Last Loyalist Free Men of Suharto's New Order", *Indonesia* 66 (Oct. 1998): 52–3.

[41] "Surat Kepala Bagian Pemerintahan Umum, H. Nursina Sipato, SH dan Walikota Makassar tanggal 15 November 1965 kepada Kepala Kecamatan dalam Kotapraja Makassar tentang Intruksi-intruksi dan pentunjuk-petunjuk", Reg. 937, Arsip Kota Madya Makassar.

[42] Airgram A353, US Embassy Jakarta to State Department, 30 Nov. 1965, Record Group 59, State Department Central Files 1964–1966, POL 2-1 INDON, National Archives and Records Administration [hereafter RG59 1964–66 documents referred to by file code and NARA].

[43] Gun, interviewed by Taufik Ahmad, 20 July 2008, Makassar, South Sulawesi.

[44] Kasman Suparlan, interviewed by Taufik Ahmad, 14 July 2008, Makassar, South Sulawesi.

Independence Day and New Year celebrations.[45] After 1 October, they were accused of being communist and their musical instruments and their homes were destroyed. Many of them left Makassar.[46]

The violence escalated to killings at different intervals across a range of locations. In Bantaeng in early December 1965, Muhammadiyah members under the command of Makassarese leaders Usman Maesa and Suaib Naba (who went on to become respected local politicians) forcibly took Muhammad Ali Yusuf, chairperson of the PKI branch in Bantaeng District, from prison. Yusuf was Makassarese and originally from Bantaeng. They took him to the Bantaeng main mosque, where he was attacked and killed and his body mutilated.[47] The same group of people, led by Usman Maesa and Suaib Naba, came around and killed Abdul Rahman Holi,[48] a financial supporter of PKI activities, in his house around 9 p.m. Abdul Syukur, the head of the Federation of Indonesian Worker's Unions (Sentra Organisasi Buruh Seluruh Indonesia, SOBSI) for Bantaeng District, was killed next, in the market by another group of people. His body was chopped up with sharp weapons. Ansor youths, under the direction of Patahuddin H. Amran, killed the head of Pemuda Rakyat in police cells in Bantaeng. Dusung, also a member of Pemuda Rakyat, hid in Bateballa but was later killed by an unknown group.[49]

Violence was intense in former Darul Islam strongholds such as Bone and Luwu Districts. Here, organisations such as Pemuda Pancasila, Ansor and HMI worked together to mobilise people to destroy the PKI. The first killing in Bone District occurred in November 1965. Kalwater, chief of SOBSI in Bone and a Eurasian, was also the head of the Bone prison. He was killed by masses mobilised by

---

[45] Anwar Abbas, interviewed by Taufik Ahmad, 14 June 2008, Makassar, South Sulawesi. For a fascinating study of how artists fared in another former DI stronghold, see Laurie Ross, "Artist Registration and the 1965 Coup in the Cirebon Region, West Java", paper presented at the 1965–1966 Indonesian Killings Revisited Conference, 17–19 June 2009, National University of Singapore.

[46] Gun, interviewed by Taufik Ahmad, 20 July 2008, Makassar, South Sulawesi.

[47] Syafrie, interviewed by Taufik Ahmad, 20 Sept. 2008, Sungguminasa, South Sulawesi.

[48] Abdul Rahman Holi ran a slaughterhouse and was involved in various social and community activities.

[49] Syafrie, interviewed by Taufik Ahmad, 20 Sept. 2008, Sungguminasa, South Sulawesi.

Pancasila Youth and Ansor. A group of angry people entered the Women's Vocational School building and killed 200 alleged PKI members who had been detained inside.[50] The actions grew.[51] People carried sharp objects and sharpened sticks of bamboo as they went to the Bone District Military Command prison.[52] Amongst the detainees were the head of the PKI, Andi Mappa, and the PKI Secretary General, Igo Garnida Heri Erianto.[53] Javanese workers who had been brought from Java to work in the Arasoe sugar mill in Bone District were also detained in the jail.[54] After being arrested, they were placed in the District Military Command prison, because their living quarters were not ready for occupation. The ethnic Chinese in Bone generally handed themselves over to the military.[55] Hundreds of Javanese and Chinese people were killed in the prison.[56] In Luwu, members of the PKI-affiliated BTI, which was widely supported in this area, also directed their anger at members of the PKI. BTI members were resentful that they were now being threatened and claimed that when they joined the BTI they had believed it was a non-communist organisation.[57]

According to my interviews with the chairman and secretary of Pancasila Youth, in the rural areas of Bone, the leadership of the

---

[50] The Vocational School building is now the Golkar headquarters. In 1968, when NU ran a training centre in this building, there were still traces of blood on the walls and floors from the 1965 killings. Idrus Husein, interviewed by Taufik Ahmad, 8 Feb. 2009, Watampone, South Sulawesi.

[51] Tj. Kadullah, interviewed by Taufik Ahmad, 26 Aug. 2008, Makassar, South Sulawesi; CB, interviewed by Taufik Ahmad, 9 Aug. 2009, Makassar, South Sulawesi.

[52] CA, interviewed by Taufik Ahmad, 18 Aug. 2008, Watampone, South Sulawesi.

[53] Idrus Husein, interviewed by Taufik Ahmad, 8 Feb. 2009, Watampone, South Sulawesi.

[54] Anwar Abbas, interviewed by Taufik Ahmad, 14 June 2008, Makassar, South Sulawesi.

[55] Asmat Riadi, interviewed by Taufik Ahmad, 1 Aug. 2009, Watampone, South Sulawesi.

[56] A US Embassy telegram received a report that in Bone "'people' had broken into [the] prison compound, killing Army guards in [the] process, and seized Chinese (presumed PKI or Communist sympathisers)". Incoming Telegram 717A, US State Department received from US Embassy Jakarta, 20 Dec. 1965, POL 23-9 INDON, NARA.

[57] Bigalke, *Tana Toraja*, p. 268.

Pancasila Youth and Ansor read out a list of names of PKI people in an open field. It has not been confirmed who provided this list of names. The Pancasila Youth and Ansor then departed from the field to commit killings based on that list. To facilitate the killings, there were "informants" in each village who identified the PKI members in their village, who were then killed or taken away.[58]

In early 1966, violence also occurred in the Javanese transmigration villages of Sidomukli, Banyuret and Lemah Abang, in the sub-district of Bone-Bone, Luwu District. The local military and police killed nine villagers, most of whom were from the BTI and the Village Defence Organisation (Organisasi Pertahanan Desa), the modern equivalent of which is the Hansip (military civil defence) network.[59] The military then determined that remaining villagers from the transmigration area must report regularly to the authorities.

Based on US Department of State telegrams, interviews and secondary sources, it seems that more than 1,000 of the approximately 10,000 followers of the PKI and its affiliated organisations were killed.[60] The violence was very uneven. According to Terance Bigalke's research in the Torajan highlands, people in this area were emphatic that there were no killings, only beatings.[61] In other areas, especially Bone District, probably hundreds were killed. Two perpetrators estimated that around 300 people perished in Bone: around 200 people were killed in the Bone Vocational School and another 100 in the detention cells of the District Military Command of Watampone.[62] Killings also occurred in the interior or hinterland of Bone District, where my interviews suggested that people were killed in almost every village. A US State Department telegram reports that

---

[58] A. Ahmad, interviewed by Taufik Ahmad, 17 Sept. 2009, Watampone, South Sulawesi.

[59] Ilham, interviewed by Taufik Ahmad, 1 Aug. 2009, Bone-Bone, South Sulawesi.

[60] An Indonesian source reported to the US the deaths of 1,000 people in Makassar in December 1965. Telegram A-391, US Embassy Jakarta to State Department, 13 Dec. 1965, containing "Confidential Memorandum of Conversation," dated 9 Dec. 1965, POL 2 INDON, NARA.

[61] Bigalke, *Tana Toraja*, p. 268.

[62] CA and CB, interviewed by Taufik Ahmad, 18 Aug. 2008, Watampone, South Sulawesi; CC, interviewed by Taufik Ahmad, 18 Aug. 2008, undisclosed location; CD, interviewed by Taufik Ahmad, 18 Aug. 2008, undisclosed location.

in December 1965, former Darul Islam supporters killed around 1,000 PKI members when the Makassar city commander released prison inmates.[63]

During this period of turmoil, it was not only the families of those killed who experienced trauma. Almost all those living in rural areas felt threatened. In recalling this terrible time, people emphasised the sense of siege emanating from PKI supporters, who were, in fact, largely passive during this period. People recalled stories of night killings by mysterious groups who used sharpened bamboo sticks to pierce the woven bamboo flooring of traditional houses. To safeguard themselves, people began storing dry twigs on the ground so they could detect if anyone slipped underneath their houses. This simple method of protection created a sense of safety. Religious teachers stopped their activities because they were afraid of possible PKI revenge attacks. Rumours identifying PKI members were also spread, heightening the sense of fear.[64]

Short- and Long-term Detention in South Sulawesi

More people were affected by the mass arrests and imprisonment than by the killings. From late 1965, the military commander of South and Southeast Sulawesi (Penguasa Perang Daerah, Peperda) arrested all known PKI members on the pretext of safeguarding them from the anger of the people. The military bureaucracy, from the Hasanuddin Command down to the Sub-regional Military Command (Komando Resort Militer, Korem), arrested all those believed to be PKI. Until the beginning of 1966, thousands of people were "made secure" (*diamankan*) and taken to the District Military Command or the nearest police station. The majority of PKI members surrendered before they were arrested.[65] The District Military Command and police jails in each district in South Sulawesi were full of political prisoners.

[63] Telegram A-391, US Embassy Jakarta to State Department, 13 Dec. 1965, containing "Confidential Memorandum of Conversation," dated 9 Dec. 1965, POL 2 INDON, NARA.

[64] Idrus Husein, interviewed by Taufik Ahmad, 8 Feb. 2008, Watampone, South Sulawesi.

[65] Anwar Abbas, interviewed by Taufik Ahmad, 28 Aug. 2008, Makassar, South Sulawesi.

From October 1965 to March 1966 the number of political prisoners increased rapidly, reaching a total of 9,765 for the whole province of South Sulawesi. This large number consisted of 9,590 civilian detainees and 175 military detainees.[66] The detainees were members of the PKI, SOBSI, Pemuda Rakyat, Lekra, the Indonesian Women's Movement (Gerakan Wanita Indonesia, Gerwani), the Indonesian Student Movement Centre (Consentrasi Gerakan Mahasiswa Indonesia, CGMI), the League of Indonesian Student Youth (Ikatan Pemuda Pelajar Indonesia), BTI, as well as trade unionists and others with no connection to PKI activities. Detainees came from various strata of society and included politicians, military personnel, government functionaries, private company employees, lawyers, teachers, lecturers, school and university students, and farmers.

PKI prisoners were held in various locations in Makassar, including Hasanuddin Military Command facilities, Military Detention Centres (Rumah Tahanan Militer), District Military Command 1408 Makassar, Lompobattang Complex (where Hasanuddin troops lived), and the Women's Prison in Dahlia Street, Makassar. The relevant District Military Commands were responsible for political prisoners outside the city of Makassar. The District Military Commands then distributed the work to the Sub-regional Military Command responsible for each sub-district. This neat and strategic structure resulted in many people being netted as political prisoners.[67]

Until the order of 11 March 1966 forcing Sukarno to hand over administrative authority to Major General Suharto, there was still some ambiguity regarding the handling of prisoners because Sukarno remained President and he continued to call for the release of political prisoners.[68] As we have seen above, some detainees were murdered in prison during this early period or released to anti-communist organisations to be killed. Yet some prisoners in South Sulawesi

---

[66] "Surat PA POM DAM XIV/HN No. R-147/TPD/7/1970 mengenai elemen-elemen militer dan sipil dalam Kommand Hasanuddin yang terlibat atau terimplikasi G 30 S/PKI, 10 Juli 1970", in the private collection of Usman Kadang (Purnawirawan Anggota Polisi Militer [POM] Kodam XIV Hasanuddin).
[67] LPR-KROB Sulawesi Selatan, "Tragedi Kemanusiaan Tahun 1965 di Sulawesi Selatan", Biro Data dan Dokumentasi DPP LPR-KROB Sulawesi Selatan.
[68] Harold Crouch, *The Army and Politics in Indonesia* (Ithaca: Cornell University Press, 1978), p. 174.

report that before March 1966, there was greater freedom and less violence with regard to interrogations and the use of torture in detention. Things deteriorated, however, after the arrest on 18 March of 15 loyal Sukarnoist cabinet ministers for their alleged role in the September 30th Movement. Go Kee Iet, a CGMI activist, was originally detained in the Makassar Metropolitan Police headquarters.[69] Before the arrest of the ministers, he was detained for his own safety and allowed to go home during the day; after the arrests, he became a prisoner and was interrogated more thoroughly. Jhonlie, a Hasanuddin University student and Lekra activist, also reported harsher treatment and an intensification of anti-Sukarno sentiment in 1966. He was arrested in May 1966 and taken to the District Military Command prison in Makassar. He was tortured by the prison guard because he would not criticise Sukarno. He then became a detainee.[70]

In September 1966, around 250 political prisoners were transferred from Kodim 1408 (District Military Command 1408) in Makassar to Makassar Prison.[71] Prison inmates received rations three times a day: breakfast was a porridge containing 7–12 corn kernels mixed with broth in a milk tin; and lunch and dinner was one serving of white rice (around 10–12 tablespoons) with green vegetables (*kangkung*) and a piece of dried salted shark meat. Every week, inmates would receive one banana and one piece of meat.[72] These rations were barely enough for survival, and several of the prisoners fell ill. Many political prisoners died in jail — for instance, Yunus LB, Bustan Emba, Karnaen, Kusman Kasman, Pamuji, Jirong Mattiro, Guntur and Ridwan Sikki.[73] Prisoners sometimes stole food from the kitchen or found ways to hide food. They also went on hunger strike, choosing not to eat rather than to receive such meagre rations.

---

[69] Go Kee Iet, interviewed by Taufik Ahmad, 26 Aug. 2008, Makassar, South Sulawesi.

[70] Jhonlie, interviewed by Taufik Ahmad, 20 July 2008, Makassar, South Sulawesi.

[71] Anwar Abbas, interviewed by Taufik Ahmad, 14 June 2008, Makassar, South Sulawesi.

[72] Abd. Waris, interviewed by Taufik Ahmad, 22 July 2008, Makassar, South Sulawesi.

[73] Sarmanto Sarmo, interviewed by Taufik Ahmad, 20 June 2008, Sungguminasa, South Sulawesi; Ir. Rasydi, interviewed by Taufik Ahmad, 27 June 2008, Makassar, South Sulawesi.

This action was designed to pressure jail authorities to increase their rations.[74]

The Regional Interrogation Team led by Major Idham Alam (from the military police) observed this resistance by political prisoners and started to think about how to deal more deliberately with the problems of the political prisoners. The deaths of political prisoners and the lack of funds to look after them led to the idea of deploying prisoners to places where they could cultivate crops under military control.

Throughout Indonesia, military commanders were facing the same issue of how to manage overcrowded prisons with insufficient funds to sustain the prisoners. The cost of feeding political prisoners was estimated to be $2 million a year.[75] Meanwhile, the economy was still in a dire state, with hyperinflation peaking. After the introduction of the prisoner classification system, the military began to process prisoners. Most Category A prisoners remained in separate detention centres awaiting trial for their alleged connections to the September 30th Movement. Trials were seriously delayed due to the overloaded judicial system. Of those tried, there were no acquittals and most received sentences ranging from 15 years' imprisonment to the death penalty. Category C prisoners, who were considered least dangerous, were generally separated from other prisoners. Some began to be released from 1966, while others were held until the mid-1970s. Category B prisoners presented the regime with the greatest challenge, for there was usually insufficient evidence to put these people on trial and link them to the September 30th Movement (Chapter 2); yet the regime felt that it would be dangerous to release prisoners who had mostly been active members of the PKI or leaders of associated mass organisations.

In 1968, the government decided to relocate Category B prisoners to prison camps or penal colonies. Here they would be separated from society and could work towards self-sufficiency. In the

[74] Muh. Tahir, interviewed by Taufik Ahmad, 2 June 2008, Makassar, South Sulawesi; Sarmanto Sarmo, interviewed by Taufik Ahmad, 20 June 2008, Sungguminasa, South Sulawesi; Gun, interviewed by Taufik Ahmad, 16 June 2008, Makassar, South Sulawesi.

[75] Justus van der Kroef, *Indonesia since Sukarno* (Singapore: Asia Pacific Press, 1971), as quoted in Fealy, "The Release of Indonesia's Political Prisoners", p. 7. This paragraph draws on Fealy, pp. 5–7.

regime's Orwellian terminology, the order issued by the Kopkamtib Commander was to complete the "securing and guidance" of the September 30th Movement detainees.[76] The military opened prison camps in various locations around Indonesia. The best-known prison camp was on Buru, a remote island in Maluku, where more than 14,000 Javanese prisoners were sent from 1969 onwards. Here prisoners worked on opening up agricultural lands and cutting down forests.[77] Isolated prison camps were also opened in Kemarau Island in South Sumatra; Argosari in East Kalimantan; Nanga-Nanga and Kendari in Southeast Sulawesi; and Nusakambangan Island, Wadas Lintang, Plantungan and Brebes in Central Java. Likewise, the Hasanuddin Military Command decided to open the Moncongloe prison camp based on the rationale of security and order, but also to economise on funding for political prisoners, isolate them from the socio-political environment, and eradicate communist teachings.

Moncongloe Prison Camp

Moncongloe was to the east of Makassar, on the border between Gowa and Maros Districts. The Regional Interrogation Team of South and Southeast Sulawesi chose this location because it was a state forest and mostly state-owned land, except for a section designated as military land. After these lands were opened by the political prisoners, they were divided among military officers, who then claimed private ownership. The forest had large stands of bamboo, which could become feed for the new paper mill in Gowa District. There were also many valuable big trees, especially in the mountains. The Hasanuddin Command had selected this area as its headquarters so as to better control the political prisoners by putting them to work on constructing the military base.

PKI prisoners began arriving in Moncongloe in March 1969. Eleven arrived first to help construct temporary barracks where the prisoners would live.[78] In April 1969, another 44 political prisoners

[76] "Petunjuk Pangkopkamtib Tanggal 16 Oktober 1968 Nomor: Pelak-002/Kopkamtib/10/68, tentang Kebijaksanaan Penyelesaian Tahanan/Tawanan G 30 S/PKI", Reg. 441, Arsip Muhammad Saleh Lahade.

[77] Amnesty International, *Indonesia: An Amnesty International Report* (London: Amnesty International Publications, 1977), pp. 90–7.

[78] Sarmanto Sarmo, interviewed by Taufik Ahmad, 20 June 2008, Makassar, South Sulawesi.

Political prisoners in front of the Moncongloe prison camp cooperative office (photo provided by a former prisoner)

came to construct more permanent living quarters. By the end of 1969, all the camp facilities had been completed. These consisted of four male barracks, one female barracks, one guard post, a polyclinic, a mosque, a hall, a church, cooperatives and a parade ground. The prison camp itself was just 150 square metres, surrounded by barbed wire. Each barrack building was around 6 by 20 metres, and could hold around 250 people. In each barrack, one person was elected as barrack commander. The barrack commander had the delicate task of both conveying the wishes of political prisoners and shouldering responsibility for any misconduct by prisoners. There were also elected team heads who coordinated the jobs of the work team members.

Political prisoners from Makassar prison and others in South and Southeast Sulawesi arrived in Moncongloe in stages until their numbers reached 911 — 859 men and 52 women.[79] Despite the

[79] Former Military Police Captain Siregar, interviewed by Anwar Abbas, 14 June 2008, Makassar, South Sulawesi (transcript provided to author).

official policy of separating prisoners, both Category B and Category C prisoners were detained in Moncongloe, perhaps to maximise the pool of labour, with each category contributing approximately half of the prisoners. Their activities were determined by the military police from the Hasanuddin Command, and the camp commander was also from the military police.

Moncongloe camp was intended as a means for the Army and its officers to exploit the prisoners. Each member of the guards company (Kompi Pengawal, Kiwal) of the Hasanuddin Command took a political prisoner as a live-in servant in his household. About 60 political prisoners worked as household servants without pay on a rotating basis, moving across different guards' houses to prevent too close a relationship developing.[80] Political prisoners were placed in corvée units, which were deployed to open agricultural lands, cut down and harvest bamboo, fell trees, and saw timber into beams and planks. When Hasanuddin Commander Brigadier General Abdul Aziz visited the camp, he came up with the idea of using prison labour for the construction of military offices and housing in Makassar.[81] As part of this project, in Lonjo Boko, Gowa District, around 300 houses were built for the Hasanuddin Command.[82] After that, the military took many prisoners out of the camp and deployed them on various military construction projects. The prisoners worked without any remuneration aside from their rations and the occasional tin of milk given as a "bonus".[83]

Each political prisoner received one hectare of land to turn into a garden. For this arduous work, they were given one hoe and a Chinese-made machete. The land they received was overgrown with elephant grass and had hard soil. Nevertheless, in the first year,

---

[80] Jhonlie, interviewed by Taufik Ahmad, 25 July 2008, Makassar, South Sulawesi.
[81] Sarmanto Sarmo, interviewed by Taufik Ahmad, 14 June 2008, Makassar, South Sulawesi; Rasjidi Amra, interviewed by Taufik Ahmad, 2 Aug. 2009, Makassar, South Sulawesi.
[82] "Construction Plans for 300 Houses for Hasanuddin Military Command in Lonjo Boko, Gowa District, 14 August 1972", personal documents of Rasjidi Amra.
[83] Sarmanto Sarmo, interviewed by Taufik Ahmad, 14 June 2008, Makassar, South Sulawesi; Jufri Buape, interviewed by Taufik Ahmad, 20 July 2008, Makassar, South Sulawesi; Rasjidi Amra, interviewed by Taufik Ahmad, 27 June 2008, Makassar, South Sulawesi.

Moncongloe already showed some results. Previously a forest, it was gradually transformed into 450 hectares of arable land.[84]

In 1972, Lieutenant Colonel Sarosa replaced Lieutenant Colonel W.R. Samallo as commander of the Hasanuddin Military Police. This resulted in the camp commander changing from Captain Rakimin to Captain Siregar. The camp was then formally designated as Moncongloe Rehabilitation Installation (Instalasi Rehabilitasi, Inrehab). There were changes to regulations, including the reduction of garden size from one hectare to a quarter of a hectare for each political prisoner. The rest of the land was given to officials. Prisoners could work in their garden only one day a week; on the other six days they had to work in officials' gardens.

For ten hours a day, prisoners worked outside their barracks. Their day began with breakfast prepared by the women prisoners, then some form of sport initiated by the prisoners themselves. After morning assembly at 6 a.m., prisoners lined up in rows and were counted one by one. Then they picked up their work tools and departed for their designated workplace. Guards read out the names of the prisoners and the gardens they would work in.[85] At noon prisoners had a food break, then they continued to work until 6 p.m. At 7 p.m., after another headcount, they had some time to socialise among themselves. Every Monday, prisoners held a flag-raising ceremony. The prisoners themselves determined who would officiate at the ceremony, raise the flag and read out the 1945 Constitution; but overall responsibility for the ceremony still rested with the prison official.[86]

In the camp's first year, some prisoners were allotted land to grow food according to a "target system".[87] The land that they opened up was then taken over by officials as their personal gardens. On

---

[84] Rasjidi Amra, interviewed by Taufik Ahmad, 27 June 2008, Makassar, South Sulawesi.

[85] Anwar Abbas, interviewed by Taufik Ahmad, 20 July 2008, Makassar, South Sulawesi.

[86] Rasjidi Amra, interviewed by Taufik Ahmad, 27 June 2008, Makassar, South Sulawesi; Anwar Abbas, interviewed by Taufik Ahmad, 14 June 2008, Makassar, South Sulawesi; Muh. Tahir, interviewed by Taufik Ahmad, 24 Aug. 2008, Makassar, South Sulawesi.

[87] Sarmanto Sarmo, interviewed by Taufik Ahmad, 14 June 2008, Makassar, South Sulawesi.

average, each official received about five hectares of land.[88] However, the heavy work in the labour teams meant that the gardens soon became neglected and tall elephant grass began to reclaim them. The prisoners tried very hard to get the gardens to produce again.

Under the command of Captain Siregar, from 1972 onwards political prisoners worked collectively on road construction between Daya and Moncongloe (a distance of some 15 kilometres) and on other roads that connected the camp with the military base. The prisoners began work at 8 a.m., arriving in military trucks, and returned to the camp at 6 p.m. They obtained materials, such as rocks, from the mountainsides south of Moncongloe. Each day about five to ten military trucks came back to the prison camp laden with rocks.[89] Political prisoners then handed over these rocks to the camp officials.[90]

Nevertheless, for the eight years from the opening of the camp in 1969 until the release of political prisoners in 1977, the military used prison labour primarily to harvest the forests. In late 1972, this exploitation was focused on the cutting of bamboo. Each political prisoner was given a target amount to be cut, usually 1 cubic metre per day. The cut bamboo would then be sold to traders in Makassar for 25 rupiah per tree.[91] If a prisoner did not meet the target, he would be hit with a piece of bamboo.[92] Camp officials competed to produce as much bamboo as possible, while the prisoners became more miserable, being forced to cut bamboo at the most rapid rate possible. Once the size of the business opportunity became apparent, the cutting teams expanded because the bamboo could also be used at the paper mill in Gowa. Military officers and camp officials suggested to the mill manager that the camp become a bamboo supplier to the mill. According to one of the prisoners, Go Kee Iet (who

---

[88] Each soldier received about five hectares of land at the Hasanuddin Guard Company (Kompi Pengawal) Home Base. Map of land distribution, Dec. 1978, signed by Guards' Commander, Captain Usman Kadang, private collection.

[89] Go Kee Iet, interviewed by Taufik Ahmad, 26 Aug. 2008, Makassar, South Sulawesi.

[90] Sarmanto Sarmo, interviewed by Taufik Ahmad, 14 June 2008, Makassar, South Sulawesi.

[91] Go Kee Iet, interviewed by Taufik Ahmad, 26 Aug. 2008, Makassar, South Sulawesi.

[92] Sarmanto Sarmo, interviewed by Taufik Ahmad, 20 June 2008, Sungguminasa, South Sulawesi.

worked in administration in the prisoners' cooperative's production section), each day an average 100 cubic metres of bamboo would be ready for sale.[93] Each night, the mill truck entered the camp to pick up the bamboo.[94] Go noted the amount of bamboo that left the camp, but the prisoners' cooperative did not receive any data about proceeds from the sales. Go estimated that at the mill, bamboo sold for around 50 to 100 rupiah per tree.

Before long, the rapid rate of felling depleted the supply of bamboo. Officers were concerned only with the amount of bamboo being felled and made no effort to regenerate the plants to ensure their sustainability. After two years, production collapsed and the bamboo-felling work teams were disbanded.

Aside from felling bamboo, prisoners were directed to go deep into the forests and mountains to cut down trees with handsaws. When the trees were cut, the prisoners handed them over to the sawing team, who turned the timber into plywood, logs and poles for houses. These timber products were then handed over to the camp officials.[95] Unsawn timber (especially from the *tumba* tree) was handed to the prisoners' cooperative to be exchanged for soap, sugar, tea, coffee and other goods. According to Go, about 50 cubic metres would be gathered each day.

Before long the Moncongloe forests had become denuded along with the bamboo stands. Large trees in the forests south of Moncongloe almost completely disappeared as they were turned into boards and poles. The land turned into hard desert ground during the dry season, and into muddy swamps during the wet season. The river became polluted and began to stop flowing in the dry season. Before the arrival of the prisoners the river had never dried up, but now this became commonplace. The camp thus not only claimed the energy and hard labour of the prisoners, but also exhausted the economic resources of the Moncongloe forests.

The environmental changes subtly influenced relations between the prisoners and the local community. At first the locals' attitude

---

93 Go Kee Iet, interviewed by Taufik Ahmad, 26 Aug. 2008, Makassar, South Sulawesi.

94 Tj. Kadullah, interviewed by Taufik Ahmad, 26 Aug. 2008, Makassar, South Sulawesi.

95 Muhammad Tahir, interviewed by Taufik Ahmad, 2 June 2008, Makassar, South Sulawesi.

had been one of fear and hatred, because they viewed the PKI as evil. However, with increased contact between locals and prisoners — for example, the prisoners assisted local people in working their house gardens and building their homes — the former became more sympathetic. Eventually the local community realised that they could no longer benefit from the Moncongloe forests and would have to instead make the long trek to the mountains. It was no longer the political prisoners who threatened their livelihood.

On and around 1 December 1976, the Indonesian government released 2,500 Category B political prisoners. Between 1977 and 1978, a further 10,000 Category B prisoners were released.[96] In Moncongloe, Category B prisoners began to be released between 1976 and 1978. Upon their release, all prisoners found themselves deeply stigmatised by the propaganda of the New Order, which designated them as "unclean" people (*tidak bersih lingkungan*). Furthermore, the government still denied them civil and political rights. Ex-prisoners had their movements monitored by the military, and they were threatened with rearrest if they were found to have taken part in political activities.[97] To avoid such stigma and surveillance, some former political prisoners changed their names and moved from place to place. Several chose to live in the city of Makassar — in rented houses, without any health care — rather than return to their hometowns, thereby becoming part of Makassar's urban poor. Some former political prisoners married local women, but if their past became known the stigma passed on to their children.

Conclusion

In South Sulawesi during the 1950s, the growth of the PKI was constrained by the firm commitment to Islam of the majority of the population and the increased emphasis on Islamic values during the period of the Darul Islam rebellion. Besides Islamic leaders, the Communist Party was also staunchly opposed by local aristocrats and

[96] Fealy, "The Release of Indonesia's Political Prisoners", p. 29.

[97] "Petunjuk Pelaksanaan Komando Operasi Pemulihan Keamanan dan Ketertiban Nomor JUKLAK-04/ KOPKAM/II/1974", dated 21 Feb. 1974, Reg. 941, Arsip Muhammad Saleh Lahade. This shows the formal mechanisms for the monitoring of ex-political prisoners.

the anti-communist military commander. Nevertheless, in the early 1960s — after the Darul Islam and Permesta rebellions had been suppressed and Masyumi banned — the Party began to attract more members, both on the strength of its support for land reform and amongst certain sections of the population such as Christians, Javanese transmigrants, fisherfolk and farmers.

In the aftermath of the September 30th Movement, Colonel Yusuf, commander of the local Hasanuddin Division, had further justification for his anti-communist stance and began to arrest members of the PKI and detain them in military facilities. The worst violence occurred in Bone District, both in the towns and in the hinterland. Ethnic Chinese and Javanese were also targeted because of their perceived links to communism. The key civilian organisations involved in the violence were the Pancasila Youth, Ansor and HMI.

Many more members of the PKI and its affiliated organisations were imprisoned. The length of imprisonment depended on the category in which the military classified the prisoners. In 1968, the New Order regime adopted a new strategy of opening self-sufficient prison camps to ensure Category B inmates remained isolated from their communities while reducing the burden on the state of sustaining so many prisoners. For many prisoners this marked a transition from short- to long-term detention. The Army's treatment of inmates at Moncongloe illustrates how the military used the tactics of arrest, imprisonment and isolation. Through the deployment of work teams for cutting down and harvesting bamboo, and logging and sawing timber, political prisoners also served the personal and institutional interests of their captors. The lands opened by the prisoners continued to be controlled by the military, limiting community access to forest resources that had previously been a source of income. Mattulada has argued that in the early New Order period the officers of the Armed Forces became the new elite in South Sulawesi, "reinforcing the social structure of the past in a kind of neo-feudalism orientated towards status".[98] In short, the military was the only group that benefited from the opening of the Moncongloe camp.

---

[98] Mattulada, *Suatu Lukisan Analitis Terhadap Antropologi-Politik Orang Bugis*, PhD dissertation, University of Indonesia, 1974, cited in Suratman and Guinness, *Transmigration*, p. 75.

8

South Blitar and the PKI Bases: Refuge, Resistance and Repression

*Vannessa Hearman**

Members of the Indonesian Communist Party (Partai Komunis Indonesia, PKI) and affiliated organisations were unprepared for the sudden attack launched on them following the September 30th Movement. Almost overnight the Party was transformed from a thriving legal organisation with autonomy and influence to an organisation with which any association was potentially fatal. By the end of 1965, the key PKI leaders Aidit, Njoto and Lukman had been killed or were missing. Surviving leaders tried to salvage what remained of the Party. They had to rethink the long-held strategy of democratic engagement within the political system and consider alternative strategies for survival. To rebuild the Party, they decided to create bases in isolated villages in south Blitar (the southwestern and south-central part of East Java province) and in other parts of Central and East Java, where the Party had strong support.

In military propaganda, the PKI bases in Blitar were depicted as "guerilla bases" or "armed bastions". An official military history referred to them as "fugitive nests" with armed troops.[1] An early scholarly account of the bases by Justus van der Kroef likewise

* Some sections of this chapter appeared in earlier form in "Guerrillas, Guns, and Knives? Debating Insurgency in South Blitar, East Java, 1967–68" by Vannessa Hearman, *Indonesia* 89 (Apr. 2010): 61–91.

[1] Semdam VIII Brawidjaja, *Operasi Trisula Kodam VIII Brawidjaja* (Surabaya: Jajasan Taman Tjandrawilwatikta, 1969), p. 16.

alluded to a sophisticated guerilla movement with "networks of covert encampments, meeting places, shelters, and even bunkers connected by underground tunnels in the Viet Cong manner".[2] By exaggerating the PKI's level of organisation and its armed capacity, the military in turn justified both the violent repression of the PKI in 1965–66 and the disproportionate firepower used in the 1968 Trisula Operation to destroy the PKI bases. Throughout the New Order regime the military also dramatised the Blitar bases to bolster its propaganda that members of the PKI were national enemies and traitors.

Drawing on extensive interviews with those who fled to or lived in the area of south Blitar, this chapter re-examines the nature of the bases, the forms of resistance in which people engaged, and the continuing repression of the PKI. It challenges the idea that the bases were functional guerilla hideouts or armed bastions. Although the Party's new strategy had envisaged building an armed capacity, its access to weapons was so limited that the bases never evolved into a guerilla operation. Some fugitives engaged in small-scale attacks against the military and Nahdlatul Ulama (NU) vigilantes in Ansor, but these attacks were rudimentary and in fact led to discovery of the bases. Most fugitives fled to the area simply to find refuge. These survivors were from diverse backgrounds, including military personnel. The experiences of those who survived the military operation reveal how the anti-communist repression affected their lives. The repression had particular consequences for women and children. In the aftermath of the operation, the military and government tried to rehabilitate those who lived in the area, bringing them under increased surveillance and control.

The Decision to Create Bases

Although the killings had subsided in Java and Bali by March 1966, surviving members and sympathisers of the PKI in Java continued to live on the run from authorities. Surabaya, an area of PKI strength before 1965, became a place of refuge for fugitives who hoped to find anonymity and protection in the big city. PKI refugees clustered

[2] Justus M. van der Kroef, "Indonesian Communism since the 1965 Coup", *Pacific Affairs* 43, 1 (Spring 1970): 41.

around areas such as Ngagel, Gubeng and Wonokromo, which had been PKI strongholds. However, such an existence was becoming more and more insecure, especially after the December 1966 arrest of Politburo member Sudisman, who had led the Party after the disappearance of Aidit, Njoto and Lukman. With continuing arrests and purges of those accused of supporting the PKI, the support networks in Surabaya were under great pressure. The surviving leadership began to consider the need for Party members to retreat from the repression and regroup in a safer area.

At first the Party reorganised into two main groups: Sudisman led one; and Rewang, chairman of the Central Java provincial committee and a candidate member of the PKI Central Committee, led the other. Rewang's group took refuge around Klaten-Boyolali in Central Java, and later in northeastern Central Java around Rembang and Purwodadi. Following Sudisman's arrest in December 1966, Rewang and Politburo member and SOBSI deputy chairman Ruslan Wijayasastra's group became the most prominent of the surviving Party leadership.[3] By 1967, the "second layer" of PKI leaders, such as Oloan Hutapea, Munir, Sukatno and Tjugito, had become more organised within Rewang's group.[4] The second layer of leaders moved to set up bases in several parts of Central and East Java. They were spurred by the pressure of military operations but were also motivated to test the possibility of other forms of struggle.

The concept of consolidating bases arose indirectly out of the remaining PKI leadership's Criticism, Self-Criticism (Kritik-Otokritik, KOK) process. The ensuing document of September 1966 was a critical analysis of why the PKI had been so vulnerable after the September 30th Movement.[5] This document helped to shape the surviving leadership's response to the intensifying political repression by questioning the legal, parliamentary struggle that the PKI had earlier chosen and the resulting neglect of the Party's capacity for armed

---

[3] SOBSI (Sentral Organisasi Karyawan Buruh Seluruh Indonesia), Indonesian Worker's Union.

[4] Van der Kroef, "Indonesian Communism since the 1965 Coup", p. 40. Oloan Hutapea was editor of *Bintang Merah*, the PKI's theoretical journal; Sukatno was a People's Youth leader; Tjugito was a PKI Central Committee member.

[5] Imam Soedjono, *Yang Berlawan: Membongkar Tabir Pemalsuan Sejarah PKI* (Yogyakarta: Resist Books and Yayasan Sapu Lidi, 2006), pp. 323–4.

struggle. After the bases' destruction, former Central Committee member Muhammad Munir explained in his defence plea on 2 March 1973 in the Special Military Court (Mahkamah Militer Luar Biasa) that the self-criticism document repudiated the PKI's previous approach of relying on peaceful, open struggle.[6] According to Munir, in the face of such serious repression, the surviving PKI leaders agreed on the need for an armed revolutionary movement to fight for popular democracy and to bring about a communist society. In formulating the strategy of retreating and rebuilding, they drew inspiration from the Chinese Communist Party and its organisation of the peasantry. Sudisman argued in the Criticism, Self-Criticism document that the PKI leadership had neglected the opportunity of stepping up the level of political organisation among the peasants.[7]

Many of the PKI members who came to south Blitar had formerly held official positions in the Party or in PKI-linked mass organisations, which made them clear targets for the military.[8] Rewang estimated that dozens of PKI members and sympathisers sought refuge in the area.[9] The military's partial list (and in some cases photographs) of those arrested during the military operation shows the diverse backgrounds of those who had come to the area to escape political persecution. They included students, Party organisers, soldiers, military officers, trade unionists, and members of the Indonesian Women's Movement (Gerakan Wanita Indonesian, Gerwani).[10] During the operation, the military arrested Politburo members Ruslan Wijayasastra, Oloan Hutapea, Munir and Rewang, and Central Committee members Tjugito, Iskandar Subekti and Mardjoko. Some of these men had held additional responsibilities within mass organisations: Munir, Mardjoko and Tjugito were officials in SOBSI; Sukatno was Chairman of the People's Youth (Pemuda Rakyat), the youth

---

[6] Muhammad Munir, "Membela Kemerdekaan, Demokrasi dan Keadilan", 2 Mar. 1973, File #286, Suparna Sastra Diredja papers, International Institute of Social History, Amsterdam. Munir was also the Secretary General of the trade union federation SOBSI in 1965. See Van der Kroef, "Indonesian Communism since the 1965 Coup", pp. 34–60.

[7] *Pledoi Sudisman: Kritik-Otokritik Seorang Politburo CC-PKI* (Jakarta: Teplok Press, 2001), p. 98.

[8] Semdam VIII Brawidjaja, *Operasi Trisula*, pp. 289–310.

[9] Rewang, interviewed by Vannessa Hearman, 14 Feb. 2009, Solo, Central Java.

[10] Semdam VIII Brawidjaja, *Operasi Trisula*, pp. 289–310.

wing of the PKI. Surachman, former Secretary General of the Indonesian National Party (Partai Nasional Indonesia, PNI), took refuge in south Blitar after the repression had extended to the Sastroamidjojo-Surachman wing of the PNI.[11] Also arrested were East Java PKI leaders Gatot Lestario (arrested in Jakarta in January 1969),[12] Rustomo and Suwandi (a member of the Central Committee). Gatot's wife, Pudjiaswati, and another East Java Gerwani leader[13] were arrested, as were members of the People's Cultural Institute (Lembaga Kebudayaan Rakyat, Lekra). In addition, spouses of PKI members or affiliated organisations were arrested, including Lies Sari (also known as Lies Katno and Sri Sulistyowati). She was both Sukatno's wife and a journalist with the national economic daily *Nusa Bakti*. Furthermore, military men who had allegedly deserted from the Diponegoro and Siliwangi commands in Central and West Java respectively were captured in this area. The list compiled by the military was by no means exhaustive. Based on interview material, we know that many others arrested in south Blitar were not on the list. These included Suwandi's wife, Lestari, who was a Gerwani functionary in Surabaya, and Putmainah, a Gerwani leader and PKI parliamentarian from Blitar.

According to both Rewang and Munir (in his 1973 defence speech), the base was set up primarily as a defensive move but also as an experiment to test whether it would be possible for the Party to mount a new form of opposition. Rewang explained the reasons for constructing this base:

> Our departure to south Blitar was based on the view that there were no longer any legal guarantees for communists. The possibility for peaceful struggle had disappeared. We needed to take up armed resistance, so we decided to relocate the party leadership to south Blitar.[14]

---

[11] Surachman was elected Secretary General of the PNI in 1963. The 1965 split created the Ali Sostroamidjojo-Surachman group and the Osa Maliki-Usep group. By 1968, the Osa Maliki-Usep grouping in the PNI had been anointed by President Suharto as the rightful leadership of PNI. See Angus McIntyre, "Divisions and Power in the Indonesian National Party, 1965–1966", *Indonesia* 13 (Apr. 1972): 183–210.

[12] He was known erroneously through some military and media reports as Gatot Sutaryo, but his real name was Gatot Lestario.

[13] DA, interviewed by Vannessa Hearman, 18 Feb. 2008, Surabaya, East Java.

[14] Rewang, interviewed by Vannessa Hearman, 14 Feb. 2009, Solo, Central Java.

Referring to the political repression in Java after 1 October 1965, Munir did not deny the Party's desire to regroup, but also explained in relation to the south Blitar base: "The reconstruction of the PKI was intended to shield (*memayungi*) the members and their families from armed counter-revolutionaries".[15] The armed counter-revolutionaries he refers to in this quote include the armed forces, civilian auxiliaries and militias who took part in anti-PKI operations, such as Ansor, Muhammadiyah, Pancasila Youth (Pemuda Pancasila) and PNI-linked Marhaen groups. As discussed in Chapter 5, Ansor, the youth wing of NU, and its armed auxiliary Banser (Barisan Ansor Serbaguna, Ansor Multipurpose Youth Brigade) had participated in the purges in East Java.

Individual motivations were not necessarily the same as the Party's official position for setting up the south Blitar base. In several personal testimonies, people stated they were motivated by the need to protect themselves and their families. A provincial level Gerwani leader, with whom I spoke, had acted as a courier and dealt with Party leaders while in hiding in Surabaya.[16] She found it was becoming more difficult to find safe houses. Lestari also went to south Blitar to join her husband, Suwandi. Another respondent, an engineer trained in Eastern Europe, was then in his early 30s.[17] He had just been released from Salemba Prison in Jakarta at the end of 1966. Upon returning to his home village near Blitar, he was scared of being rearrested and killed, especially after a short article appeared listing the names of supposedly communist Indonesian students from Eastern Europe. He said, "Rather than dying uselessly (*mati konyol*), I went along to south Blitar to hide there. It is better to resist (*berlawan*) than to die uselessly."[18] In a manuscript on her experiences in Blitar, Lies Katno wrote that she set out to be reunited with her husband, Sukatno.[19]

Establishing the Bases

After the 1965–66 slaughter had ceased, the Party still retained a large potential support base in Central and East Java. In East Java,

---

[15] Muhammad Munir, "Membela Kemerdekaan, Demokrasi dan Keadilan".
[16] DA, interviewed by Vannessa Hearman, 18 Feb. 2008, Surabaya, East Java.
[17] DB, interviewed by Vannessa Hearman, 22 Feb. 2008, undisclosed location.
[18] DB, interviewed by Vannessa Hearman, 22 Feb. 2008, undisclosed location.
[19] Lies Sari, "Blitar Selatan yang Dilupakan", unpublished manuscript, n.d.

an area where there was strong support for President Sukarno, there were divisions within the military over the fate of Sukarno and evidence of discontent during the transition to the New Order. From October 1965 leading up to the Trisula Operation in mid-1968, the press reported defections from the military, weapons thefts and armed robberies.[20] Members of the military assisted in hiding PKI members and supporters, particularly where there were familial ties between soldiers and those whom they assisted. In April 1967, Major General Muhammad Jasin took over from Major General Soemitro as Brawijaya commander (Kodam VIII/Brawijaya) and moved more aggressively to deepen the process of the "New Orderisation" of East Java, replacing military officers thought to be pro-Sukarno. Jasin complained in mid-1967 of schisms in the military. He held meetings with commanders of the Navy and the Marines in Surabaya to halt what he termed "the Cold War between the Army and the Marines".[21] Jasin explained that there were soldiers, who he suggested were supporters of Sukarno or the PKI during this period, who "took off their uniforms" to avoid being targeted in purges against sections of the military, such as the Marines and the Air Force.[22] Based on the Trisula Operation's list of those who were arrested, it is evident that some soldiers and officers joined the PKI base in south Blitar. Lieutenant Colonel Pratomo, formerly a Siliwangi officer and commander of the Pandeglang District Military Command (Kodim), was the highest ranking among them. Divisions in the military allowed civilian groups such as Banser to continue to play a role in operations against the PKI.

The Blitar base project was one of several bases being built in Central and East Java, including the area on the slopes of Mount Semeru in East Java and the poverty-stricken Gunung Kidul region in Central Java and the Special Region of Yogyakarta. South Blitar was chosen, according to Rewang, for its isolated location, which

---

[20] From the beginning of 1968 until August of that year, the *New York Times* reported that 200 soldiers had deserted in East Java alone. "Reds in Indonesia Renew Campaign", *New York Times*, 11 Aug. 1968.

[21] Muhammad Jasin, *Saya Tidak Pernah Minta Ampun: Sebuah Memoar* (Jakarta: Pustaka Sinar Harapan, 1998), p. 69.

[22] Muhammad Jasin, interviewed by Vannessa Hearman, 2 Feb. 2009, Jakarta.

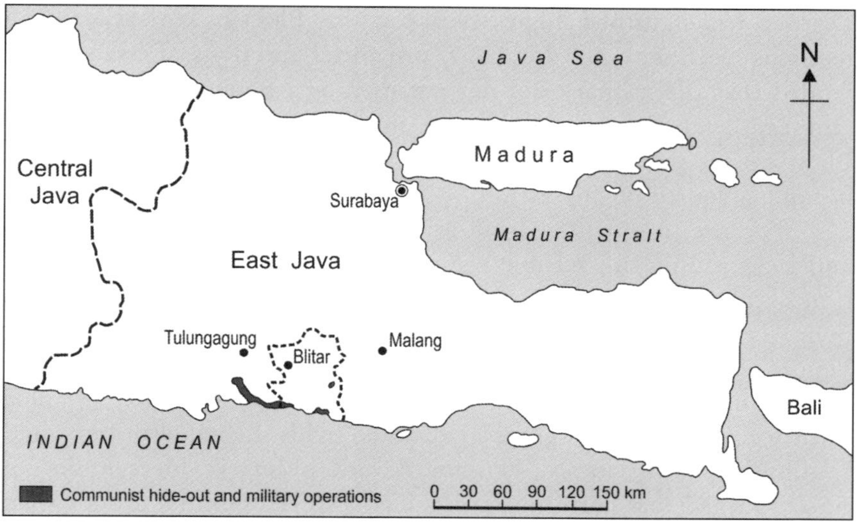

Map of the area of Blitar in East Java

attracted little government attention.[23] Before ordering large numbers of people to assemble in south Blitar, an advance party from the PKI's East Java Regional Council (Comite Daerah Besar, CDB) went to investigate conditions there. Rewang contrasted the fate of the "sleepy backwater" of south Blitar with that of Pare and Kediri, about 70 kilometres to the north, where land disputes were sharper and in 1965–66 thousands perished in the anti-communist killings.[24] The PKI's mobilisation and active strength in Pare and Kediri, and indeed other militant areas such as Klaten in Central Java marked these areas for special attention in the repression.[25] Though Blitar

[23] Rewang, interviewed by Vannessa Hearman, 14 Feb. 2009, Solo, Central Java.
[24] For accounts of the killings in Kediri and Pare, see Hermawan Sulistyo, *Palu Arit di Ladang Tebu: Sejarah Pembantaian Massal yang Terlupakan (Jombang-Kediri 1965–1966)* (Jakarta: Kepustakaan Populer Gramedia, 2000), and Pipit Rochijat, "Am I PKI or non-PKI?" trans. Benedict Anderson, *Indonesia* 40 (Oct. 1985), pp. 37–56.
[25] The Plantation Workers' Union of the Republic of Indonesia (Serikat Buruh Perkebunan Republik Indonesia, Sarbupri) was SOBSI's strongest union, with a claimed membership of 600,000 in 1957. See Iskandar Tedjasukmana, *Watak Politik Gerakan Serikat Buruh Indonesia*, trans. Oey Hay Djoen (Jakarta: Trade Union Rights Centre, 2008), p. 132.

District had returned high votes for the PKI in both the 1955 national elections and the 1957 provincial elections, Rewang contended that the military did not regard it as a potential base of militant resistance. Moreover, the low number of plantations in south Blitar meant there was not a strong presence of organised labour to become a source of opposition.

Because south Blitar is an arid area of limestone hills and caves and lacks a uniform, reliable water supply to enable wet rice cultivation or plantation development, the population has historically been poor. Leftist mass organisations such as the Indonesian Peasants' Union (Barisan Tani Indonesia, BTI) and Pemuda Rakyat already existed in the area. Performers in local *ludruk* or *ketoprak*, Javanese theatrical performance groups, affiliated with Lekra also cemented relationships with locals. Hasyim Asyari, a former local leader of Ansor, alleged that performances by Lekra-linked cultural groups were blasphemous and anti-religious and insulted Muslims.[26] In 1965, NU and Ansor members shut down some performances, in some cases using violence. Even so, the purges in south Blitar after 1 October were relatively minor. Party cadres and structures remained generally intact.[27] Markus Talam's testimony about the area in the final months of 1965 attested to the relatively safer situation. A civil servant who was detained for being a member of the All-Indonesia Forestry Workers' Union (Serikat Buruh Kehutanan Seluruh Indonesia, Sarbuksi), Talam escaped to south Blitar, where his parents lived. He explained: "This area was pretty safe. There was no operation here. There were visits by the military, along with civilians, those from Banser and Ansor, but they came here just to burn houses. You could say, over the three years to 1968, it was very safe."[28]

Party members proceeded to south Blitar by various forms of transport and, at times, for safety reasons, by circuitous routes. PKI members and sympathisers lived with the local population. The

---

[26] Hasyim Asyari, interviewed by Vannessa Hearman, 10 Feb. 2009, Blitar, East Java.

[27] André Liem, "Perjuangan Bersenjata PKI di Blitar Selatan dan Operasi Trisula", in *Tahun yang tak Pernah Berakhir: Memahami Pengalaman Korban 65: Esai-esai Sejarah Lisan*, ed. John Roosa, Ayu Ratih and Hilmar Farid (Jakarta: Elsam, 2004), p. 171.

[28] Markus Talam, interviewed by Vannessa Hearman, 10 Feb. 2009, Ngrejo, Blitar, East Java.

houses PKI leaders chose to accommodate those on the run were often far from main roads, military posts and civil administration offices. Locals helped the fugitives to familiarise themselves with the area and would often accompany the visitors, "as there was the thinking that cadres were priceless".[29] Those on the run used a system of couriers and "posts" to gather information and to organise meetings. Couriers included local youths who carried messages from villagers to the fugitives.

The PKI tried to rebuild itself through outreach activities and the construction of cells. Two of my respondents worked closely in such a cell. One of them explained that her work entailed seeking out former PKI members and sympathisers in the district she was assigned to. She then travelled by train and other forms of transport to locate them and to try to reorganise them.[30] One spoke of how leftists assassinated military and anti-communist figures,[31] but there has not been widespread acknowledgement among informants of these actions. Understandably, some former members of the base hesitate to acknowledge the use of any violence. Lestari and Putmainah cited childcare responsibilities as their reasons for not being politically involved and argued that they were in south Blitar only to avoid capture.[32] Lies Katno denied that the PKI was attempting to rebel (*memberontak*) and labelled this accusation as government propaganda.[33] She wrote that the group there had no weapons and that no deserters from the military ever joined it. Lies Katno maintained that traitors (*cecunguk*), PKI members who were arrested and then in interrogations betrayed the Party by agreeing to collaborate with the military, concocted claims of armed struggle.[34] Rather, according to her, the south Blitar group was motivated by the desire to seek refuge and to search for family members.

The PKI set up structures to train members in handling weapons, but at the time of the Trisula Operation the training and preparation seem still to have been rudimentary. According to Rewang, the Blitar

[29] DB, interviewed by Vannessa Hearman, 22 Feb. 2008, undisclosed location.
[30] DA, interviewed by Vannessa Hearman, 16 Feb. 2008, Surabaya, East Java.
[31] DB, interviewed by Vannessa Hearman, 22 Feb. 2008, undisclosed location.
[32] Lestari, interviewed by Vannessa Hearman, 26 Apr. 2007, Jakarta; Putmainah, interviewed by Vannessa Hearman, 1 Mar. 2008, Srengat, Blitar, East Java.
[33] Sari, "Blitar Selatan yang Dilupakan", p. 2.
[34] Sari, "Blitar Selatan yang Dilupakan", pp. 25–6.

base was supposed to support two primary tasks. The first, which was achieved, was to reconstruct the PKI by establishing an Emergency Central Committee (Comite Central Darurat). The second task was to build an armed capacity.[35] With regard to the latter, Rewang said they had succeeded in forming only one detachment with very few weapons. This is consistent with military records showing that they found just 34 old rifles and a few blowpipes amongst supporters of the base.[36]

Rewang realised that the Blitar base could not exist alone. If the PKI was serious about regrouping, there had to be several such bases. He gave examples of areas in East Java that the leadership had identified as potential bases, including the mountain areas of Kelud, Arjuno, Pandan and Lawu. The Emergency Central Committee had agreed to hold a conference attended by the Provincial Party Committees in Java to reach a formal agreement of when armed struggle would begin. This conference never took place, because the rebuilding work was interrupted by military operations.

There were differences within the PKI regarding the role of violence and when it could be most effectively deployed. To what degree "security incidents" such as hold-ups, armed robberies and killings should be blamed on the presence of PKI members in the area remains uncertain. There is some evidence of revenge attacks being carried out during this period. Though not a PKI leader as such, one young cadre claims to have taken part in several attacks. The targets were police and military posts, and civilians accused of carrying out anti-communist activities:

> At the time, we first needed to understand the situation. We had to be able to choose the right target, an easy target, something that could be done quickly and without leaving any trace. We could not carry any personal items that could be traced back to us. These actions could involve night-time robberies. Also other actions. For example, there was a military unit that we had, "our people" who wore military uniforms. We would go to the place of the [anti-communist] killers and say, let's go on operation in

[35] This paragraph draws on Rewang, interviewed by Vannessa Hearman, 14 Feb. 2009, Solo, Central Java.

[36] Semdam VIII Brawijaya, *Operasi Trisula*, p. 27.

> the south. On the way, when we thought it was safe, they would be killed.[37]

The cadre was critical, however, of the place and timing of the attacks. His criticisms were not about the use of violence, which he felt was justified.[38] Rather, his criticisms were against engaging in anti-military attacks "near the entry points into our [hiding] area, because that disadvantaged us; our access points were then closed off."[39] In Rewang's view, the fugitives' mistakes during this period were "leaks and uncontrolled actions leading to the government being suspicious".[40] The "uncontrolled actions" to which he referred were actions that attracted attention, that were too close to where the fugitives were hiding, and that led the military and its spies closer to their bases.

Such incidents did not escape the attention of either the military or the religious party and organisation the Revival of the Islamic Scholars (Nahdlatul Ulama, NU). The latter compiled a list of 60 cases of murder, robbery and kidnapping that were committed against its followers in East Java between June 1967 and February 1968.[41] NU members kept a close watch on any signs of the PKI's continuing existence. According to Agus Sunyoto, Banser members primarily acted as *hansip* (civilian defence guards) alongside the military.[42] They also acted as spies prior to the operation. In a 1996 interview, Romdhon, a founder of the Banser branch in Blitar, listed the religious leaders and government officials killed in revenge attacks.[43]

---

[37] DB, interviewed by Vannessa Hearman, 22 Feb. 2008, undisclosed location.

[38] DB, interviewed by Vannessa Hearman, 22 Feb. 2008, undisclosed location. DA, interviewed by Vannessa Hearman, 16 Feb. 2008, Surabaya, East Java.

[39] DB, interviewed by Vannessa Hearman, 22 Feb. 2008, undisclosed location.

[40] Rewang, interviewed by Vannessa Hearman, 14 Feb. 2009, Solo, Central Java.

[41] "List of NU Victims from the Second G30S/PKI: Killings, Robberies and Kidnappings in East Java", unpublished manuscript in Arsip Nasional Republik Indonesia, cited in Andree Feillard, *NU vis-à-vis Negara: Pencarian Isi, Bentuk dan Makna* (Yogyakarta: LKiS, 1999), p. 70.

[42] Agus Sunyoto, *Banser Berjihad Menumpas PKI* (Tulungagung: Pesulukan Toriqoh Agung, 1996), pp. 170–2.

[43] These were Kiai Maksum of Plosorejo, Kademangan; Susanto, a PNI figure and school principal from Panggungasri; Sastro, the head of the Department of Information in Binangun; as well as two Banser members in Panggung Duwet who were on duty as village guards. Sunyoto, *Banser Berjihad Menumpas PKI*, p. 166.

Romdhon pointed out that some of the local military commanders had no interest in Banser's concerns and they were forced to lobby other military commanders, who were more sympathetic with the goal of eradicating the PKI. According to one source, Banser acted independently of the Army and sent around 500 members to the villages of south Malang to investigate the Blitar leadership's suspicions about a resurgent PKI. In my interview with Hasyim Asyari, a former Ansor local leader in south Blitar, he confirmed that NU had infiltrated the PKI and possessed information about PKI membership.[44] During his command, however, Brawijaya commander Muhammad Jasin spearheaded a large-scale anti-PKI operation.[45]

With reports of attacks on police stations and local community leaders as evidence, pressure grew for Jasin to move against alleged PKI bases in the south Blitar and south Malang areas. The military began to arrest people working as couriers for the fugitives. Markus Talam had spoken of south Blitar as being peaceful in the latter part of 1965 when he first arrived there after fleeing the Blitar city authorities. Talam recalled clearly when this tide began to turn: "After 1966, the military, with those Islamic masses (*massa*), began to conduct operations here. This was because the government alleged here was the nest of PKI people."[46] Until just before the Trisula Operation in June 1968, the bases survived with support from local villagers, but the villages of south Blitar were coming under pressure by 1967. Ansor gangs conducted raids into various villages. Tensions grew as allegations mounted that "PKI remnants" were trying to rebuild. Hasyim Asyari confirmed that the military arrived in 1967 in response to news of the presence of PKI members. Hasyim gave information in his interview that clarified aspects of the relationship, and the tensions, between Ansor and the military. When I asked if there was a military operation there between 1965 and 1966, he replied:

> No, they only came from 1967 onwards ... In 1967 ABRI from Pasuruan, not even from Blitar, came but only stayed in the village. They didn't go out and search for PKI. The people (*rakyat*)

[44] Hasyim Asyari, interviewed by Vannessa Hearman, 10 Feb. 2009, Blitar, East Java.
[45] Harold Crouch, *The Army and Politics in Indonesia* (Ithaca: Cornell University Press, 1978), p. 233.
[46] Markus Talam, interviewed by Vannessa Hearman, 10 Feb. 2009, Blitar, East Java.

> did the searching. Ansor were the ones who searched. The result was that ABRI detained those we captured, but we were the ones who went out looking.[47]

Hasyim was contemptuous of the military, because he felt the military was riddled with PKI supporters. Second, in his opinion, Ansor and NU worked harder than the military in surveillance and investigation, only for the military to claim the glory. As a lifelong NU supporter, Hasyim felt that the organisation knew the community well and that the military alienated the community through its harsh tactics and thereby damaged NU's chances of winning them over after the military operation. He emphasised that Ansor declined to kill those they captured and placed ultimate responsibility for the death of any captured detainee on the military: "When we captured anyone ... we gave them to ABRI. We told our people, don't let them be killed (*jangan sampai dibunuh*). Hand them in (*disetorkan*)."[48] Although Ansor men were involved in many killings in the post-September 30th period there was a shift from early 1966 after NU leaders, under pressure from the military, began to discourage their members from participating in further killings (Chapter 5). While supporting the operation to rout out communists, Hasyim worried about the impact of the military strategy on relations between NU and local people.

A failure to arrest large numbers of people and put a decisive end to the communist presence, however, led the military to mount a more serious operation. The military began to overhaul the Hansip network, a key institution that provided an advance warning system for the PKI.[49] Previously, local people worked as Hansip. A cadre explained the PKI's reliance on the Hansip:

> We used the Hansip for our protection. The Hansip included "our people". Each time they [the military] entered, they failed. There was an idea [among our opponents] then that the old

---

[47] Hasyim Asyari, interviewed by Vannessa Hearman, 10 Feb. 2009, Blitar, East Java. ABRI denotes the Angkatan Bersenjata Republik Indonesia, Armed Forces of the Republic of Indonesia.

[48] Hasyim Asyari, interviewed by Vannessa Hearman, 10 Feb. 2009, Blitar, East Java.

[49] DB, interviewed by Vannessa Hearman, 22 Feb. 2008, undisclosed location.

> Hansip were the ones informing us. They were dismissed and the military brought their own [Hansip] from outside the area.[50]

Hansip who were not fully trusted by the military were dismissed and replaced by members of Banser, some of whom came from outside the Blitar area, who had agreed to work with the Army. The breakdown in the Hansip network helped to weaken the south Blitar base. Local government officials were replaced by "caretakers", who in the main were members of the military. In Pasiraman village, for example, nine village functionaries at various levels had military backgrounds.[51]

Trisula Operation

By early 1968, the military leadership in East Java had decided that anti-guerilla tactics were needed to deal with the fugitives — but it was not until May that the operation was launched.[52] The delay was attributable to doubts among the Army leadership in East Java about the extent of troop loyalty to the New Order in the Brawijaya command. On 20 May 1968, at a military briefing in Malang, Brawijaya Commander Jasin declared his decision to go ahead with a full-scale military operation that would rely heavily on infantry troops.[53] It was called the Trisula (trident) Operation in accordance with the trident symbol of the 18th Airborne Infantry Brigade (Brigif Linud 18/Trisula), the lead brigade in the operation, which was attached to the Army Strategic Reserve Command (Komando Cadangan Strategis Angkatan Darat, Kostrad). Colonel Witarmin, commander of this brigade, was in charge of the overall operation. At the final briefing on 31 May, Jasin assured platoon commanders that the operation was sanctioned under the 1966 Provisional People's Consultative Assembly (MPRS) decree banning the PKI. Witarmin advised soldiers who had "any doubt" in their minds against taking part in the operation.[54] It seemed unlikely that any soldier would draw attention

---

[50] DB, interviewed by Vannessa Hearman, 22 Feb. 2008, undisclosed location.

[51] DC, interviewed by Vannessa Hearman, 1 Mar. 2008, Blitar, East Java.

[52] Semdam VIII Brawijaya, *Operasi Trisula*, p. 43.

[53] Semdam VIII Brawijaya, *Operasi Trisula*, p. 46; Jasin, *Saya Tidak Pernah Minta Ampun*, p. 91.

[54] Semdam VIII Brawijaya, *Operasi Trisula*, p. 64.

to himself by withdrawing from the operation, so Witarmin's words constituted a warning.

Some days before the operation commenced, south Blitar was declared a closed area. Hansip and *wanra* (*sukarelawan rakyat*, "people's volunteers") maintained checkpoints, which were placed 300–400 metres apart.[55] The operation zone was divided into sectors, each of which was allocated to an infantry battalion. The Army deployed logistical support units such as the engineering, equipment, transport and field hospital corps, as well as religious advisers to the centre of the operation in Bakung. According to Army figures supplied to the *New York Times*, there were around 5,000 Army personnel from six battalions backed by Kostrad armour units and commandos, and some 3,000 "militia and village vigilantes armed with bamboo spears".[56] The operation formally ended with a ceremony on 7 September 1968.[57] The speed and size of the military response were key factors in the operation's success, as was the fact that they were dealing with largely unarmed civilians.

The way in which political fugitives and local villagers experienced the Trisula Operation is seldom discussed in New Order accounts. The population of south Blitar was subjected to much disruption, such as the redesign of villages and their relocation. Because of the relationship fostered between the fugitives and villagers, the operation focused on alienating the local people from the communists. The military argued in its propaganda that locals were being manipulated by communists and were thereby "caught in the crossfire". A propaganda poster depicted a communist man armed with a knife with his hand around the neck of a peasant, with the slogan in Javanese, "You should all understand that you are being used as bait."[58] The military's treatment of locals demonstrated, however, that they considered villagers as accomplices in supporting the fugitives.

---

[55] Semdam VIII Brawijaya, *Operasi Trisula*, p. 46.

[56] "Reds in Indonesia Renew Campaign", *New York Times*, 11 Aug. 1968.

[57] Mohammad Irsjad Sudiro, "Kenangan ketika Almarhum Pak Bas di Blitar Selatan", *Angkatan Bersendjata*, 11 Jan. 1969, cited in Dasman Djamaluddin, *Jenderal TNI Anumerta Basoeki Rachmat dan Supersemar*, 2nd ed. (Jakarta: Gramedia Widiasarana Indonesia, 2008), p. 108.

[58] Semdam VIII Brawidjaja, *Operasi Trisula*, picture 280 [no page number].

The military pointed out that the local population resisted cooperation with the military.[59] Local men interviewed in my research all testified to disappearing into the forest during daylight hours to avoid contact with the military.[60] For example, Markus Talam remembered:

> Every time there was an operation, I ran to the forest to avoid the operation. If there was no operation, I went home to eat. If there was, then I stayed away for two to three days. Based on experience, everybody would be forced to take part. The operation was crazy like that, so everybody ran away to avoid taking part.[61]

The military rooted out such intractables through a combination of persuasion and force. They dropped leaflets and pasted posters on trees throughout the area to convince people to support them. They cajoled and threatened locals. During the operation, a simple slogan of "3M" was adopted: *membantu*, *menyerah*, *mati* (assist, surrender or die). This outlined the options for both fugitives and local people: assist the military, surrender "with your weapons and ammunitions" or be killed.[62] The military drafted locals into day- and night-time patrols and enforced night curfews. As locals understood the terrain better than the military, they were forced to participate in fence-of-legs patrols to flush out fugitives in the forests. During these operations the military forced civilians to carry out acts of violence. Some villagers, who were implicated and placed on *wajib lapor* (obligation to report to the authorities), were forced to hit prisoners on the back of the head with iron bars to plunge them into deep vertical caves such as Luweng Tikus (Rat Hole).[63] Local men were

---

[59] Semdam VIII Brawijaya, *Operasi Trisula*, p. 86.

[60] DC and DD, interviewed by Vannessa Hearman, 1 Mar. 2008, Pasiraman, Blitar, East Java; Markus Talam, interviewed by Vannessa Hearman, 10 Feb. 2009, Ngrejo, Blitar, East Java.

[61] Markus Talam, interviewed by Vannessa Hearman, 10 Feb. 2009, Ngrejo, Blitar, East Java.

[62] Semdam VIII Brawijaya, *Operasi Trisula*, pp. 277–8.

[63] Mrs S, interviewed by Farid and Rukin, 17 Dec. 2005. Transcript of interview kindly provided by Blitar branch of Lakpesdam NU (Lembaga Kajian dan Pengembangan Sumber Daya Manusia Nahdlatul Ulama, Institute for Research and Human Resources Development) [hereafter Lakpesdam interview collection].

also required to dig mass graves and then fill them once the prisoners had been shot.[64]

The military evacuated whole villages to choke sources of support for the fugitives. On 23 June 1968, for example, local people were rounded up by Infantry Batallion 511 and placed in holding camps in Sukorejo and Maron villages.[65] Those the military considered to be "involved" were interrogated immediately. On the first day, according to one military account, 4,280 people were held, but only ten people were found to be involved in guerilla activities.[66] Villagers recalled these evacuations. A woman from Ngrejo village related how thousands of evacuated villagers were concentrated in Bakung village in August 1968.[67] The displaced people tore up a whole field of sweet potatoes to sate their hunger.[68] They had been told to bring their own food provisions. She recalled:

> In Bakung there was a whole field of sweet potatoes, all gone, ravaged by the refugees. What to do? People were hungry. No one dared to stop them, so the whole field disappeared. Tens of thousands of people were there from all over Bakung subdistrict, not just people from my village.[69]

According to the woman, in Bakung village, sounds of refugees being tortured were amplified across the fields. The military also infiltrated the ranks of refugees in order to undermine solidarity and arouse mutual suspicion. While the villages were evacuated, some of those on the run returned for supplies and found that soldiers were occupying their villages. Many who returned were shot.

The military's account of the nature of PKI resistance emphasised the communists' use of *ruba* (an acronym for *ruang bawah tanah*, underground spaces), which ranged from naturally occurring

---

[64] Paijo, interviewed by André Liem [n.d.], transcript and recording held at Indonesian Institute of Social History (Institut Sejarah Sosial Indonesia), Jakarta.
[65] Semdam VIII Brawijaya, *Operasi Trisula*, p. 102.
[66] Semdam VIII Brawijaya, *Operasi Trisula*, p. 103.
[67] Mrs J, interviewed by Farid and Rukin, 10 Dec. 2005, Blitar, East Java. Lakpesdam interview collection.
[68] Semdam VIII Brawidjaja, *Operasi Trisula*, p. 206.
[69] Mrs J, interviewed by Farid and Rukin, 10 Dec. 2005, Blitar, East Java. Lakpesdam interview collection.

caves to underground tunnels. This is represented in a diorama at the Museum of Communist Treachery in Jakarta, a museum established by the Armed Forces History Centre in 1981 to perpetuate the idea of the continuing threat of communism.[70] Visitors are shown a diorama of two soldiers taking part in the Trisula Operation walking on a hill. The soldiers are oblivious to the communists' underground tunnel beneath them, but the tunnel is visible to the museum audience.[71] Through such depictions, this military museum attempts to show the cunning and organisation of the communist "guerillas". The use of underground tunnels bolstered the idea that the Blitar base was a full-fledged guerilla movement comparable to the Viet Minh in Vietnam, an idea that the military promoted well after 1968.[72] Though underground bunkers were indeed deliberately constructed in some instances, Lies Sari maintained these were built as places to hide *after* the Trisula Operation commenced, not as a means to conduct guerilla operations. She wrote, "Before that, the term *ruba* had never been heard of before. We were all above ground (*di atas bumi*), [we] never hid underground (*tidak pernah sembunyi di bawah tanah*), what for?"[73] The fugitives hid in caves simply because they were naturally occurring features on the limestone south coast of East Java.

The rapid arrest of several key PKI leaders provided an early breakthrough when some of these men were convinced to provide information and work with the military. After his arrest on 9 June, East Java PKI leader Suwandi became a military "trophy" and the operation's mouthpiece to convince others to give themselves up.[74] Photographs are displayed in the Brawijaya Museum in Malang of his arrest, of the destruction of his underground hiding place, of the subsequent interrogation (with his hands bound with thick rope) and

---

[70] Katharine McGregor, *History in Uniform: Military Ideology and the Construction of Indonesia's Past* (Singapore: SEA Series, NUS Press, 2007), pp. 193–210.

[71] Pusat Sejarah ABRI, *Buku Panduan Monumen Pancasila Sakti Lubang Buaya* (Jakarta: Pusat Sejarah ABRI, 1997), p. 21.

[72] See, for example, Markas Besar Angkatan Bersenjata Republik Indonesia and Pusat Sejarah dan Tradisi ABRI, *40 Tahun Angkatan Bersenjata Republik Indonesia*, vol. 2: *Masa Pembangunan dan Pemantapan ABRI (1965–1985)* (Jakarta: Pusat Sejarah dan Tradisi ABRI, 1985), p. 15.

[73] Sari, "Blitar Selatan yang Dilupakan", p. 10.

[74] Semdam VIII Brawidjaja, *Operasi Trisula*, pp. 91–2.

finally of his speeches at village meetings exhorting people to stop assisting his former comrades.

According to the military, Suwandi identified the location of the hiding places of a number of PKI activists, including that of his wife, Lestari.[75] Similar tactics were used against other arrested prisoners. A Gerwani leader recounted how, while she was in detention, the military asked her to write a statement to convince others to surrender.[76] She refused, as in her opinion it was a pointless exercise: "You see the lack of respect with which people treated Suwandi and his words out there." She informed her captors that young people in the villages tore down and ground into the dust posters containing Suwandi's exhortations, showing disgust at what they perceived as his treachery. The military nevertheless used important detainees to break morale among those on the run. Former political prisoners expressed frustration at the decision by some of their leaders to cooperate with the military. But they also recognised that, in any case, with these arrests, the military was gaining the upper hand.

The participation of Banser in the operations led to differences between local leaders and the military. As noted above, Hasyim Asyari pointed out that NU leaders saw an opportunity to win over villagers and rank-and-file supporters of the banned mass organisations, but the military's approach was harming their cause:

> We suggested to our ranks that they had to study closely who was really PKI and what other groups were "made out to be PKI". If there was an ordinary farmer whose hat bore the letters BTI, they were usually saved, because they knew nothing. *If we were to follow ABRI's instructions, these ordinary people would have been finished.* But with NU there, these farmers came to us voluntarily.[77]

Although Hasyim is no doubt motivated to depict NU favourably, his comments reveal some of the tensions among those who were ostensibly fighting for the same cause, to eradicate communism from south Blitar.

---

75 Semdam VIII Brawidjaja, *Operasi Trisula*, pp. 91–2.

76 DA, interviewed by Vannessa Hearman, 16 Feb. 2008, Surabaya, East Java.

77 Hasyim Asyari, interviewed by Vannessa Hearman, 10 Feb. 2009, Blitar, East Java; emphasis added.

By early July, the net was closing in. On 12 July 1968, Surachman, the former Secretary General of the PNI, was found and killed.[78] With the killing and arrests, PKI activists fled the villages and many went westwards into Tulungagung District through the forests on the south coast.[79] When she decided to flee into the forest, Lestari left her months-old baby with a villager whose own child had recently died. As the patrols came closer, the villager became very frightened and abandoned the baby at the entrance of the local cemetery in the hope someone else would look after her.[80] On the morning of 2 August 1968, Lestari was eventually arrested with two other women and their guard, a young man. They were all winched out with ropes from the cave they were hiding in because of the steep angle.[81] Many fugitives hid in the teak forests near the villages. To intensify the pressure, military intelligence agents directed people to uproot edible plants in and around the forests to starve the fugitives. Three respondents spoke of eating raw cassava, cassava leaves, sweet potatoes and snails collected from people's forest gardens to avoid starvation while they were on the run. One explained how they survived in the forest: "Usually at night, we stole plants belonging to local people, for example sweet potatoes, which we then roasted. In the afternoon, we hid. At night we made a fire, we roasted snails and ate them".[82] After escaping encirclement at Gayas Cave, where Putmainah was arrested, DB survived in this fashion for eight days before being captured on 28 July in the southern part of Tulungagung District, in an area called Besole.

DA spoke of the experience of evading capture in the Ilik-Ilik teak forests. Her remarks demonstrate chaos, distress and a sense of time dissolving:

> We kept being chased everywhere. The last operation, where we should head ... I no longer had any idea of the terrain, where we should head for safety. We had to walk everywhere.
>
> We rested on the edge of a forest. Dawn arrived. There was a shepherd passing by, and he reported us to the nearest village.

---

[78] Semdam VIII Brawijaya, *Operasi Trisula*, p. 113. On p. 116 he is named as a PKI leader.

[79] Semdam VIII Brawijaya, *Operasi Trisula*, p. 116.

[80] Lestari, interviewed by Vannessa Hearman, 26 Apr. 2007, Jakarta.

[81] Semdam VIII Brawijaya, *Operasi Trisula*, p. 152 reports this arrest.

[82] DB, interviewed by Vannessa Hearman, 22 Feb. 2008, undisclosed location.

> Dozens of people arrived. Some of us ran to the right, I ran to the left. I spent three nights in the forest. I ate raw cassava that people were growing in their gardens. In the morning I stayed still and hid again in the bushes.
>
> In the end, I saw a light in the distance. I thought it must have been a village. I went there. When I arrived, a farmer came out. He said (in Javanese), "What are you doing here? All your friends left this afternoon".[83]

My interviewee, who was sheltering in the area, understood the farmer to mean that he knew of her fugitive status and was informing her that the military had captured her comrades earlier on that day, 13 July 1968. She was arrested not long after this encounter with the farmer, when some local villagers reported her presence to the military and the Civilian Defence Guards. She, like other women arrested in this area, was transported to Malang Women's Prison.

By the end of July, key PKI leaders had been arrested and were then sent to prison. Ruslan Wijayasastra was captured on 13 July 1968, while warming himself in the kitchen of a local villager during an unseasonal downpour.[84] Munir was captured on the same day in one of the underground emplacements. Rewang was captured on 20 July during a military operation. Many of the men and women who were associated with the PKI were tried, and served long jail sentences (including some life sentences) or received the death penalty for crimes against the state. Those executed in the mid-1980s included Muhammad Munir, Gatot Lestario, Joko Untung, Pratomo and Rustomo.[85] In their trial in the district capital in 1975, seven years after their arrest, two of my respondents (DA and DB) were accused of actively trying to resurrect the PKI. In their sentencing, prison time already served was not taken into account. They were not released until the early 1990s.

Prisoners of the south Blitar operation were treated more harshly than other political prisoners. Several detainees in the Malang Women's Prison stopped menstruating for two years due to severe malnutrition. The Trisula Operation reverberated in prisons in Java,

---

[83] DA, interviewed by Vannessa Hearman, 16 Feb. 2008, Surabaya, East Java.

[84] Semdam VIII Brawidjaja, *Operasi Trisula*, p. 137.

[85] United Nations Economic and Social Council, "Report by the Special Rapporteur, Mr. S. Amos Wako, Summary or arbitrary executions", Commission on Human Rights, Forty-second session, Agenda item 12, 7 Feb. 1986.

such as Kalisosok in Surabaya, where prisoners remembered being treated worse during this time.[86] Many of the male south Blitar prisoners served their time in Pamekasan Prison on the island of Madura. Local people in south Blitar generally served shorter sentences or were required to report regularly to local military authorities.

The military's official tallies from the operation were 257 arrested and three people (a "PKI leader" and two Army corporals) killed.[87] From accounts of Army shootings and burnings of caves, the actual figure is likely to be much higher. The *New York Times* published a figure on 11 August 1968, most likely supplied by the Army, of 2,000 "party members" killed or arrested over a period of four months leading up to August 1968.[88] The career of Lieutenant General M. Jasin, the Brawijaya Commander, shone with Trisula's success. Jasin was promoted in rank and position, and in 1968 Suharto presented him the Sam Karya Anugraha award for service excellence.[89] By December 1972, Jasin was Deputy Chief of Staff of the Indonesian Armed Forces.[90]

Local women experienced the operation in a way that was different from men. According to one woman, women in south Blitar suddenly "became widowed" when the men fled into the forests.[91] For many women, being widowed in a figurative sense quickly altered into being widowed in a real sense. Around August 1968, after shooting her husband dead in the family's field, soldiers forced a woman, then 20 years old, to strip to her underwear and lie face down on a wooden bench in her kitchen. The soldiers beat her and examined her for a "stamp" that Gerwani members were rumoured to carry on their bodies. After the operation ended, the woman had to report to the military authorities in Ngrejo village and was forced to cook for the soldiers every morning for one month. Another young woman was widowed when her husband disappeared while in custody in 1968. She was forced to be a concubine of the military

---

[86] See Adam Soepardjan, *Mendobrak Penjara Rezim Soeharto: Kisah Nyata Anak Manusia* (Yogyakarta: Ombak, 2004), pp. 268–70.

[87] Semdam VIII Brawidjaja, *Operasi Trisula*, p. 127.

[88] "Reds in Indonesia Renew Campaign", *New York Times*, 11 Aug. 1968.

[89] Jasin, *Saya Tidak Pernah Minta Ampun*, p. 99.

[90] Jasin, *Saya Tidak Pernah Minta Ampun*, p. 95.

[91] This paragraph draws on Mrs J, interviewed by Farid and Rukin, 10 Dec. 2005. Lakpesdam interview collection.

village head for the duration of his seven-year posting. The soldier promised that he could keep her brother out of prison if she agreed to be his concubine, though this promise never eventuated. The woman developed a deep attachment to her only child, the legacy from her marriage, and carried this child wherever she went. She forbade her soldier "husband" from having anything to do with the child, an important form of control she could exercise. Her highly protective behaviour probably reflected her concern that the authorities would remove the child from her (see below).

Rehabilitation

What happened in south Blitar once the guns were silent? As a result of the operation, the area long remained stigmatised. East Java Governor Mohammad Noer and the district head of Blitar set up offices in Bakung to oversee a programme of "rehabilitation".[92] This altered the local way of life, and not necessarily for the better. The end of the operation spelled the beginning of more permanent removal, rather than just temporary evacuation, of villagers from their original places of residence.[93] The local government relocated villages closer to the main roads to enable surveillance. The villagers were thus moved farther away from their food-growing areas near the forest, besides which the military required them to take an armed military escort when tending to their gardens.[94] This displacement created a problem with land tenure and food cultivation. Markus Talam returned from his imprisonment in Buru Island to find that a dozen families were occupying his parents' land.[95] These families had been moved there after the Trisula Operation and had received new land certificates from local officials. A state primary school occupied another part of the land. According to Talam, after the fall of Suharto in 1998 some families returned to the lands abandoned during the forced relocation.

Road construction throughout the area opened up south Blitar to trade and commerce, which brought benefits and lessened the area's isolation. Initially built to enable the military to conduct its

---

[92] Djamaluddin, *Jenderal TNI anumerta Basoeki Rachmat dan Supersemar*, p. 110.
[93] Semdam VIII Brawidjaja, *Operasi Trisula*, p. 206.
[94] Semdam VIII Brawidjaja, *Operasi Trisula*, p. 168.
[95] Markus Talam, interviewed by Vannessa Hearman, 10 Feb. 2009, Ngrejo, Blitar, East Java.

operations, in particular to use military vehicles, these roads were constructed out of limestone.[96] They were then improved and widened. The paths that villagers used earlier were either closed off or patrolled, thus forcing the population onto the newly constructed or repaired major roads and enabling greater surveillance of movements in the area.[97]

During the rehabilitation phase, the military recommended that children whose parents (mainly fathers) were killed in military operations be removed from the community. These orphans were considered a future threat. In the military's view:

> The high number of orphaned children as a result of this physical [military] operation is an issue that needs special attention. In the process of returning south Blitar to the realm of Pancasila [the Indonesian national philosophy], it was worrying that the education of these children, orphaned as a result of the physical operation, could result in the desire for revenge for the deaths of their fathers, if the education continued to be left to their mothers. This will create more disorder. Therefore the best thing to do would be to collect them together in a holding place (*penampungan*) with special guidance to be provided.[98]

The practice of removing children from families in which the fathers had been killed may have continued into the early 1970s.[99] The East Java Social Services Agency oversaw the practice of removing children and placing them in foster care with families outside of the south Blitar region. The majority of 55 families surveyed in 1971 by a joint team from the Social Services Agency and the Teachers' Training Institute (IKIP) in Surabaya, however, were unwilling to surrender their children, and the survey team recommended ongoing visits to convince families to participate in the "foster scheme".

---

[96] Team Survey Dinas Research Disorganisasi Sosial, *Laporan survey masalah kurang makan, salah makan di desa Bakung, Sumberdadi dan sekitarnya, Blitar Selatan, Jawa Timur tahun 1970* (Yogyakarta: Balai Penelitian dan Peninjauan Sosial, Departemen Sosial Republik Indonesia, n.d.).

[97] Semdam VIII Brawidjaja, *Operasi Trisula*, p. 192.

[98] Semdam VIII Brawidjaja, *Operasi Trisula*, p. 221.

[99] Institut Keguruan dan Ilmu Pendidikan (IKIP), Surabaya and Balai Penelitian Pendidikan, "Laporan Pelaksanaan Survey Foster-care tentang Anak-anak Korban G.30.S/P.K.I. di daerah Blitar Selatan dan Tjalon Keluarga Asuhan di Ketjamatan Bagor Kabupaten Ngandjuk dan di Kotamadya Blitar" (Surabaya, 1971).

Conclusion

In his defence plea, his last opportunity to reflect on the disaster that had befallen the PKI and also an address to any remaining followers, Muhammad Munir dubbed south Blitar "the new seat of the PKI Politburo during the epilogue to the September 30th Movement".[100] In this way, Munir linked the south Blitar phase of the PKI's history directly to the aftermath of the September 30th Movement, to the killings and the wave of arrests of PKI members and sympathisers. These mass killings obliged the surviving leadership of the PKI to identify where the PKI had made mistakes and to consider how the Party could be salvaged. They established the Blitar base for two main reasons: to evade the arrests and killings in Java and to rebuild the Party. Nevertheless, by the time of the military operation in 1968, the bases were still in a fledgling state. The few arms, uniforms and resources of those involved in the base reveal how exaggerated was the military depiction of the bases as guerilla hideouts. As two US Consulate officials reported after their visit to south Blitar, the Trisula Operation was a resounding success because south Blitar was a "soft target".[101] The bases were primarily attempts by the surviving Party leadership to establish refuges from the violence and to formulate new ways of resisting after the failure of the strategy of democratic engagement. My interviewees, however, claimed they fled to this area only for self-protection.

Military representations of the Blitar bases as guerilla hideouts, of the bases' inhabitants as traitors and of the Trisula Operation as a decisive victory over the PKI have been instrumental in the way the episode has been understood ever since. This is true even for supporters of the Communist Party who did not participate in the bases.[102] What transpired in south Blitar quickly became a forgotten, stigmatised history rather than a heroic and almost unarmed last stand.

---

[100] Muhammad Munir, "Membela Kemerdekaan, Demokrasi dan Keadilan".

[101] Department of State Airgram A-12, "Inspection Trip to South Blitar", Report from DT Kenney, US Consulate Surabaya to American Embassy Jakarta, 29 June 1969, Record Group 59, State Department Central Files 1964–1966, POL 18 INDON, National Archives and Records Administration.

[102] For a discussion of the contested views about the base amongst former political prisoners, see Vannessa Hearman, "Guerrillas, Guns, and Knives? Debating Insurgency in South Blitar, East Java, 1967–68", *Indonesia* 89 (2010): 61–91.

9

West Bali: Experiences and Legacies of the 1965–66 Violence

Mary Ida Bagus

Although the armed repression against the Indonesian Left ended with the military-led operations against Communist bases in Blitar and Purwodadi in 1968 and 1969, for long after this people associated with the Indonesian Communist Party (Partai Komunis Indonesia, PKI) continued to suffer persecution in prisons, prison camps and society. Former prisoners and the families of those associated with the Left were barred from working in the civil service and subjected to continuing state and community surveillance. For 32 years of the New Order regime, Indonesians were indoctrinated to believe that members of the PKI were dangerous subversives, treacherous and traitorous. As demonstrated in Chapter 2, there were inconsistencies in the official versions of the September 30th Movement; yet one constant message was that followers of the PKI were miscreants who had brought disaster to their families, their communities and the nation. Within local communities, however, attitudes towards those targeted in the post-September 30th violence were often more complicated.

This chapter examines how and why people in one community in Jembrana, west Bali, experienced or participated in various forms of violence, including murder, rape, destruction of property, imprisonment and exile. There are very few written accounts of these actions by witnesses or perpetrators in Bali. Interviews therefore provide a rich source of information about people's experiences of and responses to the violent social upheaval after September 1965. My research, based on interviews and discussions between 1982 and 2009 with hundreds of Balinese people, reveals complex and varied personal experiences, including stories of terror, survival, complicity and victimisation as well as patterns of mourning, remorse and commemoration that are attached to particular sites of memory. Although many survivors of the violence did become social outcasts in accordance with the will of the Suharto regime, others found ways of reintegrating into local communities. Despite official legitimisation of the violence, some people also experienced difficulties in reconciling themselves with their experiences of witnessing or participating in such brutality.

The ambiguities in the way people think about the violence in Jembrana are highlighted by the common usage of President Sukarno's term "Gestok" (October 1st Movement, Gerakan Satu Oktober) to describe the period of anti-communist purges that began in late 1965 and continued into 1966.[1] In Jembrana Gestok refers to multiple events and circumstances, including arrest, torture, murder, rape, suspicion and the enduring social stigmatisation that attached to affiliation with the PKI. It elicits the traumatic period of localised violence that followed the murder of the generals in Jakarta, rather than the initial murders that officially became the catalyst and justification for the anti-PKI purges and regime change. The Balinese expressions "kena Gestok" and "seda Gestok" refer to public censure or death for PKI affiliation. "Kena Gestok" implies victimisation, though not necessarily empathy for the victims. The generalised term "Gestok" avoids implicating anyone in the violence. "Seda Gestok" includes the polite Balinese word for death, *seda*. This is clearly a euphemism, because people didn't just die during Gestok, they were murdered.[2] The term is ambiguous because although it also obscures the actions of the perpetrators, the polite form honours and humanises victims

[1] See the discussion of "Gestok" in Chapter 1 of this volume.

[2] Groups of victims sent to other areas to be killed were euphemistically called "allotments" (*jatah*). I Ngurah Suryawan, *Ladang Hitam di Pulau Dewa: Pembantaian Massal di Bali 1965* (Yogyakarta: Galangpress, 2007), p. 225.

murdered during the anti-communist purges. As this example suggests, nuance was one way to undermine and circumvent the official socio-symbolic identity imposed on PKI affiliates. Some people in Jembrana used "seda Gestok" subversively as a statement of personal experience, empowering families and communities to recall the loss, grief and fear of those times. Their anger and regrets are embedded in the language, publicly indiscernible but always present.[3]

Jembrana was the first point of the outbreak of violence in Bali. Although the atrocities committed in Jembrana were repeated all over Bali, the region is atypical because it is so far from insular Bali and so close to Java. In addition, it has a large established Muslim population. By 1965, Jembrana had produced two major political leaders: Bali's first Governor, Anak Agung Suteja, who was associated with the PKI, and Guru Wedastra Suyasa, the leader of the Balinese branch of the Indonesian National Party (Partai Nasional Indonesia, PNI). In the period preceding the Gestok purges, these particularities created unusual local political conditions that had ramifications for the rest of Bali. After discussing these local political conditions, the chapter concentrates on experience and memory of the violence in Jembrana. The case studies focus on one Hindu village about 2 kilometres from the capital of Jembrana District, Negara, but I also refer to people, events and places in other parts of Jembrana.

Politics in Jembrana before Gestok

Although regarded as a backwater of Bali, Jembrana in the 1960s was a hotly contested political space. Political and social influences flowed from Java across the Bali Strait and national-local, modernist-traditionalist and leftist-conservative political dichotomies predisposed gangs of young men to violent factional clashes.[4] The Dutch and Japanese occupations, and the subsequent independence struggle

---

[3] See Degung Santikarma, "Menulis Sejarah dan Membaca Kuasa: Politik pasca-1965 di Bali", in *Perspektif Baru: Penulisan Sejarah Indonesia*, ed. Henk Schulte Nordholt, Bambang Purwanto and Ratna Saptari (Denpasar: Yayasan Obor Indonesia, KITLV-Jakarta and Pustaka Larasan, 2008), pp. 201–15.

[4] See Geoffrey Robinson, *The Dark Side of Paradise: Political Violence in Bali* (Ithaca and London: Cornell University Press, 1995), pp. 264–71.

against the Dutch of 1945–49, entrenched violence as a male rite of passage and an important component of manly social interactions.[5]

Locals in Jembrana usually followed the political affiliations of their kin and caste. This is not to deny that some individuals had strong ideological views, but according to my informants, the majority of locals in Jembrana exhibited loyalties that reflected patron-client relationships, expressed in hierarchical caste relations as well as in vertical relations from parent to child, older male sibling to younger siblings and educated/wealthy males to less fortunate extended family.

Although Suteja, a charismatic modernising aristocrat (*triwangsa*) from the Negara royal family (Puri Negara) ostensibly abnegated all ties with class and caste,[6] many people followed Suteja's political leanings and joined the PKI precisely because of their traditional client group (*panjak*) relations. Suteja's cousin Agung Denia was the local leader of the PKI in Jembrana, and a number of men connected with the royal family were also active in the PKI. Further entrenched rivalries between the local ruling houses ensured that rival royal families and their client groups favoured the PNI.[7]

Attitudes to aristocratic domination determined people's political affiliations. Suteja's rival Wedastera Suyasa of the PNI was a commoner (*sudra*) and active in the nascent *Pasek* commoner movement that rejected caste hierarchy.[8] In Jembrana, political allegiance was therefore most often influenced either by affirmation of patron-client affiliation with an aristocratic group or reaction against aristocratic domination.

Jembrana, traditionally a destination for exiles and migrants from other parts of Bali, displayed an inverted form of class and caste

[5] Robinson, *Dark Side of Paradise*, p. 300. Henk Schulte Nordholt, "A Genealogy of Violence", in *Roots of Violence in Indonesia: Contemporary Violence in Historical Perspective*, ed. F. Columbijn and T.J. Lindblad (Leiden: KITLV Press, 2002), pp. 81–103.

[6] Wayan Sendher, interviewed by Mary Ida Bagus, 23 Sept. 2001, Mendoyo, Jembrana, Bali.

[7] Suryawan, *Ladang Hitam*, p. 189.

[8] Adrian Vickers, *Bali: A Paradise Created* (Ringwood: Penguin Books, 1989), pp. 164–5.

politics.[9] Many from the high castes were landless peasants, and many commoners were landowners, particularly in the "outer areas" of the region, away from the established royal houses.[10] Members of commoner groups were thus often better off and better educated. Wedastera Suyasa was an example of this upward mobility. He came from the "outer" village of Penyaringan, where, prior to the rewriting of commoner genealogies in the 1950s,[11] many residents belonged to the indigenous title group Guru. After Gestok, most of the Guru kin groups associated with the PNI took on the title I Gusti Ngurah (I Gusti Ayu for women) to fit the entrenched caste classification for hereditary leaders, whilst those socially emasculated groups affiliated with the PKI retained their Guru titles. As Robinson noted, "in Bali the conflict between cultural conservatives and iconoclasts was, to some extent isomorphic with conflict based on class interests".[12]

President Sukarno appointed Suteja as Bali's first Governor in 1958. By 1965, both Suteja and President Sukarno were understood to have leftist if not communist sympathies.[13] This relationship briefly and tragically established Jembrana as a PKI stronghold with fierce opposition from the PNI and the Muslim party Revival of the Islamic Scholars (Nahdlatul Ulama, NU).

NU boasted a significant support base in Loloan, a large Muslim settlement on the outskirts of Negara town with an ethnically mixed population of Buginese, East Javanese and Madurese.[14] There were many Muslim fishing settlements along the coast as well. Reflecting this sizeable Muslim presence, Jembrana had the only NU seat in a Balinese provincial Executive Council, and two seats each for the PNI and PKI. Badung was the only other Balinese district with a balanced PNI-PKI representation. Elsewhere in Bali, the PNI

---

[9] Mary Ida Bagus, "From the Margins of History: A Long Babad of Jembrana, Bali", PhD dissertation, University of Newcastle, 2006.

[10] These previously uninhabited areas were settled during the early Dutch colonial period. Ida Bagus, "From the Margins of History", p. 107.

[11] Vickers, *Bali*, p. 164.

[12] Robinson, *Dark Side of Paradise*, p. 271.

[13] Elected members of the Balinese Regional Assembly had their own PNI candidate for Governor and opposed Suteja's appointment. Robinson, *Dark Side of Paradise*, pp. 209–10, 213.

[14] Ida Bagus, "From the Margins of History", p. 117.

was in the majority.[15] These political patterns were significant for the outcomes from 1965 onwards because in Jembrana the PNI, NU and PKI all had large, active memberships.

In 1965, Party militia (tameng) who defended both PKI and PNI party cadres were a common sight, sporting a red hibiscus flower behind one ear and a sword (*klewang*) in the belt. In Jembrana, the thuggery of PKI tameng at opposition party meetings was legendary — heckling, throwing snakes into the crowds, and starting fights.[16] They were emboldened by patronage from the Negara royal family and, by extension, the Governor of Bali. One PKI tameng in Jembrana was infamous for thrusting his sword into the woven palm walls of village homes and demanding that the terrified occupants come out and attend PKI campaign meetings. I have heard many first-hand accounts about this local PKI tameng from within his home village. This flagrant disregard for political freedom was a mimesis of the social system where despite emerging critiques of the caste system the masses were generally still bound to strict hierarchies of caste and allegiance. According to my informants, by mid-1965 social conflict and mutual suspicion pervaded village populations as they were buffeted by the political manoeuvrings of their leaders.

Gestok

After 1 October 1965, Bali was tense. Anti-communist killings had escalated in Java after Suharto's appointment as Army Commander on 16 October, reaching the town of Banyuwangi, just across the Bali Strait, by 18 October.[17] The first anti-PKI actions in Jembrana were the arrests of local PKI cadres and leaders of affiliated groups from villages in October 1965. Local village headmen used official lists to direct local PNI tameng and the drivers of military trucks from the military headquarters in Negara to the homes of victims. According to informants, these initial arrests were violent and accompanied by looting and property damage. Those detained were delivered to Toko Wong, a large warehouse in Loloan Barat, on the

[15] Robinson, *Dark Side of Paradise*, p. 216.
[16] Ibid.
[17] See Chapter 4.

outskirts of the town of Negara.[18] The property was commandeered because the police cells in Negara were unable to accommodate the initial roundup of 300 PKI leaders, ostensibly held there to keep the peace.[19] The ethnic Chinese owner, Wie Bian Chie, had disappeared[20] and, according to local rumour, been killed. Ethnic Chinese were highly visible targets due to their property holdings and their relationships with the Negara royal family through marriage and trade, but very few were murdered in Jembrana in 1965–66.

An incident in Tegal Badeng (3 kilometres west of Negara town) was the trigger for wholesale violence. On 30 November 1965 Regar, a military intelligence officer, and Suparmin and Aripin, members of the NU-affiliated Ansor militia from Loloan, were killed when they reportedly attempted to break up a secret PKI meeting.[21] However, it is not certain that PKI members killed them. I Ngurah Suryawan suggests that this story was circulated to justify an anti-PKI backlash.[22] Eyewitnesses have claimed that PKI members were sheltering en masse for protection after the October arrests. Furthermore, the victims that night may have died as a result of "friendly fire" from the ranks of a large Ansor militia that had descended on Tegal Badeng.[23] The graves for these three men in the Negara National Heroes' Cemetery (Taman Pahlawan Nasional), however, reinforce local opinion that they were indeed murdered by PKI members.

Stories surrounding the killings of these three men have shaped public perceptions of the violence that followed. In particular, their demise serves to naturalise the coalition between the military and the Ansor militia in Jembrana before the anti-PKI killings even started and to provide a more localised justification for why the PKI had to be destroyed. It was rumoured that PKI members in Tegal Badeng were meeting to plan the liberation of prisoners at Toko Wong, so on the night of the Tegal Badeng attack the 300 PKI prisoners were murdered.[24] Based on reports of the planned communist uprising

---

18 EA, interviewed by Mary Ida Bagus, 9 Oct. 2001, Batuagung, Jembrana, Bali.

19 Suryawan, *Ladang Hitam*, p. 201

20 I Ngurah Suryawan, *Jejak Jejak Manusia Merah: Siasat Politik Kebudayaan Bali* (Yogyakarta: Buku Baik and ELSAM, 2005), p. 166.

21 Robinson, *Dark Side of Paradise*, p. 295.

22 Suryawan, *Ladang Hitam*, p. 201fn22.

23 Suryawan, *Ladang Hitam*, pp. 151–2.

24 Suryawan, *Ladang Hitam*, pp. 147, 201.

and the killings of the three anti-communists, an attack began on the Party stronghold of Tegal Badeng, an area hemmed in by Loloan and the coastal Muslim communities of Pengambengan and Cupel. The mass killings had begun in Jembrana and soon spread throughout Bali.

Two days later, the Negara palace compound was attacked and Suteja's family were singled out for arrest or death.[25] On 2 December 1965, Sayid Mustafa Algadri, leader of the Loloan branch of Jamiatul Muslimin Indonesia (a local NU group),[26] led bands of "Ansor Jawa Madura" from "Loloan Jawa" (the East Javanese enclave in Loloan) to ransack the palace. Widagda Suyasa, the brother of Balinese PNI leader Wedastera Suyasa, joined Algadri with five truckloads of Balinese vigilantes from local villages.[27] At the beginning of the violence, locals attempted to balance traditional allegiances with the fast-changing political environment. Initial attacks on the palace by PNI neighbours were tentative. On 4 December, residents also bravely prevented a few truckloads of PNI supporters from Buleleng District, on the north coast of Bali, from destroying a Negara royal temple (*Pamerajan*). After a further attack, a sign was erected saying the royal family and palace was protected by the armed forces.[28] These eyewitness reports from members of the Negara royal family indicate that, initially at least, Balinese from the environs of the royal palace attempted to resist the violence that was descending on their community. The December attacks on the Negara palace destroyed the dual seats of power in Jembrana: the source of PKI influence and the pre-eminent royal house. This was a prologue for the mass killings that followed in the villages.

There is no hard evidence of the numbers killed in Jembrana. According to a US memorandum, by 9 December some 3,000 members of the PKI had been killed in west Bali.[29] Geoffrey Robinson

---

[25] Robinson, *Dark Side of Paradise*, p. 300.

[26] Suryawan, *Ladang Hitam*, p. 145.

[27] Anak Agung Ketut Parintosa and Anak Agung Made Suryawan, "Silsilah Keluarga Sri Kresna Kepakisan Puri Ageng Negara", unpublished manuscript, 1984, p. 38.

[28] Parintosa and Suryawan, *Silsilah*, p. 38.

[29] Telegram A-391, US Embassy Jakarta to State Department, 13 Dec. 1965, containing "Confidential Memorandum of Conversation," dated 9 Dec. 1965, Record Group 59, State Department Central Files 1964–1966, POL 2 INDON, National Archives and Records Administration.

quotes an eyewitness estimate of 6,000 murders during the first three days of December.[30] In the village of Batuagung alone, I estimate that at least 200 people were murdered in December 1965. Some were attacked at home, while others were "processed" by the village headman before being taken away.

According to informants, four groups worked together to facilitate the arrests and killings in Jembrana: the local military, the Ansor militia from Loloan and East Java, the local PNI militia (tameng) who led the Pancasila Front, and local village headmen. In discussions of the killings, Balinese informants mentioned the role of key characters in the killings, all of whom were Muslim, particularly Mustafa Sayid Algadari, Miskar, a Madurese military truck driver, and Lieutenant Colonel Safroni, the Javanese District Military Commander stationed at the military headquarters in Negara.

The coalition of Ansor and PNI militias was forged during the attacks on the Negara royal house. Many informants told me that the persistent presence of Ansor militia and the local military during the period of arrests and murders that took place in their villages made it difficult for families to bargain for lives, or at least for the lives of anyone who had come to the attention of the authorities. Some PKI members and affiliates were able to buy their survival with land titles and other forms of wealth.[31] The conditions for such deals were a low public profile, no local enemies and enough material assets to bribe officials. These criteria were hard to fulfil, and many PKI affiliates never arrived at official places of arrest because they were slaughtered in their homes or along the road as they tried to escape vigilante groups of neighbours.[32] Although there appeared to be no single authority that oversaw the initial killings, even the most eager local perpetrators often accused of exacting revenge on their neighbours did so with a sense of official impunity rather than spontaneous

[30] Robinson, *Dark Side of Paradise*, p. 298.

[31] One PNI village head became very wealthy from protecting PKI members. IB Tirtayasa, interviewed by Mary Ida Bagus, Feb. 2009, Melbourne.

[32] Mary Ida Bagus, "Transcending Transgression with Transgression: Inheriting Forsaken Souls in Bali", in *Celebrating Transgression: Method and Politics in Anthropological Studies of Culture*, ed. Ursula Rao and John Hutnyk (New York and Oxford: Berghahn Books, 2006), p. 107.

bloodlust.[33] As was the case elsewhere in Bali, known PKI members were forced to seek out and murder targeted PKI leaders to prove their loyalty to the new anti-PKI forces.[34] In some cases these actions saved their lives; in others they were subsequently murdered anyway.

The initial killings in Jembrana had symbolic significance for the violence that followed throughout Bali. Suteja's position as Governor of Bali, his status as heir apparent in the Negara royal house and his association with the PKI were pivotal to delaying the onset of anti-PKI violence. The devastating attacks on the royal house broke November's tense stand-off, during which Suteja initially went to ground while his associates in Bali waited for instructions,[35] and collapsed into the pogroms against the PKI membership. In Jembrana, the killings slowed with the arrival of the Army Para-commando Regiment (Regimen Para Komando Angkatan Darat, RPKAD) on 31 January 1966 (see also Chapter 4), but continued sporadically until May.[36]

A potent symbol that frames people's recollections of events in Jembrana was Miskar's truck that lumbered into their villages to collect PKI prisoners. When the ominous rumbling of its distinctive exhaust pipe reverberated through a village, families huddled indoors hoping that it would not stop outside their compound. When the truck did stop, families were left distraught as men were shackled and taken away. Those men who did not run away just waited at home for the inevitable. IB Windia, a local PKI leader who would be taken to Toko Wong, reportedly prepared his family by saying, "I'm dead, I'm already dead". An old Muslim friend from Loloan later brought Windia's ring home to the family and told them that he was dead.[37]

---

[33] Robert Cribb, "Problems in the Historiography of the Indonesian Killings", in *The Indonesian Killings of 1965–1966: Studies from Java and Bali*, ed. Robert Cribb (Clayton: Centre of Southeast Asian Studies, Monash University, 1990), pp. 33–4; Robinson, *Dark Side of Paradise*, p. 295.

[34] Robinson notes that "some community leaders simply ordered people to kill". Robinson, *Dark Side of Paradise*, p. 299. My informants suggest that known PKI affiliates were usually "ordered" to kill their leaders. Ibu Harti, interviewed by Mary Ida Bagus, 22 July 2007, Batuagung, Jembrana, Bali.

[35] Ibu Anom Dada, interviewed by Mary Ida Bagus, 12 July 2009, Batubulan, Badung, Bali.

[36] Suryawan, *Ladang Hitam*, p. 179.

[37] Biang Tut Suari, interviewed by Mary Ida Bagus, 13 May 2001, Batuagung, Jembrana, Bali.

This psychological torture of victims waiting with their families was a pervasive element of the terror of Gestok. It was a hideous prelude of fear to the inevitable acts of arrest and murder, because most people had no means of escape.

Putu, who was 16 at the time of the killings, sometimes rode with Miskar on the truck. He recounted his experiences to me in 2003, in front of a stunned audience of extended family members who had no idea of his relationship with Miskar.[38] His mother confirmed his story. Putu's high school teachers had urged him to join the PKI student organisation (League of Support for Indonesian Youth, Ikatan Pendukung Pemuda Indonesia, IPPI), but he remained with the PNI youth organisation (Movement of Indonesian Nationalist High School Students, Gerakan Siswa Nasional Indonesia, GSNI) because of his father's PNI alignment. He suffered social isolation as a result. This pressure on a secondary student to choose sides demonstrates the coercion people faced to join political groups. He described to me his sense of personal empowerment when PKI teachers and students were arrested and loaded on board Miskar's truck whilst he sat safely in the cabin.[39] I do not know whether he identified student victims for Miskar, although I suspect it to be the case. His journeys in the dreaded truck were exciting and liberating, even though the truck had carried some of his own family members to their deaths.

A respondent, who in 1965 was in his early 20s, recounted that Miskar was a violent and cruel man who loved to inflict pain on his captives.[40] In 1967, not long after the killings and arrests stopped, Miskar was struck with illness and died a terrible wasting death. According to this respondent, locals attributed this to karma and believed it was the result of Miskar's inhumane treatment of PKI prisoners in 1965–66. People's recollections of Miskar are coloured by a retrospective sense of regret whatever their political affiliation.

---

[38] Putu Raden, interviewed by Mary Ida Bagus, Sept. 2003, Batuagung, Jembrana, Bali.

[39] Robinson states that on 12 October 1965, the GSNI "called on all members to work together with ABRI … in annihilating the G-30-S". Robinson, *The Dark Side of Paradise*, p. 287fn41.

[40] EB, interviewed by Mary Ida Bagus, Mar. 2006, Turusan, Negara, Jembrana, Bali.

One informant, who was ten years old when the killings in Jembrana began, reported feeling a mixture of fearful excitement and horror when he witnessed the stoning of a neighbour from the security of a frangipani tree.[41] The innocent voyeurism of young children witnessing violence had enduring effects.

After the violence, the only teachers with jobs were those who opposed the PKI. This effectively represented a "pedagogic short-changing on that [post-killings] generation of schoolchildren".[42] The teachers who remained when the schools reopened taught a specifically New Order version of Gestok to those who had witnessed it first-hand.

Although this version of history was often accepted unquestioningly, there were many families whose experiences were at odds with the official reconstructions of the past. One informant recalled his tortured time at primary school, where his teacher regularly publicly derided him for being the child of a communist. He was punished more often and more severely than his classmates.[43] Another example is the grandchild of a murdered PKI leader who reported to me his deep sense of grief and pride when he participated in a commemorative event organised by activist and researcher I Ngurah Suryawan on 30 September 2008 in Yogyakarta.[44] The participants ate cassava grown in Jembrana fields believed to hold mass graves of PKI victims. Knowledge of the violence was often internalised, nurtured and maintained in family lore.

Several respondents also discussed sexual violence committed by PNI militiamen.[45] Having felt vulnerable to the violence of local PKI agents before Gestok, PNI vigilantes moved to dispose of their

---

[41] Ketut Tirtha, interviewed by Mary Ida Bagus, Jan. 1990, Batuagung, Jembrana, Bali.

[42] Kenneth Orr, "Schooling and Village Politics in Central Java in the Time of Turbulence", in *The Indonesian Killings*, p. 186.

[43] IB, interviewed by Mary Ida Bagus, Feb. 2003, Palungan Batu, Jembrana, Bali.

[44] Agus Jis, interviewed by Mary Ida Bagus, 13 July 2009, Batuagung, Jembrana, Bali.

[45] Discussions with a number of women in Batuagung (Jembrana, Bali) over the years 1990–2009.

competitors and to enjoy the spoils of war. Household goods, livestock and harvests were appropriated to feed the PNI and other militias who set up roadblocks and guarded roads and villages. In this setting, some PNI men also targeted women who were either members of the PKI or connected to the PKI through participation in PKI-sponsored performing arts events, or because they were the wives and daughters of PKI men. The legitimacy of coveting these women was supported by traditional Balinese practices where women could literally be "stolen" off the street and forced into marriage (*ngantén mapaksa*). Prior to the 1960s, most marriages were arranged and imposed on young women who had no choice in the matter. According to my informants, this practice was to avoid women making "inappropriate" independent choices or, worse, being "stolen" by a man with bad prospects. Due to these social traditions, PNI and non-PKI men often got away with the appropriation — and even rape — of women associated with the PKI. Widagda Suyasa, however, was eventually convicted and jailed for the rape of three women, amongst many others, "who had been accused *without basis* [of being PKI]".[46] My italics suggest the skewed logic applied at the time. If there had been any "basis" to the claims that the women had PKI connections, they and their supporters would have been silenced by fear of further anti-communist reprisals.

Local women who had danced or performed in PKI propaganda performances were particularly vulnerable to rape. In Jembrana, the PKI had successfully used popular Balinese *janger* dance performances, involving the use of allegory and social commentary, to solicit support from the uneducated masses.[47] The Army-generated propaganda about the September 30th Movement included allegations that "dancing" Gerwani (Indonesian Women's Movement, Gerakan Wanita Indonesia) women had sexually mutilated the generals kidnapped by members of the September 30th Movement. This association of Gerwani and other communist-aligned women with immorality and social danger became a pervasive element of the emerging New Order discourse and had direct repercussions for women

---

[46] Soe Hok Gie, "The Mass Killings in Bali", trans. Anton Lucas, in *The Indonesian Killings*, p. 256.
[47] Suryawan, *Ladang Hitam*, p. 115.

associated with the PKI.[48] Although sexualised torture was tolerated as punishment for such women, the appropriation of women through marriage during Gestok resonated with existing gendered local practices. Conversely, these same practices were used in some cases to protect and reintegrate PKI women into their village societies.

One example of reintegration is a janger dancer who often performed for PKI campaign rallies. During the 25 years of our friendship, this woman had only occasionally discussed her story with me.[49] Her father was a PKI tameng, and her husband was a teacher and active member of the PKI. In December 1965, when she was seven months pregnant with her first child, a mob dragged her husband from their home and she never saw him again. Her father was also arrested and murdered. The woman's advanced pregnancy protected her from rape at that time, but after her child was born she lived in fear of abduction. In 1969 an uncle who belonged to the PNI arranged her marriage to a cousin, and she was transferred back to her natal clan. In keeping with local practice, the child stayed with his patriline. With this marriage, the woman was reinvented as a wife, a returnee to her surviving extended family who were affiliated with PNI, and eventually a mother of new, "untainted" children. Her previous life as a PKI wife, mother of a PKI child and member of a PKI family was erased from the public domain. An intensely private woman, she still finds it difficult to discuss those times.

One defining outcome of the mass killings and other abuses during Gestok was that the will to speak about these experiences was overshadowed by fear of the mechanisms of state control.[50] The New Order regime often stigmatised challenges to New Order orthodoxies as communist (*komunis*), a label that equated with "subversive" in this context. These challenges included recollection of the violence and discussion of the ongoing detentions and sanctions of those labelled "communist".

---

48 Saskia E. Wieringa, "Sexual Metaphors in the Change from Soekarno's Old Order to Soeharto's New Order in Indonesia", *Review of Indonesian and Malay Affairs* 32, 2 (1998): 143–78.

49 EC, discussions with Mary Ida Bagus, 1990–2009, Batuagung, Jembrana, Bali.

50 See Ariel Heryanto, *State Terrorism and Political Identity in Indonesia: Fatally Belonging* (London and New York: Routledge, 2006).

One person who insisted on telling me her story was Ibu Harti,[51] an impoverished and sickly woman who rarely left her home in Jembrana to participate in the usual village social activities. She spent 15 years in Sulawesi as a transmigrant before returning to Bali in the 1990s with a sick daughter, who died not long after. According to Ibu Harti, this was her second child to die of poverty that was directly related to her own political affiliation so many years before.

In 1965 Ibu Harti and her husband were both primary school teachers, living and teaching in his village in the mountains about 4 kilometres from her natal home. The men in her husband's family were educated, dedicated PKI activists. One night in December 1965, a group of neighbours, including some PKI members, attacked their home and brutally murdered her husband. She hid in the garden whilst the house was being ransacked. From the news of what was happening in the village below, this violent raid had not been unexpected. With the help of a sympathetic neighbour, Ibu Harti buried her husband's body behind the vandalised kitchen to protect her children and father-in-law from the ghastly sight. Her own father, a PKI tameng, had already been trucked off to the Toko Wong in Negara, and her teenage brothers, members of IPPI, were drowned by a mob in the local river. PKI-affiliated neighbours had taken her youngest brother and mother to their home outside the village for protection. Three of her husband's brothers and various male cousins were taken away. PNI vigilantes took all her possessions, animals and food stocks. A married neighbour began to sexually harass Ibu Harti, who was now without male protection.

Ibu Harti's experience of loss and consequent vulnerability to sexual attack was common at that time. But her personal response to her situation was unusual. According to her testimony, she had nothing to lose and sought direct protection from Lieutenant Colonel Safroni, the head of the military. Her sister's husband was in Safroni's unit, and they lived at the military headquarters in Negara. Ibu Harti walked 10 kilometres with a baby on her hip and a bunch of bananas

[51] Ibu Dayu Harti, interviewed by Mary Ida Bagus, 2007, 2008 and 2009 in Batuagung, Jembrana, Bali. The following account draws on these discussions. The title "Ibu" is significant in Balinese society because in the 1960s it was an honorific title to denote a person's elite status resulting from their education in Indonesian language.

on her head. On Safroni's advice, she stayed some weeks with her brother-in-law at the military barracks, under the protection of the very authority that had created her predicament, before returning home with a letter from Safroni. Male neighbours were outraged that she had gone to the military for protection, but they left her alone. She was no longer able to teach, and PNI members of her natal family commandeered her home and land. Distant relatives with PKI affiliation sheltered her in her natal village, and she helped sell food at a roadside stall for her keep. Her two children stayed up in the mountains with surviving members of her husband's family. The baby daughter she had carried to Safroni died of untreated fever in 1966.

Ibu Harti eventually married a man from the PKI family who had taken her in. They transmigrated to Sulawesi in 1979 along with other PKI affiliates because, in her view, it was an opportunity to escape the "culture of forgetting" that was developing in their village. For her, this "culture of forgetting the violence" of Gestok failed to bring back the dead, failed to erase the PKI stamp on identity cards, and failed to reinstate her as a teacher. The Sulawesi experience, encouraged and sponsored by the government, was a form of exile, and clearly designed as further punishment.[52] There was no infrastructure for families, who on arrival had to clear the jungle, create and plant fields, and build their own shelter. Eventually, at the behest of the head of the transmigrant community, Ibu Harti organised a school for some 200 students of varying age groups.[53] She took it upon herself to visit all the families and force the children from the fields into the rudimentary classrooms provided by the community. She was never paid by the state. Her students' parents gave her produce and other material items in payment.

By the time Ibu Harti returned to Bali in the 1990s, her home village showed all the signs of the historical amnesia promoted by the New Order and encapsulated in the sign outside the Bale Banjar community pavilion: BALI – Bersih (clean), Aman (safe), Lestari (conserved), Indah (beautiful). "Bersih" insidiously implied the

---

[52] Maskun Iskandar, "Purwodadi: Area of Death", trans. Robert Cribb, in *The Indonesian Killings*, p. 204.

[53] A number of her ex-pupils have returned to Jembrana with their families and attest to her story.

"cleansing" of communists that enabled the remnants of her community to feel "safe" in the "enduringly beautiful" Balinese environment imagined by the state.[54] Based on her memory of Gestok and her associated prejudices, she found it difficult to reintegrate into the general community and had no wish to mix with people she knew as murderers. She regretted leaving Sulawesi and just stayed at home.

Ibu Harti's mother, Niang Tu, also lost everything: her husband, two sons, her home and her daughter who felt compelled to transmigrate. Eventually, she was relegated to a hut at the end of the village with her only surviving son, her youngest. She was still living in that hovel when I met her in the 1980s, and she died there destitute in the early 1990s, despite her connections to a wealthy and politically influential Brahmin family in the region. At the time of her husband's murder she was already a grandmother and, by village standards, unattractive to marauding males. Her widow status enabled her to keep her surviving son, Agus, by her side, since she was still officially a member of her husband's family.

As the case of Ibu Harti and her mother, Niang Tu, demonstrates, economic ruin was one of the lasting effects of Gestok. In the village where I concentrated my research, the most impoverished families were all associated with the PKI during Gestok. Across the villages of Jembrana there were many impoverished and articulate women and men with no visible means of support who displayed a worldliness that often set them apart from their better-fed neighbours. During the New Order, these people's daily struggles were considered fair punishment (karma) for the crimes the New Order alleged they had committed. Many survivors were transformed into an underclass of manual labourers and odd job servants who served their politically correct neighbours, but there were some exceptions.

Niang Tu's son Agus grew up with little to eat, minimal education and the ignominy of his birthright from his much maligned, violent, communist father. From an early age, he laboured for other people, developing farming skills and expertise in the practical elements of religious ritual. He married a specialist offering-maker

---

[54] This version of Bali had also already been successfully packaged for international tourism. See Degung Santikarma, "Epilog. Memasak Sejarah dan Ekonomi Ingatan '65 di Bali", in *Bali Narasi Dalam Kuasa: Politik dan Kekerasan di Bali*, ed. I Ngurah Suryawan (Yogyakarta: Ombak Press, 2005), p. 331.

(*tukang banten*), also an orphan from the killings with no formal education. In spite of the economic and social disadvantages of their childhoods, this couple's talents in the traditional arena were translated into monetary rewards as local demand for ceremonies increased and rituals became more complex. By the late 1990s, when the ultra-religious Dharma Bali movement[55] had strengthened in response to the rise of international tourism and perceived threats to Balinese "tradition", they were finally able to build a solid house with the proceeds of their ceremonial work. It was too late for Agus's long-suffering mother, but it was a clear sign that their rehabilitation in what was now a middle-class and overtly religious village was complete. This rehabilitation was enhanced in 2004 when Agus was asked to become a Brahmin priest (*pedanda*) for the extended family (*semeton*) that had thrown out his widowed mother and ignored his plight for so long. At the time of writing, he was yet to take up the offer of priesthood but continued to oversee and earn money from large ceremonies in his village.

Agus suffered extreme disadvantage as the son of a known PKI tameng. He was cast out to the fringes of society with his struggling widowed mother. He and his equally marginalised wife later became indispensable to their community and represented a new breed of Balinese villagers with cultural currency, whose expertise in complex ceremonial knowledge was desirable, was reified and translated into economic rewards.

The experiences of Ida Bagus Surya also illustrate some of the complexities of Gestok. In October 1965, his military regiment was stationed at Gilimanuk port in west Bali and he was under orders to kill PKI members escaping from East Java over the Bali Strait. By December 1965 he was arrested, tortured and imprisoned because his military unit was under suspicion of being pro-PKI.[56] During his years of imprisonment, many of his fellow inmates were taken off and shot; and he prepared to die on a number of occasions. His

---

[55] Ida Bagus, "From the Margins of History", p. 18.

[56] He was in a local Balinese unit of the Tjakrabirawa Presidential Guard, overseen in Jakarta by Lieutenant Colonel Untung. Ida Bagus Surya believes that he and others in his unit from Jembrana were targeted because of the association with Governor Suteja. Interviewed by Mary Ida Bagus, 27 June 2007, Batuagung, Jembrana, Bali.

status as a member of the military provided him with protection because the Balinese authorities categorised military political prisoners as Jakarta's responsibility. In mid-1969 he was released as a category C prisoner, meaning that no charges were brought.[57] He received an honourable discharge from the Army and a lump sum pension. It took nearly four years to receive the official decision that he had no case to answer. In his home village, it had taken only a few days for authorities and vigilantes to murder civilian PKI who had neither prior knowledge of nor involvement in the September 30th Movement in Jakarta. Although Ida Bagus Surya told me he had no personal political affiliations, members of his extended family were active in both the PKI and the PNI. His PKI father-in-law, who was also an uncle, had been murdered in his home village, as had other members of his family.

In 1979, Ida Bagus Surya transmigrated to Sulawesi, where he became a successful rice farmer and notable figure in the transmigrant community, including serving as an unordained priest (*pamangku*). Other Jembrana ex-internees from his unit also migrated to Sulawesi. They all returned to Bali, although many travelled between the islands maintaining relationships with families and tending to landholdings in Sulawesi. After nearly two decades, Ida Bagus's family invited him back to Bali to become a Brahmin high priest. At the time of writing, he held an official position of authority in the government-supported Indonesian Society for Hindu Teachings (Parisada Hindu Dharma Indonesia). This high priest's life journey, from a gun-wielding teenager in the military, to a killer of communists, to a political prisoner associated with the PKI, to a transmigrant, to a respected religious leader, illustrates the complex and arbitrary nature of the Gestok purges and their repercussions. In Balinese terms, Ida Bagus Surya's rehabilitation to the office of high priest allowed him physically to shed all his pasts, because Balinese priests ritually die a social death and are reborn (*dwijati*) as higher beings outside the usual human existence. In national terms, he was also elevated from the designation of ex-political prisoner to that of a man of religion.

---

[57] For descriptions of prisoner classifications and associated punishments, see Chapter 7.

Sites of Memory

Memory of the violence is particularly manifest in relations with the spiritual domain (*niskala*). In Bali "sekala" (the lived world) and "niskala" are generally understood as inseparable dichotomous elements of existence.[58] Despite the efforts of the New Order regime to justify and gloss over the violence, according to local beliefs and practices the past coexists with the present and is therefore inescapable.

Whilst PKI victims and their families continued to experience persecution and social alienation, some perpetrators in Jembrana also suffered for their culpability in local atrocities. In Bali the logic of karma influenced local interpretations of the Gestok purges, including a belief in *madewa pitra*, an unavoidable contract between murderer and victim, regulated from the niskala.[59] Hence, some perpetrators are understood to have suffered madewa pitra sanctions as a result of their actions, meaning they had a karmic debt representing both conscience and punishment for acts of murder. One Jembrana healer (*balian*) told Suryawan,

> I have helped a lot of ex-tameng. I know who ordered me to dispose of corpses. Now their lives are destroyed. They have gone crazy, and their families are haunted. The ones who were tameng have died hideous deaths.[60]

In 2000, when I attempted to interview a local about a sacred Chinese grave (*kongco*) on his land, he surprised me by launching into a detailed reminiscence of Gestok. In 1965, he had led anonymous PKI prisoners to mass graves by the beach at Baluk-Rening.[61] He stated that although he did not kill them, he felt sympathy for these scared and confused strangers. Not long after Gestok, he was directed through a dream to construct and care for the sacralised grave of a Chinese stranger. Since this informant associated my questions about the sacred grave site with Gestok, I can only assume that he is engaged in a madewa pitra relationship to assuage the guilt

[58] See Ida Bagus, "From the Margins of History", pp. 27–9.

[59] Ida Bagus, "Transcending Transgression", pp. 93–4.

[60] Mangku Tila, interviewed by I Ngurah Suryawan in Suryawan, *Bali Narasi Dalam Kuasa*, p. 215.

[61] ED, interviewed by Mary Ida Bagus, 1 Jan. 2001, Baluk, Jembrana, Bali.

Grave of Pak Kardi, Budeng, Jembrana, Bali (photo by Mary Ida Bagus)

and/or fear he feels due to his involvement in the deaths of PKI strangers. When telling stories around such sites, people usually cite violent and undeserved deaths. The "innocence" of victims is what gives them the power to communicate with the living or conversely causes the living to form a pact with the dead.

I visited many sacralised gravesites (*keramat* and *kongco*) in Jembrana that commemorated unnatural deaths, most often in isolated fields and gardens.[62] The gravesites Balinese Hindus cared for were the most fascinating because they indicated the possibility for close ritual ties with the dead beyond the usual ethnic and kin-group relations, even if the reasons for these ties were never clear. The only officially recognised Gestok graves were the three located in the National Heroes' Cemetery in Negara, mentioned above, commemorating not communist, but anti-communist, deaths. These "gravesites"

[62] See Ida Bagus, "From the Margins of History", pp. 197–260.

are public reminders that these deaths represent "noble sacrifices" for the nation.

Besides these official graves, Jembrana residents have identified three sacralised gravesites believed to represent PKI victims.[63] The people commemorated at these sites are Kardi, a local Muslim, a Hindu man from Tabanan and his Muslim wife from Loloan. Their graves are regularly tended by Balinese Hindus; the detritus of distinctive Hindu offerings is evidence of continuing relationships between perpetrators living in the sekala realm and their victims in the niskala.

People in Jembrana also believe that sites where bodies were dumped or buried are spiritually impure. Locals claim that the still sparsely settled area of Penginuman is spiritually contaminated. During an interview in 2000, a temple priest from a competing temple bitterly criticised the government for funding two new neighbouring temples at Penginuman. He claimed that the isolated coastal site was spiritually dangerous (*tenget*) and polluted with the bodies of PKI victims.[64] In subsequent interviews, the men who founded the new temples never revealed any complicity in Gestok murders, but each stated they had been "called" to the sites by esoteric forces. Harrowing experiences of surviving alone in the jungle led them to establish sanctuaries at the sites. Whether these men are engaged in a madewa pitra pact with victims of Gestok will never be clear, but the sacralisation of these particular sites suggests that the shrines were erected to neutralise demands from the spiritual realm.

As John Roosa has noted, there are no national monuments for the PKI victims of the purges,[65] but I have found evidence of local commemoration by perpetrators who were forced into a karmic pact with their victims. Sacralised gravesites are anathema in regular Balinese practice, because Balinese Hindus are commemorated in family shrines (*palinggih*) in the home. Those commemorated at sacralised gravesites must be from outside usual family connections, and some are victims of Gestok. Gestok-specific private Balinese shrines may

---

[63] EF, interviewed by Mary Ida Bagus, 12 Jan. 2001, Baluk, Jembrana, Bali.

[64] Mangku Lingsir, interviewed by Mary Ida Bagus, 7 Dec. 2000, Gilimanuk, Jembrana, Bali.

[65] John Roosa, *Pretext for Mass Murder: The September 30th Movement and Suharto's Coup d'État in Indonesia* (Madison: University of Wisconsin Press, 2006), p. 225.

very well exist, but the only case I have come across is a large public shrine at a junction on a mountain road that marks the site of three Gestok murders. Locals told me that the site was spiritually dangerous because it was a junction of three roads. Yet an elderly woman who lived at the junction told me that it was associated with the death of three locals whose bodies had been dumped close by.[66] This exchange was typical of the layers of memory in Jembrana. The memorial, like the sacralised graves I visited in Jembrana, was regularly endowed with simple Balinese offerings (*canang sari*), evidence of a continuing and active remembering and engagement with the past.

Other places in Jembrana also function as sites of memory of the violence. Toko Wong, for example, is an enduring symbol of the purges. Situated in Muslim Loloan, not far from the Negara palace, the two-storey building is boarded up and still standing. It is remarkable that this place where people were detained, tortured and shot was not demolished to eradicate the "evidence" and accompanying spiritual "pollution". Its edifice stands as an ominous reminder of the power of the state to eliminate its opposition. At the time of writing, the building was used as a nesting house for swallows, whose expensive nests are used for bird's nest soup. This pedestrian use of the building retains a Chinese association, while undermining the memory of victims who experienced violence within its walls. Its haunted qualities automatically provide security against potential intruders and robbers, an insidious and pragmatic use of public memory in the pursuit of business.

Some locals in Jembrana have attempted to assuage their complicity in horrific acts of Gestok violence through ritualised acts of obeisance to the dead. One telling example is that of a particularly vicious killer, a man infamous and condemned in his natal village for his barbaric behaviour during Gestok. He subsequently became a priest (*pemangku*) in the same cemetery where he committed state-sanctioned murder in early 1966.[67] To an outsider, without any knowledge of his personal history, it would seem that he was fulfilling a sacred duty to his community as priest of the cemetery temple. According to the community, he is performing a karmic duty to

---

[66] EG, interviewed by Mary Ida Bagus, 15 Dec. 2000, Masean, Jembrana, Bali.
[67] See Ida Bagus, "Transcending Transgression", p. 104.

his victims. Every day, by attending to the temple in the cemetery grounds this priest relives his own dark history for all to see. In Jembrana, collective memory operates on many levels, signified in implicit codes. The semiotics of memory are reflected in language and ritual activity.

Since the end of the Suharto period, there has been growing recognition within Indonesia that victims of the PKI pogroms did not deserve their fate (see Chapter 10). In 2000, President Abdurrahman Wahid reinstated government pensions to Independence fighters who had been stripped of their honours and livelihood because of their later association with the PKI. As the former head of NU and grandson of the founder of NU, he also apologised for the role NU played in promoting the killings.[68] By the time these official gestures began to restore a semblance of citizenship to the lost generation of 1965 communists, in Bali the perpetrators of violent "anti-PKI" acts committed out of cruelty, revenge, fear and confusion were already seen to be suffering retribution from the spiritual realm.

Since the end of the New Order in 1998, recollections of Gestok have become more explicit. Public discussion is adding to the tentative record of local events written in the 1980s by local historian Wayan Reken[69] and recorded in the Negara royal house's partial efforts at documentation of the family genealogy.[70] Reken's unpublished reports have been cited by some academics.[71] The genealogical records from the Negara royal house specify names of some of the individuals who ransacked the palace compound, but other identities are deleted. The records mention that the PKI stigma prevented some locals from attending the 1967 funeral of Suteja's father, the retired Raja, but, significantly, there is no mention of the terrible death of local PKI head and royal family member Agung Denia. He was arrested, tortured and publicly humiliated, and allegedly hanged himself by his underpants. His naked corpse was then dragged behind

[68] Gerry van Klinken, "The Battle for History after Suharto", in *Beginning to Remember: The Past in the Indonesian Present*, ed. Mary S. Zurbuchen (Singapore: Singapore University Press, 2005), p. 242.
[69] I Wayan Reken, "Collected Papers on the History of Jembrana" (unpublished manuscript, n.d.).
[70] Parintosa and Suryawan, *Silsilah*, p. 38.
[71] Robinson, *Dark Side of Paradise*, p. 298.

a truck from Negara to Tegal Cangkring.[72] I have heard the story of his demise from many Jembrana residents on both sides of politics at the time. According to my informants his suffering, like that of many others, was unjustifiable: a simple gun to the head would have sufficed. The time is approaching when his story can finally be entered into the official family genealogical record.

Conclusion

The above case studies of victims from Jembrana illustrate that there was no typical experience of Gestok but a complex spectrum of causes and effects. The decisive factor for those targeted in the killings was an association or presumed association with the suddenly illegal PKI. Survivors' recollections of this period highlight not only their successful strategies of survival but also ongoing suffering and enduring social tensions. Survivors rebuilt their lives in the context of traumas they continued to experience within their own communities. Some people found strength from networks of PKI survivors that formed among these social outcasts out of sheer necessity. Some people felt compelled to transmigrate to Sulawesi to escape the social stigma of their PKI association. Here they could again lead productive lives through farming and trading. In Bali, where marriage forms a powerful social contract, remarriage enabled many women to be reintegrated into their communities.

These stories taken together reveal that the violence and stigma of association with the PKI were perpetuated through social marginalisation and associated poverty. This is not to say that all those implicated with the PKI remained social outcasts. Being excluded from education and formal employment forced some men and women to develop skills in the traditional religio-ritual domain, allowing them in time to rise to honoured positions as ritual specialists within their communities. The victims of Gestok who were able to rise out of poverty and social sanction did so by various routes but most commonly in the form of patronage by people on the now correct side of the political spectrum.

In Jembrana, everyone who lived through the mid-1960s was affected by the violent upheaval of Gestok. The involvement of local

---

[72] Suryawan, *Ladang Hitam*, pp. 202–3.

people in vigilante action established a social contract of complicity upon which the New Order Regime based its authority.[73] Bernhard Schlink has noted wisely that "solidarity with the perpetrator leads to entanglement in his or her crime and guilt ... [and this is at] the centre of the idea of collective guilt".[74] Willing and unwilling participants in the violence and social approbation that followed were united in a programme of social readjustment that was engineered and maintained by centralist state control. Despite New Order assurances that the anti-PKI pogroms were necessary for the nation and survival, with all the supporting official propaganda of what had happened, in Jembrana collective guilt is memorialised in haunted graves and through the actions of haunted murderers. People remember these tragic events in their own ways.

Attitudes of people in Jembrana towards the violence of 1965 have become more reflective since the end of the Suharto regime in 1998. At last there has been some public airing of what happened and more open expressions of sympathy for those affected by the violence and the decades of stigmatisation. As discussed in Chapter 10, a new emphasis on human rights has even emboldened some survivors to participate in movements for justice and redress, though unresolved tensions around this haunted past have led to hostility. The tapestry of individual experiences and social relations that constitute local understandings of the violence in Jembrana help to explain why such bitter legacies will never be resolved, but they may be assuaged.

---

[73] Ida Bagus, "Transcending Transgression", p. 95.

[74] Bernhard Schlink, *Guilt about the Past* (Saint Lucia: University of Queensland Press, 2009), p. 51.

10

Mass Graves and Memories of the 1965 Indonesian Killings

Katharine McGregor

Especially since the fall of the Berlin Wall in 1989, human rights have become part of the international agenda. In countries that have made the transition from military or communist dictatorships to democracies, activists have often campaigned to ensure that the new governments pay due regard to human rights. This was certainly the case for Indonesia after the fall of Suharto in 1998, and with considerable success. In 2000 the Indonesian constitution was revised to incorporate provisions from the Universal Declaration of Human Rights. It included provisions that prohibited prosecution under retrospective legislation; but in 2000, the Indonesian government passed Law No. 26, which allowed for the formation of Ad Hoc Human Rights Courts to deal retrospectively with gross violations of human rights, including genocide and crimes against humanity. The law expanded the role of the National Commission on Human Rights (established in 1993), enabling it to conduct investigations into such crimes, after which the Attorney General could rule on whether a special court and prosecutions would commence.

Due to these legal developments, victims of the New Order regime had a basis for seeking redress for crimes committed by the military against Indonesian citizens. In doing so, they also drew upon justice models from elsewhere. Following the South African, Chilean and Argentinian models, some activists pushed for a Truth and Reconciliation Commission as a means of acknowledging historical injustice. In 2000 the Ministry of Justice and Human Rights released a draft bill on Truth and Reconciliation. As in Argentina, Guatemala and Russia, victims groups in Indonesia also sought to collect evidence of crimes perpetrated by the former regime in expectation of possible trials.

Mass graves can provide direct evidence of crimes against humanity. A criminal mass grave is one in which the victims of a crime have been concealed. It is a "demonstrable place of deliberate disposal of multiple dead within the same grave structure".[1] Since the Geneva Convention of 1949, which included the right of the dead to a marked, individual grave, mass graves have been recognised as a violation of international humanitarian law.[2] Evidence from mass graves was used after World War II to indict war criminals and then again from the 1980s onwards to investigate military-perpetrated crimes in Argentina, Guatemala, El Salvador, Chile and Peru. More recently, evidence from mass graves has been used in international criminal tribunals for the former Yugoslavia and Rwanda, resulting in increased expectations of such tribunals elsewhere in the world.

Some post-authoritarian governments have endorsed the exhumation of mass graves to demonstrate their condemnation of past crimes. The Gorbachev government in Russia, for example, sought legitimacy by allowing the victims group Memorial to proceed with exhumations of mass graves of the Stalinist period.[3] In other cases, such as that of the Spanish Civil War, there has been a growing consensus on the need to identify and exhume mass graves, even though the killings took place 75 years ago.[4]

In Indonesia since 1998, victims of the counter-revolutionary violence, most notably former political prisoners or family members

---

[1] Margaret Cox, Ambika Flavel, Ian Hanson, Joanna Laver and Roland Wessling, "Introduction", in *The Scientific Investigation of Mass Graves: Towards Protocols and Standard Operating Procedures*, ed. Cox *et al.* (New York: Cambridge University Press, 2008), p. 10.

[2] Cox *et al.*, "Introduction", p. 11.

[3] Nanci Adler, "The Future of the Soviet Past Remains Unpredictable: The Resurrection of Stalinist Symbols Amidst the Exhumation of Mass Graves", *Europe-Asia Studies* 57, 8 (Dec. 2005): 1107–8.

[4] Francisco Ferrándiz and Alejandro Baer, "Digital Memory: The Visual Recording of Mass Grave Exhumations in Contemporary Spain", *Forum: Qualitative Social Research* 9, 3, http://www.qualitative-research.net/index.php/fqs/article/viewArticle/1152/2558, accessed 6 Nov. 2010.

of those killed, have focused on researching and documenting mass graves. Although their contents have deteriorated over the decades, many graves remain intact and communities are usually aware of their location. Nevertheless, attempts to identify, exhume and memorialise these mass graves have become highly politicised. Despite some initiatives for reconciliation, memories of that bitter time still touch raw nerves and interpretations of the PKI (Indonesian Communist Party, Partai Komunis Indonesia) repression remain highly contested.

Through a case study of the first successful exhumation of a mass grave of PKI victims, this chapter explores the emergence of new alliances and sources of hope for survivors and families affected by the counter-revolutionary violence of the mid-1960s. The mass grave was located in the Situkup forest, near Dempes village, on the outskirts of Wonosobo in Central Java. Its exhumation in 2000 was remarkable in light of the fear local communities associate with such graves (see Chapter 9). The broad support for the exhumation suggested a turning point in attitudes towards the killings. Nevertheless, the subsequent violent disruption of the attempted reburial of the remains one year later, along with other efforts to block further investigations, shows that there is still intense sensitivity, particularly among Islamic constituencies and their military backers who are wary of the ramifications of possible future trials and public memorialisation of the dead.

The Wonosobo Excavation

Over the last decade victims' organisations, NGOs and the National Commission on Human Rights have begun to document the location of mass graves. The Wonosobo exhumation was carried out between 16 and 18 November 2000 by the most active survivor organisation, the Foundation for the Research into Victims of the 1965–1966 Killings (Yayasan Penelitian Korban Pembunuhan 1965/66, YPKP). YPKP was founded in 1999 by Sulami, Pramoedya Ananta Toer and Umar Said.[5] Even before the resignation of President Suharto in

[5] Sulami was formerly the second Vice-Secretary General of the Indonesian Women's Movement (Gerwani). Pramoedya Ananta Toer was Indonesia's most famous novelist. Umar Said was an exile from this period who was based in Paris for almost 40 years before his death in October 2011.

1998, these three had led an unsuccessful effort to excavate a mass grave in Blora.[6] They founded YPKP for the purpose of researching the killings, imprisonments and human rights abuses connected with the counter-revolution. From the beginning, they emphasised the need for forensic investigations and the opening of mass graves as an important means for proving that the killings took place. The Wonosobo gravesite was unusual, however, because a prison official had recorded the names of people killed at this site and, at the time of the exhumation, YPKP was in contact with Sri, a surviving family member of a person on this list.[7] This provided a rare opportunity for matching the remains in the grave with a known list of people.

YPKP was well aware of the sensitive nature of the exhumation, because ever since its foundation in 1999, its branches had often received threats from anti-communist organisations, including the military and religious groups; but it anticipated that there was growing support for opening this past. Earlier in 2000, then President Abdurrahman Wahid (also the former head of the largest Islamic organisation in Indonesia, Nahdlatul Ulama, NU), had offered a personal apology for the violence to former members of the PKI and affiliated organisations and their families. As detailed in Chapter 5, members of the youth wing of NU, Ansor, worked together with the military to kill leftists in Central and East Java and other parts of Indonesia. Wahid not only made this apology, he also proposed ending the long-standing restrictions on former political prisoners and ending the ban on communism and Marxist Leninist teachings that had been in place since 1966. The latter proposal resulted in widespread protest.[8] Together, however, these gestures gave former political prisoners and the families of those who had died in the violence some hope of possible rehabilitation and of retribution for their suffering. Furthermore, the revised constitution and new human rights laws combined with the draft Truth and Reconciliation bill led to a sense of optimism amongst members of the YPKP about addressing this past.

---

[6] "Sekitar Penggalian Kuburan Massal di Dekat [*sic*] Wonosobo", *Soeara Kita untuk Kemanusiaan Keadilan dan Kebenaran* 10 (Dec. 2000): 3.

[7] *Dateline* Television Series, "Indonesia's Killing Fields", SBS Australia, 25 Aug. 1998.

[8] Budiawan Purwadi, *Mematahkan Pewarisan Ingatan: Wacana Anti-komunis dan Politik Rekonsilliasi pasca Soeharto* (Jakarta: ELSAM, 2003), pp. 49–67.

By 2000, YPKP had also begun to work with other organisations. A direct political link was fused between YPKP and Megawati's Indonesian Democratic Party of Struggle (Partai Demokrat Indonesia-Perjuangan, PDI-P) in 1999.[9] Ribka Tjiptaning Proletariyati, a PDI-P party member and daughter of a Communist Party member, was involved in YPKP from its inception.[10] In addition, Megawati's husband, the wealthy businessman Taufik Kiemas, set up a retirement home for former women political prisoners who had been affected by the 1965 events in Kramat Street, Central Jakarta. Megawati was cautious about openly supporting former political prisoners, but her party — PDI-P — was willing to support a bill allowing victims of 1965 to become legislative candidates. In an interview, Tjiptaning noted that many former political prisoners voted for Megawati in the 1999 election because they did not want to support a candidate with a military background. This comment highlights an enduring hostility towards the military. Many former political prisoners were devoted loyalists to the former President Sukarno and thus had faith in his daughter.

In response to Wahid's apology, younger NU activists became more concerned about the role of NU in the violence of 1965–68. Throughout the New Order period, members of NU had officially celebrated their role in crushing the communists as a contribution to the Indonesian nation.[11] The role of the NU youth organisation, Ansor, in the violence had also led to deep suspicion amongst some political prisoners and survivors of the violence of Islam as a religion. Recognising this long history of hostility between former political prisoners and members of NU, activists from 18 towns in Java met in 1999 to discuss the effects of the 1965 events on Ansor. The

---

[9] The PDI, initially formed in 1971, was widely recognised as the successor party to the Indonesian National Party (Partai Nasional Indonesia, PNI), originally founded by Sukarno. The PDI-P was a breakaway faction from the PDI following government intervention to replace Megawati as the leader of the party in 1996.

[10] The rest of this paragraph draws on Ribka Tjiptaning and Sigit Herlambang, interviewed by Katharine McGregor, 26 Feb. 2007, DPR Jakarta.

[11] See Choirul Anam, *Gerak Langkah Pemuda Ansor: Sebuah Percikan Sejarah Kelahiran* (Surabaya: Majalah Nahdlatul Ulama AULA, 1990), pp. 85–99.

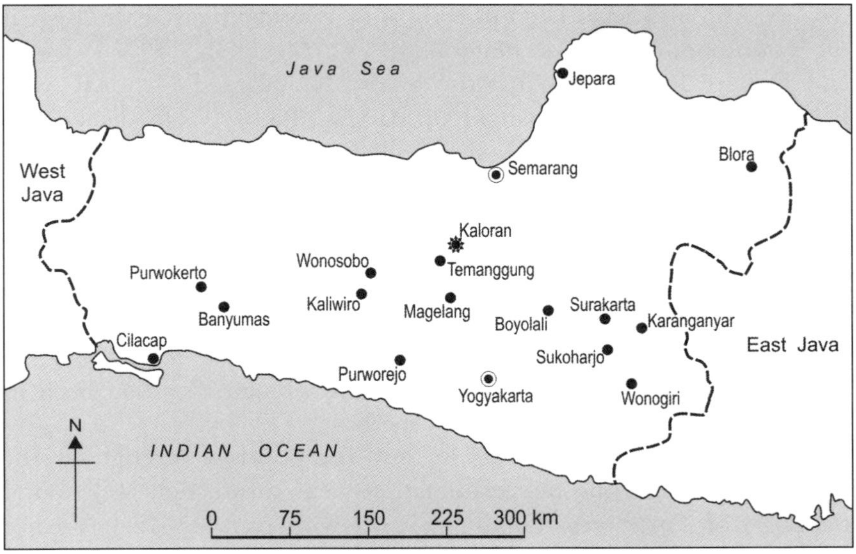

Map of Central Java and grave locations

Yogyakarta branch of Ansor followed Wahid's lead and offered an apology to victims of the violence of 1965.[12]

When YPKP decided to excavate the grave at Wonosobo, they requested Syaiful H. Shodiq, then part of this network of young NU people in Java concerned about 1965, to assist in negotiating with the local religious community before the excavation. YPKP contacted him, and he arranged to meet together with local representatives.[13] He felt that this was a difficult issue, so he requested one month to try to speak to people to "challenge the memories people had about this period", prior to proceeding with an excavation. By this, he meant challenging the stereotype of all communists as being inhumane and deserving of their fate. He gained permission from the local military and police.

[12] Umar Said, "Pernyataan GP Ansor tentang Tragedi 65", 29 Nov. 2000, http: www.hamline.edu/apakabar/basisdata/2000/11/29/0006.html, accessed 22 May 2007.

[13] Syaiful H. Shodiq, interviewed by Katharine McGregor, 22 May 2007, Yogyakarta.

Syaiful also negotiated directly with two key figures: the Regent of Wonosobo, Trimawan Nugrohadi[14] of Megawati's PDI-P party; and Deputy Regent Kholiq Arief of the NU-aligned National Awakening Party (Partai Kebangkitan Bangsa, PKB).[15] He decided to focus on the deputy because of his religious ties to NU. The Deputy Regent of Wonosobo initially asked YPKP to delay the exhumation on the grounds that their plans had not been sufficiently "socialised" to the people. He conceded only after the National Commission on Human Rights intervened and clarified that the motivation for the exhumations was humanity and justice.[16] When they presented their case to the Commission, YPKP argued they wanted to exhume the grave for the purposes of allowing Sri, the woman they had been in contact with, to bury her father properly.

Given the strong climate of anti-communism throughout the New Order, the Wonosobo exhumation went surprisingly well. Local members of Ansor were on site to assist with security. They did not wear uniforms, but they helped provide a tent for the excavation from a local Islamic school in Kaliwiro, the Tsanawiyah NU Islamic School (Madrasah Tsanawiyah NU).[17] Members of the security apparatus attached to the PDI-P also provided support. This cooperation demonstrated the wider support for YPKP's work at that time. The exhumation also attracted widespread media coverage and international attention.[18] Following a submission from YPKP, the Asian

---

[14] In 2006 in a submission to the Constitutional Court opposing the Truth and Reconciliation bill passed in 2004, Masrul Sihab, the head of a pesantren in Wonosobo, claimed that the Wonosobo exhumation had been allowed to go ahead only because Trimawan Nugrohadi's father was a political prisoner who went to Buru Island and never returned. He also claimed that his older sibling, Siswati, was a category C prisoner from 1965 and a former member of Pemuda Rakyat. *Risalah Sidang Perkara No. 020/PUU-IV/2006, Perihal Pengujian UU No. 27 Tahun 2004 Tentang Komisi Kebenaran dan Rekonsiliasi Terhadap UUD 1845, Acara Mendengar Keterangan Pemerintah, Saksi dan Ahli dari Pemohon (111)*, Jakarta, 13 Nov. 2006, p. 47.

[15] PKB was formed on 23 July 1998. Abdurrahman Wahid was one of its founders.

[16] Umar Said, "Pemakaman-Kembali Kerangka Korban 65 Digagalkan", *Soeara Kita: Untuk Kemanusiaan Keadilan dan Kebenaran* 14 (Apr. 2001): 3–9.

[17] Syaiful H. Shodiq, interviewed by Katharine McGregor, 22 May 2007, Yogyakarta.

[18] "Remains of Slain Ex-Communists found in Wonosobo", *The Jakarta Post*, 21 Nov. 2000; "24 Kerangka Anggota PKI Masih Terkatung-katung", *Gatra*, 5 Dec. 2000.

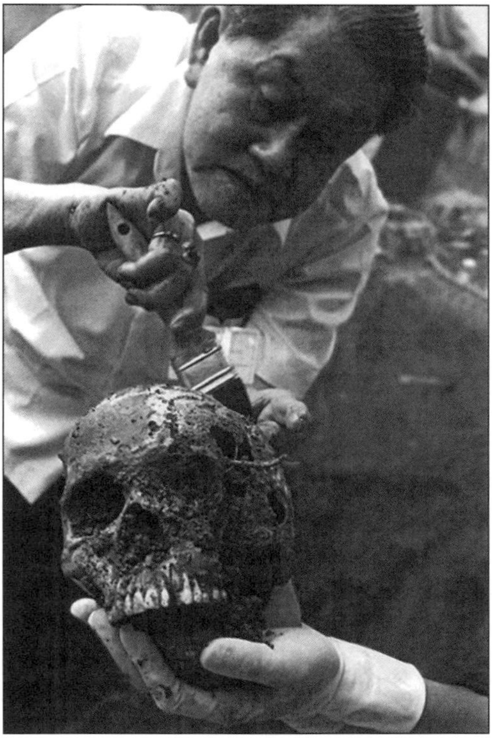

Forensic expert Dr Handoko at the Wonosobo excavation site (photo by Raharja Waluya Jati)

Human Rights Commission (a regional human rights advocacy organisation) issued a statement of urgent action calling for President Wahid and the National Commission on Human Rights to investigate the 1965–66 massacres.[19] At this stage the Commission was only authorised to investigate the human rights abuses associated with the mass imprisonments on Buru Island (see Chapter 7); earlier — in 2000 — it had refused to set up an investigation into the killings on the basis that parliament had not yet lifted the ban on Marxist-Leninist teachings.

Dr Handoko, from the Medical Faculty of the University of Indonesia in Jakarta, worked as a forensic expert on site. The excavation team identified some of the victims in the grave using the list of persons taken to the site, skeletal evidence and personal items found

[19] "Urgent Action 06-2001: 'Coffins of 65 Victims Raided by Mob'", http://www.wirantaprawira.de/ypkp/ypkp_3.htm, accessed 5 Mar. 2009.

in the grave. One woman was identified by her filed-down tooth, a red plastic comb and a silk scarf that was tied around her neck. Another person was identified by a wedding ring on which the name "Sudjiem" was written together with her wedding date of 28 June 1965.[20] Handoko determined that the killings had been carried out using short- and long-barreled rifles. The investigators suggested that these kinds of weapons were military issue rifles. Handoko concluded that 26 people were buried in this grave.

Sulami explained her motivation for opening the grave in "Indonesia's Killing Fields", a segment of Australian SBS-television's *Dateline* programme, stating "... these bones, are the bones of my comrades from 32 years ago and Indonesia has many of these spread everywhere".[21] In the television segment she spoke of the sense of responsibility she felt towards those who had died, to make Indonesians aware of what had happened during this period. She held up a human bone found in the Wonosobo grave and cried as she said, "We found evidence that what Suharto did was extraordinarily cruel (*kekejaman luar biasa*)." Her language mirrored that of the New Order and the repeated claims that the PKI were extraordinarily cruel in the way they allegedly tortured and killed the seven army victims of the September 30th Movement (see Chapter 2). As an experienced political activist, Sulami was no doubt also well aware of the visual currency that human remains have in a new era in which there is greater emphasis worldwide on human rights accountability. Television, media and even Internet audiences are, for example, now far more accustomed to images of exhumations and almost immediately equate such scenes with human rights abuses.[22] For Sulami, the physical evidence from this grave was very important as a form of proof of the killings. YPKP was, however, unable to use the physical evidence or Handoko's forensic findings for legal purposes, because without the Commission's support for investigating the killings there was no legal body to which YPKP could submit this evidence.

Looking back on this experience, several people who were part of the YPKP team realised that they had lost the evidence from this

[20] Ibid.
[21] Sulami, interviewed by Mike Carey in "Indonesia's Killing Fields", *Dateline* Television Series.
[22] Ferrándiz and Baer, "Digital Memory".

grave because they did not fully document the remains or the forensic landscape before reburial, thereby ruling out any future legal action in this case.[23] Yet YPKP had testimony from the prison guard about the location of the Wonosobo grave, testimony from a man who dug the grave, and testimony from families about the dates their family members disappeared, in addition to positive identification of several individuals.[24] Altogether, this evidence might have been sufficient to prove that those in the grave were victims from the 1965–68 killings. The fact that this evidence was not lodged according to legal procedures does not, however, mean that the exhumation served no purpose.

Above all, the exhumation had symbolic importance. Hundreds of people from East Java and Yogyakarta attended. For those whose family members were victims of the 1965 killings, the opening of this grave presented the first opportunity to witness evidence of the atrocities in which they had lost family members. Even though the remains in this grave may not have belonged to their relatives, those in attendance at the exhumation clearly wanted this past to be opened, and they wanted answers to questions that for almost 40 years they had not been able to ask, such as where their own family members had been buried. By attending this exhumation, they demonstrated their endorsement for the opening of this past.

For Sri, the woman who had been searching for her father, the recovery of her father's remains brought some sense of closure.[25] Research into the Srebrenica massacre in Bosnia reveals that families of missing persons are often driven by a strong desire to know the truth about what happened to their loved ones, yet until physical evidence is found they hold on to the belief that the missing person may be alive. At the same time, they often have mixed feelings about the identification of family members, preferring to hold on to the

---

[23] Sunarno, interviewed by Vannessa Hearman, 2 Feb. 2009, Jakarta; Yusuf Suwandi, interviewed by Vannessa Hearman, 29 Jan. 2009, Jakarta.

[24] "Remains of Slain Ex-Communists Found in Wonosobo". This article names several other people who were seeking information on their family members who had also disappeared from Wonosobo prison around the same time as the guard reported the killings took place. These included Endang Dwi Astuti (missing her father, Sandiwijoyo), Suwarsono (missing his father, Tondosuprapto) and Mrs Sarbibi Purwowihardjo (seeking her son Ibnu Santoro).

[25] Sri, interviewed by Katharine McGregor, 21 May 2007, Yogyakarta.

possibility that the missing person is still alive.[26] Margaret Samuels points out that even if a family member has been missing for a long time, "the moment of death" for that person's family is the point at which the missing person is identified through their clothes, belongings or DNA.[27] For this reason, exhumations are highly charged occasions for family members of victims.

YPKP had paid careful attention to obtaining community consent and ensuring some form of security for the people working on the exhumation, but what they had not perhaps anticipated were the psychological effects of opening the grave on those present. Based on work in forensic archaeology in many different countries, Samuels notes that reactions to exhumation and identification of remains can include trauma, withdrawal and anger.[28] In the Indonesian context, we know little about how decisions were made as to who was to be killed or imprisoned apart from a tendency towards imprisonment for those arrested in the main cities of Indonesia. For this reason members of YPKP, who are for the most part direct survivors of the violence of 1965, may feel there is some randomness in the fact that they survived while some of their comrades either died in prison or were killed. This is a source of further grief. In Sulami's memoir about her prison experiences, for example, she writes:

> However heavy the suffering the writer experienced, the writer is lucky to be alive. What about those who have already died? They disappeared from the face of the earth and from their families.[29]

Sulami suffered shock after this exhumation, and her health deteriorated rapidly due to the emotional and physical stress.[30] She died within a year.

---

[26] Mary Ellen Keough, Sara Kahn and Adrej Andrejevic, "Disclosing the Truth: Informed Participation in the Antemortem Database Project for Survivors of Srebrenica", *Health and Human Rights* 5, 1 (2000): 83–4.

[27] Margaret Samuels, "Antemortem Data Collection: Interaction with Families and Communities", in *The Scientific Investigation of Mass Graves: Towards Protocols and Standard Operating Procedures*, ed. Cox *et al.*, p. 512.

[28] Samuels, "Antemortem Data Collection", p. 511.

[29] Sulami, *Perempuan-Kebenaran dan Penjara* (Jakarta: Cipta Lestari, 1999), p. viii.

[30] "Sekitar Penggalian Kuburan Massal", p. 4; Sunarno, interviewed by Vannessa Hearman, 2 Feb. 2009, Jakarta.

The Contested Reburial in Kaloran, March 2001

The forensic team working on the Wonosobo exhumation was able to identify six of the 26 people in the grave. They returned the identified remains to their respective families for reburial.[31] The hospital staff had to wait over a month for permission from the head of police to continue with the identification process.[32] The remains of those who were not yet identified continued to be stored at Dr Sarjito Hospital in Yogyakarta. After several months, however, the hospital contacted YPKP to request them to collect the remains as soon as possible.[33] It was not clear whether the hospital was pressured to discontinue holding the remains by persons connected to the violence on the grounds that the remains constituted physical and potentially legal evidence of a crime, or whether there were more practical reasons behind the hospital's decision. It was at this point that things started to deteriorate.

YPKP was summoned by the hospital to do something within a short time period about the remains. They decided upon a reburial, accompanied by a small ceremony including multifaith prayers for those who had died. Irawan Mangunkusuma, a former political prisoner and member of YPKP, offered to donate some of his land for the reburial in the sub-district of Kaloran in the district of Temanggung, north of Yogyakarta. On 24 March 2001, the day before the scheduled reburial, members of a group by the name Kaloran Muslim Brotherhood (Forum Ukhuwah Islamiyah Kaloran, FUIK) made known their intentions to obstruct the ceremony.[34] A mob of young men blockaded the road leading to the house of Mangunkusuma. When members of the organising committee tried to flee the area in two vehicles, together with the remains of six people, a group of around 50 protesters stopped the second vehicle. They assaulted the driver and a member of the organising committee, dragged the coffins out of the vehicles and strewed the remains on the ground.

---

[31] Said, "Pemakaman-Kembali Kerangka Korban 65 Digagalkan", p. 4.

[32] "24 Kerangka Anggota PKI Masih Terkatung-katung", *Gatra*, 5 Dec. 2000.

[33] "Urgent Action 06-2001: 'Coffins of 65 Victims Raided by Mob'".

[34] Press Release, "Upacara Doa dan Penguburan Kembali Kerangka Korban Pembunuhan Wonosobo Gagal", *Soeara Kita: Untuk Kemanusiaan Keadilan dan Kebenaran* 14 (Apr. 2001), p. 3.

The skeletons were salvaged for later reburial, but the mob burnt the remaining coffins and destroyed Irawan's home.[35]

This highly charged confrontation came as a surprise to the organising committee. Recognising the continuing sensitivity to the issue of the killings, they had worked hard to ensure local authorities were in agreement with their plans. They had already reassured the religious leader Kiai Khozim, a member of the regional parliament from the PKB party, and the Temanggung police intelligence chief that the reburial would not be too "demonstrative": only six coffins would be used for the remains of the 20 unidentified bodies recovered from the Wonosobo exhumations, with the remains of two to five people in each coffin. In addition, they had opted to use smaller rather than full-sized coffins. A YPKP committee had also visited Khozim's nearby Islamic boarding school, the Sumur Blandung Boarding School (Pondok Pesantren Sumur Blandung), to gain approval for the reburial. Based on this meeting, four of the five participants agreed to the ceremony, though one person threatened he would lead an action against the planned reburial.[36] As a result, YPKP planned to cancel the reburial, but the protest went ahead.

Despite appeals from the Asian Human Rights Commission and the National Commission on Human Rights,[37] there were no arrests or prosecutions of those responsible for the violence. The violence that accompanied this disruption shocked and frightened those involved and led to a reluctance to proceed with any further exhumations of graves. For this reason, the event deserves careful analysis.

Many of the banners erected around Kaloran replicated New Order propaganda about the PKI deserving their fate and being an unclean or contaminating force (see Chapter 2). Banners reading "There is no place here for PKI skulls", "Burn the PKI skulls" and "Stop this" were erected near Mangunkusuma's house. One man from Kaloran commented to journalists who recorded the event that "this is not a PKI area, it is not a suitable place for the reburial of these

[35] "Urgent Action 06-2001: 'Coffins of 65 Victims Raided by Mob'".
[36] Press Release, "Upacara Doa dan Penguburan Kembali Kerangka Korban Pembunuhan Wonosobo Gagal", p. 3.
[37] "Urgent Action 06-200: 'Coffins of 65 Victims Raided by Mob'".

bones".[38] Umar Said, joint founder of YPKP, interpreted the disruption as evidence of "how strong the New Order's poison had been over the decades".[39] Said thus understood the opposition to YPKP's activities as being primarily a result of the success of the New Order's promotion of anti-communism, but propaganda alone does not go far enough to explain this violent opposition.

Mary Zurbuchen interpreted the disruption of the Kaloran reburial as evidence of a return to "the familiar polarisation of left and right or communism against Islam".[40] By this she referred to a rapid slide from a new openness to all aspects of history immediately after the collapse of the Suharto regime in 1998, to an unwillingness to examine this history outside of these two binary categories. She interpreted the disruption of the attempted reburial as a product of the rise of Islamist ideology in Indonesia. There was certainly a clear and visible connection between the obstruction and members of the local or wider Islamic community. The anti-communist forum behind the disruption erected banners reading "The Islamic community rejects the reburial of ex-PKI".[41] Muslim organisations were also clearly behind this action (see below). Yet contrary to Zurbuchen's interpretation, the groups behind the disruption included those with past links to the violence in addition to those with more recent origins, which were closely identified with a more strident Islamist ideology. Dating back to the killings, some Muslim leaders used ideas of Islam and specific theological concepts to justify the killings.[42] Yet there are also particular reasons why this discourse has both persisted in the rhetoric of older organisations and, as Zurbuchen suggests, been deployed by newer groups with no direct connection to this past.

---

[38] Chris Hilton, *Shadow Play: Indonesia's Forgotten Holocaust*, Hilton Cordell/Vagabond Films and Thirteen/WNET New York in association with the Australian Film Finance Corp, broadcast on SBS Australia, 2 Feb. 2003.

[39] Said, "Pemakaman Kembali Kerangka Korban 65 Digagalkan", pp. 6–7.

[40] Mary Zurbuchen, "History, Memory and the 1965 Incident in Indonesia", *Asian Survey* 42, 4 (July–Aug. 2002): 564–81.

[41] I was able to view the banners in the documentary *Shadow Play*, which includes footage of the disruption.

[42] Katharine E. McGregor, "A Bridge and a Barrier: Islam, Reconciliation, and the 1965 Killings in Indonesia", in *Reconciling Indonesia: Grassroots Agency for Peace*, ed. Birgit Bräuchler (London: Routledge, 2009), p. 216.

Syaiful H. Shodiq, the NU activist who had assisted YPKP with the attempted reburial in Kaloran, revealed a more complex scenario behind the sequence of events in Kaloran.[43] Between the time of the Wonosobo exhumation and the Kaloran incident, NU activists from 18 towns in Java had formalised their commitment to researching 1965 and working towards improving relations between former political prisoners and the wider community. They formed the organisation Syarikat (Santri Society for People's Advocacy, Masyarakat Santri untuk Advokasi Rakyat). Syaiful, who was by then a member of Syarikat, was again contacted by YPKP to assist in "socialising" the idea of the reburial in Kaloran, meaning gradually explaining the intent behind the reburial by using his existing networks within NU. Although he was given only one week to do this, he felt it would be possible because one year earlier a YPKP event had been held in Kaloran without incident. According to Syaiful's contacts in the Temanggung area, the military had tried to provoke the hard-line factions from two political parties — United Development Party (Partai Persatuan Pembangunan, PPP) and PKB — to join in on this action and to try to intimidate Ansor members so that they would not support YPKP. Here it appears the military, which had a clear interest in avoiding prosecution for its role in the violence of 1965, was able to provoke such a reaction by playing on fears within two NU-linked parties of a new alliance between NU youths and former communists.

Syaiful believed that members of the two Muslim political parties, PKB and PPP, initiated the action but that the majority of demonstrators came from the Holy War Fighters (Laskar Jihad) in Yogyakarta. YPKP's press release about the disruption also states that most demonstrators came from outside of Kaloran.[44] Laskar Jihad was set up by Ja'far Umar Thalib as a paramilitary wing of the Communication Forum of the Followers of the Sunna and the Community of the Prophet (Forum Komunikasi Ahlu Sunnah wal-Jam'ah) in January 2000 and consisted of around 10,000 young Salafi-Wahhabi

[43] Syaiful H. Shodiq, interviewed by Katharine McGregor, 22 May 2007, Yogyakarta.

[44] Press release, "Upacara Doa dan Penguburan Kembali Kerangka Korban Pembunuhan Wonosobo Gagal", p. 3.

inspired men. Members of Laskar Jihad were heavily focused on military-style training and fighting for the cause of Muslims against the Christians in the Moluccan conflict, which began in 1999. They also strongly endorsed a world view in which Zionism and communism were identified as enemies of Islam.[45] Although NU members generally held more moderate views towards Laskar Jihad followers, Noorhaidi Hasan notes that since the end of the Habibie presidency in 1999, several Islamist groups such as Laskar Jihad and the Indonesian Islamic Missionary Council (Dewan Dakwah Islamiyah Indonesia, DDII) were looking for a cause that would unite and mobilise Muslims against secular groups.[46] The name adopted by the protesting group, the Kaloran Muslim Brotherhood (Forum Ukhuwah Islamiyah Kaloran), includes the term "*ukhuwah Islamiyah*", meaning "Muslim brotherhood and solidarity", which makes direct reference to the idea of a shared Islamic cause. The term "ukhuwah Islamiyah" was central to the ideology of the firmly anti-communist Islamic party Masyumi, banned in 1960 by President Sukarno.[47] The reburial thus became a cause that would enable Laskar Jihad to try to unite with other Muslim groups.

Even so, why did the Kaloran reburial lead to such a violent response? Was it connected to "memories" or "identities" dating back to the 1960s, or was it the product of more recent political alliances and factors? Ariel Heryanto argues that the violent disruption manifested from the fact that the violence of 1965–66 "has been a crucial force in the formation of subject identities, fantasies and everyday activities of this nation for decades and it has outlived New Order rule itself".[48] For groups with historical connections to the violence, this certainly holds true. The reburial threatened a key source of identity for those who had previously claimed that their participation in the killings was a form of service to the nation or to Islam. The coordinators for the anti-communists in Temanggung were NU

---

[45] Noorhaidi Hasan, "Faith and Politics: The Rise of the Laskar Jihad in the Era of Transition in Indonesia", *Indonesia* 73 (Apr. 2002): 146–7.

[46] Hasan, "Faith and Politics", p. 160.

[47] Greg Fealy and Bernhard Platzdasch, "The Masyumi Legacy: Between Islamist Idealism and Political Exigency", *Studia Islamika* 12, 1 (2005): 78.

[48] Ariel Heryanto, *State Terrorism and Political Identity in Indonesia: Fatally Belonging* (London and New York: Routledge, 2006), p. 3.

people from the PKB. These people claimed that they rejected YPKP's efforts to "create a Heroes' Cemetery for Communists".[49] Many people from YPKP's network around Indonesia — from Bali, Banten, West Java, Jakarta and Yogyakarta — had come to Kaloran to attend the reburial, so there was to be a large gathering of people for the ceremony,[50] but there were no plans to make this site into a "heroes' cemetery". Nevertheless, the site would have been symbolic as the first case of a reburial of those murdered in the purges, and possibly it would have become the focus of ongoing commemorations for victims of the violence, for there are very few other sites that commemorate those who died during this period.

The Kaloran reburial was also threatening to groups associated with the violence because of the reburial's wider symbolic importance. The aim of the reburial was for the unclaimed remains to be reburied in a "respectful manner", with accompanying prayers to be read by Muslim, Christian and Buddhist religious officials as a sign of respect for the dead.[51] In making the representation that these victims deserved respectful burials with religious endorsement, YPKP directly challenged official New Order constructions of communists as atheists. In holding the reburial, YPKP was thus attempting to re-humanise those who had died. Indirectly, it also highlighted the lack of humanity exercised by the victims' killers in crassly dumping the victims' bodies together in an unmarked grave. In doing so, YPKP reversed the stereotype of the PKI as inhumane killers of the seven military martyrs in the September 30th Movement.[52] By highlighting the inhumanity of these deaths, YPKP also raised the possibility of prosecution for perpetrators. Indeed, Sulami's aim was to gather evidence for the purpose of prosecution. For this reason, the recovery and attempt to rebury the physical remains of victims led to an extreme reaction — possibly as a means of forewarning others against conducting further exhumations. The use of terror to deter those seeking

---

[49] Syaiful H. Shodiq, interviewed by Katharine McGregor, 22 May 2007, Yogyakarta.

[50] Said, "Pemakaman Kembali Kerangka Korban 65 Digagalkan", p. 6.

[51] Press release, "Upacara Doa dan Penguburan Kembali Kerangka Korban Pembunuhan Wonosobo Gagal", p. 3.

[52] Katharine McGregor, *History in Uniform: Military Ideology and the Construction of the Indonesian Past* (Singapore: SEA Series, NUS Press, 2007), pp. 100–2.

to address past human rights abuses has been common in the last four decades of Indonesian history.

The violent response to the reburial was also triggered, however, by national political frictions at the time of the Kaloran reburial. In March 2001, Wahid was over a year into his presidency and under threat of impeachment. One reaction to this threat had been expressions of loyalty to him from NU constituents. There were strong anti-PDI-P sentiments within the NU due to the fact that Megawati held the Vice-Presidency and it was then already a real possibility that she could take over from Wahid (which she went on to do in July 2001). So the links between YPKP and PDI-P may have fuelled resentment towards this reburial and the perceived willingness of some Ansor members to support it. In addition, members of Laskar Jihad associated Wahid with a range of conspiracy theories, including Zionist and Christian collaboration, but also the proposed revival of the Indonesian Communist Party due to his proposal to lift the ban on communism.[53]

According to Syaiful, YPKP members reacted very strongly to what had happened in Kaloran and they wanted to fight back. YPKP contacted people within the PDI-P security forces and put them on alert to be ready for a fight with the security forces linked to the PPP and the PKB. Syaiful tried to persuade them that this would be counterproductive and asked for more time to speak to members of the Islamic community to try and explain things. In a meeting with religious teachers in Temanggung, the head of the NU in Jepara, the head of Ansor for the Yogyakarta area (Nuridin Amin) and former political prisoners, Syaiful explained YPKP's ideas. He appealed to these religious leaders by stating that Wahid had asked those within the NU to fight for democracy in Indonesia. Despite the very fragile position of Wahid at this time, Syaiful was also able to draw upon Wahid's statements as a reference point to convince the religious leaders to make peace with YPKP. The religious leaders then disbanded the anti-communist group the Kaloran Muslim Brotherhood, which had appeared to oppose the reburial. A week later, a meeting was held between those who organised Kaloran and local religious leaders. They participated in an *islah* (an Islamic ceremony of mutual forgiveness) and performed a prayer (*sholat*) together.

---

53 Hasan, "Faith and Politics", p. 164.

The Legacies of Kaloran and Other Mass Grave Investigations

The Kaloran incident shocked members of YPKP and had enduring ramifications for the organisation. Many within YPKP realised that the reburial had not been well planned and that they had perhaps been overconfident about the extent of change in society's views about the events of 1965. The same year as the attempted reburials, YPKP split into two groups: YPKP and the Institute for the Investigation of Victims of the 1965 Event (Lembaga Penelitian Korban Peristiwa 1965, LPKP). Some members followed the LPKP under Sulami and others YPKP, which was led by Pramoedya. The key difference between the two organisations was that YPKP wanted to focus exclusively on research, whereas LPKP wanted to become more focused on mass organisational activities and more particularly an alliance with PDI-P.[54] In 2007, YPKP split again into YPKP HAM (HAM stands for "Hak Asasi Manusia", or "human rights") and YPKP 65, with the former devoting more time to research and the latter wishing to be more focused on 1965.[55] All three organisations have continued to document mass graves throughout Indonesia since the Kaloran incident. They have not, however, been involved in any further exhumations. Yusuf Suwandi, head of research in YPKP HAM, stated in January 2009 that the political situation did not support such initiatives because those in power were still firmly anti-communist.[56] In 2004, retired General Susilo Bambang Yudhoyono, the son-in-law of anti-communist military hero Sarwo Edhie (Chapter 4), was elected President. Asvi Warman Adam notes that Yudhoyono delayed the selection of members for the proposed Truth and Reconciliation Commission.[57] In 2006 the Constitutional Court declared aspects of the law governing the formation and operation of the Commission unconstitutional, and the Commission was never formed.

---

[54] Yusuf Suwandi, interviewed by Vannessa Hearman, 29 Jan. 2009, Jakarta.

[55] There are different versions of the causes for these splits across members and across the three organisations.

[56] Yusuf Suwandi, interviewed by Vannessa Hearman, 29 Jan. 2009, Jakarta.

[57] Asvi Warman Adam, "The History of Violence and the State in Indonesia", CRISE Working Paper No. 54, June 2008, p. 18.

Another organisation that has been active in grave identification is Shoe for Peace (Kasut Perdamaian). When Shoe for Peace workers tried to excavate a grave in 2002, they faced similar obstacles to YPKP. Esther Yusuf and Albertus Suryo Wicaksono, who run this organisation, are both too young to have experienced the 1960s directly, yet they believe mass grave identification is highly important to the process of "re-humanising" the victims. Yusuf was the coordinator for the Wonosobo excavation, but she was dismissed by YPKP 65 prior to the Kaloran incident due to strong differences of opinion about the direction of YPKP. In 2002 Shoe for Peace opened up a cave in south Blitar called "Rat Hole" (Luweng Tikus), into which bodies of those killed in connection with the communist resistance in Blitar of 1968 had been discarded (see Chapter 8). In the case of this grave, a military man actually came forward and gave testimony that he had taken people to this site for execution. Retrieving remains from the cave was very difficult due to the awkward access and the limited oxygen beyond a certain depth, so professional cavers had to be used. They estimated that there were remains of at least 41 people in the cave but were able to remove the bones of only one victim.[58] Since 2001, working with ex-political prisoners such as Putmainah — former head of Gerwani in the Blitar region and now a member of YPKP — Shoe for Peace has identified 58 graves across 13 provinces of Indonesia.[59] Suryo stated that "finding graves is part of the process of opening up the tragedy. We want them to be valued again as human beings".[60] Putmainah emphasised the need to rebury the remains respectfully, but also to try and identify the surviving family members of the victims.[61]

Shoe for Peace also attempted to "socialise" the idea of opening up the south Blitar grave with the local community for a period of seven months by meeting with local leaders and people at the grass

---

[58] Eka Sukanti, "Menguak Misteri Luweng Tikus di Blitar Selatan: Cukup Dimakamkan secara Manusiawi", *Sinar Harapan* (30 Sept. 2002), http:www.sinarharapan.co.id/berita/209/30/sh04.html, accessed 14 May 2009.

[59] "Seminar 1965 Incident Road Show", Indonesia Media On-line, 22 Sept. 2007, http:www.indonesiamedia.com/2007/10/local/Seminar.htm, accessed 27 Jan. 2009.

[60] Albertus Suryo Wicaksono, email correspondence, 23 Apr. 2009.

[61] Sukanti, "Menguak Misteri Luweng Tikus di Blitar Selatan."

roots.[62] It engaged forensic experts to confirm that the bones that had been found were human bones and to determine how these people had been killed: with firearms or with sharp weapons or blunt objects. The organisation had approval from the local village head in Blitar, but the Regent, Imam Muhadi, strongly opposed the research and opening up of this history.[63] Muhadi himself was a PDI-P man, suggesting a diversity of views on the events of 1965 within the former Sukarnoist party. The Blitar branches of a number of Islamic organisations went further than this objection by signing a joint statement opposing the plan and expressing their readiness to mobilise their members to obstruct any such exhumation. The organisations named in the statement were the Blitar branches of the Indonesian Islamic Missionary Council, the Islamic Youth Movement (Gerakan Pemuda Islam), the Association of Indonesian Islamic Students (Paguyuban Keluarga Besar Pelajar Islam Indonesia), Muhammadiyah, NU, the Association of Victims of PKI Cruelty in the Years 1967–68 in south Blitar (Paguyuban Korban Keganasan PKI Tahun 1967–68 Blitar Selatan), the National Council Presidium of Alumni of the Islamic Students' Association (Presidium KAHMI), the Islamic Students' Association (Himpunan Mahasiswa Islam, HMI), the Crescent and Star Party (Partai Bulan Bintang), the People's Mandate Party (Partai Amanat Nasional), Golkar and the Indonesian Centre for Community Studies (Yayasan Pusat Kajian Komunitas Indonesia). The last of these organisations is an anti-communist group that has mobilised protests numerous times with military support and suggests careful orchestration of protests in the name of Islamic organisations.

In response to these objections, Shoe for Peace held a press conference at the office of the National Commission on Human Rights and the Commission sent a letter to the regent of Blitar, the police and the governor of East Java and also to the Brawijaya commander asking for an explanation as to why the investigation at Rat Hole had been banned. Similar to the case of the Kaloran incident, there

---

62 Albertus Suryo Wicaksono, email correspondence, 23 Apr. 2009.

63 The Blitar branch of NU was also listed as supporting the action, but neither a signature nor an official stamp was included next to this entry on the statement of protest. Suryo also suspects some other stamps may have been forged. Albertus Suryo Wicaksono, email correspondence, 23 Apr. 2009.

was no response and no form of legal intervention. Shoe for Peace had hoped rather optimistically that the state would oversee the excavation and reburial of the remains in addition to guarding the cave and making it a commemorative site.[64] As in the case of the Kaloran reburial, the National Commission on Human Rights was supportive, but the government did not grant permission for a reburial of remains from the cave; instead, it declared that the cave was on state-owned land and that it suspected the remains of the victims were from an earlier period, before the 1960s. No progress has been made on these issues due to a lack of funds and also because Shoe for Peace is waiting for a time when it has the trust of the local bureaucracy and the local community is ready for such a project. The organisation hopes to one day construct a museum or "monument of peace" in Blitar to commemorate the victims of 1965.[65] It has already designed a monument that fits in with the landscape of the local area. Suryo stated that the planned monument "is not intended to compete with the military's Trisula monument or museum", which celebrates the people and the military's efforts to crush the PKI, but instead to "provide the public with a sign of respect for the people who died at that time who are people not animals". Shoe for Peace wants the monument to be "an alternative icon" and "a solution to this historical tragedy". It is clear, however, that such a monument would challenge the Trisula monument in south Blitar, for it was exactly this kind of memorialisation of the dead that precipitated the violent response to the Kaloran reburial. It seems that the most confrontational aspect of memorialisation of the dead, for those who object, is that it gives recognition to those who died as victims of violence. Those who defend the counter-revolutionary violence believe, on the other hand, that members of the PKI were not victims and that they were instead deserving of their fate, due to both their alleged role in the September 30th Movement and provocations towards Islamic groups prior to this (see Chapter 5). The assumption of Shoe for Peace activists that such a memorial would prevent this kind of violence ever occurring again is therefore too simplistic. Since its efforts to open up Rat Hole, Shoe for Peace has not been involved in any further grave excavations.

---

[64] Albertus Suryo Wicaksono, email correspondence, 23 Apr. 2009.

[65] "Foundation Probes 1968 Blitar Massacre", *Jakarta Post*, 14 May 2009.

In Solo, Central Java, the Joint Secretariat for 1965 (Sekretariat Bersama 65, SEKBER 65), an alliance of people concerned about the human rights abuses and ongoing effects of 1965, has been very active in identifying mass gravesites. The Joint Secretariat for 1965 was founded in 2006 in that city but now has representatives in 15 districts of Central Java.[66] It has recorded the locations of several graves in Wonogiri, Boyolali, Karanganyar, Cilacap, Banyumas and Sukoharjo Districts.[67] This organisation is also collecting data from primary witnesses to determine who carried out the killings, patterns in the killings, and information on who was killed. Based on this method of data collection, it has been able to estimate how many people are buried in known graves. From the graves it has investigated, it believes that some graves contain as few as seven victims whereas the largest grave for which it has data contains the remains of around 1,000 people. Yusuf Suwandi, of YPKP HAM, stated that in the regions only family members of victims would share information about the location of mass graves.[68] He noted, "It is usually only the victim community who will speak to them. Those outside of this group are not brave enough to do so."[69] Despite greater openness to examining the history of the killings since the collapse of the Suharto regime in 1998, there is still a sense of fear about sharing knowledge of the graves with outsiders and the possible consequences of this.

Joint Secretariat leaders point to many obstacles in their efforts to conduct this research, especially from the government bureaucracy, the military and the police. They also believe that groups who "claim to be based on religion", such as the Islamic Defenders Front (Front Pembela Islam, FPI), a vigilante group that usually focuses on crushing so-called societal vices, firmly resist their work. In response, the Secretariat has been trying to form broader coalitions with Islamic

---

[66] The districts are Wonogiri, Sukoharjo, Klaten, Sragen, Karanganyar, Boyolali, Purworejo, Magelang, Wonosobo, Temanggung, Kebumen, Banyumas, Banjarnegara, Purbalingga and Cilacap.

[67] Winarso, "Advokasi Pelanggaran Berat Ham Tragedi 1965/66", Paper delivered at the 1965–1966 Indonesian Killings Revisited Conference, National University of Singapore, 17–19 June 2009.

[68] Yusuf Suwandi, interviewed by Vannessa Hearman, 4 Feb. 2009, Jakarta.

[69] Ibid.

groups such as HMI and many other student organisations to ensure wider community support for its work. To do this, it avoids talking about ideology and instead emphasises a message of humanity. It also suggests that the continuing influence of the Indonesian military, which it claims played a key role in the killings, is another significant barrier to official support for its work.

The NU-aligned organisation Syarikat has formed strong alliances with survivor groups, yet it is also cautious about proceeding with research on mass graves. In 2007, former head of Syarikat Imam Aziz stated that excavation was meaningful for families but could be counterproductive in terms of achieving prosecutions if it was not connected with a legal process.[70]

After Aziz made this comment, new commissioners for the National Commission on Human Rights, appointed in 2007, began documenting and researching mass graves around Indonesia under a new mandate to investigate the post-30th September violence. Commissioners appointed for the period 2007–12 formed a new team, headed by Nur Kholis, to investigate more thoroughly the counter-revolutionary violence. Due to the controversies that investigations in Java raised, such as those noted above, the commissioners initially concentrated their research on islands outside of Java. The Commission, however, focused on the collection of evidence rather than proceeding to a legal investigation.[71] At the time of writing, the Commission had finished collecting formal statements from victims and survivors of the violence about patterns in the killings and related violence such as sexual abuse. This evidence was to be presented to the Attorney General.

Comparative Lessons for Indonesia

In the Wonosobo exhumation and in discussions about further exhumations, survivors and human rights activists tended to emphasise the humanitarian purposes of exhumations over their potential legal

---

[70] Imam Aziz, interviewed by Katharine McGregor, 22 May 2007, Yogyakarta.

[71] Stanley, interviewed by Vannessa Hearman, 2 Feb. 2009, Jakarta and Nurkholis; "The Role of Komnas HAM in Conducting Inquiry into the 1965–66 Killings", Paper delivered at the 1965–1966 Indonesian Killings Revisited Conference, National University of Singapore, 17–19 June 2009.

use as evidence, the latter being more likely to arouse sensitivities. Yet even when NGOs and survivor organisations stressed the humanitarian dimensions of exhumations and the planned reburial at Kaloran, their efforts met with protest. The symbolism of recognising and re-humanising those who died in 1965–66 seemed particularly confrontational to those involved in the violence, including some members of the NU, but even more so to the military as an institution, which since 1966 had every year celebrated its role in crushing communists as a watershed in the history of the nation.[72]

In countries that have overthrown repressive regimes, victims' organisations often take the lead in challenging official versions of history. Sometimes there has been almost a complete reversal in the national narrative about the past. In Argentina, for example, after the fall of the military dictatorship in 1983, victims' groups were able to dictate a new version of the past with little open confrontation until the mid-1990s.[73] In Indonesia, former political prisoners who joined victim's advocacy groups such as YPKP also tried to promote new versions of history in which they downplayed their past political activism and accentuated their suffering and their rights as victims. One goal of identifying mass graves was to provide undeniable proof of murder. Yet despite the support of some NGOs and some younger members of NU, victims' groups were continuously threatened in their efforts to challenge the national narrative that the killings and repressions were justified because of the alleged role of the PKI in the September 30th Movement. There is still a widespread view that those killed and political prisoners were deserving of their fate. Senior members of the NU and the military, for example, frequently state that had the PKI come to power, they would have rounded up those on their "death lists". In short, they promote the idea that it was an atmosphere of "kill or be killed".

Another reason for the ongoing resistance to a revised understanding of the counter-revolutionary violence is that the perpetrators were not overthrown during the Suharto regime. Instead they remain important political players. Nanci Adler notes the vital difference

[72] McGregor, *History in Uniform*, pp. 84–5.

[73] Elizabeth Jelin, *State Repression and the Labors of Memory*, trans. Judy Rein and Marcial Godoy-Anativia (Minneapolis: University of Minnesota Press, 2003), p. 37.

between post-1989 Russia and South Africa and its Truth and Reconciliation Commission or Germany and the Nuremberg trials: in the former there was no "reckoning with a victorious opponent either from without or within", and victims had little representation in positions of government.[74] In Indonesia the same dynamic is present. Soon after Suharto resigned, the military withdrew from any formal political role — but in practice it remained politically influential. Moreover, the military's former allies in Islamic organisations, including NU, returned to politics with an increased say in political matters. At the same time, the ban on communism remained in place: former political prisoners remained marginal members of society, and their families continued to be discriminated against.

The protests against the Kaloran reburial and the planned exhumation of Rat Hole were all made in the name of "Islamic organisations", thereby giving the objections the appearance of an Islamic dimension. On closer examination, however, it appears that behind the protests was a curious alliance of recently created Islamist organisations looking for a shared Islamic cause, and factions within two parties aligned with NU, a key sponsor and participant in the violence of 1965. In the case of NU, these objections related not just to the acknowledgement of victims of the violence in which NU was implicated, but also to the alliance between NU-based NGOs and survivors of the violence who jointly organised or at least supported the exhumation and reburial. Although the military is now more cautious about intimidating investigations into human rights abuses, sections of the military still endorse Islamic-sponsored anticommunism because of shared concerns about future prosecutions.

Indonesian responses to the exhumations and memorialisation of the dead have similarities elsewhere. In Guatemala, widows and orphans of those who had perished in the 1960s at the hands of the armed forces or civil defence patrols formed a committee to exhume the mass graves of family members and rebury them and then build a monument.[75] They had support from the National Coordination of Widows of Guatemala and the Guatemalan Forensic Anthropology

[74] Adler, "The Future of the Soviet Past Remains Unpredictable", p. 1110.
[75] Julie Stewart, "A Measure of Justice: The Rabinal Human Rights Movement in Post-War Guatemala", *Qualitative Sociology* 31, 3 (2008): 237.

Team. Several activists received death threats, sometimes anonymously and sometimes overtly from local soldiers. In March 1994, a grave-site monument was blown up and graves were defaced. In this case, however, the activists responded by building a bigger monument. In Russia, after several years of identifying graves, in 2002 the victim's group Memorial began to encounter resistance from the Federal Security Service of the Russian Federation, a successor organisation to the Stalin-period NKVD (The People's Commissariat for Internal Affairs), which was responsible for many of the killings.[76] It is clear from the above that support for exhumations does not necessarily increase with the passage of time since the initial violence.

In Indonesia the possibilities for further investigation, exhumation and legal action based on evidence from mass graves depend upon the response of the Attorney General to the findings of the investigation by the National Commission on Human Rights, mentioned above. The Commission completed its report in July 2011, but following discussion of the report in a House of Representatives Plenary Session the commissioners were requested to provide more specific information on the timing and locations of the crimes they had documented for the 1965–66 period. At the time of writing the Commission was still revising the report, but it was facing mounting pressure from victims and other human rights NGOs to complete its findings and release them to the public and the Attorney General. If the Attorney General's office accepts the Commission's findings, it can conduct further investigations and then recommend to the Parliament the formation of an Ad Hoc Human Rights Court.[77] Such a court could deal with the evidence located in many mass graves around Indonesia, allowing exhumations and the collection of evidence to be followed by prosecutions. Because the military is implicated in most cases of these human rights abuses, and perhaps also

---

[76] Adler, "The Future of the Soviet Past Remains Unpredictable", p. 1108.

[77] In February 2008, the Constitutional Court issued Decree No. 18/PUU-V/2007 concerning article 43 of Law No. 26/2000 confirming that the Attorney General should conduct further investigations to confirm allegations of human rights abuses before presenting these to the parliament. [AHRC Open Letter] INDONESIA: UN Working Group urged to intervene into disappearances from 1997–98, as impunity continues, http://www.ahrchk.net/statements/mainfile.php/2006statements/2274, accessed 9 June 2010.

because President Yudhoyono is not only himself a former general but also married to the daughter of Sarwo Edhie, one of the main perpetrators of the violence, he has been more reluctant to address human rights abuses than, for example, the late President Abdurrahman Wahid. In 2007, when the Supreme Court recommended to President Yudhoyono the formal rehabilitation of victims of the 1965 massacres, he did not act. Other attempts to address past human rights violations, such as the Talangsari incident of 1993 — in which hundreds died in a military attack on an isolated Islamic community in the southern Sumatran province of Lampung — as also the case of the disappearances of activists in 1997–98, have failed to result in the formation of ad hoc courts after the submission of reports to the Attorney General.[78]

While the Indonesian constitution now incorporates strong human rights provisions, the procedures for investigating and then proceeding with potential prosecutions allow for continuing political intervention. Stubborn resistance is encountered in the continuing role and influence of anti-communist figures within the central government, including the President but also retired members of the military and senior members of organisations such as NU. There is also pressure from Islamist groups who can still use communism as a rallying point. In the context of an increasingly religious society, the equation of communism with atheism further discourages Indonesian politicians from taking up the cause of investigating the events of 1965–68.

Significantly, there is little international pressure to investigate this counter-revolutionary violence, especially amongst Western nations — such as the US, UK and Australia — that were complicit in the killings (Chapter 3). This stance is in marked contrast to US pressure to hold international trials of those responsible for the killings in Cambodia during the reign of Pol Pot between 1975 and 1979. It also contrasts with pressure upon the Indonesian government from Australia in particular to prosecute those responsible for human rights abuses by the military in East Timor or in West Papua. Investigations have been convened but either not led to prosecutions or resulted in lesser charges and not against high-ranking officers.

[78] Stanley, interviewed by Vannessa Hearman, 2 Feb. 2009, Jakarta.

Nevertheless, the passage of time has allowed the release of documents in the US, UK and Australia that cast light on the destruction of the PKI, and it is likely that eventually documents will also become available in Russia and China. A fuller account of this past may be as much as can be expected. The experience of Spain, and also countries in Central and South America, suggests that until some forms of truth telling and reconciliation are achieved, antagonisms between those who carried out and those who were impacted by the violence will continue for generations. General Sarwo Edhie's acceptance of responsibility late in his life may offer a way forward. In a similar vein, as this volume goes to press, President Yudhoyono has unexpectedly signalled the possibility of making a presidential apology, before the end of his final term in 2014, for all human rights abuses.

Glossary and Abbreviations

abangan	nominal Muslim, especially in Java
aksi sepihak	unilateral action carried out by PKI-affiliated peasants to reclaim land, 1964–65
Ansor	Nahdlatul Ulama youth organisation
Banser	Barisan Ansor Serba-guna (Ansor Multipurpose Brigade), armed NU affiliate
Baperki	Badan Permusyawaratan Kewarganegaraan Indonesia (Consultative Body for Indonesian Citizenship)
Biro Chusus	Special Bureau, secret PKI organisation
BTI	Barisan Tani Indonesia (Indonesian Peasants' Union), PKI affiliate
CIA	Central Intelligence Agency (USA)
DI	Darul Islam (Abode of Islam), Islamic rebel movement in 1950s
fatwa	religious edict
G30S	Gerakan 30 September (September 30th Movement) (also abbreviated G-30-S, G.30.S)
GSNI	Gerakan Siswa Nasional Indonesia (Movement of Indonesian Nationalist High School Students), PNI affiliate
Gerwani	Gerakan Wanita Indonesia (Indonesian Women's Movement), PKI aligned
Gestapu	acronym for September 30th Movement (coined by Brigadier General Sugandhi, Director of Armed Forces daily newspaper *Angkatan Bersendjata*)
Gestok	acronym for Gerakan 1 Oktober (October 1st Movement); term coined by President Sukarno

Guided Democracy	political system proclaimed by President Sukarno in 1959
Hanra	Pertahanan Rakyat (People's Defence), civilians under the Army
Hansip	Pertahanan Sipil (Civil Defence), civilians under the Army
HMI	Himpunan Mahasiswa Islam (Islamic Students' Association), Masyumi affiliate
HSI	Himpunan Sarjana Indonesia (Indonesian Graduates' Association), PKI affiliate
Huaqiao Zhonghui	Association of Overseas Chinese
IMF	International Monetary Fund
IPKI	Ikatan Penerus Kemerdekaan Indonesia (League of Upholders of Indonesian Independence), Army-sponsored political party
IPPI	Ikatan Pemuda Pelajar Indonesia (League of Indonesian Student Youth), PKI affiliate
KAMI	Kesatuan Aksi Mahasiswa Indonesia (Indonesian University Student Action Front)
KAP-Gestapu	Kesatuan Aksi Pengganyangan Gestapu (Action Front to Crush the September 30th Movement)
KAPPI	Kesatuan Aksi Pemuda Pelajar Indonesia (Indonesian Student and Youth Action Front)
KASI	Kesatuan Aksi Sarjana Indonesia (Indonesian Graduates' Action Front)
kiai	Muslim religious scholar
Kodam	Komando Daerah Militer (Regional Military Command)
Kodim	Komando Distrik Militer (District Military Command)
Konfrontasi	Confrontation; Indonesian campaign to oppose the formation of Malaysia, 1963–66
Kopassus	Komando Pasukan Khusus (Army Special Forces Command)
Kopkamtib	Komando Operasi Pemulihan Keamanan dan Ketertiban (Operations Command to Restore Order and Security)

Korem	Komando Resort Militer (Sub-regional Military Command)
Kostrad	Komando Cadangan Strategis Angkatan Darat (Army Strategic Reserve)
Lekra	Lembaga Kebudayaan Rakjat (People's Cultural Institute), PKI affiliate
Lemhanas	Lembaga Pertahanan Nasional (National Resilience Institute)
Mahmillub	Mahkamah Militer Luar Biasa (Extraodinary Military Tribunal), used to try leaders of September 30th Movement
Manipol	*Manifesto Politik* (Political Manifesto)
Masyumi	modernist Islamic political party, banned by Sukarno in 1960
MPRS	Majelis Permusyawaratan Rakyat Sementara (Provisional People's Consultative Assemby)
Muhammadiyah	modernist Islamic social organisation, founded in 1912
Murba	national-communist political party, opposed to the PKI
Nasakom	*Nasionalisme, Agama, Komunisme* (Nationalism, Religion, Communism)
NU	Nahdlatul Ulama (Revival of the Islamic Scholars), political party from 1952 until 1973; thereafter a mass organisation
Operasi Trisula	Trisula Operation, against communist bases in south Blitar, 1968
Orde Baru	New Order; name coined in 1966 for the new Army-led regime
Orde Lama	Old Order; name coined in 1966 to refer to Sukarno-era state
Partindo	Partai Indonesia (Indonesia Party), left-nationalist political party
PDI-P	Partai Demokrat Indonesia-Perjuangan (Indonesian Democratic Party of Struggle)
Pemuda Pancasila	Pancasila Youth, IPKI affiliate
Pemuda Rakyat	People's Youth, PKI affiliate
peranakan	assimilated ethnic Chinese
Permesta	Piagam Perjuangan Semesta (Universal Struggle Charter), rebellion in Sulawesi in late 1950s

pesantren	Islamic boarding school
PII	Pelajar Islam Indonesia (Islamic Students of Indonesia), Masyumi affiliate
PKB	Partai Kebangkitan Bangsa (National Awakening Party), NU affiliate founded in 1998
PKI	Partai Komunis Indonesia (Indonesian Communist Party)
PMII	Pergerakan Mahasiswa Islam Indonesia (Indonesian Muslim Student Movement), NU affiliate
PNI	Partai Nasional Indonesia (Indonesian National Party), founded by Sukarno in 1926
PPP	Partai Persatuan Pembangunan (United Development Party), New Order "Islamic" political party
PRC	People's Republic of China
PRRI	Pemerintah Revolusioner Republik Indonesia (Revolutionary Government of the Republic of Indonesia), rebel movement/government in Sumatra, 1958
RPKAD	Resimen Para Komando Angkatan Darat (Army Para-commando Regiment)
RTM	Rumah Tahanan Militer (Military Detention Centre)
santri	student at an Islamic school; also refers to devout Muslim
Sarbuksi	Sarekat Buruh Kehutanan Seluruh Indonesia (All-Indonesia Forestry Workers' Union), PKI affiliate
SARBUPRI	Sarekat Buruh Perkebunan Republik Indonesia (Plantation Workers' Union of the Republic of Indonesia), PKI affiliate
SOBSI	Sentral Organisasi Buruh Seluruh Indonesia (Indonesian Workers' Union), PKI affiliate
SOKSI	Sentral Organisasi Karyawan Sosialis Indonesia (Central Organisation of Indonesian Socialist Workers)
Supersemar	Surat Perintah Sebelas Maret (Letter of 11 March 1966)

tameng	party militia
Tameng Marhaenis	PNI-affiliated youth organisation
Teperda	Team Pemeriksa Daerah (Regional Investigation Team)
totok	non-assimilated ethnic Chinese
ulama	Muslim Islamic scholar
wanra	Perlawanan Rakyat (People's Defence), civilians under the Army
YPKP	Yayasan Penelitian Korban Pembunuhan 1965/66 (Foundation for Research into Victims of the 1965/66 Killings)

Bibliography

Archives

Arsip Kotamadya Makassar [Makassar City Archive].

Arsip Muhammad Saleh Lahade, Badan Arsip dan Perpustakaan Daerah Provinsi Sulawesi Selatan [Muhammad Saleh Lahade Archive, South Sulawesi Province Library and Archive].

Arsip Pemerintah Kotamadya Ujung Pandang [Ujung Pandang City Government Archive].

Arsip Propinisi Sulawesi Selatan dan Sulawesi Tenggara 1946–1960 [South and Southeast Sulawesi Provincial Archive].

Guy Pauker Papers, Hoover Institution Archives, Stanford University.

Howard Jones Papers, Hoover Institution Archives, Stanford University.

John F. Kennedy Library [abbreviated JFK Library].

Koleksi Nahdlatul Ulama, Arsip Nasional Republik Indonesia.

National Archives of Australia [abbreviated NAA].

National Security Files, Lyndon B. Johnson Library [abbreviated LBJL].

United Kingdom National Archive [abbreviated UKNA].

United States National Archive [abbreviated NA].

United States Department of State, Central Files, National Archives and Records Administration [NARA], telegrams declassified through the Freedom of Information Act, Case #9100730 Indonesia Coup Attempt.

World Bank Archives.

Newspapers and Magazines

Angkatan Bersendjata (Jakarta)

Antara (Jakarta)

Berita Yudha (Jakarta)

大公報 [*Da Gong Bao*] (Hong Kong)

Duta Masjarakat (Jakarta)

The Economist

Far Eastern Economic Review

Fortune

Gatra (Jakarta)

工商日報 [*Gongshang Ribao*] (Hong Kong)
Harian Harapan (Medan)
Harian Rakjat (Jakarta)
華僑日報 [*Huaqiao Ribao*] (Hong Kong)
Indonesian Herald (Jakarta)
International Commerce
Jakarta Post (Jakarta)
Kompas (Jakarta)
New York Times
Patriot (Jakarta)
Pedoman Rakjat (Makassar)
人民日報 [*Renmin Ribao*] (Beijing)
Sinar Harapan (Jakarta)
South China Morning Post (Hong Kong)
Suara Indonesia (Denpasar)
Suara Merdeka (Semarang)
Tempo (Jakarta)
Wall Street Journal
Warta PIA
中國新聞 [*Zhongguo Xinwen*] (Guangzhou)

Books and Journal Articles

Adam, Asvi Warman, "The History of Violence and the State in Indonesia". CRISE Working paper no. 54 (June 2008).

Adler, Nanci, "The Future of the Soviet Past Remains Unpredictable: The Resurrection of Stalinist Symbols amidst the Exhumation of Mass Graves", *Europe-Asia Studies* 57, 8 (Dec. 2005): 1093–119.

Ahmad, Taufik, *Kamp Pengasingan Moncongloe*. Depok: Desantara, 2009.

Ahmadi, Aziz, ed., *Feisal Tanjung: Terbaik untuk Rakyat, Terbaik bagi ABRI*. Jakarta: Dharmapena, 1999.

Amal, Ichlasul, *Hubungan Pusat-Daerah: Kasus Sumatera Barat dan Sulawesi 1949–1979*. Yogyakarta: PAU-Studi Universitas Gadjah Mada, 1988.

Amnesty International, *Indonesia: An Amnesty International Report*. London: Amnesty International, 1977.

Anam, Choirul, *Pertumbuhan dan Perkembangan Nahdlatul Ulama*. Solo: Jatayu, 1985.

———, *Gerak Langkah Pemuda Ansor: Sebuah Percikan Sejarah Kelahiran*. Surabaya: Majalah Nahdlatul Ulama AULA, 1990.

Anderson, Benedict. "How Did the Generals Die?" *Indonesia* 43 (Apr. 1987): 109–134.

———, "Scholarship and Raison d'État: Personal Experience", *Indonesia* 62 (Oct. 1996): 1–18.

Anderson, Benedict R. and Ruth T. McVey, *A Preliminary Analysis of the October 1, 1965 Coup in Indonesia*. Ithaca: Modern Indonesia Project, Cornell University, 1971.

Anonymous. "Report from East Java", *Indonesia* 41 (Apr. 1986): 135–49.

———, "Laporan tentang Hasil Fact Finding Commission KOTI". Manuscript, 10 Jan. 1966.

Asba, Abdul Rasyid, *Kopra Makassar Perebutan Pusat dan Daerah: Kajian Sejarah Ekonomi Politik Regional di Indonesia*. Jakarta: Yayasan Obor Indonesia, 2007.

Atmowiloto, Arswendo, *Pengkhianatan G30S/PKI*. Jakarta: Sinar Harapan, 1986.

Azra, Azyumardi, "Islam and Terrorism", in *Voices of Islam in Southeast Asia: A Contemporary Sourcebook*, ed. Greg Fealy and Virginia Hooker. Singapore: Institute of Southeast Asian Studies, 2006, pp. 358–61.

Bachtiar, Harsja W., *Siapa Dia? Perwira tinggi Tentara Nasional Indonesia Angkatan Darat (TNI-AD)*. Jakarta: Djambatan, 1988.

Bigalke, Terance William, *Tana Toraja: A Social History of an Indonesian People*. Singapore: Singapore University Press, 2005.

Bird, Kai, *The Color of Truth. McGeorge Bundy and William Bundy: Brothers in Arms*. New York: Simon and Schuster, 1998.

Boden, Ragna, "The 'Gestapu' Events of 1965 in Indonesia: New Evidence from Russian and German Archives", *Bijdragen tot de Taal-, Land- en Volkenkunde* 163, 4 (2007): 507–29.

Bosra, Mustari, *Tuang Guru, Anrong Guru dan Daeng Guru: Gerakan Islam di Sulawesi Selatan 1914–1942*. Makassar: La Galigo Press, 2008.

Brackman, Arnold C., *The Communist Collapse in Indonesia*. New York: W.W. Norton and Co., 1969.

Brands, H.W., "The Limits of Manipulation: How the United States Didn't Topple Sukarno", *Journal of American History* 76 (1989): 785–808.

Bruinessen, Martin van, "Post-Soeharto Muslim Engagements with Civil Society and Democratization", in *Indonesia in Transition: Rethinking 'Civil Society,' 'Region' and 'Crisis'*, ed. Samuel Hanneman and Henk Schulte Nordholt. Yogyakarta: Pustaka Pelajar, 2004, pp. 37–66.

Bunnell, Frederick, "American 'Low Posture' Policy toward Indonesia in the Months Leading up to the 1965 'Coup'", *Indonesia* 50 (Oct. 1990): 29–60.

Bush, Robin, *Nahdlatul Ulama and the Struggle for Power within Islam and Politics in Indonesia*. Singapore: Institute of Southeast Asian Studies, 2009.

Central Intelligence Agency, *Indonesia–1965: The Coup that Backfired*. Washington, DC: CIA, 1968.

Centre for Village Studies, Gadjah Mada University, "Rural Violence in Klaten and Banyuwangi", in *The Indonesian Killings of 1965–66: Studies from*

Java and Bali, ed. Robert Cribb. Clayton: Centre of Southeast Asian Studies, Monash University, 1990, pp. 121–58.

Challis, Roland, *Shadow of a Revolution: Indonesia and the Generals*. Gloucestershire: Sutton Publishing, 2001.

Conboy, Ken, *Kopassus: Inside Indonesia's Special Forces*. Jakarta: Equinox, 2003.

Coppel, Charles, *Indonesian Chinese in Crisis*. Kuala Lumpur: Oxford University Press, 1983.

Cottle, Drew and Narim Najjarine, "The Department of External Affairs, the ABC and Reporting of the Indonesian Crisis, 1965–1969", *Australian Journal of Politics and History* 49, 1 (2003): 48–60.

Cox, Margaret, Ambika Flavel and Ian Hanson, "Introduction and Context", in *The Scientific Investigation of Mass Graves: Towards Protocols and Standard Operating Procedures*, ed. Margaret Cox, Ambika Flavel, Ian Hanson, Joanna Laver and Roland Wessling. New York: Cambridge University Press, 2008, pp. 1–36.

Cribb, Robert, ed., *The Indonesian Killings of 1965–1966: Studies from Java and Bali*. Clayton: Centre of Southeast Asian Studies, Monash University, 1990, pp. 1–36.

Cribb, Robert, "Problems in the Historiography of the Killings in Indonesia", in *The Indonesian Killings of 1965–1966: Studies from Java and Bali*, ed. Robert Cribb. Clayton: Centre of Southeast Asian Studies, Monash University, 1990.

———, "Genocide in Indonesia, 1965–1966". *Journal of Genocide Research* 3, 2 (June 2001): 219–39.

———, "How Many Deaths? Problems in the Statistics of Massacre in Indonesia (1965–1966) and East Timor (1975–1980)", in *Violence in Indonesia*, ed. Ingrid Wessel and Georgia Wimhöfer. Hamburg: Abera, 2001, pp. 82–98.

———, "Unresolved Problems in the Indonesian Killings of 1965–66", *Asian Survey* 42, 4 (2000): 550–63.

Cribb, Robert and Charles A. Coppel, "A Genocide that Never Was: Explaining the Myth of Anti-Chinese Massacres in Indonesia, 1965–66", *Journal of Genocide Research* 11, 4 (Dec. 2009): 447–65.

Crouch, Harold, "Another Look at the Indonesian 'Coup'", *Indonesia* 15 (Apr. 1973): 1–20.

———, *The Army and Politics in Indonesia*. Ithaca: Cornell University Press, 1978.

Dateline Television Series, "Indonesia's Killing Fields". SBS Australia, 25 Aug. 1998.

Davidson, Jamie and Douglas Kammen, "Indonesia's Unknown War and the Lineages of Violence in West Kalimantan", *Indonesia* 73 (Apr. 2002): 53–87.

Derrida, Jacques, *Aporias*, trans. Thomas Dutoit. Stanford: Stanford University Press, 1993.

Dhofier, Zamakhsyari, *The Pesantren Tradition: The Role of the Kiai in the Maintenance of Traditional Islam in Java*. Tempe: Monograph Series Press, Program for Southeast Asian Studies, Arizona State University, 1999.

Dinuth, Alex, *Dokumen Terpilih Sekitar G-30-S/PKI*. Jakarta: Intermasa, 1997.

Djamaluddin, Dasman, *Jenderal TNI Anumerta Basoeki Rachmat dan Supersemar*, 2nd ed. Jakarta: Gramedia Widiasarana Indonesia, 2008.

Dwyer, Leslie, "The Intimacy of Terror: Gender and the Violence of 1965–66 in Bali", *Intersections: Gender, History and Culture in the Asian Context* 10 (Aug. 2004), http://intersections.anu.edu.au/issue10/dwyer.html.

Easter, David, "British Intelligence and Propaganda during the 'Confrontation,' 1963–66", *Intelligence and National Security* 16, 2 (Summer 2001): 83–102.

———, "British and Malaysian Covert Support for Rebel Movements in Indonesia during the 'Confrontation,' 1963–66", *Intelligence and National Security* 14, 4 (Winter 1999): 195–208.

Editors, "Selected Documents Relating to the 'September 30th Movement' and Its Epilogue", *Indonesia* 1 (Apr. 1966): 134–9.

Farid, Hilmar, "Indonesia's Original Sin", *Inter-Asia Cultural Studies* 6, 1 (2005): 3–16.

Farram, Steven, "Revolution, Religion and Magic: The PKI in West Timor, 1924–1966", *Bijdragen tot de Taal-, Land- en Volkenkunde* 158, 1 (2002): 21–48.

Fealy, Greg, "The Release of Indonesia's Political Prisoners: Domestic Versus Foreign Policy, 1975–1979". Clayton: Working paper, Monash University, 1995.

———, "Ulama and Politics in Indonesia: A History of Nahdlatul Ulama, 1952–1967". PhD dissertation, Monash University, 1998.

Fealy, Greg and Katharine McGregor, "Nahdlatul Ulama and the Killings of 1965–66: Religion, Politics and Remembrance", *Indonesia* 89 (Apr. 2010): 37–60.

Fealy, Greg and Bernhard Platzdasch, "The Masyumi Legacy: Between Islamist Idealism and Political Exigency", *Studia Islamika* 12, 1 (2005): 73–99.

Feillard, Andree, *NU vis-à-vis Negara: Pencarian Isi, Bentuk dan Makna*. Yogyakarta: LKiS, 1999.

Feith, Herbert, "President Sukarno, the Army, and the Communists: The Triangle Changes", *Asian Survey* 4, 8 (Aug. 1964): 969–80.

Ferrándiz, Francisco and Alejandro Baer, "Digital Memory: The Visual Recording of Mass Grave Exhumations in Contemporary Spain", *Forum: Qualitative Social Research* 9, 3, http://www.qualitative-research.net/index.php/fqs/article/viewArticle/1152/2558, accessed 6 Nov. 2010.

Freud, Sigmund, *The Interpretation of Dreams*. London: Vintage, 2001.

Furet, François, *The French Revolution, 1770–1814*, trans. Antonia Nevill. Oxford and Cambridge, MA: Blackwell, 1996.

Gardner, Paul F., *Shared Hopes, Separate Fears: Fifty Years of United States-Indonesian Relations*. Boulder: Westview Press, 1997.

Geertz, Clifford, *The Religion of Java*. Chicago and London: University of Chicago Press, 1976.

"Gerakan 30 September" Dihadapan Mahmillub: Perkara Untung. Jakarta: Pusat Pendidikan Kehakiman A.D., 1966.

Gonggong, Anhar, *Abdul Kahar Muzakar: Dari Patriot Hingga Pemberontak*. Yogyakarta: Ombak, 2004.

Goscha, Christopher E. and Christian Ostermann, eds, *Connecting Histories: Decolonization and the Cold War in Southeast Asia, 1945–1962*. Stanford: Stanford University Press, 2009.

Green, Marshall, *Indonesia: Crisis and Transformation, 1965–1968*. Washington, DC: Compass Press, 1990.

Hadibroto, Yasir, "Tangguh dan Berbobot", in *Diantara Para Sahabat: Pak Harto 70 Tahun*, ed. G. Dwipayana and Nazaruddin Sjamsuddin. Jakarta: Citra Lamtoro Gung Persada, 1991, pp. 953–60.

Haleem, M.A.S. Abdel, *The Qur'an*. New York: Oxford University Press, 2004.

Harvey, Barbara Sillars, "Tradition, Islam, and Rebellion: South Sulawesi, 1950–1965". PhD dissertation, Cornell University, 1974.

———, *Permesta: Pemberontakan Setengah Hati*. Jakarta: Grafiti Press, 1983.

Hasan, Noorhaidi, "Faith and Politics: The Rise of the Laskar Jihad in the Era of Transition in Indonesia", *Indonesia* 73 (Apr. 2002): 145–69.

Hasworo, Rinto Tri, "Pengangkapan dan Pembunuhan di Jawa Tengah setelah G-30-S", in *Tahun yang Tak Pernah Berakhir: Memahami Pengalaman Korban 65: Esai-Esai Sejarah Lisan*, ed. John Roosa, Ayu Ratih and Hilmar Farid. Jakarta: Elsam, 2004, pp. 25–59.

Hearman, Vannessa, "Guerrillas, Guns, and Knives? Debating Insurgency in South Blitar, East Java, 1967–68", *Indonesia* 89 (Apr. 2010): 61–91.

Heidhues, Mary Somers, *Peranakan Chinese Politics in Indonesia*. Ithaca: Modern Indonesia Project, Southeast Asia Program, Cornell University, 1964.

Hendrowinoto, Nurinwa Ki S., M. Akbar Linggaprana and Tadjoer Rizal Baidoeri, *Jenderal Sarwo Edhie Wibowo: Hidupku untuk Negara dan Bangsa*. Jakarta: Yayasan Biografi Indonesia, 2008.

Heryanto, Ariel, "Where Communism Never Dies: Violence, Trauma, and Narration in the Last Cold War Capitalist Authoritarian State", *International Journal of Cultural Studies* 2, 2 (1999): 147–77.

———, *State Terrorism and Political Identity in Indonesia: Fatally Belonging*. London and New York: Routledge, 2006.

Hilton, Chris, *Shadow Play: Indonesia's Forgotten Holocaust*. Hilton Cordell/ Vagabond Films and Thirteen/WNET New York in association with the Australian Film Finance Corp., broadcast on SBS Australia, 2 Feb. 2003.

Hindley, Donald, *The Communist Party of Indonesia (1961–1965)*. Berkeley: University of California Press, 1966.

Hughes, John, *The End of Sukarno: A Coup that Misfired, a Purge that Ran Wild*. London: Angus and Robertson, 1968.

Ida Bagus, Mary, "From the Margins of History: A Long Babad of Jembrana Bali". PhD dissertation, University of Newcastle, 2006.

———, "Transcending Transgression with Transgression: Inheriting Forsaken Souls in Bali", in *Celebrating Transgression: Method and Politics in Anthropological Studies of Culture*, ed. Ursula Rao and John Hutnyk. New York and Oxford: Berghahn Books, 2006, 93–113.

Indonesia Media On-line, "Seminar 1965 Incident Road Show", 22 Sept. 2007, http://www.indonesiamedia.com/2007/10/local/Seminar.htm, accessed 27 Jan. 2009.

Institut Keguruan dan Ilmu Pendidikan (IKIP), Surabaya, and Balai Penelitian Pendidikan, "Laporan Pelaksanaan Survey Foster-care tentang Anak-anak Korban G.30.S/P.K.I. di Daerah Blitar Selatan dan Tjalon Keluarga Asuhan di Ketjamatan Bagor Kabupaten Ngandjuk dan di Kotamadya Blitar". Surabaya: 1971.

"Interview with Henry L. Heymann" by Charles Stuart Kennedy, 15 July 1993. The Foreign Affairs Oral History Project of the Association for Diplomatic Studies and Training, http://memory.loc.gov/cgi-bin/query/D?mfdip:1:./temp/~ammem_mMF4, accessed 18 May 2010.

Iskandar, Maskun, "Purwodadi: Area of Death", trans. Robert Cribb, in *The Indonesian Killings of 1965–66: Studies from Java and Bali*, ed. Robert Cribb. Clayton: Centre of Southeast Asian Studies, Monash University, 1990, pp. 203–13.

Jasin, M., *Saya Tidak Pernah Minta Ampun Kepada Soeharto: Sebuah Memoar*. Jakarta: Pustaka Sinar Harapan, 1998.

Jelin, Elizabeth, *State Repression and the Labors of Memory*, trans. Judy Rein and Marcial Godoy-Anativia. Minneapolis: University of Minnesota Press, 2003.

Johnson, Rossall J. and Dale McKeen, *Business Environment in an Emerging Nation: Profiles of the Indonesian Economy*. Evanston: Northwestern University Press, 1966.

Jones, Matthew, *Conflict and Confrontation in Southeast Asia, 1961–1965: Britain, the United States and the Creation of Malaysia*. Cambridge and New York: Cambridge University Press, 2001.

Kadane, Kathy, "Ex-Agents Say CIA Compiled Death Lists for Indonesians", *States News Service*, 19 May 1990.

Kahin, Audrey, *Rebellion to Integration: West Sumatra and the Indonesian Polity, 1926–1998*. Amsterdam: Amsterdam University Press, 1999.

Kahin, George, *Nationalism and Revolution in Indonesia*. Ithaca and London: Cornell University Press, 1970 [Ithaca and New York: Cornell University Press, 1952].

Karby, Abdul Muis, *Sejarah Kebangkitan dan Perkembangan Darul Dakwah wal Irsyad [DDI]*. Pare-pare: Pondok Pesantren Putri Ujung Lare, 1989.

Kartodirdjo, Sartono, Marwati Djoened Poesponegoro and Nugroho Notosusanto, eds, *Sejarah Nasional Indonesia*. Jakarta: Departemen Pendidikan dan Kebudayaan, 1975.

Keough, Mary Ellen, Sara Kahn and Adrej Andrejevic, "Disclosing the Truth: Informed Participation in the Antemortem Database Project for Survivors of Srebrenica", *Health and Human Rights* 5, 1 (2000): 68–87.

Klinken, Gerry van, "The Battle for History after Suharto", in *Beginning to Remember: The Past in the Indonesian Present*, ed. Mary S. Zurbuchen: 233–58. Singapore: Singapore University Press, 2005.

Kodam-1, "Laporan Tahunan Lengkap Kodam-1/Kohanda Atjeh, Tahun 1965". No publisher, presumably compiled in 1966.

Kroef, Justus van der, *The Communist Party of Indonesia: Its History, Program and Tactics*. Vancouver: Publications Centre, University of British Columbia, 1965.

———, "Gestapu in Indonesia", *Orbis* 9 (Summer 1966): 458–87.

———, "Indonesian Communism since the 1965 Coup", *Pacific Affairs* 43, 1 (Spring 1970): 34–60.

Lasut, Jopie. "Report from Purwodadi", in *The Indonesian Killings of 1965–66: Studies from Java and Bali*, ed. Robert Cribb. Clayton: Centre of Southeast Asian Studies, Monash University, 1990, pp. 214–26.

Lee Kam Hing, *Education and Politics in Indonesia, 1945–1965*. Kuala Lumpur: University of Malaya Press, 1995.

Lembaga Ketahanan Nasional, *Bahan-Bahan Pokok G-30-S/PKI dan Penhancurannya*. 1969.

Liem, André, "Perjuangan Bersenjata PKI di Blitar Selatan dan Operasi Trisula", in *Tahun yang Tak Pernah Berakhir: Memahami Pengalaman Korban 65: Esai-esai Sejarah Lisan*, ed. John Roosa, Ayu Ratih and Hilmar Farid. Jakarta: Elsam, 2004, 163–200.

LPR-KROB Sulawesi Selatan, "Tragedi Kemanusiaan Tahun 1965 di Sulawesi Selatan". Biro Data dan Dokumentasi DPP LPR-KROB Sulawesi Selatan.

Lyon, Margo L., *Bases of Conflict in Rural Java*. Berkeley: Center for South and Southeast Asia Studies, University of California, 1976.

Mackie, J.A.C., "Anti-Chinese Outbreaks in Indonesia, 1959–68", in *The Chinese in Indonesia: Five Essays*, ed. J.A.C. Mackie. Honolulu: University Press of Hawaii, 1976, pp. 77–138.

Markas Besar Angkatan Bersenjata Republik Indonesia, Pusat Sejarah dan Tradisi ABRI, *Bahaya Laten Komunisme di Indonesia*, vol. 4: *Pemberontakan G30S/PKI dan Penumpasannya*. Jakarta: Yayasan Telapak, 1995.

_______, *40 Tahun Angkatan Bersenjata Republik Indonesia*, vol. 2: *Masa Pembangunan dan Pemantapan ABRI (1965–1985)*. Jakarta: Pusat Sejarah dan Tradisi ABRI, 1985.

May, Brian, *The Indonesian Tragedy*. London: Routledge and Kegan Paul, 1978.

McDonald, Hamish, *Suharto's Indonesia*. Blackburn: Fontana/Collins, 1980.

McGregor, Katharine, *History in Uniform: Military Ideology and the Construction of the Indonesian Past*. Singapore: SEA Series, NUS Press, 2007.

McGregor, Katharine E., "A Bridge and a Barrier: Islam, Reconciliation, and the 1965 Killings in Indonesia", in *Reconciling Indonesia: Grassroots Agency for Peace*, ed. Birgit Bräuchler. London: Routledge, 2009, pp. 214–32.

McIntyre, Angus, "Divisions and Power in the Indonesian National Party, 1965–1966", *Indonesia* 13 (Apr. 1972): 183–210.

McVey, Ruth, "Teaching Modernity: The PKI as an Educational Institution", *Indonesia* 50 (Oct. 1990): 5–27.

_______, "A Preliminary Excursion through the Small World of Lt. Col. Untung". Unpublished manuscript, n.d.

_______, "The Great Fear in Indonesia". Unpublished manuscript, n.d.

Melvin, Jessica, "A Silent Massacre: The Indonesian Communist Party and the Mass Killings in Aceh". BA honours thesis, University of Melbourne, 2009.

Moertopo, Ali, *Akselerasi Modernisasi Pembangunan 25 Tahun*, 2nd ed. Jakarta: Yayasan Proklamasi and Centre for Strategic and International Studies, 1973.

Mortimer, Rex, *Indonesian Communism under Sukarno: Ideology and Politics, 1959–1965*. Ithaca: Cornell University Press, 1974.

Mozingo, David, *Chinese Policy toward Indonesia, 1949–1967*. Ithaca: Cornell University Press, 1976.

Muhamad, T.W.H., *Perlawanan Pers Sumatera Utara Terhadap Gerakan PKI*. Medan: Yayasan Pelestarian Fakta Perjuangan Kemerdekaan Republik Indonesia, 1996.

Mulyadi, M. Hari *et al.*, *Runtuhnya Kekuasaan "Kraton Alit": Studi Radikalisasi Sosial "Song Sala" dan Kerusuhan Mei 1998 di Surakarta*. Solo: Lembaga Pengembangan Teknologi Pedesaan, 1999.

Munir, Mohammad, "Pledoi Mohammad Munir", 2 Mar. 1973. Dokumen-dokumen Pengadilan Munir, http://www.library.ohiou.edu/indopubs/1995/09/23/0005.html, accessed 2 Mar. 2009.

Naipospos, Coki, ed., *50 Tahun Indonesia Merdeka Dan Problem Tapol/Napol*. Jakarta: Masyarakat Indonesia untuk Kemanusiaan, 1995.

Nasution, S.B., *Kisah Nyata Aksi Massa Pemuda Sumatera Utara dalam Penumpasan Gerakan 30 September/PKI di Sumatera Utara*. Medan: Yayasan Pembaharuan Pemuda Indonesia, 1992.

Noer, Deliar, *The Modernist Muslim Movement in Indonesia, 1900–1942*. Kuala Lumpur: Oxford University Press, 1973.

Notosusanto, Nugroho and Ismail Saleh, *The Coup Attempt of the 'September 30 Movement' in Indonesia*. Jakarta: Pembimbing Masa, Aug. 1968.

———, *Tragedi Nasional Percobaan Kup G30S/PKI di Indonesia*. Jakarta: Intermasa, 1989.

Nurkholis, "The Role of Komnas HAM in Conducting Inquiry into the 1965–66 Killings". Paper delivered at the 1965–66 Indonesian Killings Revisited Conference, National University of Singapore, 17–19 June 2009.

Oei Tjoe Tat, *Memoar Oei Tjoe Tat: Pembantu Presiden Sukarno*, ed. Pramoedya Ananta Toer and Stanley Adi Prasetyo. Jakarta: Hasta Mitra, 1995.

Oppenheimer, Joshua and Michael Uwemedimo, "Show of Force: A Cinema-Séance of Power and Violence in Sumatra's Plantation Belt", *Critical Quarterly* 51, 1 (2009): 84–110.

Orr, Kenneth, "Schooling and Village Politics in Central Java in the Time of Turbulence", in *The Indonesian Killings of 1965–1966: Studies from Java and Bali*, ed. Robert Cribb. Clayton: Centre of Southeast Asian Studies, Monash University, 1990, pp. 177–87.

Panggabean, M., *Berjuang dan Mengabdi*. Jakarta: Pustaka Sinar Harapan, 1993.

Parintosa, Anak Agung Ketut and Anak Agung Made Suryawan, "Silsilah Keluarga Sri Kresna Kepakisan Puri Ageng Negara". Unpublished manuscript, 1984.

Pelzer, Karl J., "The Agrarian Conflict in East Sumatra", *Pacific Affairs* 30, 2 (1957): 151–9.

———, *Planter and Peasant: Colonial Policy and the Agrarian Struggle in East Sumatra, 1863–1947*. 's-Gravenhage: Martinus Nijhoff, 1978.

Pledoi Sudisman: Kritik-Otokritik Seorang Politburo CC-PKI. Jakarta: Teplok Press, 2001.

Pohlman, Anne, "Ashes in My Mouth: Women, Testimony and Violence during the 1965–1966 Massacres in Indonesia". PhD dissertation, University of Queensland, 2011.

Purwadi, Budiawan, *Mematahkan Pewarisan Ingatan: Wacana Anti-komunis dan Politik Rekonsiliasi pasca Soeharto*. Jakarta: Elsam, 2003.

Pusat Penerangan Angkatan Darat, *Fakta2 Persoalan Sekitar 'Gerakan 30 September'*. Jakarta: P.N. Balai Pustaka, 1966.

———, *40 Hari Kegagalan "G-30-S" 1 Oktober–10 November*, 2nd ed. Jakarta: Staf Pertahanan Keamanan, 1966.

Pusat Sejarah ABRI, *Buku Panduan Monumen Pancasila Sakti Lubang Buaya*. Jakarta: Pusat Sejarah dan Tradisi ABRI, 1997.

Ramadhan, K.H., *Soemitro: Former Commander of Indonesian Security Apparatus*. Jakarta: Pustaka Sinar Harapan, 1996.

Razif, "Romusha dan Pembangunan: Sumbangan Tahanan Politik untuk Rezim Soeharto", in *Tahun yang Tak Pernah Berakhir: Memahami Pengalaman Korban 65: Esai-esai Sejarah Lisan*, ed. John Roosa, Ayu Ratih and Hilmar Farid. Jakarta: Elsam, 2004, pp. 139–61.

Reken, I Wayan, "Collected Papers on the History of Jembrana". Unpublished manuscript, n.d.

Rescher, Nicholas, "Aporetic Method in Philosophy", *Review of Metaphysics* 41, 2 (Dec. 1987): 283–97.

Ricklefs, M.C., *A History of Modern Indonesia since c. 1200*, 3rd ed. Hampshire: Palgrave, 2001.

______, *Mystic Synthesis in Java: A History of Islamisation from the Fourteenth to the Early Nineteenth Centuries*. Norwalk: EastBridge, 2006.

Risalah Sidang Perkara No. 020/PUU-IV/2006, Perihal Pengujian UU No. 27 Tahun 2004 Tentang Komisi Kebenaran dan Rekonsiliasi Terhadap UUD 1845, Acara Mendengar Keterangan Pemerintah, Saksi dan Ahli dari Pemohon (111). Jakarta: 13 Nov. 2006.

Robinson, Geoffrey, *The Dark Side of Paradise: Political Violence in Bali*. Ithaca and London: Cornell University Press, 1995.

Rocamora, Joel, "Nationalism in Search of Ideology: The Indonesian Nationalist Party, 1946–1965". PhD dissertation, Cornell University, 1974.

Rochijat, Pipit, "Am I PKI or non-PKI?" trans. Benedict Anderson. *Indonesia* 40 (Oct. 1985): 37–56.

Roosa, John, *Pretext for Mass Murder: The September 30th Movement and Suharto's Coup D'État in Indonesia*. Madison: University of Wisconsin Press, 2006.

______, "President Sukarno and the September 30th Movement", *Critical Asian Studies* 40, 1 (2008): 143–59.

Roosa, John, Ayu Ratih and Hilmar Farid, eds, *Tahun yang Tak Pernah Berakhir: Memahami Pengalaman Korban 1965: Esai-esai Sejarah Lisan*. Jakarta: Elsam, 2004.

Ross, Laurie, "Artist Registration and the 1965 Coup in the Cirebon Region, West Java". Paper presented at the 1965–1966 Indonesian Killings Revisited Conference, National University of Singapore, 17–19 June 2009.

Ryter, Loren, "Pemuda Pancasila: The Last Loyalist Free Men of Suharto's New Order", *Indonesia* 66 (Oct. 1998): 45–73.

Said, Umar, "Pernyataan GP Ansor tentang Tragedi 65", 29 Nov. 2000, http://www.hamline.edu/apakabar/basisdata/2000/11/29/0006.html, accessed 22 May 2007.

______, "Pemakaman Kembali Kerangka Korban 65 Digagalkan", *Soeara Kita: Untuk Kemanusiaan Keadilan dan Kebenaran* 14 (Apr. 2001): 6–7.

Samuels, Margaret, "Antemortem Data Collection: Interaction with Families and Communities", in *The Scientific Investigation of Mass Graves: Towards Protocols and Standard Operating Procedures*, ed. Margaret Cox, Ambika Flavel, Ian Hanson, Joanna Laver and Roland Wessling. New York: Cambridge University Press, 2008, pp. 498–515.

Santikarma, Degung, "Epilog. Memasak Sejarah dan Ekonomi Ingatan '65 di Bali", in *Bali Narasi Dalam Kuasa: Politik dan Kekerasan di Bali*, I Ngurah Suryawan. Yogyakarta: Ombak Press, 2005, pp. 328–38.

———, "Menulis Sejarah dan Membaca Kuasa: Politik Pasca-1965 di Bali", in *Perspektif Baru. Penulisan Sejarah Indonesia*, ed. Henk Schulte Nordholt, Bambang Purwanto and Ratna Saptari. Denpasar: Yaysan Obor Indonesia, KITLV-Jakarta and Pustaka Larasan, 2008, pp. 201–15.

Sari, Lies, "Blitar Selatan yang Dilupakan". Unpublished manuscript, n.d.

Schlink, Bernhard, *Guilt about the Past*. Saint Lucia: University of Queensland Press, 2009.

Schulte Nordholt, Henk, "A Genealogy of Violence", in *Roots of Violence in Indonesia: Contemporary Violence in Historical Perspective*, ed. F. Colombijn and J.T. Lindblad. Leiden: KITLV Press, 2002, pp. 81–103.

Scott, Dominic, *Plato's Meno*. Cambridge: Cambridge University Press, 2006.

Scott, Peter Dale, "The United States and the Overthrow of Sukarno, 1965–1967", *Pacific Affairs* 58 (1985): 239–64.

Sejarah Rumpun Diponegoro dan Pengabdiannya. Semarang: Dinas Sejarah Militer Kodam VII/Diponegoro and C.V. Borobudur Megah, 1977.

"Sekitar Penggalian Kuburan Massal di Dekat Wonosobo", *Soeara Kita untuk Kemanusiaan Keadilan dan Kebenaran* 10 (Dec. 2000): 3–4.

Sekretariat Negara Republik Indonesia, *Gerakan 30 September: Pemberontakan Partai Komunis Indonesia: Latar Belakang, Aksi, dan Penumpasannya*. Jakarta, 1994.

Semdam VIII Brawidjaja, *Operasi Trisula Kodam VIII Brawidjaja*. Surabaya: Jajasan Taman Tjandrawilwatikta, 1969.

Setiyono, Budi and Bonnie Triyana, eds, *Revolusi Belum Selesai: Kumpulan Pidato Presiden Sukarno 30 September 1965 — Pelengkap Nawaksara*, 2 vols. Semarang: MESIASS, 2003.

Siauw, G.T., *Lima Jaman: Perwujudan Integrasi Wajar*. Jakarta: Yayasan Teratai, 1981.

Siegel, James, *The Rope of God*. Berkeley: University of California Press, 1969.

Simpson, Bradley, *Economists with Guns: Authoritarian Development and US-Indonesian Relations, 1960–1968*. Stanford: Stanford University Press, 2008.

Slamet Effendy Yusuf, Mohamad Ichwan Syam and Masdar Farid Mas'udi, *Dinamika Kaum Santri: Menelusuri Jejak and Pergolakan Internal NU*. Jakarta: Rajawali, 1983.

Soe Hok Gie, "The Mass Killings in Bali", trans. Anton Lucas, in *The Indonesian Killings of 1965–1966: Studies from Java and Bali*, ed. Robert

Cribb. Clayton: Centre of Southeast Asian Studies, Monash University, 1990, pp. 252–8.

Soedjono, Imam, *Yang Berlawan: Membongkar Tabir Pemalsuan Sejarah PKI*. Yogyakarta: Resist Books and Yayasan Sapu Lidi, 2006.

Soeharto, *My Thoughts, Words, and Deeds: An Autobiography*. Jakarta: Citra Lamtoro Gung Persada, 1991.

Soepardjan, Adam, *Mendobrak Penjara Rezim Soeharto: Kisah Nyata Anak Manusia*. Yogyakarta: Ombak, 2004.

Southwood, Julie and Patrick Flanagan, *Indonesia: Law, Propaganda and Terror*. London: Zed Press, 1983.

Staf Pertahanan Keamanan, Lembaga Sedjarah, *40 Hari Kegagalan "G.30.S"*, 2nd ed. Jakarta: Pusat Sejarah Angkatan Bersendjata, 1966.

Steedly, Mary Margaret, *Hanging without a Rope: Narrative Experience in Colonial and Post-colonial Karoland*. Princeton: Princeton University Press, 1993.

Stewart, Julie, "A Measure of Justice: The Rabinal Human Rights Movement in Post-War Guatemala", *Qualitative Sociology* 31, 3 (2008): 231–50.

Stoler, Ann Laura, *Capitalism and Confrontation in Sumatra's Plantation Belt, 1870–1979*. New Haven: Yale University Press, 1985.

Subekti, Iskandar, "G-30-S Bukan Buatan PKI". Indonesian Exiles of the Left Collection, International Institute of Social History in Amsterdam, the Netherlands.

Subritzky, John, *Confronting Sukarno: British, American, Australian and New Zealand Diplomacy in the Malaysian-Indonesian Confrontation, 1961–1965*. New York: St. Martin's Press, 1999.

Subroto, Hendro, *Perjalanan Seorang Wartawan Perang*. Jakarta: Pustaka Sinar Harapan, 1998.

———, *Sintong Panjaitan: Perjalanan Seorang Prajurit Para Komando*. Jakarta: Kompas, 2009.

Sukanta, Putu Oka, *Merajut Harkat*. Jakarta: Pustaka Pelajar, 1999.

Sulami, *Perempuan-Kebenaran dan Penjara*. Jakarta: Cipta Lestari, 1999.

Sulistyo, Hermawan, *Palu Arit di Ladang Tebu: Sejarah Pembantaian Massal yang Terlupakan (Jombang-Kediri 1965–1966)*. Jakarta: Kepustakaan Populer Gramedia, 2000.

Sundhaussen, Ulf, *The Road to Power: Indonesian Military Politics, 1945–1967*. Kuala Lumpur and New York: Oxford University Press, 1982.

Sunyoto, Agus, *Banser Berjihad Menumpas PKI*. Tulungagung: Lembaga Kajian dan Pengembangan PW GP Ansor Jawa Timur and Pesulukan Thoriqoh Agung, 1996.

Suratman and Patrick Guinness, *Transmigration in South Kalimantan and South Sulawesi*. Yogyakarta: Working paper, Population Institute, Universitas Gadjah Mada, 1977.

Suryawan, I Ngurah, ed., *Bali Narasi Dalam Kuasa: Politik dan Kekerasan di Bali*. Yogyakarta: Ombak Press, 2005.

———, *Jejak Jejak Manusia Merah: Siasat Politik Kebudayaan Bali*. Yogyakarta: Buku Baik and ELSAM, 2005.

———, *Ladang Hitam di Pulau Dewa: Pembantaian Massal di Bali 1965*. Yogyakarta: Galangpress, 2007.

Taufik, Adnan Amal, "Gurutta K.H. Abdul Rahman Ambo Dalle (c. 1900–1996) Ulama Besar dari Tanah Bugis", in *Transformasi Otoritas Keagamaan: Pengalaman Islam di Indonesia*, ed. Jajat Burhanuddin. Jakarta: Gramedia Pustaka, 2003, pp. 199–219.

Team Survey Dinas Research Disorganisasi Sosial, *Laporan survey masalah kurang makan, salah makan di desa Bakung, Sumberdadi dan sekitarnya, Blitar Selatan, Jawa Timur tahun 1970*. Yogyakarta: Balai Penelitian and Peninjauan Sosial, Departemen Sosial Republik Indonesia, n.d.

Tedjasukmana, Iskandar, *Watak Politik Gerakan Serikat Buruh Indonesia*, trans. Oey Hay Djoen. Jakarta: Trade Union Rights Centre, 2008.

Tim Jarah Dam XIV Hasanuddin, *25 Tahun Kodam XIV Hasanuddin 1957–1982*. Makassar: Angkasa, 1982.

Tim Penyusun Jawa Pos, *Lubang-Lubang Pembantaian Petualangan PKI di Madiun*. Jakarta: Grafiti Press, 1990.

Toer, Pramoedya Ananta, *Nyanyi Sunyi Seorang Bisu: Catatan-catatan dari P. Buru*. Jakarta: Hasta Mitra, 2000.

Tovar, Hugh. "Sukarno's Apologists Write Again", *International Journal of Intelligence and Counterintelligence* 9, 3 (Fall 1996): 337–57.

Triyana, Bonnie, "Peristiwa Purwodadi: Kasus Pembunuhan Massal Anggota dan Simpatisan Partai Komunis Indonesia di Kabupaten Grobogan Tahun 1965–1969". BA thesis, Universitas Diponegoro, 2003.

Tsai, Yen-ling, "Through a Building Darkly", *Inside Indonesia* 95 (Jan.–Mar. 2009), <http://www.insideindonesia.org/edition-95/through-a-building-darkly>.

United Nations Economic and Social Council, "Report by the Special Rapporteur, Mr. S. Amos Wako, Summary or Arbitrary Executions". Commissions on Human Rights, Forty-second session, Agenda item 12, dated 7 Feb. 1986.

US Department of State, *Foreign Relations of the United States, 1964–1968*, vol. 26: *Indonesia: Malaysia-Singapore; Philippines*. Washington, DC: United States Government Printing Office, 2001.

———, *Declassified Documents Quarterly*, 1975, 53D.

Velthoen, Esther, "Hutan and Kota: Contested Visions of the Nation State in Southern Sulawesi in the 1950s", in *Indonesia in Transition: Rethinking 'Civil Society', 'Region', and 'Crisis'*, ed. Samuel Hanneman and Henk Schulte Nordholt. Yogyakarta: Pustaka Pelajar, 2004, pp. 147–74.

Vickers, Adrian, *Bali: A Paradise Created*. Ringwood: Penguin Books, 1989.

Walkin, Jacob, "The Moslem-Communist Confrontation in East Java, 1964–1965", *Orbis* 13, 3 (1969): 822–47.

Webb, R.A.F. Paul, "The Sickle and the Cross: Christian and Communist in Bali, Flores, Sumba and Timor, 1965–1967", *Journal of Southeast Asian Studies* 17, 1 (May 1986): 94–112.

Weiner, Tim, *Legacy of Ashes: The History of the CIA*. London and New York: Allen Lane, 2007.

Welfield, John, *An Empire in Eclipse: Japan in the Postwar American Alliance System*. London and Atlantic Highlands: Athlone Press, 1988.

Wertheim, W.F., "Suharto and the Untung Coup: The Missing Link", *Journal of Contemporary Asia* 1, 2 (Winter 1970): 50–7.

Westad, Odd Arne, *The Global Cold War: Third World Interventions and the Making of Our Time*. New York: Cambridge University Press, 2005.

Wieringa, Saskia E., "Sexual Metaphors in the Change from Soekarno's Old Order to Soeharto's New Order in Indonesia", *Review of Indonesian and Malaysian Affairs* 32, 2 (1998): 143–78.

______, *Sexual Politics in Indonesia*. New York: Palgrave, 2002.

______, "The Birth of the New Order State in Indonesia: Sexual Politics and Nationalism", *Journal of Women's History* 15, 1 (Spring 2003): 79–81.

Wilson, Forbes, *Conquest of Copper Mountain*. New York: Atheneum, 1981.

Winarso, "Advokasi Pelanggaran Berat Ham Tragedi 1965/66". Paper presented at the 1965–66 Indonesian Killings Revisited Conference, National University of Singapore, 17–19 June 2009.

Winters, Jeffrey, *Power in Motion: Capital Mobility and the Indonesian State*. Ithaca: Cornell University Press, 1996.

"Urgent Action 06-2001: 'Coffins of 1965 Victims Raided by Mob'", http://www.wirantaprawira.de/ypkp/ypkp_3.htm, 5 Mar. 2009.

Yoga Sugama, *Memori Jenderal Yoga*. Jakarta: Bina Rena Pariwara, 1990.

Young, Kenneth R., "Local and National Influences in the Violence of 1965", in *The Indonesian Killings of 1965–66: Studies from Java and Bali*, ed. Robert Cribb. Clayton: Centre of Southeast Asian Studies, Monash University, 1990, pp. 63–100.

Žižek, Slavoj, *Violence*. London: Profile Books, 2009.

Zurbuchen, Mary, "History, Memory and the 1965 Incident in Indonesia", *Asian Survey* 42, 4 (July–Aug. 2002): 564–81.

Interviews

Interviews with people who wished to remain anonymous are listed with a code in the chapters, and no further details of these interviews are provided here.

Abbas, Anwar, interviewed by Taufik Ahmad, 14 June, 20 July and 28 Aug. 2008, Makassar, South Sulawesi.

Agus Jis, interviewed by Mary Ida Bagus, 13 July 2009, Batuagung, Jembrana, Bali.

Ahmad, A., interviewed by Taufik Ahmad, 17 Sept. 2009, Watampone, South Sulawesi.

Amir, interviewed by Theodora Erlijna, 23 Aug. 2007, Solo, Central Java.

Amra, Rasjidi, interviewed by Taufik Ahmad, 27 June and 2 Aug. 2009, Makassar, South Sulawesi.

Asyari, Hasyim, interviewed by Vannessa Hearman, 10 Feb. 2009, Blitar, East Java.

Aziz, Imam, interviewed by Katharine McGregor, 22 May 2007, Yogyakarta.

Baidowi, Hamid, interviewed by Greg Fealy, 5 Aug. 1991, Jakarta.

Buape, Jufri, interviewed by Taufik Ahmad, 19 June and 20 July 2008, Takalar, South Sulawesi.

Dada, Anom (Ibu), interviewed by Mary Ida Bagus, 12 July 2007, Batubulan, Badung, Bali.

Go Kee Iet, interviewed by Taufik Ahmad, 26 Aug. 2008, Makassar, South Sulawesi.

Gun, interviewed by Taufik Ahmad, 16 June and 20 July 2008, Makassar, South Sulawesi.

Harti (Ibu), interviewed by Mary Ida Bagus, 22 July 2007, Batuagung, Jembrana, Bali.

Hasyim, Yusuf, interviewed by Greg Fealy, 26 Oct. 1991, Jombang, East Java.

Herlambang, Sigit, interviewed by Katharine McGregor, 26 Feb. 2007, Jakarta.

Husein, Idrus, interviewed by Taufik Ahmad, 8 Feb. 2009, Watampone, South Sulawesi.

Ida Bagus Surya, interviewed by Mary Ida Bagus, 27 June 2007, Batuagung, Jembrana, Bali.

Ilham, interviewed by Taufik Ahmad, 1 Aug. 2009, Bone-Bone, South Sulawesi.

Jasin, Muhammad, interviewed by Vannessa Hearman, 2 Feb. 2009, Jakarta.

Jhonlie, interviewed by Taufik Ahmad, 20 and 25 July 2008, Makassar, South Sulawesi.

Joosten (Father), interviewed by Dirk Buiskool, 23 Feb. 1993, Medan, North Sumatra.

Kadullah, Tj., interviewed by Taufik Ahmad, 26 Aug. 2008, Makassar, South Sulawesi.

Lestari, interviewed by Vannessa Hearman, 26 Apr. 2007, Jakarta.

Lingsir, Mangku, interviewed by Mary Ida Bagus, 7 Dec. 2000, Gilimanuk, Jembrana, Bali.

Mahmud Yusmanor, interviewed by Taufik Ahmad, 8 Aug. 2009, Polewali Mandar, West Sulawesi.
Mangku Lingsir, interviewed by Mary Ida Bagus, 7 Dec. 2000, Gilimanuk, Jembrana, Bali.
Masyhuri, Aziz, interviewed by Greg Fealy, 26 June 1992, Jakarta.
Mawardi, Chalid, interviewed by Greg Fealy, 14 Aug. 1991 and 25 Feb. 1992, Jakarta.
Munasir, interviewed by Greg Fealy, 14 Sept. 1991, Mojokerto, East Java.
Munir, interviewed by Taufik Ahmad, 10 Dec. 2009, Barru, South Sulawesi.
Muslich, interviewed by Greg Fealy, 26 Sept. 1991, Jakarta.
Paijo, interviewed by André Liem, no date or place.
Putmainah, interviewed by Vannessa Hearman, 1 Mar. 2008, Srengat, Blitar, East Java.
Putu Raden, interviewed by Mary Ida Bagus, n.d. Sept. 2003, Batuagung, Jembrana, Bali.
Rasydi, interviewed by Taufik Ahmad, 27 June 2008, Makassar, South Sulawesi.
Rewang, interviewed by Vannessa Hearman, 14 Feb. 2009, Solo, Central Java.
Riadi, Asmat, interviewed by Taufik Ahmad, 1 Aug. 2009, Watampone, South Sulawesi.
Sanusi, interviewed by Taufik Ahmad, 20 Dec. 2008, Watampone, South Sulawesi.
Sarmo, Sarmanto, interviewed by Taufik Ahmad, 14 and 20 June 2008, Sungguminasa, South Sulawesi.
Shodiq, Syaiful H., interviewed by Katharine McGregor, 22 May 2007, Yogyakarta.
Silalahi, Harry Tjan, interviewed by Greg Fealy, 12 May 1992, Jakarta.
Siregar, interviewed by Anwar Abbas, 14 June 2008, Makassar, South Sulawesi.
Sjahruni, Amsah, interviewed by Vannessa Hearman, 27 July 2007, Jakarta.
Soepardio, interviewed by David Jenkins, 10 Sept. 1998, Jakarta.
Sri, interviewed by Katharine McGregor, 21 May 2007, Yogyakarta.
Stanley, interviewed by Vannessa Hearman, 2 Feb. 2009, Jakarta.
Suari, Biang Tut, interviewed by Mary Ida Bagus, 13 May 2001, Batuagung, Jembrana, Bali.
Subchan, interviewed by Harold Crouch, 16 Apr. 1970.
Subroto, Hendro, interviewed by David Jenkins, 11 Sept. 1998, Jakarta.
Sulaiman, Syafi'i, interviewed by Greg Fealy, 1 July 1992, Surabaya, East Java.
Sunarno, interviewed by Vannessa Hearman, 2 Feb. 2009, Jakarta.
Suparlan, Kasman, interviewed by Taufik Ahmad, 14 July 2008, Makassar, South Sulawesi.
Suwandi, Yusuf, interviewed by Vannessa Hearman, 29 Jan. and 4 Feb. 2009, Jakarta.

Syachruddin, Eki, interviewed by Greg Fealy, 13 Mar. 1992, Jakarta.

Syafrie, interviewed by Taufik Ahmad, 20 Sept. 2008, Sungguminasa, South Sulawesi.

Tahir, Muh., interviewed by Taufik Ahmad, 2 June and 24 Aug. 2008, Makassar, South Sulawesi.

Talam, Markus, interviewed by Vannessa Hearman, 10 Feb. 2009, Ngrejo, Blitar, East Java.

Tirtayasa, IB, interviewed by Mary Ida Bagus, Feb. 2009, Melbourne.

Tirtha, Ketut, interviewed by Mary Ida Bagus, Jan. 1990, Batuagung, Jembrana, Bali.

Tjiptaning, Ribka, interviewed by Katharine McGregor, 26 Feb. 2007, Jakarta.

Tjokroatmodjo, Sukotjo, telephone interview by David Jenkins, 4 Mar. 2009, Jakarta, and 30 Oct. 2009.

Waris, Abd., interviewed by Taufik Ahmad, 22 July 2008, Makassar, South Sulawesi.

Wayan Sendher, interviewed by Mary Ida Bagus, 23 Sept. 2001, Mendoyo, Jembrana, Bali.

Yoe Sim Boen, interviewed by Dirk Buiskool, 21 Aug. and 17 Sept. 1994, Medan, North Sumatra.

Yusmanor, Mahmud, interviewed by Taufik Ahmad, 8 Aug. 2009, Polewali Mandar, West Sulawesi.

Contributors

Taufik Ahmad completed his master's degree in history at Universitas Hasanuddin, Makassar, South Sulawesi. His thesis was published as *Kamp Pengasingan Moncongloe* (Desantara, 2009). He is currently affiliated with Universitas Negeri Makassar and the Institute of People for Advocacy and Education (Lembaga Advokasi dan Pendidikan Anak Rakyat).

Greg Fealy is Fellow and Associate Professor at the College of Asia and the Pacific, Australian National University. His PhD research at Monash University (1998) was on the history of Nahdlatul Ulama, published in Indonesian under the title *Ijtihad Politik Ulama: Sejarah NU, 1952–1967* (LKiS, 1998). Fealy has published widely on Indonesian Islam.

Vannessa Hearman is completing her PhD at the School of Historical and Philosophical Studies, University of Melbourne, focusing on political violence in East Java from 1965 to 1968. She has published in *South East Asia Research* (with Katharine McGregor), *International Journal of Asia Pacific Studies*, *Indonesia* and *Review of Indonesian and Malaysian Affairs.*

Mary Ida Bagus is Conjoint Fellow at CAPSTRANS (Centre for Asia Pacific Social Transformation Studies) at the University of Newcastle. Her PhD dissertation in anthropology (University of Newcastle, 2006) was titled "From the Margins of History: A Long Babad of Jembrana Bali". Bagus has published many articles and book chapters on Bali.

David Jenkins graduated in law and arts from Melbourne University and spent many years as a foreign correspondent in Southeast Asia. His publications include *Suharto and His Generals: Indonesian Military*

Politics 1975–1983 (Cornell Modern Indonesia Project, 1984) and several articles. He is currently writing a life-and-times study of President Suharto, focusing on his rise to power.

Douglas Kammen is Assistant Professor in the Department of Southeast Asian Studies, National University of Singapore. He is co-author with Siddharth Chandra of *A Tour of Duty: Changing Patterns of Military Politics in Indonesia in the 1990s* (Cornell University Southeast Asia Program, 1999, and Equinox, 2010).

Katharine McGregor is Senior Lecturer at the School of Historical and Philosophical Studies, University of Melbourne. Her first book was *History in Uniform: Military Ideology and the Construction of the Indonesian Past* (NUS Press, 2007). She completed work on this edited volume as part of an Australian Research Council-funded project, "Islam and the Politics of Memory in Post-Authoritarian Indonesia" (DP 0772760).

John Roosa is Associate Professor in history at the University of British Columbia and a researcher at the Indonesian Institute of Social History in Jakarta. He is the author of *Pretext for Mass Murder: The September 30th Movement and Suharto's Coup d'État in Indonesia* (University of Wisconsin Press, 2006) and co-editor of *Tahun yang tak Pernah Berakhir: Memahami Pengalaman Korban 65: Esai-esai Sejarah Lisan* (Elsam, 2004).

Bradley Simpson is Assistant Professor in history at Princeton University. His first book, *Economists with Guns: Authoritarian Development and U.S.-Indonesian Relations, 1960–1968* (Stanford University Press, 2008), explored the intersection of anti-communism and development thinking in shaping US-Indonesian relations and the emergence of the Suharto regime in the 1960s.

Yen-ling Tsai is Assistant Professor in the Department of Humanities and Social Sciences, National Chiao Tung University, Taiwan. Her PhD dissertation (University of California, Santa Cruz, 2008) was titled "Strangers who Are Not Foreign: Intimate Exclusion and Racialized Boundary in Urban Indonesia". She has published in the *Taiwan Journal of Southeast Asian Studies* and *Inside Indonesia.*

Index

abangan, 91, 111, 159
Abdulgani, Ruslan, 19
Aceh (also Atjeh), 14, 16, 26, 59, 103, 133, 135, 139, 143, 145–6, 147, 151–5
  Bireuen, 151
  Lhokseumawe, 151
Achmad, kiai, 120
action fronts, 29n8, 116, 128, 150–2; *see also* KAP Gestapu
Adjie, Ibrahim, Brig. Gen., 80n7
Aidit, D.N., 33–4, 36, 38–9, 43–44, 49, 182, 184
Air Force, Indonesian (AURI), 87, 188
  Information Centre, 100
al-Irysad, 107, 120
Alam, Idham, Maj., 173
Algadri, Sayid Mustafa, 215
Amal, Ichlasul, 160–1
American Indonesian Chamber of Commerce, 72
Amin, Nuridin, 251
Amran, Patahuddin H., 167
Andalas school, 136–7, 144, 148
Anderson, Benedict, 37
Angkatan Bersendjata, 30, 97, 165
Ansor, 14, 17, 84, 92, 100, 106, 113–4, 117–26, 129, 142, 162, 165–9, 181, 183, 187, 190, 193–5, 214–6, 237–40, 248, 251
  clashes with military, 119, 125–6
  clashes with PNI, 142
  clashes with Pemuda Pancasila, 142
  coalition with the army, 92, 106, 119–20, 123–4, 165–6, 194–5, 214–5
  coalition with Muhammadiyah, 165, 187
  coalition with Pemuda Pancasila, 162, 165–9, 181, 187
  coalition with PNI, 84, 216
  formation of, 113
Antonov-12 aircraft, 100
Antara, 132–3
anti-communism, 3, 10–1, 46, 56, 67, 83–4, 84n33, 97–8, 161, 180–1, 183, 247, 254
  anti-communist alliance, 9, 16–9, 139, 141–2, 155, 157, 162–3
  and Chinese, 132–3, 137–8, 143–5, 150–2, 154, 214
  conflict, 88–93, 104, 126, 129, 189, 192–3, 209–10, 213–5, 220
  in the West, 51–2, 56, 60, 69, 73
  remembrance of, 228, 231
  and Army, 104, 109, 114–9, 122–3
  youth involvement, 61, 76–7
Argentina, 234–5, 258
Arief, Kholiq, 240
Arifin, As'ad Syamsul, kiai, 120

Aripin, 214
aristocracy, 10, 14
in Bali, 14, 211–2
in northern Sumatra, 133
in South Sulawesi, 157–9, 161, 180–1
Armed Forces, Indonesian, 51, 159, 204
Armed Forces History Centre, 30, 200
intra-military tensions, 98, 188
Military Police Corps, 81
purges within, 11, 20, 49, 95, 102, 188, 209–10
army, Indonesian
artillery units, 78
cavalry, 78, 94n73
First Cavalry Brigade, 83
Second Cavalry Battalion, 79
engineering units, 78, 100
General Staff, 42
high command, 29, 32, 42, 49, 58, 82
Infantry Brigades
Fourth, 78–9
Fifth, 78
Sixth, 78–9, 85n38, 86
18th Airborne, 196
infantry battalion, 78, 197
Army Information Centre, 85
intelligence, 39, 98, 202, 214
nationalism of, 12, 65
personnel/troop transfers, 79
Presidential Guard (Tjakrabirawa), 28, 35, 76, 225n56
purges within, 33, 41–2, 46–7, 140
Regional Military Command
II/Bukit Barisan (North Sumatra), 140, 141, 151, 153–4
VI/Siliwangi (West Java), 80, 98–9, 161, 165, 186
VII/Diponegoro (Central Java), 75, 77–8, 87, 96, 159, 186
VIII/Brawijaya (East Java), 97–100, 117–9, 123, 126, 129, 159, 188, 194, 196, 200, 204, 254
XIV/Hasanuddin (South Sulawesi), 156, 157, 161, 163, 165, 170–1, 174, 176, 181
XVI/Udayana (Bali and Nusatenggara), 99–100
Sub-regional Military Command, 78, 106, 117, 119, 170–1
Army Para-commando Regiment (RPKAD), 2, 16, 21, 44–5, 59, 76–7, 80–97, 103
Battalion I, 81–2
Battalion II, 78, 81–2
Battalion III, 81–2, 87, 92
conflict with Diponegoro Command, 76, 87, 95–6
in Bali, 99–102, 217
in East Java, 97, 99
Army Strategic Command (Kostrad), 77, 196–7
Suharto as commander, 1, 75
arrests, 7, 16–7, 29n9, 44, 46, 59, 64, 85, 90, 94, 97, 124, 139n31, 163, 166, 170–2, 181, 184–8, 194–5, 200–7, 213–6, 218, 225, 231
Asian Human Rights Commission, 240–1, 246
Association of Southeast Asian Nations, 73
Asyari, Hasyim, 190, 194–5, 201
atheism, 41, 111, 121, 250, 261
Attorney General, 19, 26, 49, 234, 257, 260–1
Australia, 37, 58, 67, 72, 85, 95, 242, 261

authoritarian(ism), 49, 111, 234
regimes, 4
rule, 23
Western support for, 51
Aziz, Abdul, Brig. Gen., 176
Aziz, Imam, 257

Baguio Chiefs of Mission Conference, 56
Bali, 8–9, 14, 17–8, 29n9, 99–103, 129, 183, 208–33, 250
Badung, 212
Buleleng, 215
Cupel, 215
Denpasar, 100n93, 101
Gianyar, 101
Gilimanuk, 225
Jembrana, 22, 101, 208–33
Kapal, 101
Klungkung, 101
Loloan, 212, 214–7, 229–30
Pengambengan, 215
Penginuman, 229
RPKAD in, 99–102
Tegal Badeng, 214–5
west, 208–33
Ball, George, 55
Banjarmasin, 128
Banser, 14, 118, 120, 187–8, 190, 193–4, 196, 201
formation of, 113–4
Bantaeng, 167
Banten, 250
Baperki, 84, 132, 142, 150–1, 155
and 10 December killings, 143–5
detention of members, 147–50
establishment of, 135–6
establishment of branches, 136–7
alleged link to September 30th Movement, 139–43
Basic Agrarian Law of 1960, 14, 112, 161
Batak, 133–4, 133n5, 146, 148n63
Batujajar, 81–2
Berita Yudha, 30, 36n25, 93, 165
Bigalke, Terance, 169
Bisri, Mohammad Cholil, kiai, 125
Bogor, 3
books, banned, 26, 49
Bosnia, 243
Brazil, 74
Brawidjaja, *see* army, Indonesian, Regional Military Command
Brezhnev government, 54
Britain, British, *see* Great Britain
Buddhism, 104, 111, 250
Budiardjo, Ali, 71
Buginese, 158, 161, 212
Bundy, McGeorge, 50, 55, 74
bureaucracy, 8, 108–9, 133, 135, 255–6; *see also* civil service
Buru Island, 157, 205, 240n14, 241

Caltex, 54–5, 68
Cambodia, 261
Catholic Party (Partai Katolik), 83, 92
cemeteries, 214, 228, 230–1, 250
Central Java, 1–2, 16–7, 19, 21, 28–29, 36, 41–5, 59–62, 75–97, 101–3, 106, 114, 129, 174, 184, 256
Banyumas, 97, 256
Blora, 97, 7
Boyolali, 84–5, 87, 90–2, 97, 184, 256
Cilacap, 92, 97, 256
Demak, 87–8, 92–3, 97
Dempes village, 236
Gombong, 96
Jepara, 97, 251
Kaloran, 245–59

Kaloran Muslim Brotherhood, 245, 249, 251
attempted reburial of remains at, 245–51
Kartosuro, 81, 85, 87, 97
Kebumen, 96, 256n66
Klaten, 30, 84, 97, 184, 189, 256n66
Kudus, 87–8, 92, 97
Magelang, 78, 81, 84–5, 256n66
Mount Merapi, 79, 94
Pati, 92, 97
Purwodadi, 21, 45n41, 97, 184, 208
Purwokerto, 87–8, 97
Purworejo, 81n19, 256n66
Salatiga, 28, 97
Semarang, 75, 77, 79, 81, 83–5, 87–8, 93, 97
Surakarta, 83–5, 87, 94, 97
Surakarta Joint Security Staff, 87
Sukoharjo, 256
Temanggung, 245–51, 256n66
Wonogiri, 84, 256
Wonosobo, 97, 236–44, 253, 257–8
mass grave exhumation, 236–45
Chalid, Idham, kiai, 111, 115
Chang Hsi Sek, 136, 137fn25, 144
Chasbullah, Wahab, kiai, 111, 115
children, 46, 128, 180, 183
experience of violence, 30, 46, 148, 219, 221–5
forced removal of, 22, 205–6
Chile, 74, 234–5
Chinese, ethnic, 21, 131–4, 139n31, 142–3, 155
anti-Sinicism, 132, 145, 151–5, 166
anti-Chinese riots, 1963, 137
"alien", 135–7, 151–3
Association of Overseas Chinese (Huaqiao Zhonghui/華僑總會), 137
"Chinese beating" (*pa denlan*), 144–5
violence against, 1966, 150–5, 214
rape of Chinese women, 145
refugee camps, Medan, 152–3
schools, 136–7, 139, 142, 144, 149, 150–1, 153
Christians, 91, 129, 158, 181, 249–51
CIA, 1, 40, 47, 56–7, 62, 93
civil service, 190, 208
purges in, 11, 20, 129
"civil war", 15, 53
class, social and economic, 104, 157–8, 136, 161, 211, 224–5
Cold War, 6, 11, 51, 74, 104
commemoration, 155, 209, 219, 228, 250, 255, 259
monuments, 229, 255
museums, 200
Commonwealth governments, 53
communism, ban on, 237, 241, 249, 259
Confrontation, with Malaysia, 14, 51–3, 55, 65, 68, 73, 78–9, 128, 134, 140
Constitution, Republic of Indonesia, 12, 49n49, 177, 234, 237, 252, 261
"Constitutional route", 20
Coppel, Charles, 131
Council of Generals, 1, 6, 82
Counter-revolution, 1, 3–4, 11–9, 30, 117, 130, 187, 236–7, 255–6
coup, 31, 43–5, 50–3, 76–7, 79, 88, 91, 95
attempted, 31, 41–2
coup d'etat, 6–7, 28

"creeping coup", 7
generals' coup (alleged), 1, 6, 15, 32, 38, 41, 76
Sukarno as instigator, 5, 39–40, 43
court, human rights, 234, 260
Cribb, Robert, 6, 131
crimes against humanity, 234–5
Crop Sharing Law of 1959, 112
Crouch, Harold, 5n6, 20, 37
Crush Malaysia Campaign, *see* Confrontation

Dalle, Abdul Rahman Ambo, kiai, 161
Darjatmo, Brig. Gen., 140–1
Darul Dakwah wal Irsyad pesantren, 162
Darul Islam, 14, 18, 20, 157–60, 162, 165–7, 170, 180–1
Dayaks, 21
death toll, 3, 5, 10
by end 1965, 95
in East Java, 106
in North Sumatra, 143–4, 146
in South Sulawesi, 169
democratisation, 22–3, 182, 207
demonstrations, against the PKI, 43–4, 141, 152, 165
Denia, Agung, 231–2
detainees, 4, 34, 83, 118, 120, 168, 171–4, 203
classification of, 11, 157, 176
elimination of, 18–9, 47–8, 195
hunger strikes by, 172
processing of, 46, 94, 147–9, 195, 213
detention, 17, 20, 60, 77, 89, 97, 130, 146–50, 155, 221
budget for, in North Sumatra, 147
detention centre(s), 21, 94, 124, 147–8, 171, 173
short-term, 7, 17, 20, 171–3
long-term; imprisonment, 12, 20, 132, 156, 171, 173–4, 181; *see also* prison, camps
Dewan Dakwah Islamiyah Indonesia, 249
Dharma Bali movement, 225
Diponegoro, *see* army, Indonesian, Regional Military Command
Djakarta, *see* Jakarta
Djamin, Awaluddin, 72
Djuanda Order, 1957, 136
Djufri, kiai, 120
Dr Sarjito Hospital, 245
Dusung, 167
Duta Masjarakat, 3n2
Dutch, 47, 72, 133, 210–1
colonial troops, 136
Islamic policy, 108
Dwikora, 134n9

East Java, 9, 14–9, 21, 29n9, 45, 60, 62, 78n8, 94–5, 97–100, 104–30, 149, 182, 184, 186–9, 192–3, 196, 200, 205–6, 216, 225, 237, 243, 254
Bangil, 118–22
Banyuwangi, 112, 119–20, 213
Blitar, 21–2, 42, 119–20, 129, 182–208, 253–5
south Blitar, 21–2, 182–3, 185–91, 194–7, 201, 203–7
graves, 253–5
Jember, 112, 119–20
Jombang, 112, 119, 122–4
Kediri, 112–3, 118–20, 122–5, 128–9, 189
Kertosono, 120

Lawu, 192
Madiun, 46, 80, 85, 87, 98, 105, 109, 112, 117, 122–3, 159
Malang, 119, 122, 127, 127n66, 194, 196, 200–1, 203
Mount Lawu, 21
Paiton, 120
Pasuruan, 62, 120, 122, 127, 127n66, 194
Ponorogo, 122, 119–20
Rembang, 125, 184
Sidoarjo, 20
Tulungagung, 62, 202
East Timor, 103, 261
economy, 10–11, 52, 54, 64, 72, 74, 166, 173
economic crisis, 55, 57, 162, 67, 69
Indonesian commercial loans, 67
inflation, 173
education, 13, 108, 136, 206, 222n51, 232
elections, 238
1955 national election, 105, 108–10, 189–90
1957 regional elections, 105, 109, 190
1971 national election, 109
absence of, 13
El Salvador, 235
Emba, Bustan, 172
Erianto, Igo Garnida Heri, 168
ethnic cleavages, 8, 126, 154
ethnicity, 24, 106, 134–5, 148, 153, 157, 161, 212, 228
execution(s), 17, 47–8, 59, 120–5, 147, 198, 155, 217, 253
execution squads, 122, 124
nightly quota, 146
patterns, 47, 122, 157, 256–7
periodisation, 8, 12, 49, 161, 162, 171, 255
1965–66, 4, 137, 163
forced to kill, 198, 217
"silent killings", 142

Fact-Finding Commission, 9, 29n9
Fatayat (NU affiliate), 128
fatwa, 121
Federspiel, Howard, 63
Federation of Indonesian Workers' Unions, 13, 167
feudalism, 181
"fifth force", 54
films, 155
floating mass, doctrine, 12
forensic investigation, 237, 241–4, 254, 259–60
Fortune, 72
France, 72
Freeport Sulphur, 70–2
Freud, Sigmund, 27
Front Pembela Islam, 256
Furet, Francois, 11

G30S (also G.30.S, G-30-S), 4, 30n10, 77, 86
Galbraith, Francis, 61, 89
generals, 1, 2, 6, 30–3, 38, 45–7, 60, 63, 65, 76–7, 82, 88, 129
Council of Generals (alleged), 1, 6
murdered, 1, 25–7, 37, 40–1, 57, 80–1, 114, 123, 162, 209
autopsies of, 30
Geneva Convention, 235
genocide, 131, 234
Gerakan Pemuda Islam, 254
Gerakan Siswa Nasional Indonesia, 218
Germany, 95, 259
Gestapu, Gestapu-PKI, 2, 3–4, 7 16, 29n8, 116; *see also* G30S

Gestok (October 1st Movement), 3–4, 19, 209–10, 212–3, 218–9, 221–2, 224–32
Gilchrist, Andrew, 58
Go Kee Iet, 172, 178
Goodyear, 54, 68, 147
Gorbachev government, 235
graves, 22, 214, 227–30, 233, 257–62
  exhumation, 236–7, 239–44
  mass, 32, 41, 47, 119, 199, 219, 234–6, 252–7
  reburial, 245–51
Great Britain, 23, 52–5, 58
  Commonwealth Relations Office, 55
  consul in Medan, 64
  declassified documents, 23, 56
  Foreign Office, 53
  Information Research Department, 56
  operations, secret, 51
Green, Marshall, 10, 58, 59
Guatemala, 74, 235, 259–60
Guided Democracy, 4, 5, 9–11, 13, 15, 45, 109–11, 115
Guntur, 172

Hadibroto, Jasir, Col., 79
Halim Perdanakusuma Air Force Base, 1, 28, 76, 114
Hamengkubuwono IX, Sultan, 19
Handoko, Dr, 241–2
Hanra, 93
Hansip, 93, 169, 193–7
Harian Harapan, 137, 137n23, 142
Harian KAMI, 45n41
Harian Rakjat, 35, 160
Harriman, Averell, 53
Harseno, Kentot, 1st Lt., 81
Harti, 222–4
Harvey, Barbara, 159
Hasan, Noorhaidi, 249
Hasyim, Yusuf, 106n3, 112, 115, 122
Heryanto, Ariel, 46n46, 249
heroes, 102, 214, 228, 250, 252
Heymann, Henry, 127
Himpunan Mahasiswa Islam, *see* Islamic Students' Association
Himpunan Sarjana Indonesia, 165
Hindus, Hinduism, 91, 110, 210, 226, 228–9
Hokkien, *see* Chinese
Holi, Abdul Rahman, 167
Holland/Netherlands, 53, 68, 72, 136
Huaqiao Zhonghui, 137–9, 142, 144, 151, 154
Human Rights Courts (Ad Hoc), 234, 260
Husein, Jasin, Col., 79, 168n50
Hutapea, Oloan, 184–5

ideology, 12, 247, 249
  ideological differences, 125
  state ideology, 34, 110
Idris, Kemal, Brig. Gen., 138
Ikabepi, 114
Ilyas, Muhammad, 111
IMF, 52, 65, 69
Indonesia Raya, 45n11, 149
Indonesian Communist Party (PKI), 2–4, 11–4, 75–6, 131–2, 182–6, 236
  affiliated organisations, 2, 13–4, 30, 36, 54, 62, 77, 85, 92, 110, 117–9, 128, 139, 156–7
  ban on, 45, 150, 162, 237, 241, 251, 259
  Central Committee, 34, 39, 184–5, 192

destruction of, 2, 9, 11–2, 16, 27, 45, 48, 56–64, 95, 98–9, 117, 128n71, 129, 262
disbandment of, 45, 77, 119, 141, 165
and education, 13, 222, 232
members/cadres, 63–4, 94, 99, 114, 141, 190–3, 213
membership, 63, 194, 217
members of parliament, 110
policy, 44, 63, 134–5
Politburo, 33, 34, 38–40, 183–4, 207
property attacked, 7, 118, 140–2, 152, 155, 166, 208, 213–4
resistance to the violence, 44–5, 47, 87, 89, 172–3, 186–7, 191–4, 207, 215, 253
Special Bureau, 15, 33–8
stigmatisation of, 4, 8, 180, 205, 207, 208–9, 221, 231–3, 239
as traitorous, 25, 183, 191, 208
violence by, 14, 87, 123, 191–4
Indonesian Graduates' Association (HSI), 165
Indonesian Herald, 54
Indonesian National Party (PNI), 11, 75–6, 126–8, 202, 212–5, 219–220
and army
left wing (Ali-Surachman), 127, 186
right wing (Osa Maliki-Usep), 20, 186n11
Indonesian Peasants' Union (BTI), 159, 190
Indonesian Socialist Party (PSI), 160
Indonesian Society for Hindu Teachings, 226
Indonesian Student Movement Centre (CGMI), 171–2
Indonesian Women's Movement (Gerwani), 13, 85, 128, 171, 185, 236n5
alleged sadism of, 2, 30, 220
"Indonesia's Killing Fields", 242
intellectuals, 14, 90
Muslim, 112
Western-oriented, 51
interrogations, 36–7, 46, 59, 89, 94, 147–8, 172–4, 191, 199–200
Islamic Students' Association (HMI), 120, 143, 161, 165, 181, 254
Ismoyo, Argo, 84
IPKI (also IP-KI), 138, 146, 153
IPPI, 218, 222
Islam, 14, 89, 92, 104–14, 120–3, 143, 158–60, 165–70, 180–1, 193–4, 236, 238–40, 247–9, 251–5, 259–61; *see also* Nahdlatul Ulama, Muhammadiyah

Jails, 89, 168, 170–3
Jakarta, 1, 6, 27–8, 38, 42, 46, 51, 72–4, 76–82, 97, 117, 128, 137–9, 153, 163, 226, 238
janger, 220–1
Japan, 57, 59, 65, 67–9, 70–2, 74, 81n19
Japanese occupation, 31, 210–1
Jasin, Muhammad, Maj. Gen., 188, 194
Java, 1–2, 9, 16, 20–1, 78, 102, 110, 116, 137, 168, 183–4, 187, 203–4, 213, 238–9, 257; *see also* Central Java, East Java, West Java
Javanese, ethnic, 82, 106, 133–4, 158, 159, 166–9, 174, 190, 197, 212
transmigrants, 181, 222–6

Jhonlie, 172
Johnson, Lyndon, 50, 62
administration of, 55, 64, 73
Jones, Howard, 56
Jones, Sidney, 128
Jusuf, Andi Muhammad, Col., 161
Juwono, Budi, 61

KAHMI, 254
Kalimantan, 78, 174
West, 8, 21, 42
Kalwater, 167
KAMI, 45n41, 46, 153
KAP-Gestapu, 29n8, 116, 128, 150–2
KAPPI, 46, 153
Kardi, 228–9
Karnaen SH, 172
KASI, 46
Kasman, Kusman, 172
Kasman, Suparlan, 166
Kasut Perdamaian, 253–5
Katamso, Col., 28
wife and children of, 30
Kayat, 81, 84–5, 96, 100n93
Khozim, kiai, 246
kiai, 105–9, 112, 120–5
Kiemas, Taufik, 238
killings, *see* execution(s)
Koanda (Interregional Command), 138, 140
Kodam, *see* army, Indonesian, Regional Military Command
Kodim, *see* army, Indonesian, District Military Command
Komnas HAM, *see* National Commission on Human Rights
Kopassus, 103
Kopkamtib, *see* Operations Command to Restore Security and Order
Korem, *see* army, Indonesian, Sub-regional Military Command
Kosasih, R.A., Maj., 81
Kowani, 128
Kroef, van der, Justus, 182–3
Kuomintang, 136–7
Kusumowidagdo, Suwito, 72

Lahade, Saleh, 159
Laksus (Pelaksana Khusus), *see* Operations Command to Restore Security and Order
land, 158, 174, 176–7, 179, 181, 189, 205, 255
ownership of, 174, 212, 216
landlords, 14, 112, 130, 161
reform, 112–3, 159–61
Lampung, 19, 128, 261
Laskar Jihad, 248–9, 251
Latief, Col., 36, 39, 42
Latin America, 70, 73
laws and regulations, 12, 14, 16, 49, 69, 71, 106–7, 112, 133, 156n2, 159, 161, 177, 234–5, 237, 252, 260n77
Lekra, *see* People's Cultural Institute
Lemhanas, 34–5
Lesser Sunda Islands, *see* Nusatenggara
Lestari, 186–7, 191, 201–2
Lestario, Gatot, 186, 203
letter of March 11 (Supersemar), 150
Lirboyo pesantren, 122
London, 50–1, 55, 64
LPKP, 252
Lubang Buaya, 28
Lubis, Abdul Rahman, 47–8
Lukman, 182, 184

Madurese, 119, 212, 216
Maesa, Usman, 167
Machrus, Ali, kiai, 112, 120
Malay, 7, 134

Malaysia, 14, 21, 52, 68, 78, 128, 134
Sarawak, 21
Malik, Adam, 71, 95
Malik, Djamaluddin, 111
Maluku, 157, 174
Mandar, 158
Mangunkusuma, Irawan, 245–6
Manipol, 44
Mappa, Andi, 168
Mardjoko, 185
Marhaenis Youth, 84, 92, 101
Marines, 19, 95–6, 127–8, 188
marriage, 180, 205, 214, 221–4, 261
forced, 22, 220
remarriage of victims, 22, 232
Maryono, Lt. Col., 77, 94
Marxism-Leninism, 237, 241
Marzuki, Syafi'i, 120
mass killings, 2–10, 16, 19, 23, 44–6, 49–51, 60–2, 76, 95, 99–102, 139, 140n32, 142, 155, 163, 207, 215, 221
"bring under control", 18, 19, 84, 142
Masykur, 111
Masyumi, 20, 92, 105, 108–11, 160–6, 181, 249
Mattiro, Jirong Dg., 172
Mattulada, 181
Mawardi, Chalid, 106n3, 115
McVey, Ruth, 10, 37
media, 3, 7, 23, 29, 56, 77, 115, 240, 242
newspapers, 1, 2, 29, 30–4, 45, 2, 83, 92, 134, 160–5
memorial, 235, 260
Merapi-Merbabu complex, 21
military, Indonesian, 5, 15, 20, 21, 23, 59, 60, 64, 69, 98, 159, 257; *see also* army, Indonesian
militias, *see* paramilitaries, civilian
Miskar, 216–8
Moncongloe prison camp, 174–80
Mojowarno, 124
Mokoginta, Maj. Gen., 134, 138–40, 143, 145–7, 153
Mortimer, Rex, 13
Muchadi, 81
Muchdi, H. Abdul, 121
Muchlis, Aminuddin, 163
Muhadi, Imam, 254
Muhammadiyah, 83, 92, 107, 109n9, 120, 108, 165, 167, 187, 254
Munasir, 112, 115–6
Munir, Muhammad, 184–7, 203, 207
Murba Party, 95
murder, *see* execution(s)
Muslimat, 128
Muslims, 14, 59, 88–91, 106–14, 117–23, 128–9, 134, 139, 143, 157–9, 166, 190, 210–7, 230, 247–50
Muzakkar, Kahar, 158–9, 162, 165

Naba, Suaib, 167
Nahdlatul Ulama (NU), 54, 76, 83, 114n20, 194, 212, 231, 238–40; *see also* Ansor
1955 election, 110, 126
"accommodationists" in, 111, 114–5
Anti-communism, 104–130
apologies for the violence, 231, 237–9
Central Board, 115, 117, 125, 130
guilt for the violence, 124
Jamiatul Muslimin Indonesia, 215
"militants" in, 113–6, 123
Multi-purpose Brigade (Banser), 14, 113–4, 118, 120, 187–96, 201

Organisation Security Coordinating Body, 116
Religious Council (Syuriah) 117, 121
Surabaya branch, 117–21
and Army, 105–6, 115, 117, 125–6, 129, 183, 195, 214–6, 258
Nasakom, 44
Nasution, A.H., Gen., 3, 19, 59–61, 67, 76, 95, 118, 129, 150
daughter of, 42n37
National Commission on Human Rights, 234, 236, 240–2, 246, 254–5, 257, 260
nationalisation
of foreign enterprises, 68
in 1957, 133
of oil companies, 54, 66–7
nationalists, 16–7, 88–9
nationalist parties, 12, 83, 142, 160, 212, 218
Navy, Republic of Indonesia (ALRI), 126–7, 188
Nebritex factory, 62
Negara, 210–7, 222, 228–32
National Heroes' Cemetery, 214, 228
royal palace and family, 211, 213–7, 231
neo-colonialism, 4, 14
New Order, 5, 12, 23, 102–3, 180–3, 188, 196–7, 219–24, 227, 231–3, 238, 242–50
New York Times, 99, 197, 204
Noer, Muhammad, 205
non-governmental organisations, 22, 72, 236, 258–9
North Sumatra, 8, 14–20, 29n9, 47, 54, 59, 64, 78, 131–55, 140n32, 146n56
Asahan, 136, 146
Bandar Betsy, 15n35, 134
Belawan, 145, 152–3
Kabanjahe, 137
Karo, 133n5, 140, 146
Kisaran, 136, 148
Labuhan Deli, 145
Langsa, 151
Medan, 20, 54, 61–2, 64, 131–55
10 December riot, 143–6
Rantau Prapat, 146
Sibolga, 140
Tarutung, 136
Tembung, 145
Notosusanto, Nugroho, 30–3, 37, 41
Nugrohadi, Trimawan, 240
Nuremberg trials, 259
Nusatenggara
East, 19
West, 17

Oei Tjoe Tat, 148
oil, 54–5, 61, 66–72
Old Order, 12
Operation Merapi Command, 94
Operations Command to Restore Order and Security (Kopkamtib), 2, 147, 163, 174
Special Task Force (Laksus), 147
Oppenheimer, Joshua, 47–8

Paguyuban Keluarga Islam, 254
Paguyuban Korban Keganasan PKI, 254
Paiso, 163
Pamuji, 172
Panjaitan, Brig. Gen., 42n37
Papua, 26, 53, 261
paramilitaries, civilian, 16, 21, 24, 94, 97, 100, 113, 248
Parisada Hindu Dharma Indonesia, 226
Parman, Maj. Gen., 39

Partai Amanat Nasional, 254
Partai Bulan Bintang, 254
Partai Kebangkitan Bangsa (PKB), 240, 248, 250–1
Partai Persatuan Pembangunan (PPP), 248, 251
Partindo (Partai Indonesia), 142, 149
Pasek, 211
PDI-P, 238, 240, 251–4
peasants, 12–4, 54, 112, 133, 160–1, 185, 212
  organisations, 114n20, 147, 159, 190
Peck, Edward, 53
Pemuda Pancasila, 61, 138, 142–5, 162, 165, 166n40, 167–9, 181, 187
Pemuda Rakyat, *see* People's Youth (PKI)
Pemuda Tanah Rentjong, 145
Penyaringan, 212
People's Consultative Assembly (MPR), 3, 20, 196
People's Cultural Institute, 13, 160, 171–2, 186, 190
People's Republic of China (PRC), 52–4, 58, 63, 73, 133, 134, 136, 140–6
  allegations of weapons from, 33, 113
  Consulate, Medan, 140, 143, 145, 155
  Radio Beijing, 143
  ships sent to Indonesia, 152
People's Youth (PKI), 13, 77, 141, 163, 167, 171, 184n4, 185, 190
Pepelrada, 134n9
peranakan, 137
Permadi, 9
Permesta, 14, 51, 111, 159–62, 181
Peru, 235
pesantren, 106–12, 117–23, 129, 162, 240n34, 246
Petanu, 114n20
PKB (National Awakening Party), 240, 246–51
plantations, 54, 68, 132–6, 140, 146–7, 154–5, 189n25, 190
Poerwanegara, Solichin Guatama, Lt. Col., 161, 165
pogroms, 3, 8–10, 15–7, 101, 131, 139n31, 217, 231, 233
Pol Pot, 261
police, Indonesian, 19, 44, 84, 87, 99, 101, 128, 143, 151, 169–72, 192, 194, 214, 239, 245–6, 254, 256
police, military, 81, 83, 98, 173, 176–7
political parties, 12–3, 19–20, 60, 73, 110, 112, 160–1, 248, 251, 259
Pranoto, 43
Pratomo, Col., 188, 203
Presidential Guard, *see* army, Indonesian
Pretext for Mass Murder, 27, 37, 49
prison, 20, 23n47, 38, 156–7, 168, 170–4, 178, 187, 203–5, 208, 237, 244
  Buru, 157, 174, 205, 241
  camps, 156–7, 173–5, 178, 181, 208
  Cipinang, 38
  Kalisosok, 204
  Makassar, 172–5
  Malang Women's, 203
  Moncongloe, 174–80
  Pamekasan, 204
  Salemba, 187
prisoners, 17, 171, 208
  classification of, 156–7, 173, 176, 180–1, 226
  ex-prisoners (*tapol*), 180
  execution of, 7, 17, 34, 44, 59, 90, 203

labour, 20, 156–7, 176–9, 190
political, 23, 37, 147–8, 163, 170–81, 201, 203, 235–9, 248, 251, 258, 259
rations, 172–3, 176
release of, 180
Proletariyati, Ribka Tjiptaning, 238
propaganda, 3, 7, 19, 25–6, 30–4, 40–9, 161, 180–3, 197–8, 208, 223, 246–7
PKI, 220
Sukarno's protests about, 30
Western, 58
property, 7, 118, 166
destruction of, 84, 101, 152, 155, 166, 200, 208, 213
seizure of, 17, 141–2, 151–3, 154, 214
PRRI, 14, 51, 111
psychological warfare, 29, 75
Pudjiaswati, 186
Putmainah, 186, 191, 202, 253
Putu Raden, 218

radio, 25, 28–9, 35, 39, 42–3, 56, 79, 116–7, 133
Republic of Indonesia Radio (RRI), 1, 76–7, 116
Radio Beijing, 143–4
Rahmat, Basuki, 118–9
Rakimin, Capt., 177
Ramelan, 1st Lt., 81, 83n27, 96
rape, 204–5, 208–9, 220–1
of ethnic Chinese, 145
Reddaway, Norman, 51
refugees, 152–3, 183, 199
Regar, 214
Regional Investigation Team (Teperda), 163
rehabilitation centre/installation, *see* detention centres
Reken, Wayan, 231
religion, 108–13, 130, 170, 197, 224–6, 232, 246, 250–1
religious differences, 8, 157–62, 190
religious groups, 14, 16–9, 104–5, 237–40, 256–7
religious parties, 12, 83–8, 193
relocation, forced, 7, 21, 80, 173, 197, 205
Republic of Indonesia
Central Bank, 68
Department of Religious Affairs, 108
foreign investment law, 69–71
foreign policy, 10, 21, 64
Ministry of Justice and Human Rights, 235
Ministry of Manpower, 72
Ministry of Mining, 70
Ministry of Trade, 153
state policy, 44, 73–4, 134–4, 176
State Secretariat, 31–2, 48
Res Publica University, 136
Revolution, Indonesian (1945–49), 1, 4, 12, 28, 40, 47, 104, 109, 138, 210
Revolutionary Council, 28, 42–3, 75–8, 82
regional councils, 43, 75, 189
Rewang, 184–6, 188–93, 203
rice, 59, 63–5, 172, 190
Robinson, Geoffrey, 215
Roosa, John, 15, 25, 56, 229
Rostow, Walt, 62, 70
rubber estates, 54, 64, 147
Rusk, Dean, 58, 66
Rustomo, 186, 203

Safroni, Lt. Col., 216, 222–3
Sahirman, Col., 77, 94
Said, Umar 236, 247

Saito Shizuo, 59
Saleh, Chaerul, 54, 66
Saleh, Ismail, Lt. Col., 31, 33, 37, 41, 45
Salim, C., Capt., 81
Samallo, W.R., Lt. Col., 177
Samuels, Margaret, 244
santri, 106–11, 121–4, 148
Sarawak, 21
Sarbumusi, 122
Sarbupri, 133, 189n25
Sarekat Islam, 109
Sari, Lies, 186–7, 191, 200
Sarosa, Lt. Col., 177
Sartono, 127
Sarwo Edhie Wibowo, Col./Brig. Gen., 9, 17, 59, 77, 80–90, 92n61, 93–4, 97, 101–3, 154, 252, 261–2
  on death toll, 9, 84n33, 92n61
Sastrodibroto, Usman, Lt. Col., 78
schools, 81–2, 92–3, 105–7, 133, 136–9, 142–4, 148–51, 153–4, 162, 168–71, 193, 205, 219, 223, 240, 246
Scott, Peter Dale, 97
Seda, Frans, 54, 68
Sejarah Nasional Indonesia, 31
SEKBER 65, 256–7
Sembiring, 81, 94n73, 96
September 30th Movement, 25–49
  aims, 7–12
  collapse of, 28–9, 30, 35, 41–4, 49–52, 57, 79, 116
  in Central Java, 1, 17, 21, 28, 29n9, 77–80
  as internal Army affair, 28, 35
  military personnel involved, 36–8, 42–3, 94
  organiser, 33, 38, 41, 43
  PKI as mastermind (alleged), 2, 7, 25–6, 29n8, 31, 35, 36n26, 162
  radio announcement, 1, 28, 35, 42–3, 79, 117
  reasons for failure of, 37, 50, 77
Serikat Buruh Kereta Api (SBKA), 85
Share-cropping Law, 1959, 14
Shell Oil, 54
Shodiq, Syaiful H., 239–40, 248, 251
Shoe for Peace, *see* Kasut Perdamaian
Siauw Giok Tjhan, 135
Siddiq, Abdullah, 120
Siddiq, Ahmad, 112
Sikki, Ridwan, 172
Siliwangi, *see* army, Indonesian, Regional Military Command
Sinar Harapan, 45n41
Singapore, 51, 56, 149
Singunkarya, 81
Siregar, Capt., 175n79, 177–8
Sisnodo, Heru, Capt., 81–2
Sitepu, Ulung, 133, 140–1
Sjahruni, Asmah, 128
Sjam, 36–9, 43
Sobiran, Brig. Gen., 141–2, 147
SOBSI, 13, 167, 171, 184–5, 189n25
Soemitro, Maj. Gen., 99, 128, 188
Soenarso, 165
Soeprapto, Lt. Col., 78–9
Solo, *see* Central Java, Surakarta
South Africa, 234–5, 259
South Sulawesi, 14n33, 17–8, 20, 156–81
  Banyuret, 169
  Bone (also Watampone), 160, 167–9, 181
    PKI branch, 160
  Bone-Bone, 169
  Cenrana, 160
  Gowa, 174–8
  Lemah Abang, 169
  Luwu, 167–9

Makassar, 156, 158, 162–7, 170–80, 169n60
Makassarese, 158, 161, 167
Maros, 174
Sidomukli village, 169
Toraja, 159, 169
Torajan, 158
South and Southeast Sulawesi, 156n2, 160, 170, 174–5; *see also* South Sulawesi
Soviet Union (Russia, USSR), 52–4, 57, 63, 73, 149, 235, 237, 259–60, 262
Spanish Civil War, 235
Special Bureau (Biro Chusus), 15, 33–8, 49
Srebrenica, 243
Stalinist, 35, 235
Stannard, R.E., Jr, 88–9
Stanvac, 54, 66
state, 25–6, 71, 103, 111, 203, 223, 255
central organs, 3, 20
civil service, 11, 20, 129, 208
provincial, 3, 16, 76, 104, 133, 136, 138, 142, 184, 187, 190, 192, 253
state of war, 87
Subandrio, 55, 138
Subchan, Z.E., 112, 115–6, 120
Subekti, Iskandar, 38–9, 185
Subroto, Hendro, 77n5, 83, 102n106
Sucipto, Urip, Capt., 81–2, 94n73
Sudisman, 36, 184–5
Sudjatmoko, 90
Sudjono, warrant officer, 15n35, 134
Sudra, 211
Sudradjat, Edi, 1st Lt., 81
Suharto, 1–10, 16–22, 25–9, 32–3, 45–7, 60–6, 103, 116, 242
autobiography of, 35n24
explanation for killings, 130
regime, 4–5, 12, 15–6, 20, 25–9, 35–6, 44, 46–9, 68–9, 73, 110, 115, 209, 221, 227, 233, 247, 256; *see also* New Order
resignation in 1998, 22–3, 236–7, 259
Sukanta, Putu Oka, 23n47
Sukardanu, Widjaja, Col., 118
Sukarno, 1–24, 25, 28, 29n9, 39–45, 50–5, 57–60, 62–70, 73–4, 76, 90, 95, 111–5, 137, 150, 188, 238
assassination attempts on, 30, 40
Sukarnoism, 11, 20, 44, 68, 74, 150, 155, 172, 254
Sukarno Front (Barisan Sukarno), 19, 150
Sukarnoists, 11, 20, 44, 68, 74, 150, 172, 254
Sukatno, 184–7, 184n4
Sulami, 236, 242–4, 250, 252
Sulistyo, Hermawan, 122–3
Sumardi, 119
Sumatra, 8, 14n33, 19, 64, 78, 134, 134n9, 136, 138, 261; see also *North Sumatra*
East Coast, 5, 133–4, 146, 154
northern, 8, 131, 149–50
southern, 8, 261
South, 174
West, 19
Sumual, Herman Nicolas Ventje, Lt. Col., 159
Sumur Blandung pesantren, 246
Sunariyadi, Brig. Gen., 119
Sunyoto, Agus, 193
Supardjo, Brig. Gen., 37–9, 42–3
Suparmin, 214
Supreme Operations Command (KOTI), 19, 144n47
Surabaya, 13, 15, 62, 98, 107, 110, 117–9, 121, 126–9, 137–9, 183–8, 204–6
Port, 126

Surjosumpeno, Brig. Gen., 77–80, 83, 85n38, 87
surrender, 198, 201
  voluntary by PKI members, 44, 166, 170
  of September 30th Movement troops, 28
survivors, 22, 163, 183, 209, 224, 232–3, 234–8, 244, 257–9
Surya, Ida Bagus, 225–6, 255n56
Suryaman, Asep, 38
Suryawan, I Ngurah, 214, 219, 227
Suteja, Anak Agung, 14, 210–2, 212n13, 215, 217, 225n56, 231
Sutomo school, 144
Sutowo, Ibnu, 68
Suwandi, Yusuf, 186–7, 200–1, 252, 256
Suyasa, Guru Wedastera, 210–2, 215
Suyasa, Widagda, 215, 220
Syaichu, Ahmad, 115
Syamsuri, Bisri, 112, 120
Syarikat, 248, 257
Syukur, Abdul, 167

Tahija, Julius, 55, 68
Taiwan, 23, 137
Talam, Markus, 190, 194, 198, 205
Talangsari, 261
Tameng, 213, 216, 221–2, 225, 227
  Marhaenis, 101
  guilt for the violence, 227–8
Tan Fhu Kiong (Tan Fuk Kiong), 137n23, 142
Tan Ho Lan, 136–7, 149
Tanjung, Feisal, 1st Lt., 81, 92
Taylor, Ross, 62
teachers, 124–5, 144, 148, 170–1, 218–9, 221–3, 251
  organisations, 12–3, 206
technocrats, 14, 51–2, 69, 90, 112; *see also* intellectuals
Tedjo, Lt., 81, 84–5, 94n73, 96
Tendean, Lt., 42n37
Teochiu Huikuan, 147–8
Thalib, Ja'far Umar, 248
Tin, 64, 68
Tiwari, B.K., 90–1
Tjokroatmodjo, Sukotjo, Maj. Gen., 81
Tjugito, 184–5
Toer, Pramoedya Ananta, 157, 236
Toko Wong, 213–4, 217, 222, 230
torture, 7, 16, 21, 33, 88, 103, 147, 172, 199, 209, 211, 218, 221, 225, 230–1, 242
totok, 137
transmigration, 22, 169, 222–6, 232
trials, 20, 36, 45, 157, 173, 203, 235–6, 259, 261
Trisula Operation, 22, 183, 188, 191, 194, 196–205, 207
  Monument, 255
Triwangsa, 211
Truth and Reconciliation Commission, 234–7, 252, 259
Tsanawiyah madrasah, 240
Tu, Niang, 224

Udayana, *see* army, Indonesian, Regional Military Command
ulama, 105–8, 112, 121, 128–30, 161
unilateral actions (*aksi sepihak*), 14, 112–3, 119, 123
unions, 13, 54, 62, 2, 159, 167
  peasant, 14, 54, 113, 114n20, 149, 159, 170, 197
  plantation workers, 54, 147, 189n25
  labour (manufacturing), 122, 133
United Nations, 53
United Press International, 88

United States
aid to Indonesia, 50, 59–62, 64–73
Consulate, Medan, 54, 61, 143–5
Consulate, Surabaya, 15, 62, 119–21, 126–7
Embassy, Jakarta, 57–8, 61, 66–7, 70, 72, 85, 87, 89, 91, 96, 97, 100
and Indonesian Army, 58–64, 67
interests, 50–74
covert operations, 51, 56, 95n77
National Security Council, 70
praise for Suharto, 60
State Department, 14, 56, 59, 63, 65, 71, 106
Universal Declaration of Human Rights, 234
University of Indonesia, 241
Untung, Lt. Col., 1–2, 7, 28, 35, 39, 42, 76–8, 203, 225n56
capture of, 36
interrogation report of, 36
testimony in court, 37–8
US Rubber, 58, 68
Usman, 78, 94, 160, 167, 171n66
Uwemedimo, Michael, 48

Van Sickle Associates, 71
victims, 6–9, 11, 23, 32–3, 42, 47, 62, 99n91, 101, 119, 124–5, 129, 131, 145, 209n2, 213–26, 229–32, 235–44, 250–60
Vietnam, 52–5, 61, 73–4, 104, 183, 200
National Liberation Front of, 73, 183
Village Defence Organisation (OPD), 169
village head(man), 205, 213, 216, 254
violence
forms of, 4, 7–8, 12, 22, 24, 208
in official accounts, 3, 23, 25
mass, 8, 12, 34–5, 51, 61, 118
military coercion, 198–9
perpetrators of, 9, 12, 17, 34, 48, 169, 209, 216, 227, 229, 231, 233, 250, 261
narration of, 29–48
on property, 118, 140–2, 152, 155, 166, 208, 213–4
regional variation, 10, 12, 24, 132

Wahid, Abdurrahman, 231, 237–9, 240n15, 241, 251, 261
personal apology, 231, 237–9
Warouw, Jacob Frederick, 159
Washington, 50–62, 64–8, 71, 74, 93, 146
Wertheim, W.F., 37
West Irian, 70; *see also* Papua
West Java, 14n33, 17–8, 21, 59, 80, 137, 158, 186, 250
Bandung, 13, 59, 82
Batujajar, 81–2
Indramayu, 21
Wicaksono, Albertus Suryo, 253, 255
Widjojo, 71
Wie Bian Chie, 214
Windia, IB, 217
Witarmin, Col., 196–7
women, 8, 12, 129, 180–3, 232, 238
violence against, 22, 90–1, 177, 203–4, 220–1
rape, 145–6, 208

women's organisations, 2, 13, 30, 85, 114, 128, 171, 185
workers, 12, 14, 42, 54, 86, 124, 133, 140, 147, 168
organisations, 13, 54, 62, 85n38, 189n25, 190
World Bank, 52, 70

Xin Hua (China News Agency), 132
Xinghua Chinese, Association of, 148–9, 154

Yani, Achmad, Gen., 6, 27, 76–8, 80–1, 86
Yayasan Pusat Kajian Komunitas Indonesia, 254
Yoe Sim Boen, 136, 149
Yogyakarta, 19, 28, 83, 85, 87–91, 93, 97, 188, 219, 239, 243, 245, 248, 250–1
Youth Action Command(s), 138–40, 145, 154–5
YPKP, 65, 236–53, 256, 258
Yudhoyono, Susilo Bambang, 77n3, 252, 261
Yugoslavia, mass violence, 235
Yunus, LB, 172
Yusmanor, Mahmud, 160
Yusuf, Esther, 253
Yusuf, Muhammad Ali, 167

Zaini, kiai, 120
Zionism, 249, 251
Zuhri, Saifuddin, 111
Zurbuchen, Mary, 247